AMERICAN HISTORY MADE SIMPLE

BY

JACK C. ESTRIN, M.A.

Chairman, Social Studies,
Richmond Hill High School, N.Y.C.

MADE SIMPLE BOOKS

DOUBLEDAY & COMPANY, INC.

GARDEN CITY, NEW YORK

ABOUT THIS BOOK

Of the writing of history there is no end; and it is right that this should be so. It is of the very nature of the subject that there can be no single, *final* work which renders all subsequent historical writing unnecessary. Historical events, of course, are not altered by the passage of time (although our *understanding* of them is, as they are illuminated and clarified by research and discovery). Men cannot tamper with the past to suit their fancy or the passing needs of faction and party—at least they cannot do so in a democratic society. But if the past does not change, our *relationship* to it does, its *meaning* for us does. It becomes therefore the constant obligation of each generation to examine its historic past anew, to seek out its significance and its signs, so that it can better determine where it is, and where it is going.

There is a special urgency to probe the American past now—now when we seem to have reached a kind of climax in our national development. Only yesterday (as historical time goes) a minor colony facing a vague and undistinguished future, the United States has become a great power on a world scale, possessing immense authority and bearing immense responsibilities. It is a thought that must give pause to thoughtful persons; and historical writing is, after all, a way of taking stock in the pause that nations must take properly to assess themselves.

It is with this in mind that this book has been written. Better to achieve my purpose—which is to bring the American past to bear on the American present—I have attempted to portray the whole view of American history: to treat the complex pattern of the nation's growth—its political, social, economic, cultural history—as the composite movement of a people towards maturity. If I have succeeded, then it is my hope that the reader will gain a sense of *witnessing*, of *participating* in the panorama and excitement of the American saga. Only to the extent that we know our past can we expect to live effectively in the present and meet whatever challenge of the future.

—JACK C. ESTRIN

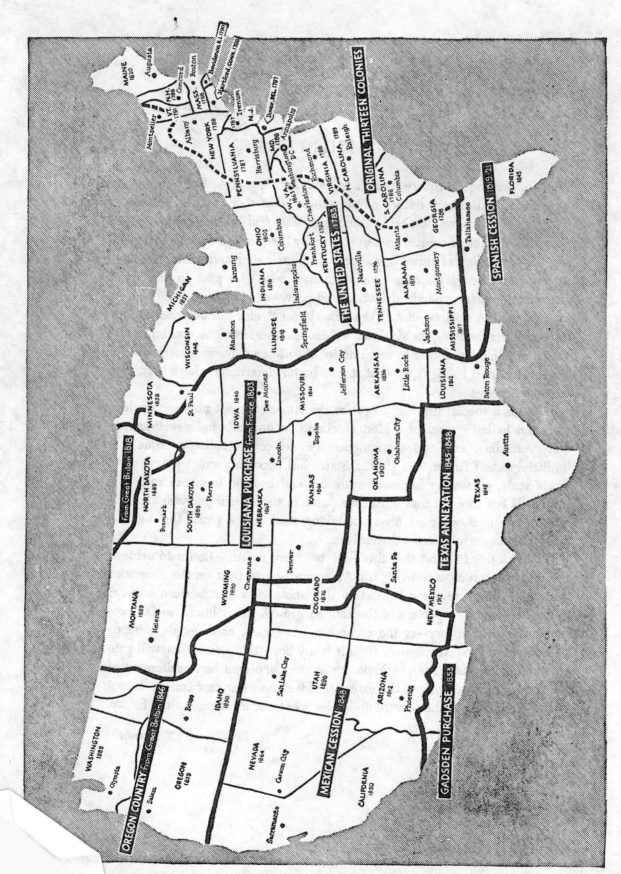

Political and Territorial Map of the United States

4

TABLE OF CONTENTS

CHAPTER IV

CHAPTER V

CHAPTER VI

CHAPTER XX

CHAPTER XXI

CHAPTER XXII

CHAPTER XXIII

INTRODUCTION

EUROPEAN BACKGROUNDS

It is customary to begin American history with Columbus' discovery on October 12, 1492. There are many good reasons for beginning here. Certainly, all honor is due to this brave but mistaken sailor who found the "new world" but died ignorant of his discovery. And Columbus' voyage enables the historian to reveal all of the historical forces which drove Columbus *westward* in search of the spices, jewels and gold of the fabled Indies.

The historian can consider, for example, the collapse of feudalism under the assaults of the new middle classes and other modern forces; the expansion of Mediterranean commerce and modern technological and scientific developments. No one can deny the importance of these and other forces *as preparations for an American history*, but, strictly speaking they are not part of the history of America. (For want of another name, we shall use **America** to signify the territory of the present United States.) American history could not begin until men and women in large numbers left Europe to settle in America. Not discovery, nor exploration, but **settlement is the key to American history.**

Spanish Settlement. America was settled by the Spanish, the French, the Dutch, the Swedes and the English; but English settlement was destined to prevail. Why? In the 17th century, Spain was well established along the southern rim of America from California to Florida; yet this wide expanse of settlement had disappeared by the first quarter of the 19th century. Historians explain the failure of Spanish settlement in various ways. Spanish *conquistadores* (conquerors) were impelled by many motives: the search for gold and silver (specie), the desire for *encomiendas* (large landed estates), the hope of locating more "westward passages" to the South Sea (Pacific Ocean), and the missionary drive to convert the "heathen."

But as they conquered, they enslaved. The result was that they provoked fierce resistance to their forward movement and were forced to pour a large part of their ill-gotten gains into war and defense. Immense quantities of specie were sent back to Spain; reinvestment in the New World was slight in comparison. The cost in human lives in extracting this specie was fearful. **Total population in Spanish-held territories** declined, thus preventing permanent settlement.

Other forms of wealth—grazing and agriculture—failed to produce any significant surplus. **Peonage** (in effect, slavery) was an inefficient labor system; the home government handcuffed free trading with self-defeating **mercantilist restrictions;** the selling price of goods was prohibitively high because of high transportation charges and oppressive **taxes.** Manpower was in constant short supply because immigrants were few. What Europeans would come overseas to a land where a few gentry owned most of the sparsely watered land? Moreover, **immigration was restricted to Roman Catholics;** hence the Spanish domain in America could become no haven for the persecuted. Nor was there any freedom in Spanish America; all Spanish lands were bound into the system of **political absolutism** that prevailed at home.

Spanish Contributions. Failure in the permanent settlement of America and the ruthless destruction of native Indian civilizations should not be permitted to obscure the **Spanish heritage in American civilization.** Spanish exploration was ceaseless and many of the pathways to the west were opened by her adventurers. **Spain initiated the economic development of America;** her gold production gave all of Europe a specie base for expansion overseas. She introduced a great number of European, African and Asiatic crops into the New World; transplanted sheep, cattle, horses and mules; and located the land and water resources of the country.

In spite of harsh measures in the conversion of the natives, Spanish missionaries instituted some popular education and attempted to restrain excessive brutality in Spanish governors. **The "oldest town in the United States," San Augustin in Florida, was founded by the Spanish in 1565.** Spanish settlers built houses, churches, hospitals and monasteries—all of which had a civilizing influence. They influenced architectural styles in America—the severe **Spanish mission style,** the use of **stucco relief,** the **baroque style** and the ornate **churrigueresque.** Imported books helped spread European culture. Finally, Spanish words mingled with American-English and are, today, recurrent reminders of the Spanish past in America.

French Settlement. French failure was even more pronounced than the Spanish. In 1608 CHAMPLAIN gave the French a beachhead for continental conquest and settlement at Quebec; but, though thereafter the French scoured the American interior from the Great Lakes to the Gulf of Mexico, no permanent settlement resulted.

France, too, restricted her settlers to Roman Catholics; granted vast tracts to *seigneurs* (nobles) and subjected other settlers to feudal conditions; extended French despotism to the regions overseas; and hampered enterprise with rigid mercantilist regulations. French farmers were given no inducement to leave home and take up with Canadian winters, hostile Indians, limited economic opportunity and the harsh policies of Finance Minister Colbert. By 1750 only 50,000 French had gone to the New World and these were mostly *voyageurs* and *coureurs de bois* (travelers and wood-runners) searching for fur. These rootless Frenchmen, who often married and merged with the Indians, offered France no permanent population base in the New World.

French Contributions. Like Spain, France left a heritage to American civilization. Her books on philosophy, science and engineering advanced the state of knowledge in regions like New Orleans, St. Louis, St. Charles and Mobile. Jesuits spread their faith and schools in French-held areas. Long after the French were expelled from the continent, their influence lingered in the laws of Louisiana and in the customs and *patois* of the Creoles (recorded by the "local colorists" in American literature, George Cable and Grace King).

Dutch Settlement. Following upon the discovery of HENRY HUDSON in 1609, the Dutch settled along the Hudson River from New Amsterdam (Manhattan) to Fort Orange (Albany). While they exploited the fur trade successfully, they were unable to build up a permanent deposit of settlers. They, too, instituted a **feudal pattern of settlement (the "patroon system")**, entailing religious discrimination, political absolutism and mercantilist restriction. Their history in America was brief but picturesque and was permanently captured in the prose portraits of WASHINGTON IRVING, who "naturalized" Dutch folklore so that it, too, became American.

Dutch influence lingered in many aspects of American life: in place and family names; in the system of public schools (the New Amsterdam elementary school of 1638 under ADAM ROELANTSEN was the oldest in America); in **American architecture** —the brick gable and gambrel roof, the gutter, the multicolored planks, the halfway doors and the high stoops; in the recreational customs of sleighing, skating, coasting, golfing and bowling; in holiday customs like Santa Claus and Easter eggs.

English Settlement. The objective student of American history acknowledges Spanish, French and Dutch contributions readily enough—and then asks the main question: Why did the English succeed where the others failed? **One reason is that conditions in England prompted large numbers of English men and women to migrate even though people are generally reluctant to leave an established homeland.**

Historians stress four general motives for the mass exodus that took place during the 17th century. Beginning with James I, the Stuart kings proclaimed themselves rulers by "divine right" and therefore absolute and infallible. When they coupled this claim with oppressive taxation without consent and with arbitrary arrest, those who suffered most were ready for flight. **By fleeing to the New World, they were actually going into a freer land for those absolute rulers permitted them to take their "rights of Englishmen" with them.**

The split in the Christian faith had created the Church of England with the English King at its head. Support of this church was required of all Englishmen (no matter what their faith). But in the religious struggles that followed upon the Reformation, men's religious convictions had deepened. Differences with the official faith abounded—**Puritans** sought to "purify" the Anglican Church of England of "popish" (i.e., Roman Catholic) practices; **Separatists** rejected the Anglican concepts entirely; and **Catholics**, of course, rejected any faith that foreswore allegiance to the Pope. **Anglican discriminations, persecutions and restrictions provoked dissenters to emigrate.**

In the early part of the 17th century **an economic depression gripped England.** With their eye upon a favorable wool market, English landlords secured Parliamentary permission to drive the yeomanry off the land and fence in their farms for sheepherding. Thus dispossessed, these farmers drifted as unemployed, "surplus" population into the cities. Those who were fortunate enough to be employed found themselves at the mercy of an inflation caused by the influx of Spanish gold. Finally, there were highly individual motives for flight such as those of the **disinherited younger sons** of the English nobility, or those stirred by the tales of RICHARD HAKLUYT to adventure, or those who could obtain release from prison if they emigrated.

THE THIRTEEN COLONIES

The "Tobacco Provinces." Virginia. After SIR HUMPHREY GILBERT and SIR WALTER RALEIGH both failed to establish permanent colonies in Virginia, the London ("joint-stock") Company made a third attempt in **1607** at **Jamestown**. This attempt succeeded through the efforts of CAPTAIN JOHN SMITH, the reinforcement of the settlement with immigrants and provisions, the discovery by JOHN ROLFE of the cure of tobacco, and the wisdom of SIR EDWIN SANDYS who forced the substitution of private for communal production and introduced the first measure of home rule in the New World.

Maryland. LORD BALTIMORE received a charter from Charles I which made him **proprietor** of the colony of Maryland. Baltimore's aim was to found **a haven for his Catholic co-religionists.** The success of this settlement (1634) was guaranteed when Baltimore opened his lands to settlement by Protestants (after protecting the Catholics with a **Toleration Act**) and when the colonists turned to the profitable production of corn, tobacco and livestock immediately.

NEW ENGLAND COLONIES

Plymouth. Plymouth was settled in 1620 by a group of **Separatists** who had fled to Holland from Scrooby, England, to seek religious freedom. Financed by the **Virginia ("joint-stock") Company**, they sailed to the New World in the **Mayflower** under leadership of JOHN ROBINSON and WILLIAM BREWSTER. They landed at Plymouth which was outside the legal limits assigned by the charter. Being "squatters" on untitled land, they drew up the **Mayflower Compact** to give themselves legality. A year later they secured legal title from the **Council of New England,** a company which had replaced the Virginia Company. Their success was ensured by the captainship of MILES STANDISH, the governorship of WILLIAM BRADFORD and their group perseverance in discharging their debts. In 1691, however, they were absorbed by their more powerful neighbor Massachusetts.

Massachusetts. Massachusetts as an area of settlement attracted some **Puritan** gentry and in 1629 they organized the **Massachusetts Bay Company** to finance a large-scale venture. They received a royal charter which omitted naming a location for the annual meeting. The directors of the company therefore decided to meet in the colony—a move which virtually freed them from royal control. By itself this could not insure the success of the venture. Between 1630 and 1640, however, persecution of Puritans was increased in England by Archbishop Laud. This caused the **great migration to Massachusetts of 25,000 Puritans**—an influx that guaranteed economic success and permanency.

Rhode Island. The Puritans established a "Bible Commonwealth" or **theocracy** (that is, rule of the state by the clergy) in Massachusetts. The Massachusetts colonist ROGER WILLIAMS, however, refused to accept the Puritan imposition of religious belief. In his opinion, the paths to salvation were many; **freedom of worship must be tolerated; above all, the church and state must be separated.** Hounded for these heretical beliefs, Williams fled Massachusetts and settled in **Providence, Rhode Island.** Two years later (1637) he was joined by MISTRESS ANNE HUTCHINSON and her followers who had stirred a hornet's nest in Massachusetts by preaching that the Puritan Saints were leading the commonwealth to damnation. **Complete religious freedom, peaceful relations with neighboring Indians and economic prosperity ensured the success of this venture.**

Connecticut. THOMAS HOOKER also quarreled with the Massachusetts Puritan governors. In 1636 he left Massachusetts to found Hartford. Others followed him and communities were set up at Wethersfield, Windsor, Springfield and New Haven. In the Charter of 1662 these many towns were united into the **Connecticut Colony** and prospered under a liberal government set up by the Fundamental Orders, the first written constitution in the New World.

Maine and New Hampshire. The areas of Maine and New Hampshire were granted as **proprietories** to SIR FERDINANDO GORGES and CAPTAIN JOHN MASON in 1623. Both were unsuccessful in settling the territory. However, settlers joined JOHN WHEELRIGHT (a follower of Anne Hutchinson) when he moved into that area from Massachusetts. Massachusetts thereupon laid claim to Maine and New Hampshire. In 1679 New Hampshire was able to shake loose from these claims and become a royal colony; but Maine continued as a Massachusetts province until 1820.

THE MIDDLE COLONIES

New York. In 1664 Charles II granted to his brother, the Duke of York, the land in the New World held by the Dutch (New York State). The Duke thereupon dispatched a task force of four frigates to New Amsterdam and compelled the surrender of the Dutch Governor PETER STUYVESANT. By 1668 the English were in possession of all the Dutch settlements. New Amsterdam thus became **New York** and under English rule settlement and prosperity advanced rapidly.

New Jersey. The Duke of York gave a generous portion of his proprietory grant to two favorites, SIR GEORGE CARTERET and LORD BERKELEY, which they divided into **East** and **West Jersey.** Because freeholds were granted on easy terms, these colonies were rapidly settled by families from adjacent colonies. They were united as a royal colony in 1702.

Pennsylvania. WILLIAM PENN, proprietor and Quaker, received his grant to Pennsylvania in exchange for a royal debt owed to his father. He wanted a haven in the New World for the universally persecuted Quakers. Instead, **Penn launched the colony as a "holy experiment" in religious and political freedom. The Frame of Government (1682) and the Charter of Privileges (1701) granted complete freedom of religious worship and a government in which most of the power was lodged in a unicameral (one-house) legislature.** Pennsylvania was a privileged area and as a result attracted numerous European immigrants, particularly from Germany.

Delaware. Penn bought Delaware from the Duke of York to protect the southern river-approach to Pennsylvania and, although permitted a large share of local autonomy, Delaware remained a possession of Pennsylvania until the American Revolution.

THE "DEEP SOUTH" COLONIES

North and South Carolina. The Carolinas were founded by eight proprietors. Their charter "established" the Anglican Church and placed restrictions on freedom of worship. The proprietors retained the English philosopher, JOHN LOCKE, to draw up a model government. Called the *"Grand Model,"* it was a fantastic array of carefully divided aristocracies. The plan was discarded and, eventually, a traditional plan of government was adopted. The success of the Carolina plantation was insured by the rapid spread of rice-planting in the south and free-farming in the north. When the proprietors surrendered their charter to the crown in 1729, two colonies were made from the grant.

Georgia. In 1732 George II of England wanted a buffer state north of Florida to protect the English colonies from the Spanish in Florida. In the same year, JAMES OGLETHORPE sought a proprietory grant to build a colony for the unfortunates in debtors' prisons. It was to be a model community where no rum was swilled and no slaves toiled. He secured his grant—but Georgia did not prosper. Debtors would not migrate in large numbers, land holdings were restricted, Negro slaves were prohibited, other labor was unavailable and constant border warfare discouraged all but the hardiest. In 1751 the grant was surrendered to the crown.

Summary. From this brief recital we can gather certain important information. The English colonies were founded by three different methods: **joint-stock company ventures, proprietory grants and splinterings from some parent colony.** A large number of colonies were turned back to the crown to become **royal colonies** ruled by governors appointed by the king. These included Virginia, Massachusetts, New York, New Jersey, New Hampshire and Georgia. In 1775, three were still proprietory—Maryland, Pennsylvania and Delaware. Only two of the colonies were **completely self-governing**—Rhode Island and Connecticut at the time of the Revolution.

CHAPTER I

COLONIAL FOUNDATIONS OF AMERICAN INSTITUTIONS

The English Base. The mighty surge of English into the colonies during the 17th and 18th centuries settled the cultural destiny of America. By 1790 their number was in excess of 2,500,000 and comprised about 80% of the total population. They had expanded not only by immigration but by natural increase as well. Their sheer numbers set the cultural pattern that eventually absorbed all non-English elements. The **English language became** practically universal—the means by which cultural developments in Europe were transmitted to the New World. American universities were patterned after the English, and the religious conflicts and settlements reflected those of England. Everywhere in this part of the New World, **English ideas and practices, laws and liberties were transplanted and took root.** This is a proper emphasis; but it would distort American history to ignore the many non-English tributaries that fed this broad English river.

". . . that strange breed of men . . ." Large numbers of immigrants speaking non-English tongues, practicing non-English faiths and pursuing non-English ways poured into the colonies from **North and South Ireland,** from **Scotland and France,** from **Germany and Switzerland.** And the **Dutch and Swedes** were already settled. Each group gravitated to its own community. The Scotch-Irish settled along the eastern foothills of the Appalachians in Virginia and the Carolinas; the Germans concentrated first in Pennsylvania and then migrated to New York, Maryland and points south; the French in South Carolina, the Swiss in Pennsylvania and North Carolina, the Irish in the Middle colonies and Maryland and the Jews in the seacoast towns. The customs which these people brought with them—their foods and fashions, their songs and stories, their habits and habiliments—were, for the most part, modified after several generations by the stronger English trends, but their distinctiveness flavored the English heritage. America's historic mission of cultural absorption and fusion had begun. The almost constant internal folk-movement into the frontier areas made commingling inevitable; intermarriage did the rest. Thus, from its founding day, **America was a melting pot of people and a haven for the persecuted.**

Motives For Immigration. Each century in history has produced more than its share of oppression and persecution. The seventeenth century in Europe was no exception. And when these struck, men fled. Thus the Germans fled the devastation resulting from the Thirty Years War that left in its wake decimated populations and ruined cities; they fled, too, from the confiscations and terrors unleashed by Catholic princes against their Protestantism and from the low subsistence level to which they were condemned as a result of the concentration of land and wealth in 17th century Germany.

The French who fled were wealthy Hugenots, who under the Edict of Nantes in 1685 enjoyed a measure of toleration. The revocation of this Edict, resulted in a ban on worship and home services, and in imprisonment and massacre.

The Scotch-Irish left North Ireland in droves to escape the oppressive acts of English landlords who crippled their thriving cattle and woolen industries, trebled their rents and excluded them from political office. The lot of their southern neighbors, the Irish Catholics, was even worse. Emigrants from Scotland had suffered humiliation and defeat in an effort to preserve their independence and clan-system; acts of expropriation had ruined them.

The Swiss fled from privileged aristocracy and lack of economic opportunity. As for the Jews, segregation and persecution were their unending lot. **The fundamental motive that drove the non-English in this century and those to follow to American shores was escape from pauperism, from political persecution, from religious discrimination and from oppressive social distinctions and prejudice. To the New World they looked for political freedom, for the right to worship freely, for a fluid class structure that would permit one's children to advance in social status and, above all, for economic opportunity and security.**

COLONIAL FREE ENTERPRISE

Early Obstacles to Free Enterprise. All the colonists who came to American shores sought to exploit its bountiful economic opportunities upon the basis of free enterprise. Free enterprise meant the private ownership of land and capital and the free use of both for private profit.

Serious obstacles impeded this motive. First was the **corporate nature** of the early settlements. Settlers, financed in their emigration by joint stock companies had to work as **company servants**, store their produce in a **common hold**. Their surplus-over-subsistence was shipped overseas for sale in Europe. Without incentive to produce a surplus, none appeared; and when profits failed, the company was compelled to sell or transfer land to individuals for private use. **This was a vital turning point in American history.**

A second obstacle to free enterprise was the grant of **royal monopolies** over the production or distribution of goods to individuals or companies. But colonists, with small accumulations of capital—individual or in partnership—ignored these monopoly assignments and **set up private trading posts** in the New World and **private channels for the disposal of goods abroad.**

Thirdly, in some of the colonies when land was granted to individuals it was limited by feudal entailments such as **quitrents** (a landlord's feudal fee) and **primogeniture** (the requirement that the first-born inherit *all* the property of his sire). It was not until the end of the Revolutionary War that these restrictions were permanently removed.

A final restriction to free enterprise existed in the **mercantile regulations** that flowed from England and served to exclude the colonists from certain occupations as well as to establish a single destination—England—for the flow of American goods abroad. But here we are dealing with a basic cause of the American Revolution. Mercantile restrictions were frequently evaded by the colonists.

Free Enterprise In Agriculture. There was great wealth to be gained from the vast stretches of arable soil in the New World. The first necessity was to **develop a self-sustaining agriculture.** All the colonists who became landowners produced the basic cereals; raised poultry and hogs; herded cattle; cut down forests for building material, fuel and tools; grew flax and wool for domestic manufacture; and concocted an impressive variety of alcoholic beverages. All this was accomplished against fearful odds: clearing a planting area took the most arduous toil; tools were very primitive; scattered fields and poor transport consumed precious time; without adequate fertilizer, planting itself was primitive and wasteful; blight, pest, disease and weather destroyed herd and crop.

Under the most favorable conditions, moreover, self-sustaining farming does not yield surplus for sale.

Colonial farmers were therefore forced to resort to "cash" crops. Such crops appeared most abundantly in all of the colonial sections but New England. From the middle or "bread" colonies of New York, New Jersey, Pennsylvania and Connecticut came wheat, corn, flour, flax and vegetables; and these were supplemented by livestock, pork and furs. The prime cash staple, **tobacco,** was produced in great abundance in Virginia and Maryland and in lesser quantities in North Carolina. North Carolina did, however, find a cash source in tar, pitch and turpentine. Rice and dye-producing indigo filled the coffers of South Carolina and Georgia.

Free Enterprise In Industry. Industrial enterprise was inevitable in a land so bountiful in natural resources. Natural harbors together with unlimited forests produced a prospering shipbuilding industry. Into the shipyards of the northern coast poured planks and timbers and masts; pitch and tar and turpentine; and barrel-staves. Abundant iron deposits led to the construction of bloomeries and forges; and to the manufacture of nails, chains, hardwares and tools. The sea, too, was a source for industrial enterprise. Fishing fleets combed the Newfoundland Banks for the primary catch, then brought them home for curing in preparation for shipment abroad. The whale's precious oil was vital to the candle-making industry. Of exceptional importance was the production of rum and whiskey, the pivot of an important cash-producing commercial venture.

Free Enterprise In Commerce. Colonies held a special place in the 17th century English **mercantilist theory of trade.** In this theory, **trade was a means for the accumulation of precious metal.** With luck metal would be discovered and mined abroad; alternatively, the way to secure sizeable quantities was to maintain a favorable **balance of international trade—balances paid for in gold.** To secure a favorable balance, England and all other western powers discouraged imports by imposing prohibitive tariffs; encouraged exports by granting bounties (subsidies), patents and monopolies, and fostered construction of large merchant fleets and protecting navies. **Colonies served the double purpose of providing essential raw materials and also a vital market for the disposal of goods manufactured in the mother country.**

Out of this theory came the **British navigation laws** that legislated the following restrictions upon colonial trade: certain "enumerated" articles (sugar, tobacco, cotton, wool, ginger, dyestuffs, rice, molasses, naval stores, copper ores, beaver skins!) could be exported to England only; when shipped, they had to be shipped in English ships manned by English crews. In 1733 a tax was placed on imports of sugar and molasses from the French and Dutch West Indies so that British West Indies sugar growers might have a monopoly; and Parliamentary Acts limited or forbade the production of iron and hats in the colonies so that there would be no competition with manufacturers at home. Were each of these acts enforced not an ounce of precious metal could leave the British Empire.

These measures had some good effects in the colonies: for example, they encouraged the shipbuilding industry and, for certain commodities, gave the colonists a guaranteed market. The British navy protected colonial commerce against piracy, tariff duties were lower on colonial products vital to British needs; the colonists also received bounties and many products not required by the mother country could be shipped outside the empire. But, the favorable balance of trade was maintained against the colonies as well as against foreign nations. The result was that the colonies suffered a continual shortage of specie (gold and silver).

To recover their losses the colonists were forced to establish lanes of commerce leading to a favorable balance for them, e.g., the "triangular traffic." Colonial products were traded in the West Indies for sugar, molasses and gold. The sugar and molasses were converted into rum and then shipped to Africa along with other products. In Africa, the ships were loaded with slaves, spices and gold. The slaves were then returned to the West Indies for more sugar, molasses and gold. When the triangular traffic was declared illegal by England and when, in addition, colonial efforts to issue paper money to replace lost specie were officially prohibited, the problem of free enterprise in commerce had obviously ceased to be only economic; it had become also political.

THE LABOR PROBLEM

Free enterprise meant not only private ownership and private profit but the ability to employ labor. There was, however, a labor shortage because of the small amount of capital required to become an entrepreneur. In spite of high wages and virtual full employment free hired hands were few in number and employers had to resort to forms of bonded labor.

Bonded labor fell into two groups: white servants and Negro slaves. White servants bonded themselves to a master for a fixed number of years in exchange for transportation from Europe to the colonies. They signed contracts called "indentures" and hence were known as "indentured servants." Such agreements were in the main voluntary, but not always so. A large number of indentured servants became such because, as debtors, criminals or paupers, they were sentenced to service in the colonies; and still others, chiefly children, were simply "spirited" (kidnapped) abroad and sold into service. The terms of service were from four to fourteen years.

Treatment of servants was modified by the need for them and since the need was steadily great, treatment was reasonably fair. Thus, in various colonies servants could vote and exercise the rights of legal "persons" (sue, be sued, buy, sell, etc.). Despite this, however, the servant was not free: his physical movements were restricted and he was subject to severe punishments. Once he was freed from his indentures, he entered the community without stigma and might, indeed, within a short while become an owner of servants himself.

The Slavery Problem. Bondage for the slave, however, was permanent. It is difficult, therefore, to read the history of slavery with an unbiased eye. The moral issue involved in human slavery and permanent bondage is inescapable. It is strange, then, to learn that the moral issue appeared only as a Quaker protest during the whole of the colonial period. The colonial attitude seems to have been that labor was needed; that slaves were available after 1619; and that slavery was more profitable than indentured servants in areas where there was extensive farming. So they were bought for the rice plantations of Georgia and South Carolina and the tobacco plantations of Virginia and Maryland. That was that!

Settlers of all religious faiths bought and sold slaves; even the Quakers did so until DANIEL PASTORIUS organized the Germantown, Pennsylvania Brothers to protest that slavery was contrary to Christian principle. This protest resulted immediately in the elimination of slaveholding among Quakers and eventually, in 1776, to the first formal demand in America for its complete abolition.

Enslavement of the Negro succeeded where efforts to enslave the Indian failed. History records that the Indian in the West Indies died in enslavement, while those on the continent of America proved so intractable and defiant that the experiment of enslaving them had to be abandoned. The Negro, on the other hand, could, apparently, be compelled to submit to his wretched fate. That some did nevertheless revolt is evident in the harsh codes adopted throughout the colonies which stripped the slave of all freedom of movement, and virtually permitted a master to put a recalcitrant slave to death.

Many reasons have been advanced to account for the "acceptance" of his lot by the Negro slave. The racialist explanation that the Negro is "by nature" servile is not worth consideration. Perhaps nearer the truth are the arguments that slaves were carefully conditioned in the West Indies before they were brought to the continent; economic necessity forced a degree of humanitarianism upon slave-holders; as an "old familiar" the slave was accorded some degree of status within the plantation system. Whatever the reasons, the fact is that the Negro slave was the base on which the whole pyramid of Southern society came to rest.

COLONIAL ADVANCES TO POLITICAL FREEDOM

The English Heritage. The economic motive to emigrate to the colonies is obvious. But what of the political motive? Political freedom was inbred in the 17th century Englishman. The charters under which they settled usually guaranteed the "rights and liberties" of Englishmen. This was no meaningless phrase. Rights and liberties defined for them the limits of government. Government, to the settler, meant a King with limited power—the limits being defined by **Magna Carta,** the **Common Law** and a **representative Parliament. Magna Carta** had limited the King's power by asserting that there was to be no taxation without consent of the taxed and no punishment without trial of the accused by his own peers. The **Common Law** further limited royal power by judicial protection of private property, by provision for trial by jury, by curbs upon arbitrary arrest through insistence upon proper warrant and the ready grant of the **writ of habeas corpus.**

Parliament was opposed to royal control of the treasury. Indeed, it was during the first century of English settlement in America that the issue of Parliamentary control was settled. The Civil War between the Puritan forces of Parliament and the Stuart kings resulted in the **"Glorious Revolution"** of 1688 and the **Bill of Rights** of 1689 which guaranteed to Englishmen the basic freedoms of speech, press and assembly as well as all the rights of fair trial. These, then, were the rights of Englishmen as the colonists knew them. However, they had to be adjusted to colonial conditions.

The Pattern of Colonial Freedom. Colonial freedom began its course in 1619 when the Virginia Company granted its colony a measure of home rule. A local government was to be set up consisting of a governor, a council selected by the governor and a House of Burgesses made up of two representatives from each settlement elected by the set-tlers themselves. **This marked the beginning of representative government in colonial America.**

When the company charter was revoked in 1624 and a royal governor was appointed, the colonists were permitted to keep their assembly. The powers of the assembly were quite extensive; it could make general laws, levy taxes, appropriate money for public purposes, and determine the salaries of the executives. The assembly was permitted to maintain a colonial agent in England to lobby for the interests of the colony. **This model of colonial legislature spread to all of the thirteen colonies and each one became a school for legislators.** In these assemblies men were trained in the art of practical government —in voting, in electioneering, in framing legislation, in debate, and the like. Independence did not find them unprepared.

DEMOCRATIC ADVANCES

The colonial assembly was a grant from above— the company, the proprietor or the crown. But when the Pilgrims drew up the Mayflower Compact, they **created a distinctly American concept of freedom.** In their historic voyage across the Atlantic, the Pilgrims were blown off course, outside the limits of the London Company. When they landed, it was without a charter, without some governing instrument. Since some form of government was required, before they disembarked they drew up this compact in which they pledged allegiance to the King and to any laws they themselves might agree upon. Herein lay **the principle of self-determination, the powerful idea that government must issue from the consent of the governed.**

This idea took root in the colonies with many variations. Thus, in Connecticut it appeared in the **Fundamental Orders, the first written constitution to appear in the New World,** with the elaboration that "consent" is a specific, limited and recorded grant of power. It appeared again in the New England **Town Meeting,** a device for the administration of purely local affairs and for the election of members to the colonial assembly. **To the Town Meeting came all the citizens to make laws directly. This was the ultimate in consent of the governed** and in this day of indirect, representative government it remains the model of a "perfect" or "pure" democracy.

Obstacles to Democracy. In spite of these notable and prophetic democratic advances, there were many barriers to complete democracy. The primary sources of these barriers were **English Councils appointed to make and execute law for the Empire;**

the colonial governor appointed by the crown or the proprietor (only Connecticut and Rhode Island had election of chief executives); and the existence of an effective aristocracy in the elected bodies in the colonies.

The restrictions upon the freedom and authority of the colonial legislatures that came from Crown Council and colonial governor were numerous—among others, the power to impose law upon the colonists without their consent and to set aside colonial law that conflicted with imperial or gubernatorial interests. This led to almost ceaseless conflict over matters of church, taxes, land sales, defense of the frontier areas, rents, and the like. From these conflicts derived a fundamental cause of the American Revolution—the demand of the colonists for legislation framed by their own representatives.

Representation was to be the issue for many years following the Revolution since the bulk of the colonists were unrepresented even in the colonial legislatures. Property qualifications for voting and holding office as well as religious restrictions kept more than sixty percent of the colonists disenfranchised and permitted government to rest in the hands of an aristocracy of wealth.

RELIGIOUS DEVELOPMENT IN THE COLONIES

A Paradox. A considerable number of English colonists came to the New World to worship freely, not to establish freedom of worship for everybody.

This paradox will puzzle the twentieth-century mind brought up in the ways of religious tolerance. But it made sense in the seventeenth century when men felt that an "unorthodox" path to God was a danger to the community. To "protect" the community against this danger of "heresy," colonial religious leaders bound the church to the state. Religious difference was thus converted into political crime and became punishable by the state.

Established churches became the rule. In the South the Church of England was made official; church attendance was required by law; believer and non-believer were taxed for its support; and the more "radical" faiths were punished or banished.

A better example is the Puritan domination of New England. The Puritan grip on the state was complete. In the early years of the Massachusetts colony a virtual theocracy (i.e., church-state) was created, and was dominated by a handful of elect "freemen." Not only was religion made a qualification for political activity, but for community existence itself. The Puritan "divines" (as the clergy were called) legislated the daily habits of its parishioner-citizens with a long series of notorious "blue laws." Intolerance reached its peak in the enforcement of blue laws. Roger Williams and Anne Hutchinson were only the most famous of the thousands who were whipped, banished or killed because of differences in belief. In these cases, church and state worked as one. The church excommunicated and the state punished by flogging, mutilation or exile. The state supported the clergy in their pursuit of the "sinful," of those who traveled or played games on the Sabbath, of those who blasphemed, of those who were inattentive during divine worship. There was a branded scarlet letter for the adultress. These were "normal" punishments. Occasionally, however —as in Salem, Massachusetts in 1692—religious hysteria and fanaticism rose against "witchcraft" and "witches" to such an extent that twenty innocent people were put to death on the basis of hearsay alone—the notorious witchcraft trials.

Calvinist Theology. How did the Puritans justify such excesses? Puritanism was transplanted Calvinism. Calvin's Protestantism was a rigorous theological system derived from the basic assumption that God's sovereignty is complete, that He is the source of all good and that obedience to His will must be absolute. In the beginning man was good, but he fell from grace in the Garden of Eden. Man fell into a state of total depravity, into sinfulness from which he could not work out his own salvation. The sacrifice of Jesus made possible the redemption of man. God "elects" to save whom He will without regard to faith or good works. He knows beforehand who will be saved since all things, past-present-future, are in His mind at once. Each man is predestined to election or damnation. Those who have been "elected" have full power to do the will of God, indeed, they have no choice but to do His will. Who are the "elect"? Calvin insisted upon "character" as an outward evidence of election and character was based upon rigid conformity with the standards set forth in the Bible, as interpreted by John Calvin.

The Puritan Variation of Calvinism. While the Puritans retained Calvin's central doctrines of total depravity of man, unconditional election of "saints," the limited atonement of Christ, irresistible grace and perseverance of the saints (that is, no saint could lapse from grace)—Calvinism itself underwent modification when transplanted to American soil. God's supremacy was basic, but His "arbitrariness" was limited by "covenants" made with men. These covenants were manifest in men's institutional devices—the family, the state and the church and could be discovered by close attention to the Bible and the world of nature, as interpreted by the clergy.

The concept of "covenant" thus raised man's dignity somewhat, though his end was still predestined. Within the church, the covenant appeared as a "congregation," a union of the elect gathered in a church body which had to be small in size, self-constituted, independent of other churches and not established by superior authority. Here an element of democracy appeared within the limits of "election."

Civil government emerged from the church as another covenant. This agreement provided that church membership was to be a prerequisite for citizenship and that only church members could participate in government. Church membership—the "elect"—rested on knowledge of the principles of religion, a pure life and open confession of faith and repentance of sin. One of the "elect" was to be minister and he, on behalf of the elders, "advised" (virtually, dictated) policy to the congregation which, in turn, could discuss and contradict—but rarely did so until the days of the Puritan decline. Here, then, was the base for the theocracy that dominated New England for more than half a century and whose effects have still not been entirely erased from the American culture.

The Collapse of the "One-Hoss Shay." The optimistic, fluid and democratic conditions in the New World could not for long sustain this pessimistic, rigid and theocratic system. Men and women arose within the Puritan fold who challenged all of the basic precepts of Puritan dogma. Immigration brought such a profusion of faiths to the New World that retention of an exclusive group became physically impossible. Puritanism undermined itself: its emphasis upon business and work led to concentration upon accumulation of wealth in *this* world rather than riches in the *next*. Its encouragement of learning and scholarship opened the Bible itself to critical examination, individual interpretation and even to hostile criticism as in the case of ETHAN ALLEN.

Moreover, its emphasis on *covenant* stirred the democratic sentiments of its membership and led to the rejection of God as "Absolute Monarch"; and where church and state were united, political struggles against Puritan control led inevitably to an attack upon its religious base. The work of Roger Williams in Rhode Island, William Penn in Pennsylvania and Lord Baltimore in Maryland established permanently the possibility of official tolerance of many faiths and the practicability of the separation of church and state. These colonies were havens for the persecuted and the Puritan fury was therefore easy to escape.

The Spread of the Enlightenment. But the most decisive blow to Puritanism and other dogmatic faiths came from the spread to the New World of the European Enlightenment. The substance of the Enlightenment was a new view of man, with the emphasis upon the freedom of his will and his infinite possibilities of achieving perfection. Arminianism for example, stressed that everybody could be saved, by the exercise of free choice, and that there could be "heaven on earth" if men agreed to live by a humane ethical code. Practical benevolence was the stress in Quakerism.

In the religious movement called the "Great Awakening" which began about 1730, reason was to a great extent abandoned for emotion. GEORGE WHITEFIELD, first of the great revivalists in America, toured the country preaching in an unorthodox manner, calling upon all who heard him to repent and be saved and to follow his "New Light." Nor could Calvinism resist the trend. In the ministry of JONATHAN EDWARDS (perhaps America's greatest theologian, whose sermons and other writings not infrequently rise to the status of literature) overwhelming emotion entered its spirit. Edwards still hammered at man's sinfulness and denied the idea of free will in true Puritan fashion, but he insisted that religion was not a matter of reason but of emotion, that through emotional release the beauty of God would be revealed as a spiritual and divine light immediately imparted to the soul.

Religion flourished through this movement; but another result was a deep split in the official churches. Impelled by the revivalist movement, Congregationalists moved into the Baptist fold, lukewarm Anglicans entered the more intense Methodist church and the stern Presbyterian church was split between "Old Light" and "New Light" groups. Heterodoxy now reinforced official toleration to produce the American religious way of life.

RELIGION AND INTELLECTUAL LIFE

The strong religious impulse during colonial times extended far beyond the church and over many more days than the Sabbath. It served to shape many of the institutions which are now considered primarily secular.

Religion and Education. In its inception, American education was parochial. The first primary school and "high school," mandated by the state of Massachusetts, were public. In 1642 the General Court of Massachusetts ordered charity schools set up; and in 1647 it decreed that in towns of 50 families a teacher of reading and writing must be provided; while in towns of 100 families a Latin Grammar school must be set up. But, the purposes of these schools were sectarian. The "abecedarians" (teachers) were required to pass rapidly from the ABC's to dogmatic instruction in religious doctrine. The universal New England text, for example, was that little Bible called *The New England Primer*, an ABC book. The entry under the letter "A" indicates the tone of the volume: "In Adam's Fall/We sinnèd all." The method was as severe as the curriculum and the best teacher was too often the readiest thrasher. Neither purpose nor method varied in the "high" school; these were college preparatory schools and the sectarian college curriculum dominated secondary studies.

Higher Education. For all practical purposes, colleges in colonial days were divinity schools. Harvard, the first to be founded (1636), was created to train Congregationalist ministers. William and Mary (1693) was intended to produce Anglican ministers. When the Harvard faculty turned toward a more rationalistic approach to learning, Yale was created (1702) to uphold Puritan orthodoxy.

Out of the "Great Awakening" in religion came Princeton for Presbyterians, King's College (Columbia) for Anglicans, Brown for Baptists and Rutgers for the Dutch Reformed. The course of studies varied little from that established in medieval Europe: much Latin and Greek, some Hebrew for Biblical scholarship, Aristotelian logic, rhetoric for the pulpit, and, of course, theology. More of the colleges, however, admitted Christians of various sects. But there was no breath of the liberal and practical arts until Franklin's College of Philadelphia. Religion dominated: five out of seven graduates became preachers.

Religion and Literature. If literature includes theology, history, chronicles and private journals, the literary productivity of the colonists was enormous. This mountain of writing remains a valuable store for those interested in old American ways of thought and life, and in historical documents. But its value *as literature* is far less. Religious obligation was primary; literature was at its service.

In essence, there was no distinction between a poem and a sermon; both had to be useful, purposeful and pious. One does not find "literary" probing of human motive and emotion in Puritan literature. What happened to the inner or outer man was simply another proof of God's righteousness. ANNE BRADSTREET, one of the few poets of the period wrote, when her husband left for England, "Lord, let my eyes see once Again/ Him whom thou gavest me,/ That wee together may sing Praise/ For ever unto Thee." Only such a view could produce MICHAEL WIGGLESWORTH's "Day of Doom," which was little more than a Calivinist tract in verse. That religious poetry can rise to artistic heights only when it is *in the first place poetry* is revealed in the works of EDWARD TAYLOR, a Puritan poet, who made God's beauty and goodness the subject matter of genuine poetry. But he is a solitary peak in a dismal valley.

Sermons. Of sermons there was no end. Nor were the topics confined to theology and dogma: in a day when there was no universal press, the pulpit served as one and the sermon often dealt with political, social and economic themes. But whatever the theme, the substance remained fixed—God's providence in a corrupt and sinful world. Not only the substance, but the form was fixed: the text was announced; its moral was drawn with proof and illustration; and then the message was driven home. All the figures of speech were employed to dramatize and make vivid the text. But even here, the preacher could not wander too far from the text—above all, doctrine must be clarified; the *what* not the *how* of the sermon was primary.

In spite of these conventions, the sermon could rise to literary merit and in the hands of a COTTON MATHER or THOMAS HOOKER or JONATHAN EDWARDS often did. These men could on occasion powerfully render the drama of the conflict between God with the forces of Satan; and there are few pieces as "alive" as Edwards' "Sinners in the Hands of an Angry God," which contains the famous sentence: "The God that holds you over the fire of hell, much as one holds a spider or some loathsome insect over the fire, abhors you."

History. Cotton Mather described the task of the Puritan historian when in the *Magnalia Christi Americana* he wrote: "I write the Wonders of the Christian Religion, flying from the depravations of *Europe*, to the *American Strand;* and assisted by the Holy Author of that religion, I do with all conscience of Truth, required by Him, who is the Truth, itself, report the wonderful displays of His infinite Power, Wisdom, Goodness and Faithfulness, wherewith His Divine Providence hath irradiated an Indian Wilderness." What interested the Puritan historian was to show Christ's marvels in America, to trace the hand of God in the course of events, and to record the historic mission of the new Israelites in a new Canaan. This is not to deny that much of the record of colonial settlement is brilliantly recorded; but they were hardly historians in our sense.

SECULAR TRENDS IN COLONIAL INTELLECTUAL LIFE

Literature. The Colonial atmosphere was predominantly, but not exclusively, religious. Secularism—the concern with *this* world—appeared as a secondary strain. In the travel literature, in the diaries of such observers as SAMUEL SEWALL, SARAH KEMBLE KNIGHT and WILLIAM BYRD, in the increasing number of essays—there was faithful rendition of the current scene, and portrayal of people and customs. This may in part be accounted for by the rise of an enlightened and democratic spirit that had begun to sweep eastward from the frontier areas and that demanded speech suited to the common man.

Diffusion of Knowledge. Mid-18th century America hungered for knowledge. New media of communication arose to fulfill this need. Subscription and public libraries were founded. In 1704 the *Boston News-Letter*, a four-page, two-column newspaper appeared and almost immediately became the vehicle for news, opinion and gossip; pulpits for secular preachers called editors. With the rise of the newspaper began a battle for freedom of the press since the great issues of the day were becoming increasingly political.

A great victory for the free diffusion of knowledge was won in the famed case of PETER ZENGER (1734), editor of the *New York Weekly Journal* who had attacked the Governor of New York in his editorial pages. Long before Governor Cosby of New York, Governor Berkeley of Virginia (1671) had set the official attitude toward the press with his utterance: "I thank God there are no free schools nor printing, and I hope that we shall not have any these hundred years; for learning has brought disobedience, and heresy, and sects into the world, and printing has divulged them, and libels against the best government. God keep us from both!" In Zenger's defense, however, Andrew Hamilton, his lawyer, pled for "the cause of liberty—the liberty both of exposing and opposing arbitrary power by speaking and writing Truth." The jury acquitted and the cause of a free press was founded by the historic decision.

The Fine Arts. No Puritan painter, or painter of Puritans, painted a nude. The dominant theme in painting was the Puritan himself, completely robed and severely austere—as befits one of the "elect."

Hampered by the absence of tradition or an atmosphere congenial to the production of significant art, the tendency among the finest American artists was to go abroad to study and work. This was the case with ROBERT FEKE, BENJAMIN WEST and JOHN SINGLETON COPLEY, among others. Among the serious artists only CHARLES WILSON PEALE remained, painting in the realistic tradition with great vigor and mature craft.

American architecture was of necessity derivative, importing the major European styles. Utility determined style; but as wealth and stability increased, more elaborate modes were employed, often recklessly: *Elizabethan, Restoration, Georgian* and other styles co-existed, uneasily but assertively.

THE NEW DAY DAWNING

The Rise of American Science. The works of Copernicus and Galileo and Newton had shattered the medieval conception of the universe, introducing rational, empirical science. Francis Bacon had proclaimed the supremacy of the inductive method and from the scientific societies in England, France and Italy had appeared the first efforts to analyze the physical and chemical universe. This scientific spirit could not but affect the New World.

Among those colonials most interested in the new science were the Puritans themselves. For them, there was no necessary conflict between science and theology. God was the architect of the universe and universal lawfulness was a testimony to his nature. Puritans, therefore, made minute investigations of the flora and fauna of the New World, collecting specimens and writing papers on botany and animal husbandry. Later, in the "enlightened" rational and scientific tradition came the remarkable pioneer work of DR. BENJAMIN RUSH in mathematics and medicine; of DAVID RITTENHOUSE with the pendulum, thermometer and mathematical instruments; and of JOHN BARTRAM, one of the foremost botanists of his day. From their work came the first American scientific society, the **American Philosophical Society**, devoted to promoting the applied sciences, practical arts and philosophy; to letting "light into the nature of things"; and to increasing the "power of man over matter."

Benjamin Franklin: The "New Man." The new day produced the new man—epitomized in the life of BENJAMIN FRANKLIN. He was equally effective as printer, editor, man of letters, inventor, scientist, philosopher, social theorist, diplomat and cosmopolite. From his scientific genius came important studies of air-currents, electricity and ocean currents; from his inventive genius, a stove, a sheet lamp and a lightning rod; from his social vision, the first liberal arts college in America, the first subscription library, the first scientific society; from his literary gifts, the "Poor Richard" almanacs, collected aphorisms, political pamphlets, letters and the *Autobiography;* from his diplomacy and statesmanship, a plan of union, a declaration of independence and a constitution. This is far from an exhaustive listing.

The source and stimulus of Franklin's activity was an emergent America, sharing in the Age of Enlightenment and Reason that was the dominant atmosphere in Europe. From these he derived his guiding concept that the **Creator was basically benevolent —a "reasonable" God, whose creatures lived in a world of infinite possibilities, the best of all possible worlds.** Man was, unfortunately, full of faults, irrationalities and superstitions; but he was infinitely perfectible. If man would but develop the habits of

thrift, **industry, self-discipline, sobriety and diligence he would realize his potential.** Franklin demonstrated how he himself had done this—it was all **up to the individual. Franklin opposed all restraints upon individual freedom and expression, whether by the state, as in mercantilism, or upon an individual, as in slavery.** Franklin's break with the past was not complete. For example, he did not arrive at the doctrine of the natural rights of man; he distrusted complete democracy; he opposed the rising commercial spirit and advocated a "physiocratic" (agricultural) society. But despite his inconsistencies, **Franklin was the bridge from the age of colonial dependence to that of national independence.**

CHAPTER II

THE FACTORS IN THE AMERICAN REVOLUTION

The British Factor. The "Glorious Revolution" of 1688 resolved the seventeenth century conflict between the British aristocracy and the British middle classes. Parliament had emerged the ruler of the nation and the landed nobility shared with the mercantile classes the leadership of Parliament. Both groups were concerned with maintaining *restricted* representation in Parliament and with using Parliament to protect and extend their profitable ventures in world trade. The colonial plantations in America were at once a menace and a promise: a menace in that their products could compete with English goods; and a promise in the many opportunities offered for speculation with surplus capital.

To eliminate the menace and to foster the promise Parliament created a Board of Trade made up of landlords and businessmen to guide the Parliamentary Ministry and especially the colonial secretary (known as the Secretary of State for the Southern Department) in the needs of British business. The needs of British business and colonial business were often in conflict. For example, the colonies profited from *world*-wide trade, England from *empire*-wide trade; English landlords fattened on colonial quitrents and the colonials refused to pay them; colonials sought a limitation on the slave trade to prevent a glut on the slave market, while English traders sought to redouble the number of slaves imported; colonial debtors wanted cheap paper money and English creditors wanted stable, hard currency; and so on.

Open conflict was delayed between 1688 and 1763 because of a period of "salutary neglect" or the failure of the Board of Trade to have its way in the colonies—this in spite of the many constitutional channels that existed for compelling colonial obedience (the governor's veto, judicial review by the Privy Council, the King's veto, etc.). **Salutary neglect resulted from the fact that colonial secretaries were frequently changed, that corrupt politics was the order of the day, that enforcement agents were unpaid or poorly paid, and that there was confusion of authority in the matter of colonial control.** But the day would come when the existing controls would be enforced and eventual crisis was inevitable.

The Factor of Colonial War. That climactic day was speeded by the outbreak in 1689 of a series of "world wars" that deeply involved the American colonies. France and England were the major contestants in these wars for empire control and the North American continent was a major area of warfare. In 1689, the English were limited in North America to the area of the thirteen colonies. North and West of this area, Canada and the Mississippi Valley were claimed by the French and France sought as well to gain the New England Colonies as a source of food and lumber.

Anglo-French Conflict. British (and colonial) eyes turned northward and westward for fish and fur, the attractive settlement areas in the Ohio Valley and the chance to break through the French encirclement. Even before the Anglo-French war in

Europe in 1689, the English had begun to penetrate Canada and the Ohio Valley, organizing a Hudson Bay Company to capture the fur trade. In 1689, King William's War began with a French offensive against New York and New England. The war was indecisive and the Treaty of Ryswick (1697) reestablished the *status quo ante bellum* (the state in which things were before the war). But in 1701 "Queen Anne's War" began and continued for twelve years. In the Treaty of Utrecht (1713) the future was forecast when France was compelled to surrender to England the Hudson Bay area, Newfoundland and Nova Scotia. But there was still no decision on the Ohio Valley. Nor was there any in "King George's War" (1744-1748) for in the Treaty of Aix-la-Chapelle the conquests made by both sides were returned.

The Military Aspect. But a final struggle was taking shape. The French had certain advantages in meeting this final struggle: they had a line of powerful forts extending in an arc from Quebec to New Orleans; they commanded as allies large forces of Indians; they possessed stronger land forces, brilliantly commanded; and they had the support of an absolute and highly centralized government.

On the other hand, the English outnumbered the French and Indians 1,500,000 to 100,000; their strategic position was more compact against assault and for a radiating offense; their supply lines were more certain because of command of the sea; they held the food-producing areas in America; and they too developed a number of brilliant commanders. Realizing that an important weakness existed in the division of their American territory into thirteen separate colonies, the English attempted a unification in 1754. The colonies were invited to send delegates to Albany to consider uniform action for defense of the empire. An **Albany Plan of Union** suggested by Benjamin Franklin failed of adoption by the several colonies and the aim of the Union to win the Iroquois (who had been alienated by English advances into the Ohio Valley) also failed. Colonial disunity hampered England in the war that ensued. When the war ended, England determined to eliminate the hazard of this chronic separateness. The consequences were not pleasant.

The "French and Indian War." The conclusive "French and Indian War" exploded in the Ohio Valley. Some Virginians had organized an Ohio Company to exploit a 200,000 acre grant of land from the crown for its fur and settlement value. Pennsylvanians had earlier built a fortified post in that territory but it had been destroyed by the French. To make intrusion permanently impossible, the French now began to build a new series of forts of their own from Lake Erie to the Ohio Forks. These were to pivot on Fort Duquesne (Pittsburgh). Since the Ohio Company claimed the Forks as its own, they sent GEORGE WASHINGTON to order the French away. He did; and a skirmish resulted which sparked the war.

French strength dominated the first three years: BRADDOCK and his armies were defeated; MONTCALM took two important British posts; and all efforts to invade Canada failed. But the tide turned when WILLIAM PITT, the British Prime Minister, strengthened the armed forces and overwhelmed the French navy. Generals AMHERST and WOLFE launched the final thrust at Quebec on the Plains of Abraham. British victory there doomed Montreal (as well as Wolfe and Montcalm).

By 1763, the French were thoroughly beaten and in the Treaty of Paris ceded to England all claims to Canada and the land east of the Mississippi River —except New Orleans. To Spain was given Louisiana (with New Orleans) and French territory west of the Mississippi. Only two tiny fishing islands, St. Pierre and Miquelon, remained in French possession. Nor was this the full measure of French defeat. She was driven from India by the British Clive and from her lucrative slave-trading posts in Africa. England now stood astride four continents.

The "Problem of Empire." England's "problem of empire" was enormous. To acquire an empire she had spent vast sums and colonial upkeep was a burdensome expense. Moreover, she had inherited everywhere diverse peoples, with diverse customs, languages and even stages of civilization. How were these to be brought together into some form of imperial unity? How much freedom could she permit the new lands? How was such a vast area to be defended and policed?

The war had revealed her essential weakness in the American colonies. When she had requisitioned men and money for the vital campaigns, the colonists had rejected or evaded the requests. When she had tried to enforce the mercantile system against the enemy, France, the colonists continued with the triangular traffic. French armies in Canada were openly supplied with food by New England. Everywhere evasion, disobedience and downright disloyalty. What was more, she had the uncomfortable feeling that these obstreperous colonies were no longer dependencies but *rivals* in the economic areas of agriculture, manufacturing and commerce. She must take steps; she did and released a holocaust.

The Mercantilist Factor. The steps taken by England after 1763 were in a colonial world whose economy had emerged as a strong rival to England's own.

Like England's, it was accumulating surpluses for investment; it demanded an expanding economy for the profitable employment of money and men. But it was forced by the mercantilist system to seek expansion areas where British capital had not penetrated. Tobacco had exhausted the land, and tobacco planters were turning to grain production and land speculation. Colonial merchants competed for the trade in the sugar and molasses plantations of the West Indies. Capital might have gone into manufacturing but restrictive legislation like the Iron Act of 1750 prevented the construction of rolling mills and steel furnaces. The end of the French and Indian War brought new hope to these investors.

The Factor of the Western Lands. Prior to the elimination of the French, the English encouraged westward settlement by the colonists. It was profitable for the British (and American) land speculators and was useful as a defensive buffer against the French. With the French out of the way, the British sought to exploit their advantage. The eastern seaboard needed intensive cultivation. English creditors found it impossible to pursue their debtors beyond the frontier. And **Pontiac's Conspiracy** in 1763 showed that westward movement would create a continuous Indian problem.

The colonial viewpoint was, of course, a conflicting one. Virginia planters had already set up new land companies prepared to take up millions of acres of unsettled western land. But these had been secured from colonial governments, not from England. Such titles were under fire from two sources: (1) from competing colonial claims to the same territory; and (2) from colonies that had no western claims. The latter in particular were eager to remove the western lands from competition and had petitioned Parliament to set up new colonies in that area. Parliament seemed so inclined, and the new land companies hastened to get in their bids for land grants. Parliament wavered and then made a fateful decision.

The "Aristocracy" Factor. Though America began as a western frontier of Europe, an area of escape from a "closed" European society, she had developed her own pattern of stratification as a result of the unequal accumulation of wealth. By 1763, the eastern seaboard had produced a colonial "aristocracy." Compared with that of the Old World, it was untitled and very fluid; but it did represent a controlling group that strove to maintain its control at all costs.

English traditions that served to foster this control were retained; thus, feudal practices like entail, **primogeniture** and quitrents prevailed, as did imprisonment for debt and barbarous prison practices. The franchise was restricted by property and religious qualifications; representation favored settled as against frontier areas; and church and state were united.

Needless to say, such measures antagonized the unpropertied. The propertied and powerful were haunted by fear of a revolt of the "lower classes," and they were being undermined by England herself. Competing British capitalists were closing off investment opportunities; threats to enforce the navigation acts doomed a favorable balance of trade; their burden of debt to British creditors had become tremendous.

The Factor of the "Lower" Classes. The so-called "lower classes" were a varied group—small farmers, small shopkeepers, urban artisans, frontiersmen, indentured servants and slaves. Each group suffered grievously under the severities of British rule, and in each, discontent grew.

But the most forceful leveling element was the frontier itself. Pressures on the eastern seaboard drove many old-time settlers to the margins of civilization—at that time, the Appalachian region—and new Scotch-Irish and German immigrants went there directly to avoid the settled communities of the East. The harsh environment produced a new type of American: the self-reliant individualist who scorned privilege and class distinction. They pushed ever westward into the Mohawk, Shenandoah and Susquehana Valleys, ignoring prohibitory law, proclamation and court order, "squatting" without legal title when necessary—always in conflict with the British land speculator.

CRISIS AND UNITY

By 1763 the crisis had begun to develop. Certainly John Adams was right when he wrote: "The revolution was in the minds of the people, and the union of the colonies, before hostilities commenced. The revolution and union were gradually forming from the years 1760 to 1776." "The minds of the people" were repositories not only of grievances but of democratic sentiments and ideas deposited during the many years of resistance to royal and clerical absolutism.

Now, in the mid-18th century, there came from England and from France a new democratic emphasis through the doctrines of LOCKE, MONTESQUIEU, VOLTAIRE, ROUSSEAU, ADAM SMITH and BECCARIA. From Locke came the doctrine of the "natural rights" of man to life, liberty and property; from Montesquieu, the relativity of government to time and place and the need for a separation of the powers of government to prevent tyranny; from Voltaire, **attacks on superstition;** from Rousseau, **a defense of revolution;** from Smith, **the great attack on mercantilism;** from Beccaria, **a philosophy of humanitarianism.**

The Proclamation of 1763. "Pontiac's Conspiracy" made the problem of the western lands an immediate one. A Royal Proclamation sealed off the Western lands beyond the Appalachians. In this way England extinguished the hopes of land speculators for new investment, and the dreams of pioneers for a thrust westward.

The Grenville Program. GEORGE GRENVILLE, named Prime Minister in 1763, was an honest though mediocre man. He discovered in the colonies shockingly dishonest practices: smuggling in defiance of the Acts of Navigation; disregard of British law in general; and inefficient, wasteful customs collection. He returned to England determined to remedy these conditions.

The Troop Shipment. First he sent ten thousand troops to America. The colonists, he argued, ought to welcome and support this force. The question was, defense against whom? Against the Spaniards and Indians? Then certainly the troops should be stationed along the frontier; instead they were lodged in the large cities of Boston, Halifax and New York. The colonists reasoned that the troops must have been sent, not for defense, but for customs collections.

The Sugar Act of 1764. As a "just and necessary" measure to raise revenue for the defense of the colonies, a Sugar Act was passed, levying new duties on sugar, wines and other imports. It lowered the duty on molasses (the chief item in the smuggling traffic) but arranged for its efficient collection.

Enforcement of Trade. To strengthen the acts of navigation and to end smuggling, Grenville provided a new bureaucracy armed with new powers. All absentee officials were ordered to the colonies as supervisors. **Writs of Assistance** (general warrants of search) were revived. Customs officials were made legally immune if they made false arrests. **The burden of the proof was on the accused.** Smugglers could be tried in England.

The Currency Act of 1764. An earlier Currency Act was revived which prohibited the establishment of land banks. (A land bank was the colonial practice of printing bills of credit which were then loaned to farmers who pledged their property up to half of its assessed value.) Bills of credit could not be offered in payment of debt—particularly inter-empire debts.

The Quartering Act of 1765. In the colony in which troops were stationed, barracks or quarters, rations and transport were to be provided by the local inhabitants.

The Stamp Act of 1765. Duties in the form of stamps ranging from half-a-penny to ten pounds were to be placed on all legal and commercial documents, newspapers, pamphlets and almanacs.

The Reaction to the Grenville Program. One is tempted, in analyzing this program, to say that the revolution was plotted in London and carried out in America. Every colonist was in some way injured by this program. In the urban areas violence broke out as artisans and their intellectual leaders, organized into groups known as the "Sons of Liberty," intimidated would-be stamp collectors, wrecked the houses of customs officials and stamp collectors, burned stamp collectors in effigy and tarred and feathered them in reality.

Less radical elements sought an appeal to reason. Of particular significance was the call by the legislature of Massachusetts for an inter-colonial assembly to consider ways and means to effective action. Nine colonies responded to the call and met in New York in 1765. The declaration drawn up by this first successful effort at colonial unity is so significant that it warrants summary:

The Declaration of the Stamp Act Congress began with an unqualified pledge of allegiance to King and Parliament. It then asserted the "inherent rights and privileges" of Englishmen. Among these is the right that "no taxes should be imposed on them, but with their consent" given personally or through representative; that not the British House of Commons but their own legislatures represented them and that they alone may levy taxes; that trial by jury cannot be denied; that the Stamp Act perverts English liberties; that the duties levied (in the Sugar Act) cannot be paid because of the lack of specie; that duties are unnecessary since colonial profits ultimately center in England to pay for manufactured goods; that the recent trade restrictions will make the purchase of such goods impossible. Therefore, the colonies demanded the repeal of the stamp duties and other acts restricting American commerce.

The Constitutional Debate. The fundamental question had been raised: What is the nature of true representation in a federal system such as that represented by a mother country and her colonies? The British view was that representation was "virtual," that is, a member of Parliament stood for all Englishmen. An English law had the same validity in England, Scotland and Massachusetts. The colonies, as corporations, could be created and dissolved at will. Their legislatures were subject to the will of the King (and Parliament). The colonists denied that an "imperial Parliament" exists. **Laws, they held, derive their validity from enactment by representatives of the governed.**

The Repeal of the Stamp Act. Neither reason nor violence achieved the repeal of the Stamp taxes—but an effective colonial boycott of British goods did. Parliament was petitioned for repeal by merchants whose business losses had been severe. The Parliamentary act of repeal was accompanied by a **Declaratory Act** which reaffirmed the British concept of representation by stating that the King and Parliament had the right to "make laws . . . of sufficient force and validity to bind the colonies and people of America . . . in all cases whatever."

The Townshend Acts. The climax of united action approached swiftly with the imposition, two years later (1767), of the **Townshend duties on glass, lead, tea and paper.** The Stamp Act scene renewed itself and, if anything, with redoubled violence. The distinction discovered by Townshend that this was no *internal* but an *external* tax, one that only Parliament could levy, was angrily rejected. The boycott was resumed, attended by violence in Boston. On March 5, 1770, British troops committed the **Boston "Massacre"** (five killed and several wounded). Counting the cost of collecting the new taxes too expensive, a new Prime Minister, LORD NORTH, repealed the Townshend duties—except that on tea.

The Boston Tea "Party." For Lord North tea was the symbol of the power and prestige of Parliament. But SAMUEL ADAMS, American propagandist and patriot, converted it into a symbol of tyranny and a standard for revolt. Time and circumstance favored Adams. The British East India Company was in serious financial straits. Because of a threepence duty upon tea, the colonists were boycotting it. Parliament decided to intervene on the Company's behalf. It eliminated an export tax required for any shipment to the colonies and in this manner made the East India Company tea the cheapest the colonists could buy. Parliament was rarely so generous and so considerate of consumer interest. Some American merchants were injured by this transaction for the Company was also given a monopoly over the distribution of the tea inside the colonies. But most Americans would benefit. The ships sailed for the major ports.

When the British ships bearing tea arrived they were met in New York, Philadelphia, Boston and Charleston by well-organized bands of patriots. In some cases they persuaded captains to about face, in others the tea was forced into warehouses and was not distributed. In Boston, Samuel Adams incited the Sons of Liberty to action and on the night of December 16, 1773, they dumped the tea into the ocean—the episode famous in history as the "Boston Tea Party."

The Intolerably Coercive Acts. Parliament responded with a severe enactment known in England as "Coercive" and in the colonies as "Intolerable." The Port of Boston was to be closed until the dumped tea had been paid for. The Massachusetts legislature was virtually shut down. Trials of Englishmen for crimes committed in the colonies could be removed to England. A new **Quartering Act** was inflicted upon the Bostonians and four new regiments arrived to keep peace and order. British General Gage was made Governor of Massachusetts.

The Quebec Act. Colonial indignation over the treatment of Massachusetts rose and protests thundered from legislature and pulpit. This was the moment England selected to promulgate the **Quebec Act,** to resolve the western lands question; to make some provision for the Catholic French Canadians; and to channel the fur trade to Montreal. All territory south of what is now Canada to the Ohio and Mississippi Rivers was incorporated with the province of Quebec. Government there was to be of the more absolutist form to which the Canadians were accustomed. The effect of this action upon Americans can be readily guessed.

At the Meeting of Roads. Boston became the cause of all America. Samuel Adams had earlier conceived the idea of **"Committees of Correspondence"**—a tight organization of dedicated men who were determined to bring the issue to the people. The Virginia patriot, PATRICK HENRY, set up such a committee there and before long a network of committees appeared in all the colonies.

A second such agency was the **Continental Congress**—a representative and federated group that had been so effective in the Stamp Act crisis. Patrick Henry proposed that an annual meeting of the group consider inter-colonial affairs. The Massachusetts Legislature concurred and in 1774 sent out a call for a meeting to be held in Philadelphia.

The Continental Congresses. In this manner the First Continental Congress was born. In the historic meeting in **Carpenter's Hall** the following was accomplished: resolutions were passed denouncing the treatment of Massachusetts; colonists were called upon to resist similar treatment and to fight if necessary; in a declaration of grievances, the rights of Englishmen were reasserted; the case against Parliament was duly documented; and, finally, the groundwork for the most intensive boycott (called the **"Continental Association"**) of British goods was laid.

Although the Congress called for another meeting if grievances persisted, there was still hope of a reconciliation. Britain responded however by cutting many of the colonies off from all trade except with Britain proper and from the Atlantic fisheries; and then General Gage commanded a troop of regulars to confiscate military supplies which he believed were being stored in Concord. This was the historic day of April 19, 1775, the day of the "RIDE OF PAUL REVERE" and WILLIAM DAWES and the "shot heard round the world."

Military "supplies" were first encountered by the British at **Lexington** in the form of "minutemen" (armed colonists) who blocked their path to Concord. The first blood was drawn. Nonetheless, the British pushed on to **Concord**—and to even greater resistance. After destroying some military supplies they began a long and disastrous trek to their base. The road was ambushed by minutemen. In Boston colonial militia gathered outside the city. The moment of pitched battle had arrived.

The **Second Continental Congress** met on May 10, 1775, their minds still divided—but the movement of events was beyond their control. Their task was difficult: They had no legal or official status, but the times called for action and unity. They supplied it—brilliantly. They appointed as Commander-in-Chief of the armed forces, George Washington; they raised armies, created a navy and commissioned merchant vessels to serve as privateers; they taxed and borrowed money at home and abroad; they set up a treasury system and a postal system; they issued currency; they negotiated alliances with the Indians and with European nations; they drew up two historic documents: The **Declaration of Independence** and the **Articles of Confederation.** And they fought a war to the point of victory.

THE BIRTH OF A NATION

The "Hesitant Gentlemen." It is difficult for us to understand the reluctance of the colonists to declare their independence. In reading Patrick Henry's noble address to the Virginia House of Burgesses on March 23, 1775, one is struck by his hostile references to the gentlemen who, though able and patriotic, suffer the "illusions of hope," who ignore England's obvious military preparations, who shut their eyes to England's harshness, who long for reconciliation and who cry "Peace, Peace—when there is no peace." His utterance was prophetic. But when, in May, the Second Continental Congress drew up the **"Declaration of the Causes and Necessity of Taking up Arms,"** it read in part:

We mean not to dissolve the union which has so long and so happily subsisted between us. Necessity has not yet driven us to that desperate measure or induced us to excite any nation to war against them (England). We have not raised armies with ambitious designs of separating from Great Britain and establishing independent states.

Clearly, independence was a thought harbored only by a few daring and radical spirits in the year 1775.

From Hesitation to Decision. Independence was an act of necessity, not choice.

The awful reality was that of spreading war and mounting dead. In May, **Ticonderoga** was assulted and taken; in June, a colonial army was routed from **Breed's Hill** overlooking Boston; in July, Washington took command of 14,000 troops; in August and September, there was war in Canada; in December, hostilities commenced in Virginia. Why? Because a state of war in fact existed. England refused to negotiate. On July 5, 1775, an "olive branch" petition to George III drawn up by JOHN DICKINSON on behalf of the American people pleaded for reconciliation on the basis of British suspension of hostilities. It was rejected out-of-hand. Instead, the colonies were declared to be officially "in rebellion" and Hessians (hired mercenaries) landed to press the hostilities.

Mission Abroad. The colonies had said: "necessity . . . . has not induced us to excite any other nation to war." Little "excitement" was required since all of England's enemies were already absorbed with the conflict. The advantages of a military defeat of England in its European wars were immediately apparent. France welcomed the agents sent by the Continental Congress to purchase war materiel. The Americans, Benjamin Franklin and Silas Deane and the Frenchman, Beaumarchais, were arranged for outfitting privateers and large shipments of arms and powder. If these measures were to be continued a declaration of independence had to be made.

Within the colonies radical elements ejected royal governors and "loyal" proprietors from government. Independent state governments were created on more democratic foundations. Recognizing the trend, the Congress issued a call for their creation to all the colonies. The contradiction of independent states within a dependent nation needed to be resolved.

"Common Sense." Such were the material pressures that drove the Continental Congress to a declaration of independence. At the crucial moment, in January, 1776 appeared THOMAS PAINE'S pamphlet *Common Sense*—a passionate and compelling cry for independence. Paine did not want to *argue* the case; he wanted only to *state* it. Government, he asserted, is at best a necessary evil, and, at worst, intolerable. Monarchy is at best absurd and, at worst, in the form of George III, brutish and tyrannical. This "Royal Brute of England" rules an island and, absurdly, the island rules a continent. Sever the connection—for it is in fact severed. America's is the cause of all mankind. "The sun never shined on a cause of greater worth. . . . Freedom hath been hunted around the globe. Asia and Africa have long expelled her. Europe regards her like a stranger, and England hath given her warning to depart. O! receive the fugitive, and prepare in time an asylum for mankind." The effect of Paine's cry was tremendous.

The Declaration of Independence. On June 7, 1776, RICHARD HENRY LEE moved in the Congress "That these United Colonies are, and of right ought to be, Free and Independent States." The motion was passed after a month of furious debate. A drafting committee was constituted consisting of THOMAS JEFFERSON, JOHN ADAMS, BENJAMIN FRANKLIN, ROGER SHERMAN and ROBERT LIVINGSTON. On July 4, 1776, the Declaration of Independence, written by Thomas Jefferson and amended by the others, was read and adopted.

This declaration, born from a moment in history, had the quality of eternity about it. It has sections of special pleading, a long list of "abuses and usurpations" on the part of the King of England; but these sections are today unread, dated, and, in the light of modern historical scholarship an incomplete and sometimes inaccurate presentation of the causes which impelled the colonies to separation. What gives the declaration its special quality is its philosophic assumptions—"self-evident truths," truths which are "axiomatic." Let us restate them here:

When in the Course of human events, it becomes necessary for one people to dissolve the political bands which have connected them with another, and to assume among the powers of the earth, the separate and equal station to which the laws of Nature and of Nature's God entitle them, a decent respect to the opinions of mankind requires that they should declare the causes which impel them to the separation.
We hold these truths to be self-evident,
—that all men are created equal,
—that they are endowed by their Creator with certain inalienable Rights,
—that among these are Life, Liberty and the pursuit of Happiness.
That to secure these rights,
—Governments are instituted among men,
—deriving their just powers from the consent of the governed,—
That whenever any Form of Government becomes destructive of these ends,
—it is the Right of the People to alter or to abolish it.
—and to institute new Government. . . .

WAR AND PEACE

The Revolutionary War. Only in retrospect does the Revolutionary War seem orderly. One cannot adequately record the terrible pain and suffering. The years from 1776 to 1778 do, however, seem like a unified stage in the war. Washington's chief objectives were to keep an army in the field; to control the hinterland while the British held large, fixed points; to harass and confuse the enemy; to avoid a major battle until he was ready for it. He had many advantages: he was campaigning on familiar soil; his men were good marksmen and were equipped with a superior rifle; his opponents, the mercenaries, were not the most enthusiastic warriors; the British were forced to keep close to their overseas supplies; and the opposing general staff did not adapt easily to the tactics required in the New World.

With all these advantages, why did victory not come sooner? The reasons are numerous: enlistments were short-term; recruits were reluctant to fight away from home; supplies were in constant shortage; large numbers of the colonists were either indifferent or opposed to the struggle; his men were almost always outnumbered and he was without a navy.

A British plan for the capture of New York provided Washington with the opportunity he sought. The plan was three-pronged. Two of them failed to materialize and the north-descending General Burgoyne was outnumbered by the Americans under General Gates at Saratoga. It was October 17, 1778, a day of decisive victory and a turning point in the war.

Diplomacy. The second phase of the war hinged on the diplomatic isolation of England. The victory at Saratoga brought France into the war in spite of her fears of bankruptcy and of unleashing the American spirit of equality among her own oppressed subjects. On February 6, 1778, France and America signed two treaties, one of commerce and one of alliance. The independence of the United States was recognized and military aid was to be forthcoming until independence was secured. Mutual conquests were to be recognized and neither was to sign a separate peace treaty. France then brought Spain into the war by dangling the hope of recovering Gibraltar, Minorca and Florida. And now that France was at war, neutrals began to suffer from England's naval reprisals. To protect themselves, they organized a **League of Armed Neutrality** which embraced Russia, Prussia, Denmark, Sweden, the Netherlands and the German Empire. Against England they enforced the principle that neutral ships carry only neutral goods. In 1780, England declared war on Holland and her isolation was complete.

Victory. The new alliances offset many of the initial disadvantages: the Americans now had a navy, the British supply line was even more precarious; England's energies were divided and she had to look to a possible invasion of her own country; supplies poured into the New World; foreign military leadership (VON STEUBEN, KOSCIUSKO, LAFAYETTE, etc.) improved the quality of the army. A series of maneuvers brought the British army into the South under the command of Lord Cornwallis. With brilliant combined generalship by Washington and NATHANIEL GREENE, Cornwallis was forced into a trap at Yorktown. The possible escape to the sea was cut by the Comte de Grasse and the French navy and Cornwallis surrendered. The war was over and won.

The Peace of Paris 1783. Peace negotiations soon revealed what a "marriage of convenience" the Franco-American alliance had been. Each side pursued its own advantage. When the American peace commissioners—Franklin, Jay, Adams and Laurens—were convinced that France and Spain were negotiating privately to the disadvantage of the colonies, they signed a separate peace treaty with England.

England recognized the independence of the United States. The boundaries were fixed: from the Atlantic Ocean to the Mississippi River and from the Great Lakes to the northern boundary of Florida. The Mississippi was to be open to British and American commerce. Creditors were given permission to collect their debts without legal impediment. The United States promised that it would recommend to the state legislatures the restoration of loyalist properties (confiscated during the war). England granted the United States fishing rights off the coast of Newfoundland. The battle was long, but the rewards were great.

The Secondary American Revolution. The Declaration of Independence had widened the great gulf between patriot (or Whig) and loyalist (or Tory). The ranks of these anti-Americans, the loyalists, were numerous. They were drawn from wealthy merchants who enjoyed special British privileges under the mercantilist system; from aristocratic-minded gentlemen who genuinely feared and abhorred "mobocracy"; from the royal governors and their numerous retinue; from royalist-oriented proprietors and their armies of bureaucrats; from the Anglican clergy and their parishioners; from normally conservative lawyers to whom revolution was illegal and, oddly, from small farmers whose landlords were patriots. Patriots confiscated the estates of loyalists, barred them from professional practice, tarred and feathered them in more generous moods, and killed them when aroused. One hundred thousand loyalists were driven into exile.

The expulsion of this mass of the propertied—the rulers and the aristocrats—prepared the way for reforms in the new state governments: New state constitutions were drawn up with bills of rights, provision for amendment, restriction of executive power, enlargement of the legislative power, election of governors, short terms of office and checks and balances. However, democratic advance stopped short of removing religious and property qualifications for voting.

Nonetheless, there was an extension of suffrage through an extension of land-holding. Large reserves of royal forest, proprietary holding and confiscated Tory estates were divided and sold in small parcels to depressed farmers. With these changes went all feudal vestiges—entail, primogeniture and quitrent. With the Quebec Act eliminated, the western lands were thrown open for speculation and settlement. Many more states moved toward a separation of church and state.

Schemes were set afoot for the abolition of slavery on a voluntary or gradual basis. Wide reforms were instituted in prison practice. In some states capital punishment was limited to murder. In others there was a modification of imprisonment for debt.

INTELLECTUAL ASPECTS OF THE AMERICAN REVOLUTION

Revolution and Enlightenment. The American Revolution was one concrete manifestation of the philosophic "Enlightment" of the 18th century. But Americans did not produce any significant or original philosophic system. They were practical philosophers and their most characteristic product was the political pamphlet, which borrowed freely from current European ideas of natural rights, religious liberty, liberal religion, freedom of thought and universal progress. Their thought was derivative, but translation of thought into action was their great contribution.

Doctrinal. Enlightenment and Revolution had these ideas in common: They were both magnificent protests against authoritarianism; both were products of a new faith in man and in man's rational powers; both repudiated the division of mankind into "superior" and "inferior," into privileged and dispossessed; both drew upon certain Newtonian concepts. SIR ISAAC NEWTON had posited in his universal system a conception of the physical world governed by discoverable law and mathematical harmony. To discover these universal laws one does not require any special or divine revelation. Human intelligence is sufficient. Man's institutions were a species of natural law. Man, too, was a product of "*nature's* God" and as such is conditioned by his environment, the sum total of all his experience. He was no "fallen," depraved creature; quite the contrary. He is capable of infinite perfection through a program of planned improvement.

Religion. The Enlightenment appeared in American religious thought as an emphasis upon God's essential benevolence. Everywhere the universe exhibits evidence of God's architectural design, His rationality. But religion must stand the test of man's reason. In a "natural religion" God loves all people and seeks their happiness. Since this is so, man must himself seek it. Happiness is the absence of personal sinfulness and social evil. In a natural, "enlightened" religion, theology is practical ethics.

From the "natural religion" of such clergymen as SAMUEL JOHNSON, JOHN WISE, JONATHAN MAYHEW and CHARLES CHAUNCEY to the extreme "rationalism" of the early Franklin, Ethan Allen and Thomas Paine (*The Age of Reason*) was an almost inevitable step. During the Revolution, Deism took root among American intellectuals. The universe, in this conception, was a perfect, self-operating machine which God had created, set in motion—and then retired from. That this system of belief aroused bitter hostility is understandable; but it was popular with many of the leaders of the Revolution and its influence was correspondingly strong.

Natural Rights. Revolutionary writers sought universal principles in the doctrine of natural rights. The fundamental concept in this doctrine was that of "social contract." In the original state of nature—went this theory—there was no civil authority; there were only individuals possessing the rights of life, liberty, property and pursuit of happiness. But the oppression of the weak by the powerful forced men to abandon this condition and to substitute a state of collective freedom. The creation of government was a voluntary act and was incorporated in a "social contract" which provided that the civil authority would undertake to protect the rights of men and that men would in exchange obey the civil authorities. Government originated, then, in the consent of the governed; theirs is the ultimate sovereignty; and the right of revolution is to be exercised when their rights are denied or destroyed. Many influences supported and augmented this doctrine: the chartered origins of the colonies; congregational church practices; the foundation of the first local governments; and wide reading of Blackstone's *Commentaries* (on law) and John Locke's *Essay on Human Understanding*.

Humanitarianism. The doctrine of natural rights was linked in the Revolutionary Mind with that of universal progress. In the view of the "rational" man progress was "inevitable." Here were the colonies moving from bondage to freedom; the growth of science and medicine, the spread of literacy, the accumulation of wealth, the rise in standards of living. So the prevailing mood was optimistic. However, this doctrine of inevitable progress had to confront the fact of widespread human misery. The task was clear: human misery must be eradicated and those forces in the environment which produced misery must be modified or changed.

Learning, Literature and the Arts. One effect of the Revolutionary War was to restrict the intellectual life of the colonies. American scholarship, for the most part, enlisted in the public service; scientific apparatus and libraries were wantonly destroyed; the flow of English books stopped; and the Tories—repository of much of the creative talent in the colonies—were driven out or silenced.

Toward a National Literature. Under these conditions, American literature could hardly thrive and it did not. Writers produced sterile, imitative works, few of which have survived except as documents of historical interest. But though their literary merit was slight, these works contributed to the birth of American nationalism, of the shedding of British modes of language and of the effort to achieve a literature which would be more native, more American.

Political Pamphlets. Men of letters entered the pamphlet war—the ideal literary form for revolutionary propaganda. In the process, however, the pamphleteers, notably JAMES OTIS, JOHN DICKINSON and THOMAS PAINE, rose above the issues of the moment to explore the new political theories of the Enlightenment—the basic problems of constitutionalism, federalism, democracy, freedom and order, government and restraint. From this developed many of the basic concepts that found expression later in the Constitution of the United States.

Poetry. The poets PHILIP FRENEAU, JOHN TRUMBULL, JOEL BARLOW and TIMOTHY DWIGHT and the group of satirists known as the "Hartford Wits" were similarly instrumental in fostering American nationalism. Though they usually produced works slavishly imitative of classical models (Freneau is the sometimes brilliant exception), they nonetheless helped instigate a movement for a "national" literature.

Painting. Nor was American painting altogether dormant. JOHN TRUMBULL (who was also a painter) fused realism with romanticism in his efforts to capture some crucial events of the war (Bunker Hill, the signing of the Declaration of Independence and the surrender at Yorktown). GILBERT STUART painted some excellent portraits.

What is an American? This new pride was eloquently revealed in an essay written in 1782 by ST.

JOHN DE CREVECOEUR. "What then is the American, this new man?" asked Crevecoeur. "He is either an European, or the descendant of an European, hence that strange mixture of blood, which you find in no other country. . . . Americans are the western pilgrims who are carrying along with them that great mass of arts, sciences, vigour and industry which began long since in the east; they will finish the great circle."

CHAPTER III

CONFEDERATION AND CONSTITUTION

THE ARTICLES OF CONFEDERATION

Confederation. Colonial determination to be independent was manifested in still another proposal made by RICHARD HENRY LEE—that a plan of confederation for the united colonies be issued for consideration and approval. John Dickinson headed the committee which drew up and submitted, on July 12, 1776, a report on "Articles of Confederation and Perpetual Union." After five years of intermittent consideration the Articles were adopted on November 15, 1777 and sent to each state for ratification.

The Substance of the Articles. The Articles numbered thirteen, the first giving to the new country its permanent name, "The United States of America." The second stated that "Each state retains its sovereignty, freedom and independence" along with all powers not delegated to the United States. The third declared that the independent states were entering into "a firm league of friendship . . . binding themselves to assist each other, against all force offered to, or attacks made upon them. . . ."

The free inhabitants of any one state, said the fourth article, shall be entitled to all privileges and immunities of free citizens in the several states. Full faith and credit were to be granted in each of the states to the "records, acts and judicial proceedings" of every other state. Fugitives from justice were to be delivered up.

The fifth dealt with delegations to Congress. They were to be (virtually) ambassadors from the states and subject to recall by the states. In the Congress each state was to have one vote. Freedom of speech and debate in Congress was then guaranteed to the delegates. In the sixth article a state was forbidden to enter into foreign alliances, accept or grant titles

of nobility, make interstate alliances, levy tariffs contravening Congressional trade treaties, keep navies or armies in time of peace (except "well-regulated militias") or engage in war—unless the Congress ruled otherwise. Article VII was concerned with appointment of officer personnel for troops raised in the common defense. In the eighth it was provided that war and defense costs were to be paid by the states on a proportionate basis and that the state legislatures would levy the required taxes.

The Powers of Congress. The emphasis upon the powers of the states is readily apparent. Wartime needs, however, demanded the exercise of united power. Therefore Congress was given the power in matters of peace and war, to send and receive ambassadors, to make treaties and alliances (provided they did not restrict the commercial powers of the states!), to serve as court of last resort in interstate disputes, to regulate money, to fix standards of weights and measures, to deal in a limited way with Indians, to establish post offices, to make officer appointments for national armed forces, to appoint interim committees and executive committees, to appropriate and borrow money, to issue bills of credit, to raise armies and a navy by requisition upon the states. For any Congressional action nine of the thirteen states had to agree.

The tenth article returned to the interim committee. The eleventh, somewhat optimistically, made provision for the entrance of Canada into the union. The twelfth was concerned with debts accumulated prior to the union. And the last predicted that the "union shall be perpetual," and provided that a unanimous vote of the states was required for any amendment.

The Results. The Articles of Confederation served

as the government of the United States from 1781 to 1789. Why did this "perpetual union" prove so temporary?

That some central government was required to successfully wage war was not disputed; so, broad powers were granted to Congress adequate for that purpose and in the sixth article, important national powers were denied to the states. But, though the Congress had *powers*, it had no *power*. Sovereignty resided in the states. This was stated precisely and then reinforced as follows: the states were bound in a league of friendship; each state, large or small, populous or sparsely populated, was accorded one vote; unanimity was required for any amendment to the Articles; and the delegates were to be appointed, removed and remunerated by the states. There was clearly a prevailing fear of a strong (possibly oppressive) central government.

Under the Articles, Congress could make a law, but only if nine of the thirteen states concurred. But the Articles had failed to provide for a national executive and a national judiciary to enforce the law. Moreover, Congress was made to depend upon the states for both money and troops.

Prompted by the bitter memory of mercantalist exploitation, the Articles' framers denied Congress the power to regulate the commerce among the states. This meant that the states could levy their own tariffs (and, indeed, did so) against other American states as well as against foreign powers. And though Congress could make commercial treaties with foreign powers, it had no means to compel the states to obey.

"THE CRITICAL PERIOD": 1781-1789

The "Critical Period" in American history corresponded to that of the Articles of Confederation. Therefore it has become customary to say that the Articles *caused* the "crisis" from which the Constitution rescued it. But this is not the case.

The Post-War Depression. For example, one can hardly hold the Articles of Confederation responsible for the post-war depression. Britain had been defeated; but she remained a dominating factor. There was this difference: America had now become an independent commercial rival. During the war, with English goods cut off, American wool-growing, mining, metal fabrication and manufacturing industries had "boomed." The war over, England was eager to unload accumulated surpluses on the American market. This would serve the double purpose of easing the depression at home and of crippling her infant competitor. She therefore extended easy credit to American distributors who, in a wave of victorious optimism, overbought and were then compelled to make hasty sales through auction. Prices fell and, with them, home industry.

American productive power had increased under the impetus of the war and traders looked forward to large exports of tobacco, wheat and flour to England. But England was now treating the United States for what it was: an independent nation—and a competitor. The West Indies were shut off. Loss of the West Indies meant destruction of the triangular trade and elimination of the most fruitful source of income. When England also withdrew her mercantilist bounties and privileges, the indigo and fisheries industries were ruined. Rice production had been a war casualty. For these reasons, the post-war depression was a severe one. But the Articles were hardly responsible for it.

A Favorable View of the Articles. There is considerable evidence, moreover, that the depression was over before the Constitution was adopted. By 1787 small domestic factories had been constructed and were busily engaged; a thriving China-East Indies and Baltic trade had replaced the lost West Indies traffic; farm prices and land values were rising; states which had embarked on ruinous inflationary programs were returning to sound money; some states even offered to pay their debts.

By means of interstate agreements something like a single commercial front was being developed. Prussia and Sweden had made reciprocal commercial treaties with the Congress and Holland had also made a limited pact with the United States. Rum, that "essential ingredient" in the American Revolution, was ruined by trade discriminations; but whiskey had come to take its place. But even more cogent evidence is the resistance which met moves to scuttle the Articles.

The Unfavorable View. It is, however, also true that some saw in the Articles a threat to the survival of a united nation. These men comprised the wealthy class, upon whose fate depended in considerable measure the fate of an expanding America. To them, all the forces in the economy fostered by the Articles seemed to be moving toward restrictions upon wealth and toward fastening an agricultural economy upon the new nation.

As the Financier Saw it. National revenue was sorely needed. There was a huge war debt to be paid to domestic and foreign bondholders. Soldiers had been promised a bonus of full pay for five years. State and federal currencies had depreciated disastrously; how was money to be raised in value and stabilized? When the Congress, in 1781, asked for

$11,000,000 to meet some of its obligations, it got only $1,500,000. When it proposed an amendment to the Articles to permit Congress to levy a 5% tax on imports, Rhode Island exercised its constitutional right of *librum veto* (where one state may override all) and the proposal was defeated. How were merchants to do business with currency that consisted of a miscellaneous collection of coins of varied weights, most of them counterfeit or adroitly shaven by professional clippers? Just how was one to do business when the government was helpless to remedy these conditions?

As The Merchant Saw It. The free flow of commerce was severely handicapped by artificial barriers that could not be removed by the national government. Between 1780 and 1789 Pennsylvania had enacted fifteen tariff laws; Virginia, twelve; Massachusetts, New York and Maryland, seven each. Southern tariffs were mostly for purposes of revenue; but those of the North were protective and retaliatory. This was how the New Englanders avenged the destruction of the West Indies trade.

It was not long before the states were at commercial war with one another. Some states sought to attract British trade by a lowering of tariffs. Thus when New York imposed a retaliatory tariff on English goods, Connecticut and New Jersey responded with a general lowering. New York then extended the retaliation to include those states. England was the beneficiary and entered into commercial treaties, not with the United States, but with the separate states, recognizing the former's impotence. As a crowning reminder of the low state of national power, (now that protection by the British navy was gone) American Mediterranean commerce was subjected to raids by the powerful Barbary pirates.

As The Creditor Saw It. Economic confusion was further compounded by the inability of mortgage holders and other creditors to collect debts, especially when forced to resort to local courts with biased juries. British and Loyalist creditors, though they had guarantees from the Treaty of Paris of 1783, found it almost impossible to collect. Those who held warrants to western lands were fearful to take possession since the government was unable to provide adequate protection against Indian attack.

The View from Europe. The British attitude reflected the considerable European contempt for the United States—mixed with fear of the American democratic experiment. England withheld diplomatic recognition, refused to return captive slaves, or military and trading posts on the Great Lakes, or to negotiate the northeastern boundaries dispute and the dispute over the Newfoundland fisheries.

Further, England armed the Indians for attacks on American settlers.

Spain ignored the treaty line set for Florida (the 31st parallel) and, more seriously, closed the mouth of the Mississippi to American grain shipments bound for New Orleans. In the face of these provocations, of the actual occupation by foreign powers of American soil, of the deliberate incitement to war and destruction, the Congress of the national government was helpless.

Internal Dissension. Just as the creditor-owner had opposed the British imperial government during the war, they now opposed their former allies, the debtor-agrarians. Two events illuminated this, one was the **Jay-Gardoqui Treaty of 1786.** Some arrangement with Spain was essential. The Western farmer, in particular, had demanded that the Eastern government open the Mississippi to unrestricted shipment. Commercial men, on the seaboard, were tempted to conclude a commercial treaty that would renew the influx of the desperately needed Spanish gold specie. JOHN JAY, a spokesman for the commercial forces, was sent to negotiate with the Spanish representative, GARDOQUI. In a treaty signed on August 3, 1776, Jay, with the permission of Congress, bartered away the rights to the Mississippi. The angry outbursts from the West and from the agrarian East, the violent threats of secession caused the negotiations to collapse; but the breach was widened.

It widened even more with an incident in Massachusetts. In that State conservative merchants, shippers, and bankers were firmly entrenched in the government because of rigid constitutional property qualifications for voting and holding office. To pay off the Revolutionary debt, they had levied a heavy tax of twenty pounds on each household with five people. This hit with special force the farmers, who, failing to meet their debts, were foreclosed. As a consequence, the agrarian-debtors rose in armed revolt under the leadership of the Revolutionary War veteran, DANIEL SHAYS. Shays proposed to ease the debtor's position by capturing the legislature, forcibly ousting all appointed magistrates, cancelling the debt and issuing paper money. In this crisis, the national government was again impotent and the rebellion was crushed (in 1786) by the Massachusetts State Militia. But George Washington noted that "There are combustibles in every State which a spark might set a fire in." **Shays's Rebellion** (as the episode is known in history) had been suppressed; but its causes remained.

The Way Out. The only apparent solution lay in an increase in the national power which could be consistent with democracy. That this was possible became evident in the closing days of the Confederation. It will be recalled that the Articles were adopted in 1777 but did not become law until 1781 —the delay caused by the issue of the western lands that arose during the process of ratification of the Articles. Following the Revolutionary War, the western lands were rapidly settled. Now, seven states claimed this territory, Virginia most vigorously. The six states without claims insisted that the domain be held by the United States and, when ready, should be admitted as new states. Claimless Maryland refused to ratify the Articles of Confederation until Virginia announced, in 1781, that she was surrendering her claims. Other states followed suit and the weak Congress of the Confederation came into possession of a land area larger than the United States itself.

What was to be done with the land? Thomas Jefferson's solution is a landmark in democratic history. He rejected the 18th century practice of imperialism, of domination by a powerful nation of a weaker area and instituted a standard of the democratic treatment of territories in the Ordinances of 1785 and 1787.

The Ordinance of 1785. The Land Ordinance of 1785 began a national land policy of generous land grants at low prices. It provided that after title had been secured from the Indians, townships of thirty-six square miles were to be constituted; each was to be divided into thirty-six sections (a section being one mile square with six hundred and forty acres—thus easily divisible into half and quarter sections for easy sale); one section in each township was to be set aside for the support of schools. Land sales were to be by auction and the minimum price was set at one dollar an acre. By providing for the township system of government, common schools and reduced land prices the Land Ordinance made possible the extension of the original land system across the country. But it failed to resolve the problem of personal freedom.

The Ordinance of 1787. This was accomplished by the **Ordinance of 1787.** The Northwest Territory (Ohio to Wisconsin) was to be divided into from three to five states. The progress from dependency to equality was to be in three stages: (1) A territory with fewer than 5000 people was to be governed by a governor, secretary and three judges appointed by Congress; (2) when a territory had 5000 free males above the age of 21, the government was to be altered to include an elected House of Representatives, a council chosen by Congress from nominations made by the House of Representatives, a governor appointed by Congress and a voteless ter-

ritorial representative in Congress; and (3) when a territory had 60,000 people it would elect a constitutional convention to frame a new constitution to be submitted to Congress for approval. Such approval granted, it became a state on an equal basis with all states.

While they were in territories, the people were assured of essential liberties. These were spelled out in three separate articles: no infringement upon freedom of worship; the benefits of habeas corpus writs, proportionate representation, common law judicial proceedings, reasonable bail and punishment for crime, no deprivation of property, rights of compensation for land taken by eminent domain. Education was to be fostered and the Indains accorded humane treatment. The final article provided that "There shall be neither slavery nor involuntary servitude in the said territory . . ." Until the United States acquired overseas possession, her territories were assured by the **Northwest Ordinance** of the orderly progression from the status of dependency to that of a free people in a free state.

THE FRAMING OF THE CONSTITUTION

Commerce and Conventions. In 1785 appeared the first dim signs of recovery from depression. Some Virginians, including Washington, were interested in land development of the Ohio valley. They hoped to extend the navigation of the Potomac and link it by canal with the Kanaha—across the mountain watershed. Commissioners from the bordering states met at Washington's home in Mount Vernon. Maryland suggested that Pennsylvania and Delaware be asked to participate in the uniform codes drawn up. Virginia thereupon issued a call for a nation-wide convention to be held in Annapolis in 1786. Disappointingly, only five states responded. ALEXANDER HAMILTON suggested another attempt be made at Philadelphia, a more central location, in May of 1787. His suggestion was adopted and was passed on to the Confederation Congress, which to save face, issued the call.

The call contained Hamilton's suggestion for an agenda—a meeting "for the sole and express purpose of revising the Articles of Confederation and reporting . . . such alterations . . . as shall . . . render the Federal Constitution adequate to the exigencies of Government and the preservation of the Union." All states but Rhode Island appointed delegates. The **Philadelphia Convention** met formally in Independence Hall on the 25th of May, 1787. Though only twenty-five delegates were present, George Washington was elected as presiding officer; it was decided that a journal of proceedings be kept; and the delegates voted that locked doors and secrecy be maintained throughout the proceedings. What was to have been a "Revision Convention" became a "**Constitutional Convention.**" In reforming the old, it gave birth to the new.

Roll Call. The delegates at Philadelphia were men of substance and property: university presidents, professors, lawyers, planters, statesmen, judges, financiers, land speculators and bondholders. We have been compelled to reckon with this ever since Professor CHARLES BEARD called attention to it in his significant book, *The Economic Interpretation of the Constitution.* Beard carefully catalogued the holdings of the framers: 40 held government securities worth a fraction of their face value; 14 were in possession of vast tracts of western lands; 25 were moneylenders; 11, merchants; 15, slaveholders; and so forth. Clearly, a strong central government which would repay bonds at face value, permit exploitation of western lands and protect these lands from Indians, guarantee repayment of debts and support commerce and slaveholding would be of direct benefit to the delegates. From this arose the thesis that here were no public-spirited "demi-gods" (Jefferson's phrase), but narrow, selfish, interested parties to a conspiracy against the unrepresented democratic mass of the people. Today, most historians reject this interpretation as a distortion of the 18th century context and as an injustice to a rare collection of men who wrote a document characterized by Gladstone as "the most wonderful work ever struck off at a given time by the brain and purpose of man."

The 18th Century Context. In the context of the 18th century, "men of property" were engaged in accumulating the capital that would make possible an industrial economy. Restrictions upon property had the further disadvantage of making the new nation defenseless in a world of contending imperialisms. Nothing would have suited the European powers more than a weak, agrarian America. True independence could only result from a diversified, nearly self-sufficient economy and it was toward this goal that the propertied were striving. What is more, one must remember that "propertied" were not a fixed category. Men fell from it and rose into it. America was an "open," fluid society.

The Founding Fathers. The "context" inclined men to strive to identify self-interest with the larger requirements of "natural law" and the progress of civilization. Two civilizations contended—the static-agrarian and the dynamic-industrial. The manufacturers were not notably democratic but were groping for some political theory that would reflect their sense of national destiny. For the most part men of sound education and culture, they were students of political theory and practitioners of the art and craft of government. It was they who had formulated the theory of separation from Great Britain and along with the democratic mass of people had staked their lives and property in its cause. It was they who had built up the new state structures which rose from the ruins of royal and proprietary strongholds. Their names resound: Washington, Franklin, Madison, James Wilson, Randolph and George Mason, the two Morrises of Pennsylvania, Dickinson, Ellsworth, Sherman, the two Pinckneys, Rutledge, Paterson and Luther Martin, to mention only some of the most active. Of these, Madison has been called "**Father of the Constitution**" and for good reason. He was an extraordinary scholar, and a brilliant floor leader; and kept officially the only complete record of the speeches and proceedings of the Convention.

Their Political Philosophy. Madison was in many ways typical of American conservative leaders. Their conservatism derived in part from a repudiation of the doctrines of man's innate goodness and the inevitability of progress. They were rather inclined to see man as "naturally" selfish and contentious and government as a device to restrain man's vicious tendencies. "If men were angels" wrote Madison, "no government would be necessary."

Yet they were enlightened men, too. They believed with John Locke that government had a preservative function, that it must derive ultimately from popular consent and that it must itself be checked against abuses and usurpations. The contest resolved itself, then, into a war between men and *evil* government. Could a balance between freedom and authority be struck? In striking the balance, the founding fathers constructed a monument.

THE "BUNDLE OF COMPROMISES"

Basis for Agreement. The delegates' will to negotiate and willingness to compromise were supported by their shared acceptance of certain basic principles: that there can be no liberty where property is insecure; that a strong central government is the best guarantor of liberty; that such a government must be given clearly stated and ample powers; that it should consist of a "supreme legislative, executive and judiciary"; and that the tyranny of the many ("democracy") as well as the tyranny of the few ("autocracy") must be avoided. Three instances of negotiated compromise illustrate the prevailing spirit at the Constitutional Convention.

Large State and Small. An important difference developed early between the large, populous states and the smaller ones. EDMUND RANDOLPH of Virginia was the first to present a plan of government. The government was to be bi-cameral (two-housed): the lower house was to be elected by the people; the upper, by the lower. Such a government would be national in power and would transcend the states. To the smaller states, the **Virginia Plan** seemed little short of disaster. They feared absorption by the more populous states and that within the nation their sovereignty and equality would be threatened. Therefore PATERSON of New Jersey proposed an alternative plan of government which would enlarge the powers of Congress and make the acts of Congress the supreme law of the land, while retaining unicameral (one-house) Confederation Congress based upon the equality of states.

The issue was this: was the government to be based on people or on states? Was national power or that of the states to prevail? The common desire for a strong central government resolved these extremes toward moderation and a "**Great Compromise**" was effected. The legislature was to be bicameral; its lower branch was to be proportional to population, national in scope and elected by the people; its upper branch would contain an equal number of representatives from each of the states and its members would be chosen by the state legislatures. In this compromise, the founders created the "federal principle."

Representation and Taxation. No sooner had this controversy been resolved when another arose to alarming proportions. If the lower house was to be based upon population, was "population" to be interpreted to include slaves? Yes, said Georgia and South Carolina, else Southern representation in Congress could not be truly proportional. No, replied the Northern states, slaves were not citizens but property, and could not be counted in the population.

Previously it had been agreed that direct taxes were also to be based upon population. Again, what of slaves? Yes, said the Northern states, else Southerners would not bear their fair proportion of the taxes. No, replied the Southern states, slaves are not citizens upon whom taxes can be levied; they are properties of their Southern masters. This vexing issue was resolved by the "**Federal Ratio**"—a slave was to be counted as three-fifths of a person in apportioning both representatives and taxes.

Commercial and Agrarian. The differences that arose between the commercial North and the agrarian South resulted from the conflicts of their economies. The commercial states sought navigation acts that would protect their interests—chiefly customs duties to be levied against rivals. But the agrarian states felt menaced by customs duties that would in fact be indirect taxes levied upon those who bought abroad heavily, as did the South. Furthermore what was to prevent "misguided" northern humanitarians from using the "navigation" power to stop importation of slaves who were so vital to the plantation system. Debate had shown that many of the delegates objected to "property in men" on moral, economic and political grounds. Southern agrarians proposed, therefore, that navigation acts, if permitted, require the approval of two-thirds of Congress. Compromise settled these differences too. Northern commercial interests were to have the right to pass navigation acts under the general power to regulate commerce; and the slave trade was to be ended. While it continued, a ten dollar head tax could be levied on each imported slave. Southern agrarians were satisfied with the concessions that the traffic in slaves would be permitted for twenty years (until 1808) and that export taxes were to be made unconstitutional.

THE CONSTITUTION OF THE UNITED STATES

From the 25th of May, 1787 to September 17th the debate raged and was resolved. Gouverneur Morris prepared the final draft, which was modified slightly and approved. Three delegates, Gerry, Randolph, and Mason, refused to sign but thirty-nine did and it was sent to the Congress of the Confederation for transmission to the states. By the terms of its seventh article, it was to become operative if nine states ratified.

THE UNDERLYING PHILOSOPHY OF THE CONSTITUTION

Balance and Restraint. The constitution is a unique document in 18th Century intellectual history. It created a small universe of states revolving about a central Union and guided by principles of "natural law." Newton had taught that universal systems are held together by a gravitational force. The framers of the Constitution found such a force in society to exist in **balance and restraint**. Men, left to themselves, are driven by "natural instincts" of greed and rapacity; in society they will form self-centered property-interest groups. An instrument of government must, therefore, **balance** conflicting drives and **restrain** contending interests. The following principles of government will best accomplish this goal:

The law is above men. It must be a written law to which men can refer to determine the justice of individual and group action. It must act directly upon the individual in its sanctions and not upon other sovereignties. Colonial experience since the first charters and the Fundamental Orders of Connecticut had shown the value of a defining and restrictive document containing fundamental law.

The Division of Powers. The powers in law must be distributed carefully where there are states within a union. This was taught to the framers by their wide reading in the failures of Ancient Greek efforts at confederation. But how should these powers be divided? In solving this problem, they made an original contribution to political theory—the **Federal System of Division of Powers.**

To the central government was given a list of specific, enumerated and delegated powers (to levy taxes, to regulate interstate commerce, etc.); the states, then, were left with the remaining powers, unless they were specifically denied. Thus, for example, since powers to regulate marriage and divorce, voting and education were not delegated to the federal government, they were reserved to the states. This division created only a few exclusive powers; namely, those delegated to the federal government and denied to the states (to lay duties, to declare war, to make treaties etc.). In the non-exclusive areas, as in the power to levy taxes, powers might be concurrent, that is, exercised by both governments. Each revolving sphere in the federal universe was thus assigned its proper place.

Conflict of Interest. It was foreseen that in the future conflicts over powers would develop among the states and between the states and the union. The founders were in no sense creating a Utopia. Obviously, a limiting force was required and in the clause making the **Constitution the supreme law of the land enforceable in both federal and state courts,** a limit was placed on the possible extension of conflict.

But such an extension of power in itself threatens to upset the desired balance. Therefore, the counterweight of **amendment by the states** was written in. If the central authority proved to be destructive of the ends of justice, then by two-thirds proposal and three-quarters ratification the state legislatures could amend the Constitution and restore the scales of justice.

Republic and Democracy. The Constitution created **a republic, a representative system.** The founders felt justified in their hostility toward both monarchy and democracy from their reading in Aristotle and Plato. Monarchy and democracy were viewed as unbalancing and unrestrained forces within the "body politic." Monarchies were incorporated greed; and democracies, incorporated passion—neither were fit instruments for the rule of law. To eliminate the possibility of monarchy, offices were made elective and terms of office were limited. To prevent the excesses of democracy, only one body, the House of Representatives, was to be popularly chosen. The remainder were removed from popular control by indirect election as in the case of the Senator, the President and the Judge. Government was to be firmly lodged in the hands of "philosopher-kings," the wise and well-born men of property. For property was considered to be the primary stabilizing force. (It was JOHN LOCKE's doctrine that property was essential to liberty.)

The Influence of Montesquieu. More immediate in influence even than Locke was the French philosopher, MONTESQUIEU, author of *The Spirit of the Laws.* From Aristotle, Harrington, Locke and Blackstone, Montesquieu had distilled and formulated his concept of **the separation of powers:**

When the legislative and executive powers are united in the same person . . . there can be no liberty because apprehension may arise lest the same monarch or senate should enact tyrannical laws, or execute them in a tyrannical manner. Again there is no liberty, if the judiciary power be not separated from the legislative and executive. Were it joined . . . then the life and liberty of the subjects would be exposed to arbitrary control; for the judge would be the legislature.

From this followed the principle that the three departments of government be kept separate and distinct—a goal to be achieved through a system of **"checks and balances."** House and Senate would "check" each other in the course of legislation; the President could veto a law and could be overridden; the Court might examine a law for its constitutionality; impeachment and amendment were ultimate safeguards.

The "Elastic Clause." The founders envisioned change and provided for it. Through the "elastic clause" the delegated powers of Congress could be extended. The growth of the Union was guaranteed in the right of Congress to admit new states. Finally, change could be effected by the process of amendment.

RATIFICATION

The Great Debate: Con. Even before the document went through the trial of ratification important voices like those of Patrick Henry and Samuel Adams were raised against it. Now that it stood before the delegates elected to ratifying conventions, protest had a forum. The changes were several. It was an illegal document because it violated their express mandate to amend the Articles of Confederation and to win approval by unanimous consent. It would reduce the states to helpless sovereignties in the grip of an overwhelming central government. It was undemocratic in its manner of choosing senators, presidents and judges and in its elaborate scheme of checks and balances. It was a private instrument for the protection of landed and mercantile property. But most of all it had no Bill of Rights. The people were left with no protection against a tyrannical central ruling power; their unalienable rights were clearly in jeopardy.

The Great Debate: Pro. The Constitution was brilliantly defended by Madison, Hamilton and Jay, who wrote a series of articles in defense of ratification for New York newspapers. These have been collected into a classic volume of political theory and of commentary upon the Constitution, called *The Federalist*. Drawing upon history and philosophy, legal and political theory, they analyzed the implications of each clause of the document and left a treasure of 18th century thought. The "Federalist Papers" had the effect of winning New York to ratification. Delaware had been the first to ratify on December 7, 1787. Pennsylvania, New Jersey, Georgia and Connecticut followed in rapid succession. The fight was bitter in important Massachusetts for both John Hancock and Sam Adams were in opposition. Adoption came on February 6, 1788 after Adams' conversion, a conversion based on the acceptance by the Convention of an amendment to the ratifying resolution, which provided for a demand for a Bill of Rights. The vote was 187 to 168—close! Maryland, South Carolina and New Hampshire followed to complete nine states required for ratification. But no union was feasible without New York or Virginia. Late in June 1788, Washington, Madison and John Marshall were able to prevail in the Virginia convention over Patrick Henry and George Mason by ten votes. With Virginia in, New York, also demanding amendments, fell in line. North Carolina and Rhode Island entered only after the first Congress met and threatened to treat them as foreign powers and punish them by discriminatory tariffs.

It was thus a bitter struggle and all the more surprising since the Conventions were, because of property qualifications, in the hands of the wealthy few. The mass of the American people were unrepresented. But their presence can be detected in the insistent demand for a bill of rights. These demands were met by the first Congress. Ten amendments were proposed and quickly ratified by all the states but Connecticut, Georgia and Massachusetts (which did not get around to ratifying them until 1937!) and on December 15, 1791, the Bill of Rights became part of the Constitution.

THE GOVERNMENT IS LAUNCHED

On July 2, 1788 CYRUS GRIFFIN, President of the Confederation Congress, announced the new Constitution in effect. On September 13, New York was fixed as the site of the new government. Presidential electors were appointed by the states on January 7, 1789. In February, Congressmen were chosen and the electors balloted. March 4, 1789 the first Congress met but had to wait until April 1st for a quorum to arrive. On the 6th of April, the electoral ballots were counted and George Washington became President with 69 votes. John Adams, with 34 votes, became the Vice-President. On the 16th of April Washington left Mount Vernon for New York and arrived on the 23rd. Seven days later he mounted the steps of Federal Hall, a building at the corner of Wall and Broad Streets, to be inaugurated.

One of history's great democratic experiments was about to begin.

CHAPTER IV

THE FEDERALIST ERA

THE AMERICAN MIND: 1790

Localism. With the election of a Congress and the inauguration of a President the great experiment in republican government had begun. A tiny minority of Americans called "Federalists" (because of their strong support of the new Constitution) were attempting to create a strong national state in a hostile environment of anti-Federalists. The voiceless mass of small farmers and artisans, often with the support of wealthier agrarians, were opposed to a strong central government which could levy taxes, stabilize currency, police the distribution of new lands, enforce navigation acts and command a formidable national army to enforce its acts.

Such hostility was natural to the undeveloped sense of nationalism which characterized American society in 1790. The census of 1790 revealed the presence in America of almost 4,000,000 people, more than ninety per cent of whom were farmers with a deep attachment only to the soil and their immediate locality. The frontier farmer was isolated by roads deplorable in good weather and impassable in bad; by unbridged streams and rivers; by primitive means of transport—removed from community and organized government. How could a sense of nationhood develop in such circumstances?

Nationalism. This sentiment—such as it was in 1790—was centered in the few urban areas along the seaboard. In all, there were six cities with populations over 8,000; Philadelphia led with 42,000. Urban population was less than three per cent—but it was a powerful and influential three per cent. Men of business were building fortunes in trade and land, establishing banks of loan and discount, investing heavily in shipping and new commercial enterprises, and in state and federal securities. Their thought and enterprise were national in scope, even if they saw America as a national hunting ground for quick fortunes. The points of view and the "many" and the "few" were explosively opposed.

FEDERALISM ENTRENCHED

The political climate was favorable to the Federalist cause. The elections of 1788 were hardly contested. Anti-Federalists had been largely inactive in seeking office under the new government and the result was that those who were instrumental in framing the Constitution and in obtaining its ratification were established in the new government as Senators and Representatives. Eleven of the founders sat in the Senate. The sizeable number that sat in the House were under the expert leadership of JAMES MADISON. In the office of President was the presiding officer of the Constitutional Convention, vested by the Constitution with the all-important power of appointment.

Washington's appointments were at times politic, as in the case of his naming Jefferson as the first Secretary of State; they were always made with a view to selecting able men. But Washington was not concerned with effecting a coalition government. He preferred men who would support the principles of Federalism. All the federal judgeships, for example, were awarded to outspoken proponents of strong

central government. The machinery of power—as Charles Beard has observed—was in the hands of the men who had established it.

TOWARD A NATIONAL STATE

Money and Administration. The first Congress set in motion the machinery of economic and political power. Madison introduced a revenue measure to fill the national treasury—a tariff of five per cent which was rushed through to tap the influx of early summer imports. Influential merchants, however, managed to have it delayed so that the imports would come in duty free. Once in, the prices could be raised to conform with the new tariff and an extra-profits harvest could be reaped. The anti-Federalists took careful note of this maneuver. They noted, too, that Madison did not rush through the amendments promised at the ratification convention, but acted only when charged with bad faith. The Bill of Rights was then enacted. On the 2nd of September, 1789, Congress created the administrative departments of Foreign Affairs, Treasury and War and followed this, on the 24th, with the important Judiciary Act. Each of these measures stirred considerable debate.

The "Unwritten Constitution." The Constitution had not provided for administrative departments or a cabinet to assist the President. When Congress established the posts of Foreign Affairs, Treasury and War they were initiating a precedent that was to persist as part of the Constitution.

Washington's appointments to these posts were of cardinal importance in the development of the new government. Jefferson was recalled from Paris to become Secretary for Foreign Affairs; ALEXANDER HAMILTON, Secretary of the Treasury, General HENRY KNOX, War Secretary, and JOHN RANDOLPH of Virginia, Attorney General (a post created in the Judiciary Act). This established a check and balance system within the cabinet for Hamilton and Knox were ardent Federalists while Jefferson and Randolph were at most lukewarm.

The Judiciary Act. The importance of this act in establishing the principle of national supremacy was crucial. The Judiciary Act first supplied the Supreme Court with its personnel: a Chief Justice and five associate justices. It then created inferior courts: thirteen federal district courts, each with one judge and three circuit courts made up of the two Supreme Court justices sitting with one district court judge. Anti-federalists had opposed the creation of these inferior courts, arguing that the state courts were adequate for all cases except those assigned by the Constitution to the Supreme Court itself. But the Federalists dismissed this proposed limitation on the national power: all cases affecting it must be dealt with in national courts. They were to be sifted in the district courts and then sent up on appeal to the Circuits and Supreme Court. Not satisfied with this stress on the national power, the Federalists added provisions which joined the state with the federal courts in concurrent jurisdiction in certain cases involving federal law; and then provided that in certain cases appeals could be made from the state to the federal courts. These provisions gave life to the mandate that the Constitution was to be the Supreme Law of the Land. State courts were compelled to enforce the Constitution. The Supreme Court of the United States was to be the final judge of constitutionality.

Judicial Precedents. JOHN JAY was made the first Chief Justice and gave to the federal courts a distinct nationalist direction. In the first three years of its existence, no case came before the Supreme Court; but the district and circuit courts had begun to prepare the nation for living under the Constitution.

The first federal justices set important precedents in judicial procedure: judges would render no advisory opinions; opinions and decisions would be given only in adjudicating specific cases brought before the courts. The federal judiciary would void any laws of a state that violated a treaty or impaired the obligation of a contract; and would declare any act of Congress incompatible with the Constitution null and void.

One case—Chisholm v. Georgia—led to a restriction of the judicial power. Two citizens of South Carolina brought suit for recovery of confiscated property against Georgia. Georgia refused to appear on the grounds that such an appearance would infringe its sovereignty. The Supreme Court decided against Georgia, for the Constitution had provided that the federal courts were to have jurisdiction over "controversies between a state and citizens of another state." Georgia's sovereignty was relegated by the Constitution, reasoned the Court, to "more domestic concerns." The day following the decision, Congress proposed an eleventh amendment to the Constitution which was eventually adopted (1798) and which read: "The Judicial power of the United States shall not be construed to extend to any suit in law or equity, commenced or prosecuted against one of the United States by Citizens of another State, or by Citizens or Subjects of any Foreign State."

THE ACHIEVEMENT OF ALEXANDER HAMILTON

Philosophy. History has recorded no final judgment on the career and influence of Alexander Hamilton, who was in his lifetime and today remains a center of controversy. More than anyone else he inspired and directed the policies of the first administration. Unlike his contemporaries he was not a product of the Enlightenment. He did not believe in the "natural rights" of man or in the inevitability of universal progress. With Hobbes, he felt that all human action proceeds from self-interest; and that all states contain conflicting self-interest groups. For human society to exist at all the state must be armed with power to coerce men to restrain their bestial appetites.

All communities (he wrote) divide themselves into the few and the many. The first are the rich and well born, the other the mass of the people. . . . The people are turbulent and changing; they seldom judge or determine right. Give therefore to the first class a distinct and permanent share in the government. They will check the unsteadiness of the second; and *as they cannot receive any advantage by a change,* they therefore will maintain good government.

Since the "appetites" of the rich and well born are in check when they are satisfied, that state is best which satisfies them. "That power which holds the purse strings absolutely, must rule." Economic masters are the "natural" political masters. However, not all economic masters best serve the public welfare; only those do who use their capital properly to produce a thriving economy and stable society in which artisans and farmers are also contented. The masses do not know their own good. "The people! —the people is a great beast!" For the people if given power will destroy the foundations of their own prosperity—the rule of capital.

This view of property is "continental" or national, as opposed to local or regional. Concentration upon *union* leads to the need for a *national* system. Capitalism, as outlined by Adam Smith, in his epoch-making work, *The Wealth of Nations,* was obviously the best of systems. It was based on the full exploitation of national and human resources, on division of labor for the creation of wealth, and on the necessity for accumulating wealth into few hands to provide the essential capital. Hamilton agreed with Smith that selfish motivation can become social good; he did not, however, accept Smith's emphasis upon *laissez-faire* (an unregulated economy). A government that did not intervene directly in promoting the accumulation of wealth would be delinquent in duty. Hamilton did not deny that in the process individuals would suffer injury. But one could not be concerned primarily with justice. What mattered was power and the proper use of power.

Hamilton, as can be seen in the light of the above views, was no humanitarian; but he was convinced that he was on the side of humanity. In the long run all men would benefit from the stern measures adopted for the short run. From this philosophy flowed his economic program.

The Financial Program. Hamilton's financial program was developed in a series of reports to Congress. The first and second dealt with **public credit**, the third with the necessity for a national bank and the fourth with **manufacturing and the tariff**. Each was part of a broad and comprehensive economic program designed to restore public credit at home and abroad, to ensure the stability of the new government by winning the support of the wealthy and to advance the American economy toward capitalism.

The Public Debt. By modern standards the public debt was not large. The foreign debt, held chiefly by the French and Dutch, amounted to $11,710,378; the domestic debt, to $44,414,085 and outstanding state obligations, to about $25,000,000. But for a new government with no treasury it was an immense sum. Hamilton could have taken the path of limited repudiation, for the bonds representing the debt were selling at heavy discounts. Many of their original owners, in fact, had sold them to speculators who hoped that they might be redeemed at face value. If the government redeemed the bonds at face value, the speculators would reap a fortune. Hamilton proposed payment in full on a funding basis. New government bonds would be issued for the old; two-thirds would bear an interest rate of six per cent, one-third, of three per cent. Each year only two per cent of the bonds would be redeemable. In preparation for redemption a sinking fund was to be created and fed from the streams of customs revenues and the sale of public lands.

ALBERT GALLATIN led the anti-Federalist opposition to Hamilton's program. The program was extravagant, would benefit unscrupulous speculators who possessed the bonds by fraudulent means. Counterproposals were offered: to limit the value of the refunded bonds to those prevailing at the time of the debate and to reward the original holders in some manner. Hamilton was unmoved. It was clear, he argued, that the bonds were debts incurred by the government under the Articles of Confederation; that the Constitution had ordered the new government to honor such debts; that they must be honored at full value to "justify and preserve the confidence of the most enlightened friends of good government"; that the new bonds would serve as a basis for loans; and that this was the only means to assure future credit for the United States. Refunding at face value was adopted.

Controversy. Assumption of state debts caused the first major rift in the Federalist grouping in Congress. The division was sectional. New England had the bulk of the unpaid state debts while the Southern states had, for the most part, discharged theirs. Why, argued the South, should there be national taxation for the benefit of one section? Because, answered Hamilton, the states had accumulated these debts in the common cause; because the amount to be paid was the same whether paid by state or nation; because the manner of payment would be more efficient if a single agency were responsible; and, most important, if all the creditors receive their payments from one source, they will have the same interest in that source. Clearly, assumption was intended to "cement more closely the union of the states."

Madison broke with Hamilton and led the House opposition. This was, he argued, an unjust, unnecessary and dangerous infringement on state authority. The proposal suffered a temporary defeat on April 12, 1790. Hamilton now sought out Jefferson for assistance. He convinced Jefferson that the union was at stake. Fortunately for Hamilton's plan another major issue had arisen that could be used in some compromise offer. The South was pressing for the permanent site of the new government to be located on the Potomac; the North preferred Philadelphia. In exchange for Virginia's votes, Hamilton agreed to establishing the capital at the Southern site. Assumption of state debts became law.

The Bank Proposal. The bitterest debate was reserved for Hamilton's *Report on the Bank*. The country had but three banks. Hamilton urged the establishment of a national bank permitted to open branches everywhere. It would increase capital necessary for economic expansion; it would provide the government with facilities for borrowing money and for collecting taxes; it could serve as a government depository; it might print a circulating medium that would be uniform and stable; it would stimulate and attract vital foreign capital.

Agrarians rose in unanimous opposition. The proposal, they said, would create an intolerable monopoly over exchange; state banks could not exist in the face of such competition since the bank's issues would be favored in the payment of government obligations; debtors would be handicapped in favor of creditors; and, what is more, the proposed bank is clearly unconstitutional since there is no express provision granting Congress the power to establish a bank. Hamilton conceded this point but invoked the "doctrine of implied powers."

The Doctrine of Implied Powers. Before he signed the bank measure, Washington called upon his cabinet to submit opinions on its constitutionality. Attacking its constitutionality, Jefferson developed **the doctrine of the strict interpretation of the Constitution.** The bank, he reasoned, was not an "enumerated power" and was therefore reserved to the states. The "general welfare" clause of the enumerated powers was inapplicable since it was intended to authorize only the enumerated powers and not to give Congress a sweeping grant of power. Jefferson similarly rejected the idea that the bank was "necessary" to the foregoing powers as established in the "elastic clause." "Necessary" meant "indispensable" not "convenient." In response, Hamilton stressed the **loose construction of the Constitution.** The "necessary and proper" clause of the Constitution gave to Congress implied powers.

The criterion is the end to which the measure related is a means. If the end be clearly comprehended within any of the specified powers, and if the measure have an obvious relation to that end, and is not forbidden by any particular provision of the Constitution, it may safely be deemed to come within the compass of the national authority.

The bank was adopted.

Features of the Bank. The Bank was capitalized at $10,000,000 in 25,000 shares. One-fifth of the shares and directorships went to the government. Three-quarters of the shares could be paid for in government six-per cent bonds; one quarter had to be in specie. Foreigners might participate, but could not sit on the board of directors. Eight branches could be opened. The bank was empowered to receive deposits and to make loans. Loans could be effected by issuance of credit or of bank notes. The latter could not exceed total capitalization. Interest was fixed at six per cent.

The Excise Tax. To put his program into effect, Hamilton needed a new source of revenue. In his second report on public credit he recommended a tax on domestic distilled liquors. This was to be collected at the source, which was largely in the back country of Pennsylvania, Virginia, North Carolina and Maryland, where the farmers found the shipment of grains west too expensive to be profitable and therefore reduced their grain in bulk by converting it into spirits. Needless to say, the tax was denounced as odious, unequal, unpopular and oppressive; moreover, it would never be collected.

The tax was passed on March 3, 1791. A little over a year later the threat was translated into action. A convention was held at Pittsburgh by those most affected and resolutions were drawn up declaring that legal measures would be used to obstruct collections. The governor refused to call out the militia to suppress this "**Whiskey Rebellion.**" When, in 1794, a federal judge in Pennsylvania notified Washington that the courts were unable to enforce the law, the President ordered an army of 15,000 to the area. The rebels were scattered. The show of force demonstrated that no new Shays would be permitted to defy the central government.

The Report on Manufactures. In this paper, Hamilton projected the future of the United States. He denied that agriculture could be the base for American progress. Only manufacturing could serve that purpose. With manufacturing, there would be a tremendous surge in production and new markets would be created for agricultural goods. But manufacturing needed government encouragement and support—that is, protective tariffs, prohibitive rates, import and export quotas, bounties and subsidies, encouragement of invention and internal improvements. This most prophetic of Hamilton's projects was regarded with considerable skepticism; and his proposals were not enacted.

Coinage. Hamilton's proposals for a system of coinage, however, were full enacted in the **Mint Act of 1792.** The basic coins established were the $20 gold eagle, the half eagle, the quarter eagle, the silver dollar, half dollar and quarter. Thus a bi-metallic (gold and silver) standard was adopted. A mint was set up to provide this uniform coinage. No debate developed on this proposal.

Significance. One can hardly improve on Daniel Webster's tribute to Hamilton's genius. He "smote the rock of national resources and abundant streams of revenue gushed forth; he touched the dead corpse of public credit and it sprang upon its feet." More prosaically, Hamilton laid the foundation for the nation's prosperity; he strengthened the national government and increased its authority; he steered the economy toward capitalism; he laid the base for an expansion of the Constitution; and he created the division that was to result in America's two-party system, a system which, like the Cabinet, was to become an indispensable feature of the "unwritten" constitution.

THE BIRTH OF POLITICAL PARTIES

In their search for balance and restraint, the Constitutional Founders had relied upon the aristocratic principle that government by the "few" would provide essential stability. They did not, and in their day probably could not, foresee the upsurge of democracy, the popular demand for a direct voice in government. When they thought of the "people" over whom the Constitution prevailed, it was with fear that the people would upset the delicate constitutional balances. Their fears could not contain the democratic floodtide, but the balance remained. The two-party system was the chief element in its preservation.

The Bases for a Two-Party System. Parties will arise when the fundamental issues of the day create alternative possibilities. The controlling group operated on this set of principles: the economic order must be balanced and diversified; government must intervene to encourage finance, industry, commerce and shipping; the creditor must be favored over the debtor; the government must be strong and centralized and national in force; leadership must be in the hands of "born" leaders; the masses are incapable of governing; etc.

Opposition to these principles developed a contrary set: the "good" society is that in which there is a broad distribution of wealth; the basis of that society should be an agrarian order of individual freeholders; industrialism, urbanism and finance destroy the well-ordered state by concentrating wealth; the debtor must be protected from the creditor; centralized governments are necessarily tyrannous; local government must be the center of rule; and the rulers must be the masses of the people; etc.

The alternatives were sharp, and drove a clean wedge through the nation. To the principles of centralization, loose constitutional interpretation and capitalism gravitated a solid core of capitalists, merchants, manufacturers, financiers, lawyers, clergymen, university men—the "respectables." By 1793 they composed the **Federalist Party.** Their views were vigorously espoused in the *Gazette of the United States*, a newspaper edited by JOHN FENNO. Washington was their standard-bearer and Hamilton, their mentor. It was not a "political party" in the modern sense for they would not admit that society was divided. More truly organized as a modern political party was the **Republican Party,** sneeringly referred to by their opponents as "Democratic-Republican." Jefferson was their standard-bearer and mentor; but he was ably assisted by such men as GALLATIN, BURR, MADISON, MONROE and DEWITT CLINTON. Standing for localism, strict interpretaion of the Constitution and democratic participation of the masses in government, these men gathered about them the tobacco and cotton planters, the

small farmers, the urban dispossessed, artisans and laborers, the frontier elements, the states' rightists, whiskey rebels—the "people." They, too, had a vigorous press, *The National Gazette,* edited by the poet-pamphleteer PHILIP FRENEAU.

The Election of 1792. The full impact of the party division was not felt in the election of 1792 because Washington was persuaded to run again, precisely to avoid the impending clash. Federalists and Republicans supported him and he was chosen unanimously. But the Republicans made a bid for the Vice-Presidency with Governor George Clinton and for both houses of Congress. They failed in their first objective since John Adams, Federalist, was chosen as Vice-President; nor could they capture the Senate. They did, however, win the House of Representatives.

Foreign Policy Conflicts. Foreign problems were the dominant themes of Washington's second administration, as domestic problems had been of the first. Hamilton had shown that in coping with domestic problems one must rely upon consent, and that failing, upon coercion. But how are consent and coercion to be applied to hostile nations when one has neither prestige nor arms? Observe, for example, the problem of the Barbary pirates. To engage in Mediterranean trade, a maritime nation had to pay tribute to the Dey of Algiers or suffer the destruction of its fleet. In 1795 the United States concluded an Algerian Treaty. $642,500 was paid to these pirates for the ransom of captives and an annual tribute to the Dey.

The Indians. The movement to settle the northwestern and southwestern territories of the American part of the Mississippi Valley was encouraged by the Land Ordinance of 1785 and its accompanying Northwest Ordinance; by the payment of veterans' claims in western land; by the cheapness of land ($1 per acre, handicapped, however, by the requirement to purchase in 640 acre lots); and by the enterprising activities of new land companies at home and abroad. Settlement was hampered by defensive attacks of hostile Indians armed by the British, who still held the fur posts around the Great Lakes. An apathetic Congress was finally convinced to provide an army of 2,000 under General Arthur St. Clair to subdue these hostile neighbors. St. Clair was disastrously defeated. Congress responded by providing General ANTHONY WAYNE with three regiments. At Fallen Timbers, in 1794, the Indians were decisively routed and compelled to sign the Treaty of Greenville, ceding virtually all of Ohio to the United States. By application of the same "foreign policy" the Cherokees, Creeks, Chocotaws and

Chickasaws and their Spanish supporters were forced into treaties favorable to the United States.

France. In 1793, France could hardly be classified as an enemy; if anything, she was our friend, bound to us by a treaty of alliance and a treaty of commerce and amity. Under the former, both countries enjoyed mutual guarantees of territorial integrity; under the latter, they were pledged to grant each other trading privileges, to permit the prizes of enemy vessels seized at sea to be brought into each other's ports and to prohibit outfitting privateers for enemy nations. What is more, by 1793 the reasons for friendship between the two nations had multiplied. Our own republic was barely founded when, in 1789, the French nation erupted in a democratic revolution against a corrupt monarchy and aristocracy and feudal privilege. The French acknowledged the inspiration of the American Revolution and in their **Declaration of the Rights of Man** echoed the noble "self-evident" truths of America's **Declaration of Independence.**

The French revolutionary cause was immensely popular with most Americans. Enlightened democratic thinkers saw in it dramatic evidence of the universal progress of man toward "liberty, equality and fraternity." And they sought to extend a fraternal hand to friends across the sea. But George Washington did not: in a proclamation issued on April 22, 1793, Washington in effect repudiated the treaty of alliance and the treaty of commerce and amity. Our foreign policy in this matter was to be one of neutrality. Why?

The Reasons for Neutrality. The French people were not only engaged in a domestic revolution; they were at war with England, Austria and Prussia. England had already begun to seize American ships as enemy vessels. Hamilton stated the case for neutrality in forceful terms. War—especially with England—would be disastrous for the new nation, surrounded as it is by hostile powers. England was America's principal importer; English imports yielded by way of tariff, the chief source of the American income, and supported the entire structure of the financial and public credit programs. Moreover, there *were* no treaties of alliance and commerce and amity. These had been made with the French monarchy, which no longer existed. American conservatives—the Federalists—detested and feared the resort of the French Revolutionists to terror and confiscation of property. Now in power, they chose to forget that they had only recently themselves usurped power in a just cause.

But Jefferson enthusiastically supported the Revolution; and he denied heatedly that the treaties

concluded with the king were not binding. The treaties, he said, were made with the French *nation*, whoever ruled it, and were binding until repudiated. If not philosophically, then as a matter of expediency he agreed with Hamilton that America could not afford involvement in a European war. There was no way out but neutrality which, if it would desert the French, would not aid the English. As Secretary of State, then, Jefferson urged Washington to proclaim American neutrality without repudiating the treaties of alliance and commerce and amity. Washington issued his **Proclamation**, not using the term "neutrality." It pledged the United States to pursue a conduct friendly and impartial toward the belligerent powers and it cautioned American citizens scrupulously to respect its intent.

Citizen Genêt. EDMOND CHARLES GENÊT landed at Charleston, S. C., on April 8, 1793 and promptly added to the confusion that attended Washington's Proclamation. He was Minister of the French Republic and had come to renew the amity treaty and negotiate a new treaty of commerce. Fully confident of his position under the old treaties, he set about commissioning privateers and dispatching them to raid British vessels. He then extended his operations to organizing expeditions against Spanish and British territories in America. Since he had not yet seen the President, he traveled to Philadelphia on April 18th, not arriving until May 16th because his trip had turned into a triumphal procession. It was while en route (April 22nd) that he learned of Washington's Proclamation of neutrality—and appealed over the head of the President to the people. Washington received him with the coolest formality on the 18th of May. On August 2nd, the President asked France to recall him since, in contempt of proper diplomatic procedure, Genêt had continued to commission privateers, to grant commissions on American soil and to appeal over the head of the President to the people. This continued until a new minister, Fauchet, arrived with instructions to arrest Genêt, who appealed to Washington for political asylum and was granted it by the President. Genêt stayed in America, became a citizen and the son-in-law of DeWitt Clinton. But his brief ministry had serious consequences. Washington had drawn so close to Hamilton on the matter of the French policy that Jefferson resigned as Secretary of State, making permanent the breach between the Federalists and the Republicans.

England. England was America's best customer and most constant irritant. In spite of the fact that seven-eighths of American trade was with England, no commercial treaty existed between the two countries. England systematically violated all the provisions of the Treaty of Paris of 1783, which had concluded the Revolutionary War. Her troops occupied six forts on American soil in the area of Detroit. Now that she was at war with France, England extended her activities against the United States to include impressment of seamen into British naval service, seizure of ships carrying foodstuffs to the French, interference with the French West Indies trade and increased incitement of the Indians on the frontier. Such humiliating treatment aroused war sentiment in the United States. Washington himself commented: "If we desire to avoid insult, we must be ready to repel it; if we desire to secure peace, one of the most powerful instruments of our rising prosperity, it must be known that we are at all times ready for war."

The Failure of a Mission. But there was to be no war—yet. In a last effort to avoid war, Washington sent John Jay to London with instructions to secure a permanent enforcement of the Treaty of Paris, compensation for all vessels seized and a commercial treaty. As a weapon of persuasion, Jay was to threaten the creation of a new League of Armed Neutrality that had been so effective during the Revolutionary War. Jay found England favorable to negotiation; the European War was not going well and Sweden and Denmark had already formed a Neutrality Convention. Negotiations got under way in June, 1784. Clever and experienced British diplomats soon outmaneuvered Jay; and Hamilton stripped him of his chief weapon by assuring the British ambassador in America that the United States would never join a neutrality league of nations. As a result, the treaty accomplished nothing but the avoidance of war.

Jay's Treaty. Once again England promised to withdraw from all posts and places within the boundary lines designated by the treaty of peace; England was reassured the free use of the Mississippi; boundary lines were to be surveyed and negotiated; the United States guaranteed collection of British debts contracted before the peace; England guaranteed compensation for illegal capture and condemnation of American vessels; in regard to commerce, England was to permit seventy tons of American ships to the West Indies trade provided they did not carry molasses, sugar, cotton or coffee, to admit American commerce into British possessions in the East Indies, Europe and the continent of North America and to grant each other "most favorable nation" guarantees in the matter of tariffs. But of impressment, the return of captured slaves and

a commercial treaty with England itself, there was not a word.

In Washington's words: ". . . the cry against the treaty was like that against a mad dog." Jay was burned in effigy, Hamilton was stoned and Washington himself was scornfully designated as the "stepfather of his country." The Senate debated the treaty for seven weeks before a reluctant approval was secured. The House refused until April 30, 1796 to vote the necessary appropriations for fulfilling the treaty. Federalist prestige had suffered a mortal wound.

Spain. The most beneficial result of the Jay Treaty was the effect it had upon American relations with Spain. Spain feared that this rapprochement between the United States and England would be turned against her on the continent of North America, where her possessions included Florida and the western half of the Mississippi Valley. For years she had been harassing the Americans by inciting Indians, violating the southern boundaries and limiting navigation on the Mississippi. Moreover, since she held the mouth of the Mississippi, she would not accord Americans the right to deposit goods there for reshipment abroad without the payment of duties for entry to Spanish soil.

The Jay Treaty, the rising menace in Europe of a revolutionary France reclaiming the Louisiana Territory, and the decisive defeat by Sevier and Robertson of the southwestern Indians, convinced the Spanish ministry headed by Godoy to make a settlement with the Americans. On October 27, 1795, THOMAS PINCKNEY was able to conclude a treaty with Spain that did much to restore American prestige. The Spaniards promised to keep the Indians under control; to accept the thirty-first parallel as the southern boundary as established in the Treaty of Paris of 1783; to permit free navigation of the Mississippi; and to grant Americans the "right of deposit" on Spanish soil without payment of duty.

THE DECLINE OF FEDERALIST POWER

Washington's Farewell Address: Premonition. On September 17, 1796, there appeared in the *American Daily Advertiser* an "Address" written by Washington to his fellow citizens. It was a message of farewell and advice—premonitory advice. Washington first outlined the advantages of unity as a means of securing liberty, independence, domestic tranquillity, peace, safety and prosperity. He made a fervent appeal to the nascent sense of nationalism. "The name of American must exalt the just pride of patriotism more than any appellation derived from local discrimination." The sections are vital to the American scheme only as they reinforce its unity and add to the blessings of union the advantages of their resources.

He then asked, what causes may disturb the union? In answer, he pointed to parties organized to foster sectionalism; failure to respect and obey the Constitution, its authority and the laws derived from it; dangerous innovations in government—"time and habit are as necessary to fix the character of government as of other human institutions"; the baneful effects of the spirit of party which derives from human passions; the encroachment of one constitutional sphere upon another.

His advice followed: Cultivate religion and morality as indispensable supports of political prosperity; promote institutions for the general diffusion of knowledge; cherish the public credit; observe good faith and justice toward all nations; be alert to the encroachments of foreign influence; and "the great rule of conduct for us in regard to foreign nations is, in extending our commercial relations, to have with them as little political connection as possible." Europe's primary interests have only a remote relation to the United States, and the United States must not implicate itself by unnatural ties. "It is our true policy to steer clear of permanent alliances with any portion of the foreign world." In spite of the limitations of its world view today, Washington's **Farewell Address** is still read annually in the Congress of the United States—a tribute to its enduring appeals for peace—at home and abroad —as the necessary prior condition of democracy.

The Election of 1796. Federalist decline began with victory in the elections of 1796. After one of the most scurrilous campaigns in our history, John Adams, a Federalist, was elected as President and a working majority of Federalists was chosen for the Congress. This hardly seems like decline. But in the course of the election Hamilton, who had resigned as Secretary of the Treasury, broke with Adams and sought to maneuver Thomas Pinckney into office over Adams. When Adams unwisely retained Washington's cabinet, he was surrounding himself with Hamilton's henchmen. This division in party control handicapped Adams throughout his administration. Adams' personality, moreover, was repellent to Federalist and Republican alike. Brilliant and learned, he was also cold and arrogant. The man of the hour was Jefferson. Since the custom had not yet hardened that electors "vote the party," Jefferson had been chosen Vice-President; the result was a President of one party and a Vice-President of another, for the first and only time in American history.

The Undeclared War With France. Adams was convinced that America's existence depended on avoidance of war; yet he was brought to the brink of war almost at once. Relations with France suffered rapid deterioration after the passage of the Jay Treaty. JAMES MONROE, our Minister to France, in an excess of revolutionary fervor, had promised that no such treaty would be made; and now it was made, in open violation, the French felt, of the treaties of alliance, commerce and amity. (For his indiscretion, Monroe was recalled.)

The French thereupon launched a series of retaliatory measures against America: vessels were seized, cargoes confiscated and diplomatic relations severed. Adams called Congress into special session and asked for adequate defense appropriations; he indicated, however, that another effort at settlement would be made. Congress responded with measures to increase the navy and army and to fortify the harbors. But it held to neutrality by forbidding the export of arms and the outfitting of privateers.

To strengthen this neutral gesture, Adams appointed JOHN MARSHALL, ELBRIDGE GERRY and PINCKNEY as a commission to secure from France a new treaty of commerce and amity.

The "XYZ" Affair. Of all the humiliations suffered by the infant republic none was worse than the experience of this mission. Before the French Foreign Minister—TALLEYRAND—condescended to negotiate, he kept the commission cooling its heels for two weeks. Three French delegates (designated in dispatches as X, Y and Z) then approached the American commissioners with these outrageous proposals: that apologies be made by the United States government for certain remarks made by President Adams; that the United States make a loan to France; and that a *douceur* (bribe) be given to the French Directory of $240,000 for deigning to negotiate. These proposals were, of course, indignantly rejected. Adams informed Congress of the failure of the negotiations and submitted to it the correspondence involved.

Undeclared War. War fever rose to high pitch in the country as Federalists and Republicans rallied to the slogan "Millions for defense but not one cent for tribute." The Hamilton wing of the Federalists took the leadership to propel the country into war. Wielding his influence in Congress and the Cabinet, Hamilton succeeded in having Washington appointed as commanding general and himself as second in command. The Congress also created a Navy Department and repealed the treaties with

France. A military force of 10,000 men was ordered recruited, twelve naval craft were ordered built and merchant vessels were ordered armed. On the 20th of November, 1798, the first naval battle took place. But the President hesitated, to the dismay of the Hamiltonians. The initiative in a declaration of war should come from the French, he said.

The Peace. The war with France did not take place. The reasons went beyond Adams' scruples: within the Hamiltonian ranks there was a sordid squabble over commissions; the miserable pay impeded recruitment; new war taxes met furious resistance along the frontier; a new government loan at eight per cent brought charges of corruption; and the Republicans had become disaffected. Not only had the Republicans been excluded from all rank in the proposed army, but they had good reason to believe that Hamilton was using the war fever for personal and party advantage. They also realized that high taxes and high-interest government loans could serve their own partisan purposes in the forthcoming election of 1800.

Adams went his own fixed way. When Talleyrand indicated that a new commission would be received with respect, he appointed William Vans Murray to attempt a new negotiation. Napoleon had come to power and was eager for an opportunity to consolidate his position by reducing foreign difficulties. In a convention signed on the 30th of September the French government agreed to honor the treaties of alliance, commerce and amity; to pay indemnities for damaged ships and cargoes; and to honor the principle that "free ships make free goods." A year later the Senate ratified the convention. Adams had won his peace but there was no peace in the Federalist ranks.

The Alien and Sedition Laws. The Federalists had taken note of two facts during the course of the difficulties with France: that support for the French emanated in part from immigrants, particularly those of Irish extraction, who hated England with traditional bitterness; and that most immigrants after they had acquired citizenship drifted into the ranks of the Republicans. Unless they could stop this drift, it was clear to the Federalist that power would slip from their hands in the election of 1800. But the laws which followed from these observations destroyed the Federalist Party.

The first was a **Naturalization Act** which repealed the Naturalization Law of 1795 and raised the period of residence required for citizenship from five to fourteen years. This should—it was hoped—certainly stop the surge of "aliens" into the Republican Party. The second was the **Alien Act** which provided for deportation of all aliens "dangerous" to the peace and safety of the United States or who were engaged in "treasonable act or conspiracy" against the established government. The third was an **Alien Enemies Act** which authorized the President in the event of declared war to arrest, imprison or banish aliens who were subject to the enemy power.

These acts against aliens met with only moderate resistance, and, emboldened, the Federalists moved on to a fourth act, the Sedition Act, directed against the *citizens* of the United States. The following acts were declared to be high misdemeanors subject to fine and imprisonment: entering into unlawful combinations to oppose execution of the laws; preventing officers from performing duties; aiding insurrection, riot, unlawful assembly or combination; publishing any false, scandalous or malicious writing bringing the United States government, Congress or President into disrepute. Under the last of these provisions, ten Republican editors and printers were fined and imprisoned, the most notable being James Calleder, Matthew Lyon and Dr. Thomas Cooper.

The Kentucky and Virginia Resolutions. The Republican counteroffensive began immediately. These laws were vicious, despotic and unconstitutional. Jefferson felt that the most effective protest against them would be by means of **interposition** by the state legislatures. He and Madison therefore drew up a series of protect resolutions and had them introduced into the legislatures of Kentucky and Virginia. But why the state legislatures?

Jefferson felt that they were the logical agencies for declaring a law unconstitutional. His reasoning was that the Constitution was a compact among the states to delegate certain enumerated powers to the central government and to reserve all others to the states. If the central government assumes undelegated powers its acts are *per se* void and of no force. Since the central government cannot be the judge of its assumed powers, the parties to the compact have the right themselves to judge infractions. Each state, therefore, may nullify a law. (This is the theory of "interposition.") The Alien and Sedition Laws are a patent violation of the first amendment to the Constitution. The Kentucky and Virginia Resolutions called upon all the states to declare the Laws null and void. The states did not respond to the suggestion and the laws remained until they were voided by the Congress.

Finale: The Election of 1800. The Federalists entered the election of 1800 as an already beaten party. Washington had died in 1799 and had taken with him the spirit of Federalist unity. In the same year, JOHN FRIES had led a new Pennsylvania insurrection against the direct federal property tax levied in expectation of war with France: it was crushed, but it smouldered. The protests against the Sedition Act and the increased national debt were mounting. The country was demanding action against British impressment; but the Federalists were pro-British. Above all, the schism in Federalist ranks had not been healed. Adams had awakened to the Hamiltonian conspiracy within his cabinet and had discharged the cabinet. Hamilton and his "Massachusetts Essex Junto" were countering with a plot to prevent Adams from getting a second term.

The Republicans, on the contrary, were well knit and highly disciplined; they had efficient local organization. Their platform of peace and retrenchment was popular. Above all they reflected in their approach the rising sentiment of democracy. When the electoral votes were counted, Jefferson and Aaron Burr had secured all of the Republican ballots —each had seventy-three votes. It was fully intended by the Congressional caucus that had chosen Jefferson and Burr as candidates that Jefferson would be president and Burr, Vice-President. A tie vote required decision by the House of Representatives.

Now here was a final chance to subvert the Republicans. In the House, the Federalists threw their support to Burr—a corrupt and cynical politician— and were able to forestall Jefferson's election for thirty-five ballots. In the course of the balloting, Hamilton had to make the most difficult and courageous decision of his career. He opposed Jefferson; but he despised Burr as a profligate and extortionist. When he finally decided that Jefferson was the safer of the two candidates, Hamilton succeeded in inducing one of his Congressional friends to abstain from voting, permitting Jefferson's election.

The growth of parties had revealed a defect in the Constitution: tie votes would appear regularly so long as electors cast two ballots for party candidates. In 1803 the **Twelfth Amendment** remedied this defect by providing for **separate** election of president and vice-president and requiring that elections in the House of Representatives be from the top three candidates.

The "Midnight Judges." The executive was lost; the Congress was lost; there remained the judiciary. Why not—the Federalist strategists asked—fill this branch of the government with life-appointed judges who would check the "dangerous radicalism" of the Republicans? Thus in 1801 a Judiciary Act created sixteen new judgeships and a number of attorneys, marshalls and clerks. Adams nominated Federalists for the posts and the Senate confirmed them. The "lame ducks" (defeated candidates) had to act hurriedly before leaving office. John Adams did so; and late in the night of March 3rd he signed the commissions. One of the midnight appointments was JOHN MARSHALL. The Federalists were to have the last word, after all.

CHAPTER V

JEFFERSONIAN REPUBLICANISM

THEORY AND PRACTICE

Time-Span. With the election of THOMAS JEFFERSON as President, there began a quarter-century of Republican rule. Jefferson served two terms (1801-1809) and was succeeded by James Madison (1809-1817), James Monroe (1817-1825) and John Quincy Adams (1825-1829). With the exception of Madison's 1812 election and, in the ebbing years of Republican strength, the election of John Quincy Adams, no serious contest for presidential office developed. In fact, in 1820 Monroe was uncontested and received all the electoral votes but one (thrown away to keep the unique honor of a unanimous election as Washington's alone).

History thus set aside a generation for the testing of Jeffersonianism, ideas directly antithetical to those of Hamilton and Federalism. The long continuance in office of Republicanism would seem to indicate the triumphant vindication of Jefferson over Hamilton. Nothing could be farther from the facts. Had Hamilton not been slain by Aaron Burr, he would have lived to see his policies and predictions fulfilled by Republican hands.

Jeffersonianism. Jefferson's outlook was philosophic but he, himself, was no systematic philosopher. He produced only a handful of public statements of his philosophic position; most of his credo is derived from his immense correspondence.

Philosophical. Jefferson's philosophy originated in the fundamental assumption that **all men are born free and equal**; at birth they are endowed with inherent and unalienable rights of life, liberty and pursuit of happiness. Innately, the freeborn man is gifted with a moral instinct, with compassion and generosity; and if permitted the free exercise of these qualities—the right to individual liberty, to act and think freely, to engage in unhampered communication—he would multiply the blessings on earth for himself, others and posterity. But the barriers to the realization of his natural capacities are numerous and men must plan their social lives to eliminate such barriers. Barriers are in nature political, social and economic.

Political. The chief political barrier is the "Leviathan" state—the overcentralized, over regimented state in the hands of a ruling aristocracy exploiting the rights of men for narrow, selfish advantage. States inherently tend to grow too big, too complex, too powerful for human control; if left to themselves (and the whole of history is testimony to this truth) they become corrupt and tyrannical and violate the rights of man. Obviously then, a proper plan of government would be built on the **principle of restraint.**

Restraint can be established in two ways: by an extension of democracy, of the principle of government by consent and therefore of suffrage; and by active decentralization, by restricting most of political power to local rule. For the United States, living under its Constitution, this implied the strictest interpretation of the delegated powers of Congress and the absolute equality of the states with the central government. The government of the states must, by its very nature, be more responsive to popular direction than the mammoth central government; and, being more responsive, the forces of stability, law, order, statute and legality would yield to the more desirable forces of justice, changing conditions, public need, popular will and human rights. When the past is regarded as sacred, progress is thwarted. But the living cannot be bound by the dead and must change the past as the need arises. Mankind is in a state of constant revolution, in a constant war against despotism. Each generation produces its patriots whose blood must water the tree of liberty.

Economic. No greater threat to human rights exists than the tendency of societies to become industrial and urban. Political aristocracy—Jefferson reasoned—is always a monied class whose wealth derives from industrialization and urbanization, while the urban worker is reduced to dire poverty and the freeholding farmer is turned into a crushed peasant. This intolerable economic order can only be prevented by establishing an agrarian society of freeholders. "Those who labor in the earth are the chosen of God. . . ." The free yeoman grows rich only as the earth is rich and as he labors to extract its wealth. The United States with its great land area to the west that will not be exhausted for a millennium is the ideal laboratory for the experiment of a free society based upon agriculture. Government must further this experiment and discourage any tendency to industrialization; hence, no tariff protection, no favored tax provisions, no bounties or subsidies—no feature, that is, of Hamilton's "vicious" program for creation of men of wealth.

Social. Ignorance, inhumanity and superstition are a triple-headed barrier to realization of human rights. Since ignorance is a function of lack of educational facilities and a controlled press, the states and local communities must foster a system of publicly endowed schools and the press must be kept free. The press may abuse its freedom, it may lie and malign and be vulgar, but—this is an evil for which there is no remedy. "Our liberty depends on the freedom of the press, and that cannot be limited without being lost."

Slavery is a brutal and inhumane institution which brutalizes the master while it dehumanizes the slave. Slaves, being human, are born with natural rights which cannot be realized until they are emancipated. Any experiment in emancipation is to be encouraged.

Superstition derives from the dogmas of religion and the clergy who propagate dogma—the "tyranny over the mind of man." Therefore, government must maintain unlimited freedom of conscience and absolute separation of that "loathsome combination"—church and state. The need is for a restoration of the simple religion of Jesus without the "engrafted sophistications" derived from the "jargon of Plato, Aristotle and other mystics."

America in the World. War is natural to man in general and to European man in particular. Americans, then, must be scrupulously neutral toward Europe's conflicts, must avoid "entangling alliances" and limit its relations with Europe to peaceful trade and commerce.

Jefferson's First Inaugural Address. As March 4th, 1801 approached—the day of Jefferson's inauguration—some Federalists were convinced that the President-elect was about to usher in an era of anarchy and atheism. TIMOTHY DWIGHT, for example, foresaw a "country governed by blockheads and knaves . . . the ties of marriage severed; our wives thrown into the stews; . . . our children cast from the breast and forgotten, filial piety extinguished." But Hamilton, more temperate, was more sanguine.

It was true, agreed Hamilton, that Jefferson was fanatic and crafty, persevering and unscrupulous, hypocritical and popularity-seeking; but, "he is as likely as any man I know to temporize . . . and the probable result of such a temper is the preservation of systems."

The Federalists were reassured by the address. Jefferson made a strong appeal for unity, for social harmony, for a balance between the rights due to a prevailing majority and the protections due to an existing minority. Differences of opinion are not all differences of principle; so, "We are all Republicans —we are all Federalists." Federalist and Republican alike share the blessings of a land separated from European chaos and of a high-minded, equality-minded and God-minded people. A good government is one which is wise, frugal and leaves men alone to eat the bread they have earned. Jefferson further advocated equal and exact justice for all whatever their political beliefs; for "peace, commerce, and honest friendship, with all nations—entangling alliances with none"; for honest payment of debts.

Less comforting to the Federalists were Jefferson's proposals for support of the state governments in all their rights, for complete reliance upon a militia, and for economy in government; and the President's stress upon freedom of the press and of person was embarrassing in view of the existing Alien and Sedition Laws. Certainly, they could not object to Jefferson's demand for absolute submission to the decisions of the majority; after all, they had lost the election and might win the next. Hamilton's comment upon the address was smug; he regarded it as a pledge that Jefferson would not lend himself to "dangerous innovation" and would "tread in the footsteps of his predecessors."

Republican Government. In the first years of the Republican administration there was little done that would bear out Hamilton's prediction. The Republicans began with an intensive attack upon Federalist policies. In contrast to Washington and Adams, Jefferson adopted a simplicity of official and public behavior. He was "democratic" to the extent of receiving the British Ambassador in simple clothes and worn shoes. Albert Gallatin, his appointee as Secretary of the Treasury, looked upon the national debt as a mortgage to be paid off to prevent a select few from becoming wealthier. This was made possible by the fortunate occurrence of a British decision to permit American vessels to break a direct voyage from the French West Indies to France by landing at neutral American ports and paying duties; this converted unneutral into neutral goods. As revenue duties mounted, Gallatin effected drastic retrenchment in the army, navy, diplomatic and civil services and large savings in government outlay. With income up and expenses down he was able to cut the national debt by almost $40,000,000 in eleven years.

The Alien and Sedition Laws were allowed to expire, those imprisoned were set free and the fines imposed were repaid. Although Jefferson avoided wholesale removal of Federalists from office, all vacancies were filled with Republican partisans. The Republicans began an assault upon the Federalist judiciary. The Judiciary Act of 1801 was repealed and the new judgeships were abolished; signed and sealed commissions for office were ordered withheld; two Federalist judges, John Pickering (insane) and Samuel Chase (sane but violently anti-Republican) were impeached and Pickering was convicted and removed from office. These attacks upon the judiciary, however, were not uncontested.

Marbury v. Madison. Chief Justice John Marshall entered the lists when William Marbury, a "midnight" justice of the peace, sued in the Supreme Court for a *writ of mandamus*. This writ forced a civil officer to deliver up a signed and sealed commission for office. Power to issue such a writ had been granted to the Supreme Court by the Judiciary Act of 1789. Marshall's strategy was to avoid a struggle with Jefferson over Marbury's appointment but, nonetheless, to assert the independence of the judiciary from executive and legislative control. Marshall's great decision in **Marbury v. Madison** was over a matter of petty politics; but it was not a petty decision. The decision created a constitutional precedent that made the **Supreme Court the final arbiter in constitutional matters and co-equal with the other branches of government.** The Chief Justice proceeded in his decision without benefit of precedent; his reliance was upon logic alone. The Constitution, he reasoned, is the supreme law of the land and binds all who act under its name, including the Congress. The Congress is a body with limited powers; it is not sovereign. The Constitution is sovereign. A congressional measure, therefore, must be judged for its constitutionality and the judges of the Supreme Court are appointed for this purpose. If an act of Congress exceeds its powers as assigned by the Constitution, the judges have the duty to declare it void. Thus, the relevant section of the Judiciary Act is void for it assigns to the Supreme Court original jurisdiction not provided in the Constitution, namely, the right to issue *writs of mandamus*. Marbury lost his job; Jefferson won his political point; it took years for the country to comprehend the revolution in Marshall's decision —the right of "judicial review" of Congressional legislation, which has since become an essential feature of the "unwritten Constitution."

JEFFERSON'S GREAT REVERSAL

Pirates and Peace. Thomas Jefferson preferred peace as a national policy; the Pasha of Tripoli did not. In 1801, Yusuf Caramalli decided that an annual tribute of $83,000 from America was insufficient if one truly evaluated Tripoli's position among the pirates of the Mediterranean. He declared war on the United States. In the face of this provocation, Jefferson dispatched what remained of the navy (following Gallatin's retrenchment policy) to the Mediterranean waters. After four years of inconclusive warfare, the United States signed a treaty with the Pasha of Tripoli providing for reduced payments annually; it was not until 1816 that all tribute stopped. Thus, the President who would have no navy, initiated it.

Purchase and Property. The Tripolitan incident was a relatively minor one; major ones were to follow when, by secret treaty, Spain restored Louisiana to France in the person of Napoleon. Again there emerged a powerful, aggressive neighbor capable of nullifying the terms of the Pinckney Treaty with respect to navigation of the Mississippi and the "right of deposit" at New Orleans. An outraged and fearful clamor from the agrarian west rang across the country. So, in spite of the fact that Jefferson was the symbol of anti-British sentiment and of no "entangling alliances" he proclaimed that "The day France takes New Orleans . . . we must marry ourselves to the British fleet and nation."

But in a more practical vein Jefferson instructed ROBERT LIVINGSTON, Minister to France, to get a renewal of the Pinckney terms or, if possible, to arrange for the purchase of a tract of land in the lower Mississippi area for use as a port. Monroe was sent as reinforcement and carried even more specific instructions—from two to ten million dollars might be spent to buy New Orleans and West Florida.

The Louisiana Purchase. The time was propitious for an offer of purchase. French troops in Haiti had suffered disastrous and humiliating defeat at the hands of TOUSSAINT L'OUVERTURE (though he himself was captured and sent to die in a French prison). Could a nation unable to hold an island command a continent? Moreover, his power consolidated at home, Napoleon looked toward a new assault on the continent and England. On the 11th of April, 1803, Livingston received a proposal offering the sale of all of Louisiana; he was to name a price. He stalled the negotiations until Monroe arrived. On the 30th of April the deal was consummated—$15,000,000 for the whole, 3¢ an acre!

Jefferson was delighted with the results, but how does a "strict constructionist" purchase territory when there was no specifically delegated power in the Constitution? To derive an implied power would be to confirm Hamilton and to negate the Tenth Amendment, which reserved the undelegated powers to the states. Obviously an amendment would do it, and one was drafted; but whether Napoleon would wait while it made its rounds of ratification could not be risked. Jefferson decided to imply the power from the delegated power to declare war and to make treaties, registering his faith "that the good sense of the country will correct the evil of loose construction when it shall produce ill effects."

But ironically the Federalists, led by Thomas Pickering, now invoked the doctrine of states' rights to oppose the treaty! One provision of the proposed treaty provided that inhabitants of the Louisiana Territory should be rapidly admitted into the Union on the basis of statehood. The Federalists feared an accretion of Republican power in Congress would result from this provision; they therefore denied the right of Congress to admit new states unless every existing state gave its consent (recalling the Articles of Confederation). To complete the irony it was the Federalist judge, Marshall, who gave judicial consent to the Republican interpretation that territory might be acquired under the treaty and war clauses of the Constitution.

Expansion and Exploration. For a quarter of a century, Jefferson had fought centralization in the national government; as President, he served its cause. By the purchase of Louisiana, he had placed in the hands of Congress a territory as large as the United States itself. He could not avoid this act of centralization, for free land was vital to agrarian interest. Even before the purchase of Louisiana, Jefferson had proposed a military-scientific expedition to the foreign-held Louisiana Territory, for which Congress had appropriated money.

With the purchase, it became an official survey. Thirty-two men were organized under MERIWEATHER LEWIS and WILLIAM CLARK to explore the territory. From St. Louis the expedition journeyed up the Missouri River and down the Columbia to its mouth. Returning by the same route in 1806 they reported their finding: the land beyond the Missouri was not fit for "white" habitation or use (!). The value of this expedition was therefore indirect—a number of diaries that increased America's literary treasure and an additional claim to the **Oregon Territory**. (A con-current expedition was made by ZEBULON PIKE into Colorado and New Mexico.) A second indication of Jefferson's expansionist sentiments can be seen in his "loose" interpretation of the boundaries of the Louisiana Territory; it included, he claimed, Texas and all the land to the 49th parallel and the Pacific!

Sectional Stirrings. The purchase of Louisiana crowned Jefferson's first administration; there was a sense of prideful unity in the land. But there were also sectional stirrings among the extreme Republi-cans who felt that Jefferson had applied his "all Republicans-all Federalists" thesis too literally. South of the Mason-Dixon line, JOHN RANDOLPH had organized a group of dissidents known as "Quids" to oppose Jefferson's nationalist tendencies. They made a focal issue of the **Yazoo Land Claims Case.**

In 1795 a Georgia legislature had awarded 35,-000,000 acres of land in the Yazoo River Valley to four land companies for about $500,000. The share-holders of these land companies included many Georgia legislators. In 1796 a new legislature, horri-fied by this corrupt action, rescinded the grant. The United States acquired the disputed area when Georgia surrendered her land claims. Thereupon the United States offered the Yazoo holders five instead of thirty-five million acres; New England had a strong interest in the remainder. Jefferson's aim was to forge national unity but, when his bill for settlement was before the Congress, Randolph led his "Quids" in battle against it and defeated it.

The matter then came before John Marshall in the case of **Fletcher v. Peck.** Marshall, applying *strict* construction, held that the original (corrupt) grant was valid and the rescinding act null and void. His reasons were that a contract had been made by the first legislature and the second had impaired the obligation of contract when it rescinded the grant. The motives of legislators, he declared, are irrelevant.

Aaron Burr. Randolph's factional tirades were matched outside of Congress by the secessionist schemes of Aaron Burr. Burr's first link was with a secessionist plot hatched by Thomas Pickering and the Massachusetts "Essex Junto," a Northern Con-federation to be created consisting of the New Eng-land states, New York and New Jersey. Burr was assigned the task of maneuvering New York into secession; but first he must secure the governorship. Hamilton's successful opposition to this scheme cost him his life in a duel with Burr at Weehawken, New Jersey.

Burr now shifted his operations to the Southwest and with funds supplied by the Spanish Minister, he plotted an expedition into Spanish territory. Burr's motives in this scheme are still a matter of contro-versy. Nonetheless, he was apprehended and tried for treason. The case came before Justice Marshall sitting in the Circuit Court. Marshall, applying a strict interpretation to the treason clause, insisted upon two witnesses to an overt act of treason. This was impossible to secure, and Burr was acquitted. The nation rested more easily when he went into voluntary European exile to avoid being charged with Hamilton's murder.

THE WAR OF 1812

Jefferson, overwhelmingly elected in 1804, looked back upon his first administration as the harvest season of his life. Territorial growth had been ac-companied by economic growth: the cotton gin of ELI WHITNEY had increased cotton production which had mounted to more than half-a-million bales by 1804; other agricultural products kept pace; almost a million tons of goods were afloat, nine-tenths car-ried in American ships; and the national debt was under control despite Barbary pirates and the Loui-siana Purchase.

But the rosy dawn of the Republican administra-tion was soon scattered by the ominous war-clouds that gathered as the second administration began. In 1803 Napoleon began his war with England. Peace, commerce and diplomatic relations became entangled in this foreign struggle. In this manner arose a question that was to persist throughout American history: Can America remain neutral and prosperous in a world at war?

America was unable to remain neutral and pros-perous in the Napoleonic wars. Why?

Impressment. Because of the Napoleonic Wars, England intensified her impressment of American seamen into British service. Conditions in the British naval service were abominable. Its sailors deserted and many of them enlisted in the growing American merchant marine where wages, conditions and treat-ment were more humane. Jefferson felt that volun-tary expatriation is one of man's natural rights and if England forced desertion there was no reason why America should not supply asylum. England dis-agreed; her navy patrolled the American coast, mounted American ships at will and removed any seaman it chose to label "deserter."

Violation of Sovereignty. England treated Ameri-can claims of sovereignty rights with contempt. The **Chesapeake-Leopard Affair** was a case in point. About eight miles from the American shore a British (54-gunned) frigate, the "Leopard," stopped the

American frigate, the "Chesapeake" (her guns were aboard but had neglectfully not been mounted!), and demanded the right to call a muster of the men to search out four deserters. Commodore Barron of the "Chesapeake" refused; he knew of none and, what is more, the "Chesapeake" was a government vessel and none but her own officers could muster a crew. England answered with a broadside that was so damaging that Commodore Barron struck colors after firing a single shot. The British removed "their" four sailors and the "Chesapeake" limped back to shore. American shame and indignation were at high pitch and the pressure on Jefferson to respond in kind was great. But Jefferson did not desire war; he countered only with a proclamation forcing all British war vessels to leave American waters.

Violation of Trading Rights. France had thrown open the trade of her West Indies. At first, England had permitted this and American profits piled high. With a renewal of the conflict, England rescinded her permission and began systematic seizure of American ships engaged in this commerce. This was only a beginning of seizure. In 1806 the English issued "Orders in Council" blockading the European coast; neutral ships were forbidden to trade in the blockaded area unless they secured British clearance papers and paid an English customs duty.

Confiscation of American vessels continued as a result of this blockade. To make matters worse, Napoleon responded to the Orders in Council with his own "Berlin and Milan Decrees" that made it illegal for any vessel to clear through England. Confiscation of American vessels by the French resulted from these decrees. What were Americans to do as they watched their commerce decline to two-thirds its former value?

The Failure of "Peaceful Coercion." Jefferson could no longer avoid the issue of adequate defense measures. Necessarily, the army must be increased and the coast fortified in the event of war. This was done; but the problem was to avoid war. How could this be better achieved, reasoned Jefferson, than by withdrawing American goods, vital to both sides, from the seas? Jefferson sent a message to Congress on December 7th, 1807 in which he proposed that American ships be detained at port until England and France repealed their oppressive trade regulations and stopped seizing American vessels. Congress responded and in the Embargo Act of 1808 forbade departure of all American merchant ships for foreign ports. Vessels in the coastal trade were to post bonds to ensure the landing of cargo on American shores. Foreign vessels might carry goods into but not out of America.

The embargo policy failed miserably. American merchantmen schemed to avoid the act; smuggling in foreign products began on a large scale; legitimate trade fell disastrously; economic distress was widespread. In New England, the nullification or interposition features of the Virginia and Kentucky resolutions were revived; in Congress the "Quids" vented merciless criticism. It was Napoleon, however, who made a complete mockery of the act by "enforcing" it. All American vessels entering the ports of France, Italy and the Hanseatic towns were seized on the ground that, since the embargo was effectively enforced (sic!), any American ships must really be camouflaged British vessels! On the day he left office, Jefferson signed the repeal of the embargo. His second term had supplied him with a bitter harvest.

James Madison. The new President, JAMES MADISON, continued Jefferson's policy of peaceful coercion with considerable ineptness. Congress had passed a **Nonintercourse Act (1809)** to replace the Embargo; it provided that trade was to be resumed with all countries but England and France. However, if either of these countries would stop its violation of neutral trade, trade would be resumed with that country. England showed interest in reopening commerce and Madison concluded an agreement with the British Minister Erskine to that effect. He did not wait for official approval in England of the agreement and permitted a resumption of trade with the British. His embarrassment was great when Canning, the English State Secretary, rejected the Erskine agreement, and orders for reinstituting the embargo had to be issued.

The Nonintercourse Act being ineffective, Congress now made the full turn and in the **Macon Act (1810)** lifted all restrictions on trade; but if either England or France would remove the restrictions the embargo would be placed on the other. Again Madison acted clumsily. Napoleon informed him that beginning November 1, 1810 the Berlin and Milan Decrees would be withdrawn provided the United States "shall cause their rights to be respected by the English." Though warned, Madison did not heed the proviso and placed an embargo on the British; and was dismayed to learn that American vessels arriving at French ports were being confiscated for violating the unrepealed Berlin and Milan Decrees.

The final fiasco came when England, succumbing to the pressure of her merchants (and impressed by the defeat of her ship, "Little Belt," by the American frigate "President"), repealed the Orders in Council (1812). Peaceful coercion had finally worked. But there was, in those days, no instantaneous communication. Ignorant of England's capitulation, the Americans had declared war two days later.

The "War Hawks." Prompt communication may have made no difference; some Americans, for reasons of their own, wanted war with England in any event. After all, it was not England that declared war; she had merely provided the provocations. The war message of Madison listed these as violation on the high seas of our sovereignty, confiscation of ships, illegal impressment and blockade, destruction of trade through Orders in Council and incitement of Indians.

The candid fact is that this was not the whole story. Within the Congress there were a group of young, aggressive men from southern and western frontier areas who were the first generation never to have known British rule. They were intense nationalists and fiery patriots. Led by HENRY CLAY and JOHN C. CALHOUN they made every act of England against American commerce the occasion for a demand for war with England. England, they argued, must be eliminated from the continent; a second war for independence must be fought. If England were eliminated, it would solve several pressing problems. The Mississippi was too narrow an outlet for the productive abundance of the agricultural West—eliminating England would open dozens of new outlets; new settlers were crowding the national domain—conquest of Canada (and Florida) would provide vast new land areas; eliminate England and the Indian would be eliminated as well for the Indian survived only through English arms and could retreat to the protective custody provided by Canada and Florida. To prove their point they could cite the new uprising of TECUMSEH and his brother, The PROPHET. These two had organized a Northwestern Indian Confederacy to defy the latest of nine treaties (since that of 1795) compelling them to yield their land to American settlement. When their center at Tippecanoe had been taken, at great cost, by the Indiana governor, WILLIAM HENRY HARRISON, did they not retreat into Canada? All this would end if Canada were America's. Then—on to Canada! No wonder John Randolph baptized these firebrands the "War Hawks."

War! America was no better prepared for this "second war for independence" than she had been for the first. She had the advantage in that England was preoccupied with Napoleon and had to depend on what navy she could spare from her armada of 800 vessels; but though small in number, the American navy had excellent command and considerable experience in warfare. As for Canada, the American population was greater than hers by fifteen times.

There was the additional advantage that America controlled the interior lines of communication.

But war required an army and Jefferson's retrenchment and peace policies had resulted in a force of 7,000 men (tiny for population of 7,240,000)—badly administered, commanded and equipped. In 1811 the United States Bank had been permitted to expire and there was no centralized financial administration in the country; money had to be borrowed by public subscription. But the financial public centered in New England refused to subscribe to "Mr. Madison's War." So extreme was New England's disaffection that during the war the New England states openly supplied the English armed forces with provisions, withdrew their militias from Federal service and sabotaged enlistments.

The Home Front. The hostility of New England to the war made the home front an important battleground, but the warriors were fighting on sides opposite those they held in the last decade of the 18th century. The peace-propagating Republicans had plunged the nation into war; the war-propagating Federalists were the party of peace. The states-rights Republicans were increasing the power of the central government in ways Federalists would never have considered; the Federalists, the fathers of the centralized state, were piously proclaiming the doctrine of states-rights.

These issues came to a head in the election of 1812. The Congressional caucus chose Madison for a second term even though his record as President had considerably diminished his stature as a public figure. Federalists and Republicans combined to nominate a strong peace candidate, DEWITT CLINTON. Along the seaboard the vote was very close; 90 electoral votes for Madison and 89 for Clinton. But all the frontier states—Vermont, Kentucky, Tennessee, Ohio and Louisiana—had voted solidly for Madison and war.

The war went on and with each year of its continuation the Federalists grew more desperate. In their despair they met (1814-15) at a Hartford Convention. From the text of Madison's Virginia and Kentucky Resolutions they lifted the doctrine of state nullification or interposition and made it their own; they drew up resolutions and proposed Constitutional amendments which would have restricted federal powers over conscription, taxation, declaration of war and embargo, regulation of interstate commerce, admission of new states—in other words, the virtual repeal of all that they had considered desirable when they were in office a decade before. This Convention proved to be their dying gasp; they ran one more candidate in 1816 and then disappeared from American history.

1812. American offensive actions in the year 1812 centered on Canada, which was to be taken by a three-pronged attack moving out of Lake Champlain under DEARBORN, out of the middle region of the Niagara River under VAN RENSSELAER and out of Detroit under HULL. Hull began inauspiciously by losing his baggage train before the campaign got under way. He entered Canada but was so obsessed with fear of encirclement that he retreated hastily to Detroit. When the British threatened Detroit, he succumbed to a new fear of an Indian massacre and surrendered the town to the British without firing a shot. (He received due punishment.)

Van Rensselaer would have moved into Canada willingly enough had expected reinforcements from the New York State militia arrived as commanded. They did arrive but refused to fight outside state boundaries. Dearborn met a similar refusal while en route to Montreal. The Canadian campaign was a complete fiasco. And 1812 would have been an inglorious year had it not been for glorious naval successes. Hull's "Constitution" defeated the "Guerriere;" JOHN PAUL JONES' "Wasp" the British frigate "Frolic;" DECATUR's "United States," the "Macedonian;" and BAINBRIDGE's "Old Ironsides," the "Java." This was an incredible though not decisive record.

1813. Early in 1813, Americans organized to recapture Detroit. For this purpose William Henry Harrison was provided with 10,000 men. Harrison's campaigning discovered that while the British held Lake Erie as a line of communication Detroit could not be taken. The task of clearing the Lake was given to CAPTAIN OLIVER HAZARD PERRY. Perry's first problem was to float a flotilla in the face of complete British control. This difficult task overcome, on September 10 he set out to challenge British control. His flagship flew a battle-flag with Captain Lawrence's order inscribed: "Don't give up the ship." (Lawrence had lost the Chesapeake and his life in a battle with the Shannon.) The results of the battle were recorded in Perry's famous message: "We have met the enemy and they are ours." Having lost their line of communication on Lake Erie, the British evacuated Detroit. Harrison fought a successful battle on the Thames River in lower Canada, a battle which destroyed Tecumseh and his Confederation. But for the remainder of the year, the war settled down to a series of border raids.

1814. The surrender of Napoleon in 1814 released British troops for an offensive in America. They planned a triple attack: one from the North along the Johnny Burgoyne route, one from the South using the Creek Indians in a direct attack on New Orleans and one in the nature of harassing raids all along the Atlantic coast, coupled with an ironclad blockade. But the offensive fizzled. The northern descent was stopped by Captain Thomas Macdonough at Plattsburg Bay on Lake Champlain; the Creeks were soundly beaten and scattered by the southern forces under ANDREW JACKSON and then, after the peace had been signed and in ignorance of that fact, Jackson defeated 10,000 British regulars at the famous Battle of New Orleans.

The blockade and the raids succeeded. The British captured and burned Washington. Their foray against Baltimore was not significant as a battle but as the source of FRANCIS SCOTT KEY's "Star-Spangled Banner." The British had bombarded Ft. McHenry "through the night" and in the "dawn's early light" "the broad stripes and bright stars" were still flying.

The Peace Treaty of Ghent, 1815. By the end of 1814 it was obvious to both sides that the war had lost much of its purpose. With Napoleon defeated, impressment, Orders in Council, ship seizures and cargo confiscations were of little interest to the British. The "War Hawks," their wings badly clipped, had come to the realization that Canada could not be won. On both sides of the ocean the people were war-weary and the treasuries were exhausted. The military situation was clearly at a stalemate. An American Peace Commission had gone to Europe early in 1814 at the invitation of Lord Castlereagh; it was composed of John Quincy Adams, J. A. Bayard, Henry Clay, Jonathan Russell and Albert Gallatin. After a year of negotiation, on Christmas Eve, 1814, the Treaty of Ghent was signed. It provided for a *status quo ante bellum* (a return to things as they were before the war) and the creation of commissions to settle outstanding boundary disputes. Were these years of war in vain? Had they been completely fruitless?

WAR AND CONSEQUENCE

Historians have evaluated the War of 1812 as "futile and unnecessary" or "stupid" with "meaningless bloodshed." But war must be treated as an objective fact of history. This does not mean that historians ignore the horror of man-slaughter; they may long for the permanent abolition of war. But, whatever their moral precepts, they may be forced to conclude that a war resulted in important consequences. The War of 1812 may have been futile, unnecessary and stupid in its cause, indecisive in its course; but there is a sense in which the war did serve important national purposes.

America's international position was established and interference by foreign powers with her national expansion came to an abrupt halt. England, beyond all others, recognized this fact and was disposed to make permanent settlements of all outstanding difficulties that might lead to future war. This required that she experiment with peaceful means for the settlement of disputes. Trade discriminations were gradually withdrawn in commercial conventions. The notable Rush-Bagot agreement of 1818 provided for complete disarmament of the Great Lakes, a principle eventually extended across the entire Canadian-American frontier. A fisheries convention signed in the same year gave America permanent rights to fish along the coasts of Newfoundland and Labrador and to dry and cure fish on unsettled shores. Most of the northern boundary was peaceably disposed of by drawing a line across the 49th parallel. There was a claims dispute over Oregon; and this was settled by deferment, joint occupation for ten years, renewable. Arbitration was utilized to dispose of the lingering question of the slaves captured during the Revolutionary War. Here, then, were enduring gains.

The *national* history of America began with this war. Though in fact the nation had done no better than hold its own against the partial might of Great Britain, Americans chose to consider themselves victors, to the marked subsequent increase in national consciousness and pride.

Further, the Mississippi Valley was permanently cleared of Indians as a result of the Battle of the Thames in the Northwest and the Battle of Horseshoe Bend in the Southwest. Clearance of Indians ensured permanent occupation and released an unprecedented flood of immigration into the territory.

As the West expanded, the Northeast developed intensively. The whole policy of embargo and nonintercourse had destroyed American commerce and reduced foreign importation to a minimum. Capital became idle and sought new outlets for profitable investment. The obverse side of the embargo policy was a unique system of absolute protection for potential manufactures. Realizing this, states, counties, municipalities and special societies offered attractive bounties for any who would build factories. The War of 1812 launched the American Industrial Revolution and transformed the face and history of the nation.

Finally, the war transformed the Republicans from dogmatic localists to confirmed nationalists. In this process they absorbed Federalism into their own program and made the existence of a Federalist party unnecessary. This brought the colonial era of American history to its end. Thus the War of 1812 at once closed an era and opened a new one.

IDEOLOGICAL BATTLES OF THE JEFFERSON ERA

The battle for the Constitution having been fought and won, the Federalists turned with fury upon the basic ideas of the Enlightenment, which they regarded as the seedbeds for political instability and social chaos. The French Revolution confirmed their fears; in France, the doctrines of "Jacobinism" had been loosed. Jefferson was taking up the French cry for the equality of man, for belief in man's essential goodness, for rationalism in religion and for belief in the inevitability of progress and the necessity for change. Federalists felt that Jefferson and his French cohorts were instigators of violence, turbulence, bloodshed, property confiscation, destruction of the natural aristocracy and democratic leveling. The result was that Federalist intellectuals went into battle against American Jacobinism.

American Jacobins. The American Jacobins were men who held to the beliefs of the American Revolution. Men like Philip Freneau, Benjamin Rush, Joel Barlow and Thomas Paine considered the French Revolution a continuation of America's own great revolt against aristocracy and feudal decay. Barlow and Paine had actually gone overseas to help the French in their battle. In their absence the intellectual climate in America underwent a sudden change. Paine was therefore shocked at the reception given in America to his pamphlet, *The Rights of Man.* It was a retort to Edmund Burke's *Reflections on the French Revolution* and contained little that was novel to men of the Enlightenment.

Paine had invoked against Burke the idea of man's original state of equality with no distinction but sex to differentiate one from another. He argued that because each man individually has not the power to preserve his "natural rights," he barters them to a civil power for "civil rights," for protection and security. This civil power, or government, is a necessary evil. If one must have government, then democracy is the best form. Monarchy is no more than usurpation of power; aristocracy no better. Democracy itself will not assure protection of natural rights if it is not linked to property *in land* and commerce. Man has the right to the use of land as a *natural* right. If he confiscates it from landholding aristocrats, he is taking only what belongs to him. Democracy, too, must permit man free use of his intellectual rights—freedom of thought, utterance and conscience.

Religious Views. Paine followed *The Rights of Man* with a pamphlet titled *The Age of Reason.* Once more, he said nothing new; but few works in the intellectual history of America have been more bitterly attacked than this. The charge against it was "atheism" in spite of the fact that Paine asserted "I believe in one God, and no more; and I hope for happiness beyond this life. I believe in the equality of man and I believe that religious duties consist in doing justice, loving mercy and endeavoring to make our fellow-creatures happy."

From this position, Paine attacked all existing churches: they did not, he claimed, possess revealed truth; Jesus was a virtuous reformer and revolutionist from whose simple life a mythology was fabricated; the Old and New Testament embodies low as well as high standards of morality. The true revelation, said Paine, is the visible creation, the world of nature and man; natural philosophy (science) is the only sound theology. Scientific principles will reveal more of God's nature than the mysteries and miracles which defy man's reason. Man has but to discover his own benevolence in the natural moral order.

Freneau added little to this stock of ideas but used them as ammunition against the Federalists. He attacked Federalist officeholders, armies and navies, aristocratic ceremonial, government centralization, slavery and the like. Barlow, on the other hand, extended Paine's concept of the rights of man to include the doctrine of social responsibility. Government, he argued, has the responsibility for individual well-being. The state is the agent for all of society and not the instrument for one group; it is a public thing, a *res publica*, guarding the social heritage. Not protection of property but securing justice is the end of government. Justice demands equal opportunity and the primary agency for providing opportunity is public education. An educated public will hold government to its just purpose if permitted annual elections and the right to recall civil officers who fail to do their duty.

The Conservative Reaction. As the French inspired the Jeffersonians, so Burke inspired the Federalists and provided their arguments. Burke reasoned from the fundamental concept that God had implanted a divine order on earth, a chain of rights and duties which binds the living to the dead, and which places on society the obligation of preserving the moral traditions of humanity. The moral order derives from a transcendent justice and man was gifted with reason to plumb the depths of this justice.

What does reason reveal? That uniformity, equalitarianism and utilitarianism are contrary to the divine plan. Civilized society requires orders and classes, gradations of humanity, as of all things. All men are created equal—in their disagreeable qualities only; their abilities are far from equal. Neither appetite nor ability is a guarantor of freedom; appetite leads to tyranny of the many and ability leads to tyranny of the strong. The principle of divine justice must be sought outside mankind; and what is more enduring and stable than property? Property supported by tradition is the source of true liberty. If property is the guide, change will come, but slowly; property will permit reform, not revolution. When Providence directs, changes will be made; men must have faith in Providence and not in their own base natures.

Counterattack. These Burkean concepts attracted the able minds of men like John Adams, John Fenno, Joseph Dennie, William "Peter Porcupine" Cobbett and William Clifton. The most learned among them was John Adams. In his erudite *Essays on Davila,* Adams attacked equalitarianism as unrealistic and based on misconceptions about men, namely, that all men are equal, that they are rational and kindly, that they can be impelled by ideals, reason and altruism. The reverse is true and for this reason democracy is an unworkable system which results in anarchy. Government must be a check and coercion upon the corruption, selfishness, jealousies and natural turbulence of *all* men. But somewhere in society there are "natural aristocrats," men above greed. These must be found and made the rulers, conferred dignity and surrounded with ceremonies befitting their station. So reasoned Adams, and others.

Others devoted themselves to counterattack upon Paine and Freneau. First they identified all the ideas of the Enlightenment with Jacobinism; the Jacobinism with unbridled license, with blood that will flood the happy land, with guillotine and terror. Jacobins, for example, had advanced the idea of the equality of the sexes. Federalists equated this idea with immorality and leaped to the defense of marriage, chastity and decency, the defense of domestic virtue and feminine subordination. In this violent reaction even slavery found some defenders. The earlier flush of gradual emancipation paled as men began to emphasize property rights in slaves or the need to keep slaves apart to prevent miscegenation (intermarriage). Negro inferiority in a white environment was openly proclaimed and some among the Federalists urged a "back-to-Africa" movement.

The most bitter attacks were based on religion. To John Adams, Revolutionary France was a nation of "thirty million atheists"; Hamilton saw it as a league between disciples and apostles of irreligion and anarchy. Led by religious leaders like Samuel Hopkins, Joseph Bellamy and Timothy Dwight a crusade was begun. Religious tracts were printed in large quantities; Bible societies were founded to put a Bible in every home; Christian societies were established to war on gambling, swearing, intemperance and Sabbath-breaking; Sunday schools appeared everywhere; a missionary movement was created to spread the gospel in indifferent areas within the United States. Everywhere there was a renewed insistence upon orthodoxy. This led inevitably to a frontal attack upon science and its base, the Newtonian Universe. Gravitation was ridiculed, botany was scorned, vivisection was condemned and animal breeding denounced. Sinfulness was accounted the main cause of disease and prayer the most effective cure.

This was the conservative mind of America and it prevailed until the Jacksonian revolt in spite of the political victories of the Jefferson Republicans.

CHAPTER VI

NATIONALISM

The Force of Nationalism. American nationalism appeared in mature form only after the War of 1812. The American people came to see themselves as one, united people without regard to section or regions or vast distances that separated them. They identified themselves with the *national* community and felt that their nation was different from all others. They were different in the language they spoke, their origins, history, customs and traditions; in their belief in the "common man," in the individual, in democracy, in a free and "classless" society —and responded profoundly to appeals to their uniqueness, their "differentness." Americans were, in fact, now bound by obligations which flowed from habitation of a common soil and loyalty to a united nation which they stood ready to defend with their lives. They were proud of any American who was able to establish himself in the world of science, ideas, or culture. Intelligent nationalism—true pride without arrogance or contempt for others—is the basis of true patriotism.

The "American System." The profound impact of nationalism upon the history of the United States can be observed in economic, political and cultural spheres following the War of 1812. Formerly, each section would examine national policies from the point of view of its local interests. Proposals for a protective tariff, national bank and federal internal improvements brought dissension among competing sections. But now, there was universal approval of Henry Clay's appeal for an "American System."

Clay sought to translate national into economic unity. He had been a western "War Hawk" in his youth. With the failure of his agrarian imperialist program in the War of 1812, he moved to a nationalist, isolationist position. He proposed that manufacturing in the North be encouraged by a protective tariff, thus freeing the country from dependence upon European industry. To facilitate entry into business and to guarantee stability to established concerns, Clay suggested that the national bank be rechartered. (The First Bank of the United States had expired in 1811.) The South and West, Clay hoped, would then be linked to the North by a series of internal improvements—roads and canals—built by federal funds derived from the tariff. In this way the producers of raw materials would be brought closer to the centers of manufacture; raw materials would then find their way to their natural markets in the home industries; manufactured goods would return by the same routes to raw material centers; and, as demand for more raw materials was felt, people would migrate westward along the highways and waterways carved out by internal improvements to new sources of supply.

Congress would encourage westward migration by liberal land laws. The Constitution would be stretched by loose interpretation to accommodate the new nationalism. Out of this round of migration—raw materials—manufactures—distribution—migration—raw materials etc., in ever widening circles, the American Nation would rise to economic self-sufficiency and to a station equal to that of the world's great powers. Clay's appeal was applauded and—while the nationalist spell lasted—acted upon.

The Second Bank. There were good reasons for rechartering a Second Bank of the United States. The abandonment of the First Bank in 1811 had led to near financial crisis. State banks, no longer curbed by a central bank, flooded the country with bank notes that declined in value as the number increased. Dollar bills with fluctuating values made normal business almost impossible though for a short while farmer-debtors found them useful in discharging their debts cheaply. There was a time when Henry Clay and John C. Calhoun viewed the national scene through debtors' eyes. Nationalism changed this and both sponsored a bill to recharter the Bank.

The Bank was to have triple the capitalization of its predecessor and, for the privilege of the charter, the bankers were required to give the government a "bonus" of $1,500,000. In other respects it was to be like the First Bank with provisions for partial government ownership, for branch banking, and the like. The bill became law and men looked forward to unimpeded realization of the American System. Unfortunately, the policies of the Bank from 1816 to 1819 were those of "wildcat" banking: banknotes were issued with little regard to available reserves of gold and silver and loans were made indiscriminately and with small concern for reliable security; the bank itself speculated on a phenomenal rise in the prices of western lands.

When, in 1819, NICHOLAS BIDDLE became Bank President he managed to save it from utter ruin by completely reorganizing bank policies, that is, by contracting the note issues to conform with specie reserves and by calling in the riskiest loans. He saved the Bank, but started a deflationary spiral which precipitated a collapse of land values, an increase of foreclosures on both rural and urban real estate and helped to bring on the Depression of 1819. As a result, the debtor West—creditor East conflict broke out anew.

The Tariff of 1816. It should be noted that—ironically—the Second Bank was the creation of Jeffersonian Republicans. However, this was a *new* Republican Party, one inspired by nationalist fervor, which was still active when Clay's proposal for a protective tariff was introduced into Congress. The West and the South (somewhat reluctantly) were persuaded to support the manufacturers of New England, for whom the period following the War of 1812 was a critical one. During the Embargo and War years, investment capital, cut off from its customary outlet in the shipping industries, had made its first ventures into manufacturing. With competition virtually excluded, business—particularly textiles—boomed. Americans of necessity "bought American," even though domestic goods were more expensive. Encouraged by initial successes, New England capitalists began "mass" production of tools, clocks, woodworks, hardware, textiles, and the like. Following Eli Whitney's lead, they produced by

means of standardizing parts; they introduced ingenious labor-saving devices; and they made their first cautious moves to replace the power of the water wheel with that of steam.

The English were aware of this threat to British manufacturing supremacy. After the War, they flooded the United States with inexpensive manufactured goods. English credit was extended liberally to encourage American distributors to buy. Formerly, New England's difficulties would have been Southern and Western opportunities. Now, however, nationalist sentiment rallied the whole nation to the defense of New England. Jefferson himself abandoned half-a-century of prejudice and wrote: "We must now place the manufacturer by the side of the agriculturist. He . . . who is against domestic manufacture must be for reducing us . . . to dependence on that foreign nation (England)." (This was, of course, Hamilton's view.)

The result was that Congress passed and President Madison signed the Tariff of 1816. Duties on cloth and home-produced articles were made prohibitive; on other goods the duties averaged about 20% which, for that day, was considerable protection. But, nonetheless, the English were still able to do great damage to American high-cost manufactures. Manufacturing in New England declined sharply from 1816 to 1819 as deflation drained away the profits. The Depression of 1819 settled upon New England as it did upon the South and West.

Westward Movement. Westward settlement was pivotal to the realization of the American System. Following the War of 1812 there was a vast population movement into the western territory. Half a million people moved into the Northwest Territory; the population of the Southwest mounted from 40,000 in 1810 to 203,000 in 1820; from Europe an average of 20,000 immigrants poured annually into the United States; within three years Indiana, Illinois, Mississippi and Alabama were admitted into the Union as states.

To foster this movement into unoccupied regions Congress was forced to consider more liberal land policies. The Land Act of 1796 had fixed the price at $2 an acre and had introduced an installment plan of two payments; but it had provided that 640 acres should be the minimum purchase. In 1800, this law was amended: the number of installments was increased to four and the minimum purchase to 320 acres. In 1804 the minimum purchase was again reduced—to 160 acres. This system of land sale had not worked: installments were linked to harvest periods, and when harvests failed defaults mounted. The government held the mortgages but found that it was not politically wise to evict large numbers of defaulters. Since they were permitted to stay on the land, those who could pay the installments refused to do so. Congress reduced land prices to $1.25 an acre; the minimum sale was made 80 acres; unpaid-for land could be returned and paid-for, kept. This generous legislation accounts in great part for the mass movement westward.

Internal Improvements. But to satisfy insistent western demands that passage westward be facilitated Congress in 1811 appropriated $7,000,000 to construct **the first national highway in the United States—the Cumberland Road.** This highway was first projected during Jefferson's administration. The War and the intense objections from some states forced its temporary abandonment. But post war nationalist sentiment overcame sectional differences. In 1818 the first 600 mile long, 60 foot wide (with a 20 foot macadamized strip down the middle) "National Road" was complete from Cumberland, Maryland to Wheeling, Virginia. By 1838 it was extended to the Mississippi River at Vandalia, Illinois. However, the sentiment that initiated this notable engineering feat gradually soured as one state after another interposed local objections to its continuation at federal expense.

POLITICAL REFLECTIONS OF NATIONALISM

The Election of 1820. The issues of a national bank, a protective tariff, a liberal land policy and internal improvements produced within Republican Party ranks a substantial unity. As the election of 1820 neared, it was discovered that the choice of the Republican caucus, JAMES MONROE, would be unopposed. The Federalist Party had become extinct (or, perhaps, "absorbed"). With differences within the Republicans held, for the nonce, in abeyance, Monroe received all the electoral votes but one cast for John Quincy Adams. Back in 1817, the *Boston Columbian Centinel* had dubbed Monroe's administration "The Era of Good Feelings" and in this second election of Monroe, good feeling reached its apex.

Judicial Nationalism: John Marshall. The spirit of Hamiltonian nationalism survived in the person of John Marshall, Chief Justice of the United States Supreme Court from 1801 to 1835. Through Marshall's crucial decisions the property-centered concepts of the American Enlightenment of the 18th century passed over into the capitalistic individualism of the 19th. Marshall's primary aim was to consolidate the continent, to establish a centralized state founded upon the protection of property against all

assaults and to make the Federal Government supreme in fact as well as theory. He therefore opposed state's rights which he considered the chief threat to union; and he disliked democracy, which he considered the chief threat to property.

His motives, however, were personal as well as ideological, for Marshall was an aristocratic Virginia gentleman-businessman with wide property interests. He was a land-speculator, a corporation stockholder and a bank director. Moreover, as a Federalist judge in a Republican context, he was keenly aware that every judicial decision would have to be a deft political maneuver. Constitutional historians seem agreed that Marshall's interest in The Law as such was minimal; he was most interested in writing into permanent precedent the Federalist conception of American nationalism. This was his great contribution to the shaping of America.

With all its limitations, Federalism had a clear conception of America's destiny—constitutionalism and protection of private property. Marshall completed the Federalist contribution. In **Marbury v. Madison** he placed the Supreme Court in an impregnable position by declaring an act of Congress unconstitutional. Having established the supremacy of the Court in constitutional matters, Marshall then began to elaborate the Federalist philosophy in the many cases that came before him.

Expansion of the Contract Clause. To protect property against confiscation, the Constitution had forbidden states to enact any law which would impair the obligation of a contract. Marshall expanded the meaning of "contract." If a state made a land grant and then rescinded it, it was violating a contract and the rescinding act was void (**Fletcher v. Peck**); if a state exempted someone from taxation, this was a contract and any later act taxing the exemptee was void (**New Jersey v. Wilson**); if a state legislature transferred control of a university to a more representative board of trustees by repudiating a grant to a less representative board, the transfer was void (**The Dartmouth College Case**); if one state legislature voided or amended an agreement with another, this, too, was a violation of contract (**Green v. Biddle**); and so on. It is clear then that contracts were the base for an expansion of the Federal Government (through the agency of the Supreme Court) over the states.

Extending Appellate Jurisdiction. Before Marshall, there was some question whether decisions of the highest state courts could be reviewed in the federal courts. In a conflict between the state and the central government, which was the final arbiter? The Judiciary Act of 1789 had made the central government final. Virginia challenged this delegation of authority in two cases (**Martin v. Hunter's Lessee** and **Cohens v. Virginia**). In these cases Marshall argued that uniform maintenance of constitutionality required a single system of courts; that the Constitution had placed limits upon the state's sovereignty; and that, since the Constitution is the "supreme law of the land" the national judiciary must prevail in any conflict of authority. No decisions of Marshall were more bitterly attacked by the Republicans than these for it seemed to them that they had made the power of the Supreme Court irresponsible and tyrannical. The Court, they said, was amending the Constitution at will by a bare majority. Moreover what check was there, except by the long and difficult process of amendment, on the Court's assumption of power? These charges were, of course, to echo down the decades. But Marshall was not noticeably disturbed.

Implied Powers and the National Supremacy. Marshall reached the climax of his politico-legal reasoning in the case of **McCulloch v. Maryland** which arose in the dispute concerning the Second Bank. In 1819, the bank was at the low point of its popularity and was widely blamed for the depression of that year. States began to retaliate against the bank by illegalizing it in their constitutions or by levying discriminatory taxes upon it. Maryland had levied such a tax. The case arose when McCulloch refused to pay the tax. There were two large questions before the Court:

1. Has Congress the power to incorporate a bank?

MARSHALL: The federal government derived its sovereignty from the *people* of the states—not from the states. This sovereignty, though limited, is supreme within its sphere of action. The delegated powers create the area of federal action. Within this area, Congress has the implied power to select appropriate, necessary and proper means for carrying the enumerated powers into execution. What is "necessary and proper?" "Let the end be legitimate, let it be within the scope of the Constitution, and all means which are appropriate, which are plainly adapted to that end, which are not prohibited, but consist with the letter and spirit of the Constitution, are constitutional." Here was the ultimate in loose constructionism!

2. Can a state constitutionally tax a National bank?

MARSHALL: The Constitution (and the Acts of Congress under it) is the supreme law of the land. The Bank was a lawful act of Congress. In a conflict between an act of Congress and a state law, the act of Congress must prevail. The state tax upon the Bank is therefore void. "The power to tax is the power to destroy." How absurd it would be to permit the inferior law to destroy the supreme law.

Commerce, Broadly Interpreted. With the arrival of the steamboat on the interior lakes and rivers, there was a temporary revival of the inter-state chaos that had prevailed under the Articles of Confederation. States vied with each other in granting to favored companies exclusive privileges of navigation in inland waters. ROBERT FULTON and ROBERT LIVINGSTON had secured such an exclusive right from the State of New York and had transferred it to AARON OGDEN. Ogden, then, had the exclusive privilege of steam navigation between New York and New Jersey. Gibbons, acting under a *federal* license, challenged the monopoly. In the case of **Gibbons v. Ogden** (Marshall's last great decision), the Chief Justice defined commerce as "every species of commercial intercourse" and the power of Congress over interstate commerce is supreme. But since commerce does not stop at state boundaries, neither does the power of Congress. Congress therefore has the power to regulate commerce within state lines. To appreciate the far-ranging effects of this decision, one need but examine the powers of Congress today over "every species of commercial intercourse."

NATIONALIST FOREIGN POLICY DEVELOPS

Expansion and Elimination. By 1820, the American foreign policy of "isolation" had become fixed. The late war, the fact of geographic separation from Europe, the dominant need to exploit the continent and the position which America held as a "minor" power—all these combined to convince Americans that following Washington's advice of avoiding permanent alliances was sound. The purchase of Louisiana and the seizure of West Florida had suggested an extension of the doctrine of isolation: eliminate potential enemies from the continent by land purchases, if they could be persuaded to sell.

Florida was a case in point. Along the Georgia-Florida boundary violence was routine. Indians, runaway slaves and cattle rustlers made periodic raids into American territory and escaped from pursuit to sanctuary in Spanish Florida. General ANDREW JACKSON was sent to terminate these activities. In the course of his "policing" duties he invaded Florida, raided the Spanish archives in Pensacola, and court-martialed and executed two British instigators on Spanish soil. Spain was thus made acutely aware of her vulnerability (even though the United States apologized for Jackson's expedition). Additional pressure to sell Florida was provided by the full-scale revolt of Spain's Latin-American colonies under the leadership of SIMÓN BOLÍVAR. Henry Clay urged formal recognition of their independence from Spain. By these tactics Spain was "convinced" that she ought to sell Florida. The sale was made on February 22, 1819. The United States assumed citizen-claims upon Spain amounting to $5,000,000; in exchange Florida was turned over to the United States. Spain relinquished her claim to Oregon and the United States surrendered her claim to Texas as part of the Louisiana Purchase.

THE MONROE DOCTRINE: GET OUT AND STAY OUT!

The doctrine of nationalist isolation was crowned by the Monroe Doctrine. Behind its proclamation was a complicated foreign situation.

Quadruple Alliance. In Europe, Austria, Prussia, and Russia had constituted themselves a "holy alliance" to maintain the *status quo*, that is, to put down any attempt at revolution aimed at changing the existing state of affairs. France joined with these three in an effort to win back her international prestige lost with the overthrow of Napolean I. When revolutions broke out in Italy and Spain, the French army was assigned to suppress them, and did so. In 1823, the Latin-American colonies of Spain had successfully thrown off her yoke; Spain therefore appealed to the Holy Alliance to get her colonies back. After the Florida Treaty, the United States had begun to recognize the independence of Spain's former colonies; now she was faced with the possibility of a large European invasion of the Western Hemisphere to restore the new republics to Spain.

Russia. At the same time Russia announced her claim to the west coast of North America to the 51st parallel, a claim that brought her within the Oregon Territory. Along with this claim Russia closed all the surrounding waters to commercial shipping. John Quincy Adams, the American Secretary of State, notified the Russian government that the American continents are no longer subject to colonization and that the United States was prepared to contest any new territorial establishments.

England. England regarded Spain's loss as her gain; she would now be able to break through the Spanish mercantilist policy and win the trade of Latin America. England, therefore, denied the right of the Holy Alliance to intervene and threatened to recognize the independence of the new republics if intervention were attempted. Here then was a case for Anglo-American cooperation; in fact, the English foreign minister, Canning, had already proposed joint action against intervention. President Monroe and ex-Presidents Jefferson and Madison thought the offer a fine one and recommended acceptance.

John Quincy Adams. The American Secretary of State did not agree and recommended its rejection. He was skeptical of Canning's true intentions; he knew that with or without America England would act to prevent intervention; why then become a "cockboat in the wake of a British man-of-war." An alliance with England would remove the possibility of American annexation of Cuba; England was unconcerned with Russia's west coast moves . . . Adams was convinced, with true nationalist conviction, that the United States must act alone and create an "American System" in the Western Hemisphere.

The Monroe Doctrine. Adams prevailed after stubborn argument. Therefore, in the annual message, December 2, 1823, Monroe announced an American doctrine for the Western Hemisphere: The American continents are no longer subject to European colonization. European and American systems being essentially different and separate, the United States would consider any attempt to extend the European system into the Western Hemisphere an unfriendly act. The United States would not interfere with any existing colonies, or in Europe's internal affairs; nor would she take part in European wars.

Without England's support, Europe was unable to challenge this bold assertion. The Tsar accepted the 54-40th parallel as his southern boundary and removed his claim to Oregon. The young republic had proudly and powerfully asserted its national dignity.

CULTURAL NATIONALISM

The party battles of the past had subsided in the dawn of nationalism; the bitter party battles of the future had not yet come. Americans had leisure for self-examination and self-discovery—for some thought and art.

What kind of culture was produced?

"Who Reads an American Book?" In this period of the birth of American nationalism Americans were deeply offended by remarks such as this: "During the thirty or forty years of their independence, (the Americans) have done absolutely nothing for the Sciences, for the Arts, for Literature, or even for . . . studies of Politics or Political Economy. . . . In the four corners of the globe, who reads an American book? or goes to an American play? or looks at an American picture or statue? . . ." (Sydney Smith, 1820)

Though perhaps too harsh a statement, it contained much truth. American culture was of course immature and therefore imitative. Beginning about 1800 CHARLES BULFINCH, THOMAS JEFFERSON, PIERRE

CHARLES L'ENFANT (who planned the District of Columbia), BENJAMIN LATROBE, WILLIAM STRICKLAND and ROBERT MILLS started a Greco-Roman Revival in American architecture. First intended for state buildings, the vogue spread until the humblest homes were adorned with columns, pediments, friezes, rotundas, vaultings, domes and other features of ancient Greek architecture. Similarly, American painters were restricted and self-restricted to portraiture —imitative of the English and French masters.

Literature was dominated by popular English sentimental fiction ("soap-operas" of seduction and abandonment), or the English "Gothic novel" ("mystery" tales of ruined castles, rattling chains, ghosts and multiple murder), or the English picaresque novel (with its shifting scene and rogue-hero). Much of the verse was deplorable imitation of the great English poets of the eighteenth century. Of the attempts to explain American cultural inferiority of this period, the most convincing are those that center upon the lack of an American tradition, the inadequacy of American education, the absence of an international copyright that made it cheaper for American publishers to steal and reprint English classics than venture into printing an unknown American, and the absorption of the best American minds with political problems.

The First Stirrings. Some Americans, however, sought to create a native American culture. "Native" is hardly applicable to the development in architecture. Here a break was made with classical models; but instead of developing an original style, Americans introduced other European styles (Gothic, French Suburban, Swiss Cottage, Ancient Etruscan, Oriental and Moorish!). The results were frequently grotesque and absurd, but in an odd way liberating.

In painting, JOHN VANDERLYN became notorious by exhibiting a nude "Ariadne." THOMAS DOUGHTY, THOMAS COLE and ASHER BROWN DURAND successfully launched a school of landscape painting that featured idyllic and pastoral scenes—of the Hudson River Valley and the Catskill and Adirondack Mountains. Genre painting (scene from common life) began to appear on the canvases of HENRY SARGENT and HENRY INMAN, scenes of *American* peculiarities like whittling, barn-dancing, electioneering and eel-spearing. Genre painting led to CURRIER and IVES prints which represented *American* events. And the drama in introducing the figure of the "Yankee" into the patriotic play, made a special contribution to native American humor and popular culture.

Literature: The First Triumph. Literature provided the first major triumph of American cultural nationalism in the works of WASHINGTON IRVING, JAMES FENIMORE COOPER and WILLIAM CULLEN BRYANT. Irving's dependence upon English style, his imitation of English models of composition, his lack of invention, his ransacking among picturesque ruins abroad detracted somewhat from his genuineness as an *American* product. But in his *Sketch Book of Geoffrey Crayon, Gent*, he made America his theme: the "noble" Indian savage and the native Dutch legends of the Hudson valley. In other works he explored the historical past of New York and Astoria. He recorded American customs, if only to lampoon them. More important, though, was the fact that he wrote books that *were* read and praised by such men as Sir Walter Scott and Lord Byron—in fact he became the "darling" of cultivated Europeans. His contribution to the world's humorous literature was enduring; he is still—in some of his work—readable.

JAMES FENIMORE COOPER was America's first important novelist, the first American to exploit the American scene and past for artistic purposes. His weaknesses are those of his time and character; he spoke for a disappearing American landed-aristocracy. But he produced some considerable literature in his wilderness, sea and historical novels. His Harvey Birch, hero of *The Spy*, is a full-length portrait of an American patriot of the Revolutionary War. In Natty Bumpo-Leatherstocking-Hawk-Eye, he created a new American image—the pioneer who loves freedom and the forest and faces ever westward, quietly heroic. His Indians lack all reality, are "just Natty Bumpo daubed over with red" and the "women he draws from one model don't vary,/All sappy as maples and flat as a prairie." (James Russell Lowell.) His work is full of improbabilities, his dialogue is artificial—the accusations can be (and have been) multiplied. The point is that—in ways which are not always readily apparent—he was an artist, and the first important American novelist.

WILLIAM CULLEN BRYANT, the "first bard of the nation," wrote some beautiful and important scenic poetry. "Thanatopsis," seems a permanent part of the poetry of the English language. What is significant for this context is that the natural scene of his verse was American: the bobolink, the waterfowl and the pine (instead of the nightingale, the yew and the celandine).

THE FALSE DAWN OF NATIONALISM

But all was not well. The Bank Bill of 1816 passed the House of Representatives by a vote of 80 to 72, proof of widespread opposition to the measure. The "Voice of New England," DANIEL WEBSTER, opposed the measure. He felt that state banks served that section well enough. Western states opposed the measure; the Bank often refused to lend a new settler money because he could not put up adequate security. State banks were much more generous in their loan policies. And 34 out of 57 Southern representatives had voted against the Tariff of 1816, which made imported goods so much more costly for them and which invited foreign buyers of cotton to retaliate against American cotton producers. Calhoun argued that the South would develop its own industries; but the planters resisted. "Nationalism" was thus opposed by a strong counterforce: "Sectionalism."

Sectionalism. Sectionalism is a psychological (and politico-economic) impulse that compelled Americans, despite common nationhood, to consider themselves as **different from one another.** It was a sense of belonging to a local community—with distinct accent, origin, history, customs and traditions, pursuing a "different" way-of-life from other locales and loyal to the **state,** not the nation. Common economic interests cemented these divided communities: one was bound to cotton production produced on plantations by slave labor; another to wheat production produced on small freehold farms by free labor; a third to household manufactures or factory production or commerce, etc. Pride in cultural achievement enhanced the sense of sectionalism; all Southerners, for example, hailed an artist if he were *Southern* (being an *American* artist was less important). Local pride was a commanding sentiment.

Internal Improvements. The movement inspired by Clay for internal improvements at federal expense collapsed in the face of sectionalist opposition. In 1816 Calhoun proposed that the bonus of $1,500,000 to be paid by the Second Bank for the privilege of the charter be set aside as a fund for the construction of roads and canals. Calhoun pleaded that no "low, sordid, selfish and *sectional* spirit" be permitted to determine national policy. The bill passed Congress by the thinnest of majorities and was promptly vetoed by Madison who, a short while previously, had advocated it in his "state of the union" message. Proponents of states' rights rejoiced and the history of internal improvements became the history of state action.

The Missouri Dispute. More ominous was the issue of the admission of Missouri as a state into the Union. By 1819, Missouri had qualified for statehood under the terms of the Northwest Ordinance. A committee of the House recommended favorable action on the admission request. But James Tallmadge of New York arose to amend the bill of admission: "That the further introduction of slavery or involuntary servitude be prohibited . . . and that all children born within the said state, after the admission thereof into the Union, shall be free at the age of twenty-five years." This amendment split the nation in two—"slave states" and "free states." Men were reluctantly driven to make a choice. The debates that followed provoked passionate disagreement.

The Debate. Northerners turned their broadsides full upon the institution of slavery itself. They called it an offense to religion and morality, charging that Christians who maintain slaves are hypocrites; that Southerners sought to spread slavery throughout the Louisiana Territory in order to maintain a grip on both houses of Congress.

Southerners vehemently denied the charges, asserting that slavery—the **"peculiar institution"**—had been inherited from a long past. Cotton production which had advanced from 20,000 pounds in 1791 to 160,000,000 in 1820 had made slavery necessary. Moreover, Northerners might spout about "political domination" but it was *they* (the North) who threatened to become politically dominant. They had the House in their possession already (105-81) in spite of the three-fifths federal ratio; the Senate was tied at eleven each. Was it really asking too much to admit Missouri as a slave state and give the South a two member advantage in the Senate? Slaveholding was not illegal, they claimed; it was recognized in the Constitution and in the treaty which had transferred Louisiana to the United States. Did the North propose to confiscate Southern property? If not, what practical plan for emancipation had the North?

The Missouri Compromise. When the measure for admission came to a vote, it was defeated! The issue "went to the country" in the Congressional elections that followed. Mass meetings were held North and South; state legislatures drew up indignant petitions for and against slavery and sent them to Congress; outraged feelings were vented; but, the time for a decisive break had not yet come.

The new Congress reconsidered the issue. The state of Maine was now applying for admission. In a compromise offered by Senator Thomas of Illinois, Maine and Missouri were linked: Maine was to enter as a free and Missouri as a slave state, thus keeping the balance in the Senate. In the remainder of the Louisiana Territory all new states above the 36-30 line were to be free, those below, slave. A precarious balance was achieved and men could return to national considerations. But the issues had aroused the north and south to sectional self-consciousness. Reflecting the fury of the debate, Jefferson wrote: "This momentous question, like a fire bell in the night, awakened and filled me with terror."

The Election of 1824. The nation's turmoil registered in the election of 1824. Five "favorite sons" candidates contended for three sections. William Crawford and John C. Calhoun vied for Southern support; Henry Clay and Andrew Jackson for Western support; and John Quincy Adams was unopposed in his bid for the North and Middle states.

During the course of the campaign Calhoun withdrew his candidacy, threw his support to Jackson and accepted the offer of the vice-presidency. The electoral count revealed that Jackson had 99 votes, Adams 84, Crawford 41 and Clay 37. Since there was no majority, the vote went to the House of Representatives. As Clay was eliminated, he threw his House support to Adams. There was an immediate outcry and one Philadelphia newspaper published an anonymous letter charging that a corrupt bargain had been made between Adams and Clay. The House voted and Adams defeated Jackson, 13 states to 7. Adams appointed Clay as Secretary of State and the Jacksonian House began an investigation of the "corrupt bargain"; none was established. That fact did not matter for Jackson had already begun his campaign for presidency with the slogan "bargain and corruption" and "Clay, the Judas of the West."

The Unsung Administration of J. Q. Adams. Although he was an able and honest public servant, John Quincy Adams' administration yielded no great achievements. In his first annual message he projected a golden dream: federal road and canal construction, a national university, a national astronomical observatory, standardization of weights and measures, explorations of the West and laws to promote agriculture, commerce, manufacturing, the arts, sciences and literature. A decade earlier these proposals would have been given sympathetic hearing; now they were the victims of sectional and party politics.

As each proposal was offered in Congress, it was defeated by a coalition of supporters of Jackson, Calhoun and Crawford. When Clay sponsored a proposal of Simón Bolívar for a Pan-American Conference to consider the important matters of recognition of Haiti, regulation of the slave trade, and independence for Cuba and Puerto Rico, the measure met violent debate in which the pro-Jackson forces played upon Southern prejudices. When delegates were finally appointed, one died enroute and the other arrived at Mexico City to find the conference adjourned—a fitting symbol of a futile administration. Adams served four years, but history is more concerned with Jackson's activities during that time.

The "Tariff of Abominations." Typical of Jackson's strategy was his manipulation of the combustible tariff issue. The Tariff of 1816 had support in every section. When the depression of 1819 struck the country, New England sought relief by demanding increased duties on manufactured goods. Relief was granted in 1824, during the dying light of the nationalist flame. But when another increase was attempted in 1827 it was defeated in the Senate by Vice-President Calhoun.

It was then that Jackson's supporters in the House of Representatives planned a political tariff, one that would "manufacture a president." Such a tariff would have to win over the anti-tariff South and the pro-tariff North. How was this miracle to be achieved? A bill was introduced with fantastically high rates on raw materials. This would force the North to vote against the tariff because it would add materially to the cost of manufactured goods; the South would also vote against it on principle. Now what? In campaign speeches in the North the Jackson men would claim that they were for the tariff but New Englanders voted against it. This would gain the Northern vote. Southern Jacksonians could claim in the South that they had voted against the tariff, as they had. This would gain the Southern vote. The ruse failed. New England, to the chagrin of the Jacksonians, voted for the measure to give the country a preposterously high tariff, a "**tariff of abominations**," as it was called.

Exposition and Protest. John C. Calhoun led the outcry against the tariff. A convert to sectionalism, he relinquished his nationalist faith reluctantly. South Carolina was trying to survive by means of a single cash-crop, cotton. In better days, she had tolerated national movements for internal improvements and protective tariffs. Exhausted now, these demands upon the national treasury (attended by higher taxes) provoked her opposition. Calhoun loyally followed his state into dissent and when the Tariff of Abominations became law, he wrote his *Exposition and Protest.*

This tariff, he asserted, is discriminatory. But what mattered most was that the South had been made a permanent minority in the nation and was now completely at the mercy of a permanent and hostile majority. The Constitution could not have intended that such a state of affairs should exist ever, and had provided checks upon tyrannical majorities by placing the ultimate sovereignty in the states. Congress enjoyed only a limited sovereignty. If it exceeded its sovereign rights the states must provide the remedy. The remedy was **interposition by state convention.** When a state interposed, the

Congress could choose to repeal the law; or to amend the law; or to offer an amendment to the Constitution, that is, to test the law by a three-quarters majority of the states.

This was the state to which nationalism had fallen in the year 1828; one state could set aside the national will as represented by Congress. The lines, seemingly, had been drawn.

CHAPTER VII

THE AGE OF ANDREW JACKSON

DEMOCRACY

While nationalism and sectionalism contended, a third great force—democracy—developed. This idea was born and matured in the "frontier" areas of America—the agricultural frontier along the rim of American civilization and the urban "frontier" along the Atlantic seaboard.

The Frontier. A frontier was—in reality as well as imagination—a land of opportunity; an area where one can make a fresh start and rise in the economic scale; where there is no frozen class-structure to impede his advance. On the edge of American civilization, opportunity lay in exploitation of land and its resources; along the seaboard it lay in the chance to rise from the laboring to the employing class. The important qualities, it was felt, were **personal** ones: hard work and ingenuity. No one wanted all men to *remain* equal, only that they *begin* equal and rise according to their merits. Frontiersmen admired and were inspired by those who were successful under frontier conditions; but resented and opposed a "privileged" class that preempted opportunity for itself alone. And since such permanent classes controlled government, the frontier demanded democratic participation.

The Idea of Democracy. First they sought an extension of suffrage; and, as early as 1807 New Jersey was forced to abolish tax qualifications for voting. Between 1812 and 1821, six western states entered the Union with constitutions providing for universal, white, male suffrage and, in a wave of constitutional revisions between 1816 and 1821, four of the Eastern states followed suit. With the vote secured, further victories were secured when religious qualifications were eliminated; representation was reapportioned according to population, not taxpayers; the choice of presidential electors was transferred from state legislatures to the people; the number of elective offices was increased. In national politics, the Congressional caucus to nominate presidential candidates disappeared and, following the pattern set by the anti-

Masonic Party in 1831, the national party nominating convention took its place. Political democracy, for males anyway, had become a fact.

The rise of a new voting bloc transformed political activity. Politicians had now to cope with the "people" and they needed a new type of organization which could "get out the vote." In response to this need there arose the party "machine" headed by the political "boss" who derived his power from his command of "patronage." These men spoke a new "popular" kind of political oratory in their efforts to win their new constituents. They have ever since remained an important feature of the American political scene.

Jackson as a Symbol. Political "bossism" was baptized in the campaigns for the election of Andrew Jackson. The bosses learned that a man need not be what people see in him. People "saw" Jackson as the very type of the frontier democrat, the rough-and-ready warrior against all privilege. He had become a popular legend. They recited his brawling career with pride and told and retold of his enlistment in the Revolutionary War at thirteen, of his mutilation and capture by the British, of his gambling on horses and cock-fights, of his violent quarrels and successful duels, of his military victories during the War of 1812, of his rugged defiance of international law in Florida, of his roughhouse tactics in Tennessee politics. The frontier loved him and saw in him the heroic symbol of their own aspirations to rise from rags to riches. Jackson and his party leaders fed the legend.

The legend was grounded in solid fact but it was only one side of a complex personality. Jackson was a newly arrived gentleman-aristocrat, but once arrived he had adopted the mien and manner of the gentry. He was a prosperous slaveholder and businessman and, until bankrupted, a creditor and "sound-money" man who had consistently sided with the "haves" against the "have-nots" on the frontier. Then, he had become dignified, courtly and sentimental—a "proper" country gentleman. These characteristics, however, were political handicaps and were carefully concealed from public view by his campaign managers. The image of the fighter—"Old Hickory"—has persisted and that is an image too essential to our folklore to be much concerned with the mere fact that he had the graceful and suave manners of a Southern gentleman.

Coalition. With the nomination of Jackson, there appeared for the first time in American politics a coalition organized around a powerful personality with multiple appeal. The persistence in America of the stable two-party system was to a large extent made possible by the fact that single individuals could command the loyalties of normally opposed groups and thus present a single political front. It was exactly such a coalition that formed around "Old Hickory" in the campaign of 1828: the backcountry Scotch-Irish extending from the Piedmont to the Northern wheat fields; small grain-and-hay growers in the Middle States; poor seafarers and urban laborers along the Atlantic Coast; debtors everywhere; petty Southern planters warring against the Tidewater planters and Tidewater planters themselves, who looked upon Jackson as a fellow-slaveholder.

What bound these groups together? Primarily, they were "antis": anti-Adams, anti-British, anti-Indian and especially anti-monopoly and special privilege. Positive programs differed sharply; some were for aristocracy and hostile to "King Numbers" (rule by majorities); others hated the aristocracy. Some were "soft money" men seeking to escape debt through inflation; others were "hard money" men seeking wages that would buy the full money's worth. Some favored tariff protection for essential grains; others were for complete free trade. Only the compelling personality of Jackson and an "elastic" policy could make of these discordant elements a cohesive voting group.

The Election of 1828. The campaign of 1828 was conducted as though the forces of light were contending with the forces of darkness. Special privilege, so went the Democratic campaigning, had wrested the election of 1824 from the people and the people's choice and the people, newly armed with suffrage, must recapture their rights from the entrenched aristocrats. Ironically, this democratic upsurge was led by the aristocrats William Crawford, John C. Calhoun and Martin Van Buren who had mounted the Jackson bandwagon. Calhoun was nominated for the Vice-Presidency. A tight organization was formed extending from North to South and by oration, mass demonstrating and newspaper editorial the cry was raised, "Turn the rascals out!" Jacksonians were for the most part silent on the major issues of the day and concentrated upon the "corrupt bargain," the "dictatorship" of the Congressional caucus and the rule of the aristocracy. The tone of the campaign was violent.

The Adams-Clay Republicans played into the hands of the Jackson Democrats. They had failed to build up an effective organization and Adams did not consolidate his position by a proper distribution of patronage (i.e., political favors). Even more to his disadvantage was Adams' concrete program for internal improvements and a protective tariff; for no clear stand on specific issues could compete with the "Old Hero's" hold on the people's imagination. Jackson was swept into office.

The People are Crowned. For the common man inauguration day was a signal triumph. This was their man and their day. They had come from as far as five hundred miles south and west to hail their hero. For three days before the Inauguration the capital was in a festival fever. Now that their man was in office, they came to the White House to be greeted formally by the President. Refreshments were served. But the crush was so great that the orange punch was spilled and the glasses were splintered and the rugs and silken sofas were trampled with muddy boots. Jackson himself had to be rescued from their adoration. How could he now doubt his strength?

The Spoils System. The term "spoils system" has an odious ring to modern ears and it seems no compliment to Jackson to say that he inaugurated this practice on a wide scale. But all things are relative to their time and place. In Jackson's day government was small. There was no army of special "experts" to direct government intervention into all aspects of American life as there is today; nor were millions of employees required for the functions of government. Only a few posts required specialists. It seemed clear to Jackson that federal office must rotate with the popular will. There was no place in the American democracy for a permanent bureaucracy. Government is a simple process and all people must be given an equal opportunity to share in its management. Jackson regarded as vicious the idea of public office as "spoils." As President he was scrupulously honest in his appointments to office and he fought unrelentingly against graft, embezzlement, waste and the use of public funds for party purposes. In its origin, then, the "spoils system" was intended to extend the practice of democracy. Only as the government grew in size and the opportunities for corruption exceeded the capacity to resist temptation did the spoils system become a corruptive influence.

The Coalition and the Cabinet. The cabinet had

to serve the coalition. With an eye to reconciling Northern and Southern supporters, Jackson appointed as Secretary of State, MARTIN VAN BUREN of New York and divided the rest of the posts among relative unknowns from other regions. This was a sharp departure from tradition. In the past Presidents had sought for the Cabinet men of recognized stature. Mediocrity served to make a strong president stronger and to ensure that no Cabinet member would become strong enough to upset the coalition. To make doubly certain of this, Jackson discontinued the practice of holding regular Cabinet meetings. In fact, he sought guidance outside the official Cabinet, gathering about him into an unofficial "Kitchen Cabinet" of party leaders and journalists to write his state papers, plan strategy and keep alive his public image.

The First Break in the Coalition. The Calhoun forces representing the Southern aristocracy were the weakest link in the coalition chain. Sitting as President of the Senate, Calhoun studied the character of the new president carefully. He saw Jackson make a powerful assertion of the independency of the executive by resisting Congressional checks and balances. Conflict with Congress developed early as Jackson tried to force appointments through the Senate. The President wielded the veto power like a club and with each veto message spread the doctrine that his own energetic and self-assertive will was the "people's will."

Calhoun noted the frequency of the appearance of cartoons dubbing Jackson as "King Andrew I" and watched impeachment threats mount. There was an implicit understanding between him and Jackson that Calhoun was to be the presidential nominee in 1832; now, however, Jackson was silent on that matter; as a matter of fact, the "Kitchen Cabinet" had already begun a boom for a second term for Jackson. But one had to move cautiously; the "mob" was with Jackson. It was Jackson, however, that forced the break with Calhoun. He learned that in 1818 Calhoun had proposed a court-martial for his having invaded Florida and publicly ended his friendship with Calhoun by purging his Cabinet of Calhoun's supporters. The Vice-President resigned and was re-elected to the Senate where he would be better able to do battle.

THE POLICIES OF ANDREW JACKSON

Ideology in the Senate. For the first two years the Jackson administration failed to confront any of the nation's basic problems. The urge to make a powerful assertion of popular authority conflicted with the need to maintain the coalition. The resultant paralysis ended unexpectedly with a Senate debate. Senator Foote of Connecticut proposed to limit for a time the sale of public land. Senator Benton of Missouri charged Foote with a conspiracy to impede westward settlement; this was a New England plot to keep cheap labor in the East. Robert Y. Hayne entered the debate, ostensibly to support Benton's proposal for even cheaper western land, but really to try to make a South-West alliance within the coalition.

The Webster-Hayne Debates. Hayne pointed to the growing centralization of the Federal Government—because of it, he charged, the West was unable to have its cheap land and the South was victimized by a high tariff. Both the West and the South would do well to adopt Calhoun's theory of nullification according to which a single state might declare a federal law null and void if it was thereby injured. Had Hayne succeeded in welding the West and South to the doctrine of nullification, the course of American history might have taken a queer turn. But Hayne did not succeed and the credit for his failure goes to Daniel Webster.

Webster appreciated the unassailable logic of the Hayne-Calhoun position—*if* its major premise were granted, that the Constitution was a contract among the several sovereign states and the Federal Government was merely a creature of the states. He therefore proceeded to demolish this premise and impose his own. In answer to the question, Whose creature is central government? he replied, "It is, sir, the people's Constitution, the people's government, made for the people, and answerable to the people." The Constitution created the central government and permitted the states a small measure of sovereignty; ultimate sovereignty lay with the people and therefore the Constitution created remedies if a law of Congress should be unconstitutional: there were the federal courts, the frequent elections and provisions for amendment. How could anyone support the absurdity that there should be as many interpretations of constitutionality as there are states? One nation could not have many masters. Talk of secession was talk of treason; any effort to disrupt the Union would be met with force. Only those who made the union—the people—can dissolve it. Webster concluded with an appeal for "Liberty and Union, now and forever, one and inseparable."

Jackson and the Debate. Jackson followed the Webster-Hayne debate with close attention. Calhoun's press began to campaign for some stand by the President. Jackson knew that any statement he made would have its impact upon the coalition. He knew that there was more to the South than Calhoun. In the deep South Jackson's popularity had mounted with his decisive handling of the Indian problem. During his administration more than 90 treaties were concluded with the Indians, each one pushing them West to beyond the Mississippi; two disciplinary wars were fought (**The Black Hawk War and Seminole War**). The deep South benefited in land grabs and was duly grateful. He felt that he had the popular support to challenge Calhoun.

On April 13, 1830 at a (Democratic) Jefferson Day Dinner Jackson rose to offer a toast. His eyes squarely upon Calhoun, Jackson declared "Our Federal Union—it must and shall be preserved!" Calhoun rose and replied: "The Union, next to our liberty, most dear. May we all remember that it can only be preserved by respecting the rights of the states. . . ." The battle was joined.

The Issue of Nullification. Two years later, the tariff issue provided the test. In December of 1831 Jackson had asked the Congress to lower some of the "abominable" rates of 1828. A Congressional combination of New England and the Northwest, however, was able, in 1832, to push through a tariff which, though lower than that of 1828, was still substantially protective. Putting Calhoun's theory into operation South Carolina called a state convention in November 1832 which resolved that both the tariffs of 1828 and 1832 were "null, void and no law, nor binding upon this State, its officers, or citizens." Federal officers were forbidden to collect customs in South Carolina after February 1833. Any federal action would be "inconsistent with the longer continuance of South Carolina in the Union." That was the challenge: nullification—and that failing, secession.

Clay's Compromise. Strategically, Jackson requested Congress to lower the tariff and called upon South Carolina to act moderately, thus establishing his non-partisanship. Then he asked Congress for the power to use force to collect the duties and denounced the act of nullification, thus rallying the nationalists to his side. South Carolina found herself isolated and willing to compromise. In Congress, Henry Clay shaped the compromise: the tariff of 1832 was to be repealed; the free list enlarged; and the tariff of 1828 was to be gradually reduced to the rates of the Tariff of 1816. Accordingly, South Carolina repealed the Ordinance of Nullification and instead nullified the Force Act. This was merely a face-saving gesture; the repeal of nullification had nullified the use of force. Jackson emerged the hero and the coalition, though shaken, still stood.

The Maysville Veto. Internal improvements was a sensitive issue to the Tidewater planters and to the western farmers—the latter demanding them, the former hostile to them. Jackson satisfied the westerners by continuing assistance to the Cumberland Road, by extending road building in the territories and by giving local communities federal grants-in-aid for river and harbor improvements. The Tidewater planters did not need internal improvements since they were well supplied with rivers flowing into the Atlantic. They regarded federal aid as a burdensome tax; and to keep them within the coalition, Jackson knew that he must make some dramatic veto of an internal improvement project.

The opportunity came with the proposed Maysville Road, a project that lay wholly within the state of Kentucky, home of Jackson's arch-enemy Clay. There was but one hitch: a veto might alienate western Democratic support. Fortunately, most of the states wanted to keep the federal government out. The states were engaged in large local improvements—particularly in the construction of canals. Federal aid might assist speculators who could challenge the local builders. From this strong position, Jackson vetoed the Maysville project with the explanation that since the road lay wholly within the state, federal funds were unavailable. This doctrine was a blow to loose construction of the national power and satisfied the states rightists. It kept the Tidewater within the coalition and permitted Jackson to strike a blow against privileged groups—road contractors and land speculators. Jackson's brilliant strategy served also as a defeat for Henry Clay.

Jackson v. the Bank. Jackson's most dramatic battle was waged against the Bank. More than any other incident, it revealed his genius as a political antagonist, if not, perhaps, as a sound economist. The Bank was a central bank. As such it checked the "wildcat" tendencies of the local state banks. When the local bank over-issued notes or credit, the Bank insisted that they pay their debts in specie. Or, it suggested to the local banks that new loans be suspended until uncollected ones were repaid. In its own banking practice, the Bank was a model of conservatism. It collected its debts and when they could not be paid, it foreclosed on mortgages held as securities. While this may be sound banking, it incurred the hatred of those who were foreclosed. Most of these were Westerners.

Jackson came to share this hatred. In the early part of his administration, he seemed to favor the Bank and even hinted to Nicholas Biddle, the Bank's president, that Democratic directors be appointed to the Board of Directors. Biddle did so in the outlying branches. Later, as western hostility increased, Jackson's sentiment turned with it. Biddle wanted the renewal of the Bank's charter in 1836. Generous loans were made to Congressmen and journalists; Webster and Clay became unofficial advisers. They advised Biddle to secure recharter in 1832 to force the hand of Jackson before the election. If Jackson vetoed the Bank Bill, he was certain to be defeated in the country; the Bank Bill might even elect Henry Clay as President. Biddle, somewhat dubious, agreed. The Bill was passed easily by both houses and promptly vetoed by Jackson.

The Veto Message. Jackson's veto message is a classic and deserves study. He stated that he had informed Congress that some of the powers exercised by the Bank were unconstitutional, subversive to the rights of the states and dangerous to the liberties of the people. Since Congress ignored his advice, he had no choice but to veto the bill. The Bank was a monopoly with almost exclusive control of domestic and foreign exchange. This had raised the value of its stock above the par value and had yielded huge profits to the stockholders. The present bill would make the stockholders even richer. And who were the stockholders? "More than eight millions of the stock of this bank are held by foreigners." *Their* profits are paid by the American people. If there must be a central bank, why should not the government and the people be the beneficiaries?

Moreover, the bank is a threat to American liberty and independence. The state banks are the victims of the central bank and the central bank belongs to foreigners. Do we want foreigners to influence elections and control national affairs? An American bank "should be purely American." What of the bank's constitutionality? Marshall's decision is not the last word on that matter. "Mere precedent is a dangerous source of authority. . . ." Against the one Supreme Court decision one must balance the many Congresses and State Legislatures that have opposed the Bank. Nor does a Supreme Court decision necessarily bind the Executive. "Each public officer who takes an oath to support the Constitution swears that he will support it as he understands it, and not as it is understood by others." The Bank is constitutional, but it is for Congress and the President to decide its proper uses. At the very end of the message Jackson stated:

There are no necessary evils in government. Its evils exist only in its abuses. If it would confine itself to equal protection, and, as Heaven does its rain, shower its favors alike on the high and the low, the rich and the poor, it would be an unqualified blessing. . . . Experience should teach us wisdom. Most of the difficulties our Government now encounters . . . have sprung from an abandonment of the legitimate objects of Government by our national legislation. . . . Many of our rich men have not been content with equal protection and equal benefits, but have besought us to make them richer by act of Congress. By attempting to gratify their desires we have in the results of our legislation arrayed section against section, interest against interest and man against man, in a fearful commotion which threatens to shake the foundations of the Union.

The Election of 1832. The election of 1832 was significant in other ways. It was the first in which nominations by the major parties were made by party conventions. The National Republicans met and nominated Henry Clay, setting a precedent by adopting a **party platform** condemning Jackson's stand on the Bank and the Supreme Court and endorsing once more the "American System." The Democrats then nominated Jackson and Van Buren. Van Buren's selection by Jackson threatened the coalition and Jackson insisted that he be nominated by a two-thirds vote. (Democrats continued this precedent, the two-thirds rule, until 1936.) No platform was adopted—the bank issue, the corrupt bargain and Jackson were sufficient.

Jackson was elected 219 to 49. He now felt he had a popular mandate to destroy the Bank and ordered the discontinuance of government deposits after September 15, 1833; existing deposits would remain until exhausted. New deposits were to be made in the state or "pet" banks. There was so much opposition within Jackson's Cabinet that he had to remove two Secretaries of the Treasury until he found Roger B. Taney, a states' rights Marylander, who was willing to sign for new deposits to be made in state banks.

Hollow Victory. Jackson had scored a great political victory, but brought on serious economic consequences. The flow of federal funds into the "pet" banks and the distribution of a federal treasury surplus to state areas released a wave of reckless speculation. "Wildcat" loans, mounting inflation and unsecured indebtedness followed. Since Eastern manufacturers were unable to supply the inflationary needs, imports poured in from overseas to drain the country of specie (foreign debts must be paid in gold). As specie became short, foreign investors withdrew credit; local investors sought to cash in their holdings; the banks began to contract their loans and to call in their outstanding obligations; and, with no alternative, Jackson issued his **Specie Circular (1836)** which provided that land offices accept only gold and silver in payment for public land. A rush on the banks resulted, forcing them to suspend specie payments. The deflationary collapse began: land values disintegrated, businesses closed and agricultural products accumulated. But when the depression reached its depth, Jackson was out of office.

FOREIGN RELATIONS AND THE COALITION

Texas. Texas became a major issue during Jackson's administration; but in this matter Jackson acted without his customary vigor. Or rather, his vigor was devoted to maintaining the coalition instead of actively seeking to annex Texas, as he ardently desired to do. How had Texas come into the position where its annexation had become an explosive issue?

In 1820 MOSES AUSTIN had secured permission from Spain to settle an American colony in Texas to plant cotton. A year later the Spanish government was overthrown by revolutionary Mexicans and the grant to the Americans was renewed by the new Mexican government. Cotton planting proved so successful that in 1825 Mexico introduced the *"empresario"* system; huge land grants were made to *"empresarios"* who would import hundreds of families. Since no minimum price for land was established, the lands were disposed of cheaply and quickly.

The Mexican government grew fearful of the large foreign settlement within its borders. These settlers were peculiar. They considered themselves to be Americans, not Mexicans, and continued to deal across the border as though there were no boundary line. Thereupon the Mexican government undertook to place them under control; it banned further immigration into Mexico, tightened all customs controls, abolished slavery and severely limited the right to home rule. Texans defied the dictatorship, set up a provincial government and, when the Mexican ruler SANTA ANNA sent a punitive expedition against them, they declared their independence. After an initial defeat at the Battle of the Alamo, under the banner of "Remember the Alamo" SAM HOUSTON rallied the Texan forces and defeated Santa Anna at the Battle of San Jacinto (1836). With independence secure, the Texans organized the "Lone Star" State and President Sam Houston asked for immediate annexation by the United States.

Jackson had followed these events with great interest. But as head of a popular coalition that embraced slave and non-slave areas, Jackson could not openly endorse a move like annexation that would split the coalition. Texas had become deeply embroiled in the slavery issue. The democratic upsurge released by Jackson had been to a great extent responsible for a wide anti-slavery movement. The annexation of Texas was belligerently demanded by the slave states. This dilemma was too great even for Jackson. He merely recognized the new state of Texas and refused annexation. His successor would inherit the storm, not he.

"Shirtsleeve" Diplomacy. In foreign relations Jackson acted vigorously, instituting an epoch of "shirtsleeve" diplomacy. He forced England to take the last step in full commercial relationships with America by opening the British West Indies to American trade (1830). France was made to pay for damages inflicted on American shipping during Napoleon's "Continental System." Jackson had seized French property and severed diplomatic relations.

Van Buren. Jackson retired from office in 1837, but not from battle. His tremendous influence was thrown behind MARTIN VAN BUREN for President in the election of 1836. The Democrats still commanded the allegiance of small western farmers, backcountry southern planters and seaboard workers; but wealthier and more influential groups had left the coalition. The Jackson opposition, now calling themselves "Whigs" as a symbol of revolt against Jackson's "monarchical" tendencies, were composed of Clay's supporters of the American System, Calhoun's statesrightists, pro-Bank men, large Southern planters and Northern industrialists. But they could not agree upon a candidate and offered instead a number of candidates in an effort to send the election to the House of Representatives. Van Buren was elected. His running mate, Richard M. Johnson, failed to secure a majority in the electoral college and for the first and only time in American history the Senate of the United States chose the Vice-President. Johnson won in the Senate.

Van Buren's election occurred simultaneously with the Depression of 1837, caused by the runaway inflation. He met this crisis by removing all federal deposits from state banks and by establishing an Independent Treasury System which would hereafter hold all federal deposits in vaults or subtreasuries and make all payments in specie. Thus federal funds were divorced from banking and the government returned to a "hard money" policy. In the Congressional struggles over the subtreasury plan, Calhoun was reunited to the Democratic Party.

The disintegration of the coalition revealed the extent to which it had depended upon the force of Jackson's personality. Van Buren was a skillful and intelligent President, but colorless. Like Jackson, he avoided a commitment on Texas and on slavery; he reduced tensions with England over unofficial American aid to revolutionary Canadians (1837); he got England to agree to arbitrate the tender Maine-New Brunswick boundary following upon the bloodless

Aroostock War in that area. But the depression years that followed upon Jackson's policies obscured his achievements, such as they were, and ended the Jacksonian coalition.

The Whig Coalition. An end to the Jacksonian coalition did not mean an end to coalition politics. Jackson's enemies learned from him the art of combining discordant groups. For the election of 1840 they selected WILLIAM HENRY HARRISON and JOHN TYLER and thus combined North and South in one ticket. They avoided taking a stand on the issues of the day. They centered their attack upon the aristocratic pretensions of Van Buren the Democratic candidate; and they converted their own *true* aristocrat, Harrison, into a "log-cabin and hard-cider" candidate. They exploited slogans like "Tippecanoe and Tyler too" and "Van, Van is a used-up man."

Their campaign was distinguished by abuse, evasion, irrelevancy and misrepresentation; and they won overwhelmingly in the electoral college over both the Democrats and a third party, the Liberty Party. The Democrats had drawn up a platform and taken a concrete stand for strict construction, opposition to the bank and internal improvements, and for non-interference by Congress with the status of slavery in the territories. This was the first national recognition of the slavery issue. That slavery was becoming a paramount issue was indicated by the appearance of the anti-slavery **Liberty Party** under JAMES BIRNEY.

Harrison to Tyler. William Henry Harrison achieved no more in office than selecting a Cabinet. He chose Clay men for all but two of the posts. One month after his inauguration, Harrison died of pneumonia and was succeeded by John Tyler, a Southerner of the Old Republican school. (Tyler was the first Vice-President to succeed to the Presidency.)

The Democrats quite accidentally rose to power again with this difference: it was now founded upon the slave states. Tyler proved to be a faithful servant to the slave power—and no Whig at all. When he vetoed the Whig efforts to create a third Bank of the U. S., his Cabinet of Clay-men resigned in a body. Unruffled, Tyler appointed a new Cabinet of states-rights men headed by Calhoun as Secretary of State. Webster remained in the Cabinet long enough to complete negotiations with England over the Maine boundary. This matter was finally settled in the **Webster-Ashburton Treaty of 1842.** For the most part the existing lines were maintained with a few adjustments; other aspects provided for monetary compensation, provision for navigation rights and joint naval patrols. His job done, Webster resigned his post to Calhoun. Now began a period of Southern control of the national government, the most fateful period in the domestic history of the United States.

CHAPTER VIII

THE MATURING OF THE SECTIONS

Population. The growth of U. S. population in the first half of the 19th century was phenomenal. Natural increase and immigration swelled the population from 5.3 million in 1800 to 31.4 million in 1860. While average annual immigration in the first quarter of that century was 10,000, in the second quarter it rose to 60,000 by 1832 and 100,000 by 1842. Between 1845 and 1860 the influx was abnormally high because of crop-failure in Europe, famine in Ireland and political upheaval following the European Revolution of 1848.

Settlement. Only one-tenth of the immigrants went South. The immigrants, obviously could not afford to buy lands and slaves for cotton production and could not compete as labor against the slave. By 1860 the Southland with half the land area of the United States had but one-third the popula-tion. The Northeast and Northwest, based on free labor in agriculture and industry, shared the remaining two-thirds about equally.

Once settled, the immigrant adopted the manners and mores of his section: he became a Westerner, or Northerner or, more rarely, a Southerner. His needs and demands were those of his section. Since the Civil War arose from the conflicts among the sections, it is important to know the nature of each section.

THE WEST

The Settlement of the West. Farmers headed west in the face of great hazards and at great personal cost. It is difficult for us today to appreciate the hardships of travel in **Conestoga Wagons** or on canal and river boats; of wheels registering every rut in the crude roads or dragging at a snail's pace through endless prairie. Pioneering was no romance: it meant cutting a clearing out of timber land and river bottom; acclimating to unknown and extreme weather conditions; solving problems of seed-gathering, of primitive methods of sowing, planting and harvesting; transporting goods to distant centers; establishing communities from nothing. The miracle is that it was done and done quickly. How was the settlement of the west accomplished?

The hazards of travel were gradually reduced as the steamboat appeared on inland canals and rivers and as the first railroads were placed in operation. The greatest waves of westward movement coincided with the high points of American prosperity; hence, farmers were able to realize quick cash returns. Moreover, the ruthless elimination of the Indian heightened the sense of security. And the unrelenting flow of immigrants speeded population growth to the point where territories could enter the Union as states and participate in the nation's political life.

Eastern manufacturers discovered the market in the West and manufactured goods began to move westward to raise the primitive standards of living. Some advance in mechanization took place: new devices included **Deere's steel plow**, **McCormick's reaper**, seed drills, threshing machines (horse-drawn, of course). The trend in farm prices was steadily upward throughout this middle period. Increased efficiency reduced costs of production per unit acre. Since means of transportation were still competitive, this made for reasonable rates. There was a fairly steady national and international market to absorb production: England became a very good customer after she repealed the tariffs on grain (The Corn Laws). These, then, were some of the reasons for the rapid advance westward.

The Significance of the West. The existence in the West of an area of undeveloped land was a major influence in the course of American history, providing for a time almost boundless economic opportunity. The best land was often taken up by speculators and held for sale or rental. Its fertile areas might be settled by farmers who could raise the necessary money to go west, clear the ground and put in several crops. For those who could afford it there was considerable money to be made in cattle-raising or in tapping the abundant mineral resources. Other opportunities existed in lumbering and road-canal and railroad construction. All westerners were linked by the common bond to become successful businessmen, to produce commodities marketable at a profit.

Settlers and Squatters. Since 1796 westerners had pressed for cheaper land to be sold in smaller parcels. However, in the process of the liberalization of the land laws, the speculator was favored over the working settler—a policy which tended toward land monopolization. The farmer, with little capital, was forced to buy at inflated prices or to borrow unless he preferred renting (and he never did!). One alternative was to "squat" on the land—that is, to settle in some outlying region without purchase. Under these conditions eventual eviction was inevitable. The small farmer, therefore, turned to the national government for relief and demanded special "pre-emption laws."

Thus he secured the **Pre-Emption Law of 1841** which permitted a squatter to select 160 acres of the public domain and at a later date (after he had had a chance to farm it) to purchase the land with a cash settlement. Public auction of the land would be deferred to that date. Even this had a drawback for the small farmer, for those who could not raise the money had to borrow at high interest rates. From the small farmer's point of view, then, there was only one solution—free land. The cry for free homesteads became so insistent that political parties could no longer afford to ignore it.

Land Speculators. The west attracted surplus investment funds from land companies which could buy up lots ranging from 5,000 to 100,000 acres. Land speculators were of tremendous significance in the settlement of the west. Long before the settler reached the west, the speculator had parceled out the choice locations and surveyed them. Immigrants turned his way; he pressed hard upon the state and federal government to finance or in other ways encourage the building of canals, railroads, plank roads and river improvements to facilitate westward passage for producers and goods; he furnished an outlet for bankers since much of the land was bought with wildcat banknotes. In a very specific sense, then, the land speculator was a trail blazer, a pioneer, a necessary element in the expansion of the national realm. Like the pioneer, however, he was a temporary phenomenon—and often a destructive one. Land speculation was no way of creating wealth; it created no enduring American fortunes.

Extractive Wealth. Of more permanence (though in this Middle Period of American history of less significance) was the western wealth resulting from fur trading and mining. The great pioneer in the fur trade was JOHN JACOB ASTOR who organized the industry on a vast scale. It was he who first linked America to the Oregon Territory by way of St. Louis and the Columbia River; who subdued the Indians by employing them in the fur trade and who carved the first pathway to the west. But fur was too uncertain and Astor invested his profits in Manhattan real estate.

More certain for future wealth were the iron, silver, lead and zinc mines which were discovered early in American history. Mining and smelting of metals attracted Eastern capital and encouraged railroad construction. The discovery of gold at Sutter's Mill in 1848 swelled the population of California from 10,000 in 1848 to 100,000 in 1850. Gold did not make for great fortunes until it was dug by organized companies. Wealth in the gold areas came from the concomitants of the gold hunt—transport, trade, food supplies, mining tools, furnishings, construction, gambling and the like. The pedlar, the shopkeeper and the retail merchant were the chief beneficiaries of the **Gold Rush of '48.**

Expansionism. The western settler was no respecter of boundaries; the land "out there" had a constant allure and the problem of who owned the land was of secondary importance. Frontier pressure had caused the vast territory of Louisiana and the Floridas to come into American hands; land hunger had converted the War Hawks into agrarian imperialists, and Americans had swarmed into Texas and then separated it from Mexico. This expansionist fevor had instilled the notion that it had a "**manifest destiny**" to bring all the land up to the Pacific Ocean under American control. Texas would become American once political barriers were removed; England could be removed from Oregon; and beyond Texas was an immense terrain over which a weak Mexico ruled but did not prevail. From the west came constant pressure for possession of these areas.

The Northeast. From 1840 to 1860 the economic structure of the Northeast underwent a vital change, the elaboration of which converted America from mercantile capitalism to idustrial capitalism. But this was not apparent in 1843, for during the first half of the 19th century American industry was in an early stage and it was difficult to appreciate its ultimate significance.

Internal Commerce. Investment capital in the 1830's was inevitably attracted to road and canal construction in the northern and western states. Roads were built for the most part by **joint stock companies** which received exclusive franchises to build them, to improve them with bridges and to maintain them in repair. Profits were derived from tolls and it was natural for the joint stock companies to concentrate where the traffic was heaviest. Private investors were reluctant to build in less populated areas and demanded government subsidies for such ventures. But the possibility of federal subsidies had been cancelled by the successive vetoes of internal improvements by Madison, Monroe and Jackson; the states, however, were eager to give financial support.

Steamboats offered another important field of investment. River traffic remained slight as long as transport of goods depended upon the keelboat and flatboat. The capacity and speed of the steamboat, however, resulted in a tremendous increase in river traffic. In the early 1830's, for example, receipts at New Orleans totaled about $26,000,000; by 1850 they had amounted to $108,000,000. River traffic had the considerable advantage of "no tolls to pay, no work animals to take care of, and no bad inns at which to put up." In spite of these advantages, river traffic was no permanent source of wealth. Canals were too strong a competitor.

The Erie Canal. The Erie Canal is the symbol of all the canals of this period. New York State was early aware that it possessed in the Mohawk Valley a favorable route to the West if it could be converted into a water route from the upper Hudson River to Lake Erie. The distance to be covered was 363 miles, a formidable project even for these days. But the engineers BENJAMIN WRIGHT and JAMES GEDDES—were undaunted. They gathered about them a number of very able men (indeed, the Erie Canal was our first "engineering" school). The canal, when built, climbed by a series of locks from a point above Albany to the entrance into the Mohawk Valley. It was begun in 1817 and did not reach Buffalo until 1825. Few projects undertaken in America encountered greater natural obstacles and public hostility and it would have been abandoned many times were it not for the vision and courage of Governor DeWitt Clinton in pressing it forward. It cost New York State about $7,500,000 and was a financial success from the start. It is impossible to calculate all the effects of this mighty project, but some of them were:

It **reduced the time** for shipping freight by two-thirds and lowered freight costs from about $100 a ton to $10. It laid the foundation for the **rise of scores of cities** along its route, making New York City the nation's greatest port of entry and financial center. It made possible the **influx of western grains** to the East and forced a radical shift in Eastern farming (from grain production to truck-and-dairy farming). It created a major passageway for migrants to the West and reduced considerably the cost of westward migration. It stimulated new banking, warehouse, and factoring activities as additional outlets for surplus capital.

But, in spite of these considerable achievements,

canals did not create the opportunities for founding great fortunes. State debts mounted so dangerously that default and repudiation were inevitable. When in 1841-2 nine states stopped payment of interest on canal bonds, canal investment was struck a major blow; and when this was followed by repudiation of $40,000,000, profits were wiped out completely. Canals were overbuilt; they were constructed far in advance both of population and markets. In many cases, profits simply did not materialize. And by 1850 the railroad emerged as an invincible foe.

Railroads. The railroad rose slowly from the function of being merely a feeder for the canals. The first railroad to open for public use was the Baltimore and Ohio in 1830. Between 1830 and 1850 only 9,000 miles of track were laid. Private capital was only mildly interested and construction funds were, for the most part, supplied by the states. The problems involved in railroad construction seemed almost unsurmountable. Cast iron provided a poor material to bear the weight of the train; bridge construction was in a primitive stage; no standard gauge was used; sparks and cinders were a real menace to safety; engine power had not advanced to a point where heavy loads could be carried over inclines; and so on.

Nonetheless, heavy pressure developed from the land companies for construction of "trunk lines" into the West at federal expense. Jackson's Mayesville Veto had set a precedent for no federal aid to an *intrastate* project and this in turn limited the possibility of railroad expansion. However, private capital might be induced to invest in an *interstate* road if the government would make land-grants along the route and permit the investors the full use (timber, minerals, depot-sites, etc.) of the land. With an increase in government subsidy 20,000 miles of rail were laid between 1850 and 1860.

Commerce. Great hope of wealth was bound in with ocean commerce and the carrying trade. During colonial times commerce had been the foremost means for accumulating wealth. Freedom to engage in unrestricted commerce was a basic objective of the American Revolution. Independence did not, however, bring fulfillment of the hope. Caught in the crossfires of the Napoleonic Wars, commerce languished from 1800 to 1820. For a brief period, American shippers turned to the China trade; this, too, was short lived because the English began to produce cheap imitations of Chinese goods. What is more, coffee began to replace tea as the national beverage. There was a burst of renewed commerce in the years from 1843 to 1857 stimulated by the production of the Yankee Clipper ship, by the re-moval of restrictions on grain imports into England, by the discovery of gold in California and by the opening up of Australian, Chinese and Japanese markets for American goods. But this was the last sputter.

The clipper-ship, "the most perfect full-rigged sailing vessel ever conceived by man," could not compete with the English iron steamboat. Freight costs on steamers were lower from the start as the British government made substantial subsidies to shipbuilders. The American Congress tried to compete by offering mail subsidies. Again, British metallurgical industry was far in advance of American. The result was that the Cunard and Pacific Steam Navigation Company took the commercial lead and held it. The death-blow to American commercial hopes was delivered by the Depression of 1857. And, as shipping declined, so did the fishing and whaling industries. Anyway, Europeans were beginning to replace their fish diets with meat; and coal, oil and gas were everywhere being substituted for whale-oil.

THE TRANSFORMATION OF AMERICA

The first turning point in American history was the creation and consolidation of an independent nation founded upon written law and the idea of democracy; the second was the transformation of America from an agrarian-commercial-mercantile nation to an industrial one operating within this constitutional and democratic framework.

Industrial capitalism rested on many economic pillars: a factory system employing division of labor and power-driven automatic machinery; the free use of capital for short and long term needs; continuous production; employment of a labor force wholly dependent upon wages. Out of this combination of factors came mass production for a national and international market. The maturing of industrial capitalism was slow; it was as though all other forms had to be tried first and found wanting.

Earlier Forms. From its earliest days, manufacturing existed in America—chiefly on a household basis. Wives and daughters produced crude linsey-woolsey textiles by spinning wheel and hand loom; husbands and sons hammered and carved tools, utensils and furniture. As time went on, however, an increasing separation took place between those who farmed for market and those who manufactured as tool-owning specialists—blacksmiths, leatherworkers, cabinet makers and millers of all kinds. These manufacturers were in reality workingmen using their homes as shops. The capitalists were merchants who bought up large quantities of raw materials, distributed them to tool owners for manufacture, and collected and sold the finished wares in the market. This system was universally known as the "domestic" or "putting out" system of manufacturing and was an intermediate stage to industrial capitalism.

The Industrial Revolution. The flowering of industry occurred after the Panic of 1837 had wiped out large amounts of commercial and mercantile capital. The inspiration to invest in industry came from England. There production by industry had come to maturity as a result of invention, capital accumulation, available labor supplies and resources. American progress had been delayed because capital was dispersed over too many mercantile and commercial ventures and because labor was scattered over too large a terrain. British competition acted as a constant depressant upon American experiment with industrialization, and American capitalists were handicapped by the long history of colonialism. By 1840, however, conditions were ripe for industrial advance.

Technology. Impressive advances were made in New England textile production. In Waltham, Massachusetts, for example, all the processes of spinning and weaving were brought together for the first time in America under one roof. Production was by automatic machinery. Labor was specialized and workers were organized by departments, wages were paid in cash, output standardized, cost accounting introduced and buying and selling systematized.

Waltham's success inspired Lowell, Lawrence and Manchester to follow suit. Eli Whitney's invention of the cotton gin spurred others and, in the course of the half-century, ELIAS HOWE produced the sewing machine, CYRUS MCCORMICK and OBED HUSSEY produced a practical mechanical reaper and WILLIAM KELLY discovered, independently, the Bessemer process of decarbonizing ore with air blasts. Whitney had taken industrialization another long stride forward when, in producing an order for rifles, he elaborated a system of standardization of parts and interchangeable mechanisms. The iron industry kept pace, developing a method for the cheap use of anthracite coal in the smelting process; now it could compete with low-cost British coke-production.

Newborn industries were, at first, forced to locate near the source of supply, but with the development of cheap and rapid transportation the most profitable locations could be selected. Through most of this half-century, industry was given tariff protection as an incentive. Finally, the discovery of gold in California gave the country exportable specie which could be used to buy important machines and machine parts abroad.

The Corporation. Of great significance was the development of the Corporation as a device for multiplying small capital accumulations into large ones suitable for the heavy investments required for factories, machines and weekly payrolls. Sales to the public-at-large of shares of stock in small denominations made almost unlimited capital available. A corporation, moreover, possessed almost unlimited life, for the stock continued to exist even though its owner died. This "life-principle" in a share of stock was enhanced when the courts endowed a corporation with legal "personality" (the ability to buy and sell, sue and be sued, own and dispose of, etc.). But probably the most attractive feature of the corporation was its limited liability —that is, in the event of bankruptcy, the shareholder lost only what he held in stock; his personal belongings could not be seized to pay off the creditors.

Labor. The influx of a cheap labor supply after 1845 coincided with these mechanical and legal developments. Without adequate capital to make a westward settlement, new immigrants were forced to concentrate in the urban areas and to seek cash-paying jobs. Prior to their arrival factory operatives were mostly women and children seeking supplementary income and willing to accept low wages. Wages were high for male labor, which was in scarce supply. The new immigrants now provided a cheap labor supply of primary, family-supporting wage-earners. Industrialists took prompt advantage of this new source of profits. Wages were lowered and factory conditions deteriorated rapidly. Inevitably unions sprang up; workingmen began to organize against long hours, low wages and miserable working conditions. But the early unions were badly hampered by legal restrictions, inexperienced leadership and the boundless opportunity to accumulate some cash and make an escape from the factory.

Finally, the industrial revolution as we know it would have been impossible without the acumen and toughness of the first industrial capitalists and their families: the Lowells, Jacksons, Appletons, Lawrences, Dwights, Browns, Phelps and DuPonts. They fought against foreign enemies, suffered the buffets of sudden economic collapse and were ever forced to make new starts; theirs was an industrial frontier and they had to break new ground. Because their beginnings were small and because their successors case a brighter beam, these early industrialists are somewhat obscured in history. Their contribution, however, cannot be minimized.

THE SOUTH

The Plantation System. Five characteristics distinguished the plantation economy: it was a single-crop, cash-crop system; it could employ labor for most of the year; the labor was slave and therefore had to produce enough to maintain itself and provide a profit for the owner; the method of cultivation was extensive, that is, putting as much land under cultivation as possible in order to realize the maximum cash return; credit for productive enterprise was derived from outside the plantation.

In the long run such an economy militated against wealth accumulation. It was accompanied by waste of soil resources and tended to discourage small but necessary economies; large money returns encouraged great extravagance; the planter was normally a debtor because of his drive to expand his holdings; income tended to be concentrated in a tiny percentage of the population and therefore contributed to a general state of impoverishment; finally, it made an adequate laboring force unavailable to smaller planters and doomed them to a permanent low status and to general stagnation.

The Aristocracy. Southern society was sharply pyramided. At the apex were less than 2,500 planters who held 100 slaves or more. In an intermediary position was a group of about 45,000 planters with 20 slaves or more. In all, only one-quarter of the southern population owned slaves. 75% of the southerners, then, were "poor whites" with no important stake in the plantation system.

The severest impact of the declining plantation system fell upon the intermediary group of small slaveholders. They were usually in the upcountry, far from market and credit and therefore suffered more from higher costs than the planters in the deep South. They usually owned only male fieldhands and therefore had no "natural" increase of slaves to draw upon.

Among the non-slaveholders was the independent yeoman running a self-sufficient farm. They did a little producing for the local market. When lucky, they might be employed as overseers or mechanics on the large plantations. At the bottom of the economic pile were the utterly despised and depressed "sandhillers," "crackers" and "clayeaters" grubbing a bare subsistence from pinebarrens and sandy coastal plains.

But, whether slaveowner or not, every white Southerner became psychologically bound to the slave system. From birth he was made to perceive the world as divided in two, white and black; richest to poorest Southerners developed a color solidarity—the white was free, superior to and ruler of the black. With this indoctrinated view, the whites bound themselves to and then bled for a system that doomed most of them to the borders of poverty, to severely limited economic opportunity, to unfair labor competition and to a declining economy. One can escape most environmental barriers; but the mind can be an impregnable prison.

The Slave. Most of the Negroes were enslaved fieldhands working the plantations in gangs under the watchful eyes and ready whips of the overseers. Some secured favored service as "domestics," some herded cattle and others did household labor (carpentry, masonry, smithing, shoemaking, spinning and weaving). About a quarter of a million Negroes were free and served as constant reminder to Southerners that the premise of the Negro's "natural inferiority" was questionable. Not only were Negroes the chief source for southern handicraft industries, but many more were engaged in railroad and canal construction, in mining and quarrying, in lumbering and iron fabrication—in fact, there seemed almost nothing that the Negro could *not* do! Therefore, Southerners reinforced their theories (which they could hardly defend in view of reality) with legal enactment to freeze the slave to his status.

The greatest fear of the Southern planter was the runaway slave and the slave revolt. Such revolts were stimulated by the news which seeped into Negro communities (in spite of their total illiteracy) of successful revolts in Haiti, or of British emancipatory legislation, or of abolitionist agitation in the North. Southerners had had the bitter taste of **Vesey's Uprising** in South Carolina in 1822 and **Nat Turner's Revolt** in Virginia in 1831. Less dramatic than a slave revolt but sometimes more effective was the occasional runaway who, if successful, was a beacon for all the rest. The fact that only a tiny minority of slaves were ever involved in a runaway effort was of small significance; a single instance created a sense of universal threat to the Southern aristocracy.

As a result, Southerners were in a permanent state of preparedness and their reaction to even minor infractions by the slaves was violent in the extreme. Southern regions had the appearance of armed camps; social intercourse among the Negroes was under constant surveillance; movement was restricted to those who carried passes; no show of independence was tolerated.

This is not to say that all the slaves were subjected to brutality. This hardly seems logical or possible. Slaves were expensive property, working property and had to be physically fit to carry on. Even more important, slaves were breeders of more property, if properly cared for. It seems reasonable to assume therefore that slaves were sometimes accorded "humane" treatment by the planters.

Inhumanity derived from the vicious system itself. Thus, for example, as cotton production declined in the states of Virginia, South Carolina, Kentucky and Missouri, these states turned to slave-breeding as a commercial venture. The traffic in bred slaves was well-developed. They were bred in the northern tier of Southern states; there, auction centers developed for the sale of slaves to traders who, in turn, distributed them by auction in the far South. Now this truly was incalculably vicious when one considers that husbands and wives, children and parents were constantly separated to be sold at auction. Where profit was concerned, conscience was irrelevant.

The Southern "Defense." But conscience *was* relevant. Southerners would have preferred to argue slavery on its economic merits. It was, they proclaimed, an efficient system. "King Cotton" was the bulwark of American national and taxable wealth; the North itself was supported out of the production of cotton by slaves. Slavery, it was argued, was a thousand times more humane than "wage-slavery." But try as they might, southerners could not for long avoid the moral implications of the purchase and sale of human beings. So they cast about to prove the fundamental inequality of men; they brought in Biblical testimony to show that God "sanctioned" slavery; they argued that slaves were "child-people," held by their masters as wards. The slave system was paternalistic and the master acted with complete humanity toward his "children"—gave them dignified employment, provided them with basic necessities, cared for them in illness, trained them in civilized decencies and cared for their religious needs. Northerners may shout "democracy"; but no political system was exclusively right. Southerners pointed to the glories of ancient Greece to justify the slave basis of their society. The Southerner was a moral aristocrat acting upon a code of honor (derived from the chivalric medieval code) consisting of courage, generosity, *noblesse oblige* and the glorification of women. What more noble purpose could the slave serve than to support this system with his labor. Such were the strange mirrors through which the slave owners saw themselves.

The Great Economic Dilemma. In fact the plantation system was not doing well by the 1840's. Planters were constantly faced with the necessity of cutting costs to augment profits. The greatest single cost was his fixed, immobile investment in slaves; but freight, commissions, mortgage and interest payments, property maintenance and acquisitions of new land were also unavoidable costs. After 1840 these costs began to rise significantly. The discovery of gold precipitated a monetary inflation that increased rates and land values; sharp competition for a limited number of slaves drove prices upward; prices rose on manufactured goods bought in a protected home market. Why, then, didn't the planter boost his own prices accordingly? He couldn't because the price of cotton was determined by the world market over whose fluctuations the planter had no control.

The only alternative was a reduction in costs. Slave costs could be reduced if the laws preventing importation could be repealed; the costs of manufactured goods could be lowered if tariffs were abolished; the opening of new cheap land would reduce rent costs; commissions and interest costs could be lowered if one could break the stranglehold of the northern bankers. These were some of the needs that dictated the sectional demands of the ante-bellum South.

SLAVERY AS A NATIONAL ISSUE

Early Protest. The early development of slavery was accompanied by a wide acceptance of it. No serious objections arose during the colonial epoch; the Constitution recognized both slavery and the slave trade; as early as 1793 a Fugitive Slave Law was passed to provide for an easy return of runaway slaves. Stimulated by Quaker objections to the institution and by philosophical equalitarianism during the Enlightenment, some opposition to slavery was registered. It was prohibited from the Northwest Territory; and early in the 19th century a movement for re-colonization of slaves in Africa was begun. The debate over the admission of Missouri had revealed the explosiveness of the slavery issue, but men were inclined to be reasonable and to permit Congress to settle the matter by drawing a line across the Louisiana Territory. Moderation was fostered by the requirements of national unity.

William Lloyd Garrison. The rabid defense of slavery did not arise until the sections had become more distinct and until "abolitionism" was born in the North and West. Abolitionism was the work of a very small minority; but their agitation was enormously effective. The spiritual father of 19th century abolitionist activity was WILLIAM LLOYD GARRISON who, in 1831, founded the abolitionist journal

The Liberator. Garrison hated slavery after he had seen it at first hand and had spent time in jail for libeling a slave trader. He broke with his employer, Benjamin Lundy, on the issue of gradual versus immediate emancipation. Garrison condemned gradualism as timid, unjust and immoral and called for the "immediate enfranchisement of our slave population." The tone of Garrison's call to arms was certainly not timid. In *The Liberator* he proclaimed:

I am aware that many object to the severity of my language; but is there not cause for severity? I will be harsh as truth and uncompromising as justice. On this subject I do not wish to think, or speak, or write with moderation. No! No! . . . I am in earnest—I will not equivocate—I will not excuse—I will not retreat a single inch—and I will be heard.

He was heard. In the West James G. Birney and ELIJAH LOVEJOY began to print abolitionist journals. Birney was mobbed and Lovejoy killed. Nat Turner was inspired to launch an insurrection and sixty whites were killed. In 1833, the **American Anti-Slavery Society** was founded to spread the knowledge that "Slaveholding is a heinous crime in the sight of God, and that duty, safety and best interests of all concerned require its immediate abandonment without expatriation." THEODORE WELD, head of the Society, undertook to preach a crusade across the land and made many converts to the cause and he trained each of his converts in missionary work. WENDELL PHILLIPS, of high Boston society, joined the cause after witnessing a near-lynching of Garrison by a Boston mob. Led by Quakers, an "Underground Railroad" was organized to encourage runaways and to help them steal by night from South to North to Canada. Each year witnessed heavier traffic on the "road."

Finally, the Abolitionists turned to political action. Lobbyists were successful in securing a Congressional antislavery bloc who legislated at every favorable opportunity against slavery. In 1840 and 1844, Birney was run for presidential office. Garrison was heard, indeed! His voice made a resounding crash and forced all men to consult their consciences.

Anti-Abolitionism. Men did consult their consciences and for the most part rejected the extremism and radicalism of the abolitionists. Assaults against abolitionists and their public meetings were common in the North. Northerners and Westerners were alienated by the abolitionist proposal to wipe out in a single stroke millions of dollars in property. (Had not Garrison publicly burned the Constitution as a "covenant with death and an agreement with hell?") Moreover, the North was linked by commercial, mercantile and agricultural interests to the plantation system; were they expected to cut their own economic throats? Men of peace shuddered at the belligerent tone of the South's reaction to abolitionism and foresaw a bloody end to this agitation. Such Northerners and Westerners sympathized with Southern violence against abolitionists in their own midst; with Southern state legislation limiting freedom of expression of such incendiary ideas; with the revised "Black Codes" that ended all privileges for Negroes (some had accumulated over the years); and with a Southern move in Congress to end the flood of anti-slavery pamphlets pouring into the South through the federal mails. Southern authorities burned such mail publicly and went unreproved by Jackson's Postmaster General, Amos Kendall. Jackson himself joined in the attack on the abolitionists and recommended an act to prohibit the sending of incendiary material through the mails. This failed of passage, but Southerners pushed a resolution through the House of Representatives that anti-slavery petitions to Congress were to be tabled without a reading of or action upon them. When John Quincy Adams—no abolitionist—protested this "gag rule" as a violation of the right to petition, he was ignored; he had to fight for eight years before the "gag rule" was repealed.

CHAPTER IX

INTELLECTUAL AND SOCIAL FERMENT IN THE AGE OF JACKSON

FROM REFORMATION TO TRANSFORMATION

Utopia. Crusading individualism was the keynote to the Jacksonian reform movement. But one cannot overlook a strong cooperative undercurrent which existed in these days. Some men, in fact, regarded the whole reform movement as mere patchwork upon what was, they felt, a basically unworkable system. Social evil resulted from the competition among individuals. The greatest evil was that of existing inequalities among men.

Therefore, they argued, if men would stop competing, if they could merge their private selves into the collectivity, then they would create a utopia on earth. (Utopia was a never-never land in the minds of these social critics, a perfect society which banished evil from the earth and transformed men into angels.)

Obviously, utopia could not be accomplished for the millions of Americans in one fell swoop. But what if a small band of initiates, of inspired men and women, were to find some corner of America into which they could withdraw and in which they could build a perfect community? Would not such a community become magnet, attracting all men of good will? With some such thoughts in mind, a number of utopian seers began to build model communities in the outposts of America. These communities were inspired by either religious or humanistic sentiments, or both.

Religious Communities. A number of factors account for the rise at this time of experiments in religious communism. A great revival in religious faith occurred between 1820 and 1830. Sects arose which denied that man was a damned, depraved, and inherently sinful creature; that salvation was for an "elect." In place of this doctrine, they asserted man's inherent divinity, his infinite capacity for perfection, his "free-will" to choose a wide-open path to salvation. In the course of this debate, religious institutionalism was challenged. God's grace was pictured as freely given to all men. It was maintained that if one adores goodness, one adores God. Faith, it was held, is an individual matter between man and God and that no church mediation was required for man to "reach" God. From this, the conclusion was drawn by many that if salvation was so simple for one man, why not for all men?

From the back country arose an unsophisticated emotional religion based upon the literal interpretation of the Bible. Such literalism helped to spread abroad the belief that an immediate Second Advent was at hand. Then was it not necessary to make intensive preparation for the Last Judgment? And what better way was there than by instituting the good life here and now, on earth? Many sects arose claiming a special road to salvation based upon a literal interpretation of the Bible. To prevent corruption by the traditional faiths, such groups began to withdraw from the community. Their extreme piousness and poverty, and their belief that the ancient Christian Church practised communism led some of them to set up communist societies.

Mormonism. Millennialism and utopianism were important strands in the birth of the faith that became the **Latter Day Saints.** During the revivalist sweep of the 1820's, the founder, JOSEPH SMITH "saw" two personages announcing they were the Saviour and God the Father. Somewhat later, he was directed by a divining-stone to the discovery of a book made of golden plates which contained the creed of a new faith. Three witnesses signed affidavits to the effect that they had seen the plates and the engravings on them. From the plates, the Book of Mormon was derived. According to this book America was settled by an ancient people dispersed from the east when human tongues were confused at the Tower of Babel and by Israelites who emigrated from Jerusalem six hundred years before Christ. The Mormon Church was therefore created to continue the beliefs and practices of this rediscovered group. While the Book of Mormon includes belief in the Bible and the main tenets of Christianity, it has religious elements of its own: the nature of the priesthood, the validity of visions, prophecies, and the "gift of tongues," the imminent coming of Christ, the creation of a new Zion in the United States, the restoration of the "ten tribes," the return of the Jews to Palestine. Later, BRIGHAM YOUNG added the doctrines of celestial marriage and polygamy (now repudiated).

The history of the persecutions and wanderings of the Mormons is one of the most dramatic in American history. A "New Zion" was first set up at Independence, Missouri, by Joseph Smith. From the first, the settlement encountered hostility, persecution and violence; in 1839, the governor of Missouri expelled it. The next settlement was made at Nauvoo, Illinois. Within a few years it grew to be the richest and most populous town in the state. Envy turned to hostility and hostility to violence again; Joseph Smith and his brother were murdered while in jail on a charge of treason! Under the leadership of Brigham Young, the sect moved into the deep west and settled at what is now Salt Lake City. Here in the desert, like the Israelites departed out of Egypt, the Mormons built their first shelters and by means of irrigation planted their first crops. And the desert was made to bloom after years of incredible hardship. The latter day history of these Latter Day Saints centered on two basic conflicts: the invasion of their land by "gentiles" who were hostile to their way of life, and their efforts to enter the Union while continuing their practice of polygamy. They were defeated on both fronts, but few of the movements of the Age of Jackson exhibit so well those qualities of individualism, collectivism and millennial hope as does Mormonism.

Secular Communities. The factors which account for the rise of experiments in secular communism were equally numerous. The 1820's and '30's witnessed the birth in Europe of theories of "utopian socialism." These theories were carried across the Atlantic by immigrants who came over after the devastation of the wars of Napoleon and the revolutions of 1820, 1830 and 1848 in Europe. Of greatest importance were the theories of ROBERT OWEN and CHARLES FOURIER.

Robert Owen believed that the perfect society could be built if well-intentioned capitalists would devote their wealth to creating socialistic communities based upon a balanced economy of farm and factory. In these communities the wealth would be shared equally. After experimenting with benevolent capitalism in his cotton mills in New Lanark, Scotland, Owen came to America to try a more radical experiment. Along the Wabash River in Indiana he built a "perfect community" called **New Harmony**. It consisted of model dwellings, surrounding vineyards, orchards and wheatfields, and accompanying cotton and flour mills. Its personnel was made up of intellectuals, mechanics and farmers. Work and profits were shared and after work, discussions, concerts and balls made up the social life of the community. The experiment failed because of internal mismanagement and dissension, but something of the pattern of capitalist paternalism remained as a residue in American economic thought. Owenism had its many imitators.

Fourierism had still more. This system was less dependent than Owenism upon capitalist good-will. Fourier proposed to transform society by means of anarchistic "phalanxes." A phalanx could be formed if any 1,620 people would agree to farm in common 5,000 acres of land and engage in the handicrafts necessary to existence. Each member in the phalanx was free to find his own vocation and in so doing would add to the community's wealth. The wealth was not to be divided equally as in the Owen community and one could keep his profits after contributing to a common fund for community needs.

Brook Farm. The most spectacular experiment in Fourierism was made at **Brook Farm** established by the "Transcendentalists" at West Roxbury, Massachusetts. It was originally created by George Ripley as a joint-stock company which would profit handsomely from a rich section of land purchased at West Roxbury. Members of this joint-stock company were to live together in a model community based upon Unitarian and Transcendental principles. But in 1844 Ripley was converted to Fourierism. Brook Farm was turned into a phalanx and members were assigned to tasks according to their preference. Planned agricultural production was its economic base.

But Brook Farm was also a training school for Transcendentalist and Fourierist missionaries. As such, it attracted some of the finest minds of its day: Emerson, Hawthorne, Fuller, Dana, Dwight, Parker, Owen, Brownson, Greeley, Brisbane, Peabody, Alcott, Channing, and others. Its greatest success was in the field of education. The Brook Farm School won national recognition. It was based upon complete freedom between students and teachers who lived, worked and studied together. Classes were held whenever convenient or necessary. Traditional emphasis upon the classics and mathematics was retained but to this was added a new emphasis upon history, modern languages, philosophy, botany, drawing, dancing, music, literature, play production and dramatic readings. Life was very unconventional among the mingled scholars, farmers, seamstresses, mechanics and preachers. Work and culture were coalesced. The failure of this experiment was due to bankruptcy brought on by the Depression of 1839, to a disastrous fire, to internal dissension, to the fact that intellectuals generally avoided hard labor or deserted the community when hard labor became inevitable—in general, to the fact that the most distinguished Americans were far removed from the angelic condition. (Something of the glory and disillusionment bred by this effort at communal life is recorded in Hawthorne's *Blithedale Romance*.)

The "Golden Day." In the environment of contending nationalism, sectionalism and democracy, an American literature was born. Enduring literary classics flowed from the pens of Ralph Waldo Emerson, Edgar Allen Poe, Henry David Thoreau, Nathaniel Hawthorne, Herman Melville, John Greenleaf Whittier, Henry Wadsworth Longfellow, Oliver Wendell Holmes, James Russell Lowell and Walt Whitman; classic histories were written by George Bancroft, William Prescott, Francis Parkman and John Lothrop Motley; songs and ballads still sung arose from anonymous folk along the frontier and in the slave belts. Why one restricted period in the history of a people will produce a sudden flowering of genius is an unresolved problem; but between 1820 and 1860 American literature had a "Golden Day."

Individualism. The literature of the period brought to a head the doctrine of individualism which was implicit in American thought from the days of the Enlightenment onward. Individualism contained an unbounded faith in the "goodness" of man and in man's ability to shape the good society; it was thus linked with the doctrine of man's inevitable progress through time. Man was encouraged to become self-reliant and to realize the universe within himself. "Nothing" (taught the individualist) "is at last sacred but the integrity of your own mind." Larger-than-life man became symbolic of man's potentiality. Poe's conquering Tamerlane, Melville's demonic Captain Ahab in pursuit of Moby Dick, the frontiersman's Mike Fink and Davy Crockett are examples of the exaggerated individualism and expanded egotism that resulted from the stress upon the heroic nature of man during the Golden Day.

Democracy. Individualism brought new democratic dignity to the common man. Farmers, lumbermen, shoemakers, village blacksmiths, tenement dwellers—in short, the "people"—course through the works of Whittier, Emerson, Thoreau, Whitman and the balladists. Whitman in particular gave literary stature to the common man. He tried to create an epic for the man en masse in his **"Leaves of Grass."** Whitman's poems are virtual inventories of American types and American surroundings. His "barbaric yawps," his egoistic absorption of all humanity into himself, his efforts to enshrine spontaneity and sensuousness, his stress on sensuality and his experiments in free verse forms—all combined to make a complete break with the aristocratic European past and to produce an American statement. Literature has not produced a more splendid spokesman for universal mankind and human brotherhood.

Sectionalism. Sectionalism, too, was a literary force during the Golden Day. Indeed, much of it was a "flowering of New England." Whittier and Longfellow recorded the legends of New England; Lowell, the dialect; Holmes, the Brahmin caste-system; Melville, the whaling past; and Hawthorne, the divided soul of Puritanism. Southerners produced their own spokesmen in Longstreet, Kennedy and Simms. The popular song and folk tale were western in theme, in dialect and in essence.

Nationalism. Some writers needed broader spaces and made the nation their theme. Historians took the lead. Bancroft saw God's hand in America's history; Prescott went back to the roots of America's colonization during the Spanish Period; Parkman chronicled the French and Indian Wars and the trek northwestward up the Oregon Trail; Motley read the march of American democracy into the struggles of sixteenth century Dutch against their Spanish overlords. Emerson proclaimed in "The American Scholar" the intellectual and literary independence of America.

Transcendentalism. "Transcendentalism" was a religious and humanistic philosophy that sought to transcend or pass beyond all usual methods of communicating with God—through church, clergy or Scriptures. It sought to establish *direct* and *unmediated* contact. This was viewed as possible because God was considered to be "universal mind" and each individual was an incarnation of God's mind. By inward reflection, then, one could transcend the self and reach God. The means for this direct passage was **intuition.** All men are therefore spiritually equal. Man's intuitive knowledge transcends rational knowledge if restrictions upon it are removed. These restrictions are the dead hand of the past as it is incorporated in science, tradition, history, conventional morality and organized churches. Men must therefore cast these restraints aside and discover new knowledge and invent new institutions that will be better adapted to their present purposes.

In their applications of this theory, transcendentalists substituted for natural science a nature-mysticism; individual conscience was to be superior to conventional morality. Though most transcendentalists revolted against society and its institutions, they did not remove themselves from it. In the case of Thoreau, however, even transcendentalism proved to be too much of a restraint and he resigned from society to live at Walden Pond.

Fantasia. Not everyone could escape the workaday world via Transcendentalism or Walden. Writers like Poe, escaped into carefully created realms of the grotesque, the terrifying and supernatural; others like Longfellow into a sentimental past, or like Melville, to the South Seas. Some Southerners created a never-never land out of the Old Plantation South. The heroic red-man-tradition founded by Cooper continued to flourish.

In Sum. These artists, whatever their literary path, were *conscious* artists, interested in word, form and aesthetic effect. Hawthorne and Melville made the novel into a great art form. Poe and Hawthorne created the short story. Poe gave us the first of a line of brilliant detectives. Lowell taught Americans how to model a phrase and Emerson taught all writers to love language. Thoreau created a great prose style. Poe and Lowell founded modern American literary criticism. In sum, an organic break with Europe's past was made in the Golden Day. From that day on, no one would ever again ask "Who reads an American book?"

CHAPTER X

TOWARD SOUTHERN SECESSION

TYLER'S TRIUMPH

The Tariff and the Bank. With John Tyler's accidental ascent to the Presidency following Harrison's death (1841), the South returned to a position of political control. Tyler was no Whig, or rather, he was a Whig only in that he opposed Jackson. In his message to a special session of Congress, he supported lowering the Compromise Tariff of 1832, asked for elimination of the hard-money subtreasury system, and stressed respect for states' rights. Clay, the leader of the Whig Party, demanded a new Bank, tariff, increases and distribution to the states of the government cash surplus derived from the sale of public lands. The opposition was absolute.

A bank bill was passed by Congress but vetoed by Tyler as unconstitutional. Overnight he became a hero to the Southerners and the Jacksonians. The Whigs repudiated his leadership and resigned from his cabinet—all but Webster who stayed on to conclude the treaty with Ashburton. Tyler replaced the departed Whigs with states' rightists and set up a "kitchen" cabinet of pro-slavery propagandists. When Congress then passed a new protective tariff and a distribution-of-the-surplus bill, Tyler vetoed them as well.

Expansion. Having had their way with the bank and tariff bills, the Southerners now pressed for the annexation of Texas. Texas was independent and, with Sam Houston as President, eager to enter the Union. It was also in great difficulties: Mexico had renewed its threats, a paper inflation was in progress, England was offering a defensive alliance if Texas would remain independent and abolish slavery. Southerners felt they must not lose Texas. If it entered the Union, it could be divided into at least five states—a gain of ten "slave Senators" and a large number of "slave Representatives."

From his "retirement" Jackson kept up continuous pressure for annexation. Tyler made no secret of his desire to annex, but withheld his pressure until Webster—violently opposed to annexation—had concluded the Ashburton Treaty and resigned. In 1844, Calhoun became Secretary of State. In spite of Mexico's threat that annexation would mean war, and in spite of increased anti-slavery propaganda against annexation, Calhoun drew up such a treaty and on April 22, 1844, it went to the Senate for ratification. Southerners supported their case for annexation by appeals to nationalism (it would increase the national domain), to widespread hatred of England, to sectionalism and to pro-slavery sentiment. But voting on the measure was delayed until the nominating conventions had selected the candidates for the election of 1844.

The Referendum of 1844. The Texas Question (and the Oregon Question) dominated the political scene of 1844. Jackson's power in the Democratic Convention was very strong. Van Buren had been his man for the nomination, but Van Buren had published a letter, along with one from Henry Clay, opposing Texan annexation. He was promptly repudiated by Jackson and the Democratic Party; instead a "dark horse" was chosen, JAMES K. POLK of Tennessee. The Democratic Party platform made its position clear: ". . . the reoccupation of Oregon and the reannexation of Texas at the earliest practicable period are great American measures which this Convention recommends to the cordial support of the Democracy of the Union."

Clay was renominated by the Whigs. The Whig platform had no word about the Texas Question. The Liberty Party with Birney at the head condemned extension of slavery to the territories, but was silent on the question of annexation. The conventions over, Congress returned to vote on the treaty of annexation. It was defeated 35 to 16, thus leaving the issue to the people. If Clay had had the vote of New York, he would have had a majority in the national electoral count. But Birney's Liberty Party withdrew 15,800 votes from Clay and he lost the state by 5,000 votes; Polk was victor and now Tyler felt he had a popular mandate to proceed with the annexation. Since there was still no two-thirds approval in the Senate, Polk recommended a parliamentary device to evade the necessity of a two-thirds approval. This device is known as a **joint resolution** and requires a simple majority in both houses plus the President's signature. Texas was finally annexed by joint resolution.

The resolution admitting Texas provided that she was to be admitted to statehood without any previous territorial status; might, with her consent, be shaped into four states; would retain her public lands but pay her own debts; and would come under the 36-30 line covering slavery. This was, clearly, a victory for the South.

Slavery. Northern hostility to slavery intensified during Tyler's administration. Remaining "black codes" in northern states were repealed; abolitionists won control of some local offices and increased their influence in state governments; some states passed laws to hinder the return of fugitive slaves by making such return conditional upon according to the slave full due process of law.

In Prigg v. Pennsylvania the Supreme Court gave official blessing to these efforts to protect the runaway slave. Laws protecting the runaway slave were called "personal liberty laws" and provided for guarantee of *habeas corpus,* defense attorneys and trial by jury; it was forbidden to detain the runaway in jail pending trial; heavy fines were imposed for kidnapping free Negroes; citizens were fined if they helped federal law enforcement officers enforce the Fugitive Slave Act; slaves who were brought into free territory were declared to be free men, etc.

Slavery and the Churches. Heightening tension over slavery was felt particularly in the churches. The Presbyterians, Baptists and Methodists had national organizations. As a result of Northern pressure, these churches split into Northern and Southern wings. The division of Presbyterians was into "Old School" with fourteen slaveholding synods and the "New School" with twenty free synods. In 1843 an American Baptist Free Mission Society was founded which admitted no slaveholding members and abolished racial discrimination and segregation within the Church. The national Baptist organization remained united, however, though badly split into two non-cooperating groups. The Methodist group was divided when Southern members seceded to form the Southern Methodist Church. These schisms reflected the divisions in the hearts of the membership, and also deepened them.

Foreign Relations. As a result of England's abolition of slavery in the British West Indies (1833), Anglo-American relationships became further complicated. England set up a naval watch over efforts to reopen the African slave trade and began to search and seize vessels flying the American flag. To reduce the growing friction over this practice, England suggested a cooperative policy of search and seizure by the two governments of one another's vessels. Webster was willing if England would formally surrender the practice of impressment; England refused, and each country continued to maintain independent squadrons searching for slave ships.

More serious, though was the "Creole Affair." The "Creole" was an American vessel hauling a cargo of slaves from Virginia to New Orleans. The slaves revolted while en route, overpowered the ship's crew and drove the vessel to British-ruled Nassau. There, England set the white crew free but held the revolting slaves in custody as free men. The United States protested; but, after much negotiation, she accepted a monetary settlement for the lost slave property.

POLK'S PROGRESS

Tariff and the Bank. The South had a reliable man in Polk. It received heavy representation in the cabinet and controlled the posts of State, Treasury, Postmaster General and Attorney General. The Secretary of the Treasury, Robert J. Walker, sponsored a lower tariff, in accordance with the desires of the South, advocating that tariff revenues be limited to government revenue needs, that each item be taxed with a view to extracting only a contribution to the total revenue (and not with a view to giving favored protection), that luxuries be taxed hardest and the burdens which duties created be distributed as equally as possible among the sections.

In line with its tariff policy Congress passed the mildly protective **Tariff of 1846,** featuring a large free list (goods paying no tariff). Considerable Northern and Western resentment developed over the lowering of rates; the South was, of course, gratified. The South was content, too, with Polk's revival of the **Independent Treasury System** which had been repealed during the brief period of Whig rule. Subtreasuries were established throughout the country and circulated specie-backed notes which acted as brakes upon "wildcat" issues. This system persisted until it was replaced by the Federal Reserve System under Wilson.

Expansion: Oregon. As the annexation of Texas featured Tyler's administration, so the annexation of Oregon featured Polk's. Claims upon the Oregon territory were many and varied: French—initial ownership and exploration of the Louisiana Territory; Spanish—sea explorations; Russian—the exploits of Vitus Bering; and English—the voyages of Sir Francis Drake, James Cook and George Vancouver, and upon the land explorations by Alexander Mackenzie.

French claims were yielded with the transfer of Louisiana to the United States; Spanish claims, with the Florida Treaty of 1819; Russian claims, with a renunciation by that country in 1824. English claims, however, persisted. The United States opposed England with claims derived from the expeditions of the American ship captain Robert Gray up the Columbia River, from the discoveries of Lewis and Clark and activities of John Jacob Astor. In 1818 a tentative agreement was reached whereby the disputants would jointly govern the territory.

Americans realized that annexation of Oregon would be achieved only by direct occupation of the land by permanent settlers. Leadership in such settlement was assumed by American missionaries of whom MARCUS WHITMAN deserves special mention. Whitman, a Presbyterian minister, founded his first Oregon Mission in 1835. The beauty and wealth of the territory overwhelmed him and, when he returned East in 1842, he undertook to convince the government of its importance. He returned there with a party of settlers, thus beginning the movement of thousands of Americans up the Oregon Trail from Independence, Missouri through South Pass to Fort Vancouver. By 1844 enough settlers were located in Willamette Valley to set up a provisional government; they asked, of course, for immediate annexation by the United States.

The demand of the Oregon settlers appealed to Polk's expansionist temperament (even though the South could not benefit from this accession of territory). But the South had been temporarily appeased by the annexation of Texas. Polk requested and received permission to terminate the joint occupation. During the campaign of 1844 Democrats raised the slogan "54-40 or Fight!" but, since neither England nor the United States wished to fight an amicable agreement was reached to extend the 49th parallel to the Pacific.

Expansion: The Mexican Cession. Between Texas and the Pacific coast lay a broad expanse of territory which included Arizona, New Mexico and California. Polk felt a tremendous pull of "manifest destiny" in that direction. He justified his expansionist desires by showing that Mexico had not made any large scale effort to populate that area; that England was unquestionably interested in the annexation of California; and that Mexico had adopted a hostile and discriminatory policy toward American settlers. In violation of treaty with the United States, Mexico had arrested and even executed Americans, deported them from California, halted their immigration into Mexican territory and impeded trade along the Santa Chihuahua trail with severe regulations. Moreover, Mexico's official attitude toward the United States was hostile. They had regarded the annexation of Texas as a hostile act and had broken off diplomatic relations with the United States. They owed the United States $2,000,000 and had agreed to pay it in five annual installments; but after three payments, Mexico had stopped paying. These were Polk's arguments.

The Mexican Viewpoint. But there is a Mexican point of view which demands attention. The Texan Affair was clear evidence to them that the United States was bent upon conquest of all Mexican territory to the Pacific. The activities of Americans in California were suspicious: in 1842, an American naval officer had "mistakenly" seized Monterey; the consul in California had assured Californians that the United States would welcome a move on their part for independence (with annexation to follow); JOHN C. FREMONT had actually led a military party into California and had engaged in violent action and threats. Then, to cap it all, President Polk had sent JOHN SLIDELL to Mexico with an offer to take up all claims of American citizens against Mexico if Mexico would sell to the United States all of New Mexico and California! This was the basis of Mexico's grievances.

The Mexican War. At this point in the deteriorating relationship between Mexico and the United States, the southern boundary of Texas came into dispute. Mexico claimed it was the Nueces River, farther to the north. The United States held that it was the Rio Grande, the "obviously" natural boundary farther to the south. General Taylor was sent with an army to occupy the disputed area. To counter this move, Mexico sent General Arista into the same area with orders to fight if necessary. On the 24th of April, 1847, the first American blood was shed when a scouting expedition was caught by the Mexicans.

Congress declared war on May 13 and it was "Ho, for the Halls of Montezuma!" In less than a year, Mexico was decisively beaten. Pushing down from Texas, General Taylor won battles at Monterey and Buena Vista. The land north of Mexico City was opened wide. For political reasons, however, Taylor was kept idle at Buena Vista. A westerly thrust by Colonel Stephen W. Kearney subdued New Mexico and then linked with Fremont's forces that had moved into action two weeks before war was declared (to create an independent California). Their combined forces destroyed the Mexican garrison near Los Angeles. Finally, General WINFIELD SCOTT sailed to Vera Cruz to strike from the South. It was his force that fought its way to Mexico City over the fortified hill of Chapultepec. Mexico had no alternative now but surrender.

Peace. On February 2, 1848 Mexico signed the **Treaty of Guadaloupe Hidalgo** and ceded New Mexico and California to the United States. She also accepted the Rio Grande as the southern boundary of Texas. Generously (and perhaps guiltily) the United States paid Mexico $15,000,000 for the land taken and assumed claims against Mexico totaling $3,250,000. Southern joy was matched by Northern hostility. ABRAHAM LINCOLN came into national prominence with a bitter attack on Polk and the war; the abolitionist press proclaimed it a "war for slavery"; the Whig Party openly sympathized with the Mexicans; and some leading writers and intellectuals—among them Thoreau, Whitman, Lowell—bitterly opposed the war.

Slavery. This did not dampen Southern joy; but Judge DAVID WILMOT did. During the course of the war an appropriation bill for peace negotiations was introduced in the House. Wilmot of Pennsylvania proposed an amendment (or "rider") to the bill to the effect that peace was to be made with the understanding that "neither slavery nor involuntary servitude (should) ever exist in any part of the territory acquired from Mexico." Needless to say, this amendment now called the **Wilmot Proviso** became a storm center. The preliminary bouts were fought, however, over the creation of a territorial government for Oregon.

In the course of the battles four stands on slavery became clearly distinguished: The **extreme Southern**, that slavery is constitutional, legal, can exist everywhere, must be protected and is beyond the power of Congress to abolish; **the extreme Northern and Western**, that Congress, with its power to organize new territories, can abolish slavery there (even if it cannot touch slavery in the established states); **the moderate**, that the Missouri "Compromise Line" can be extended to the Pacific; or, that failing of acceptance, "squatter sovereignty," that is, the people of a territory can decide by vote if they want slavery or not; **the abolitionist**, that slavery is inhuman, ungodly and should be erased forthwith from territory and state without compensation.

Oregon was admitted to the Union with slavery illegalized under the terms of the Northwest Ordinance. But the problem of the Mexican Cession was not so easily resolved. A House Bill to organize these territories without slavery was held up in the Senate. Here began one of the most dramatic debates in the history of the American Congress. Led by Calhoun, Southerners one after the other denied the right of Congress to determine the status of slavery anywhere. They espoused the claim that New Mexico was really a part of Texas and that therefore slavery was as legal in New Mexico as in Texas. Northerners evoked the multitude of historic precedents that clearly established the right of Congress to control slavery in the territories. Then they demanded that slavery and the slave trade be abolished in Washington, D.C. Southerners countered with a demand for an effective fugitive slave law that would negate the personal liberty laws. So matters stood when the American people went to the polls for the presidential election of 1848.

The Election of 1848. Both parties were careful to select candidates who would not drive the extremes farther apart than they already were. The Democrats chose Lewis Cass, "a Northern man with Southern principles" and the Whigs selected "Old Rough and Ready" ZACHARY TAYLOR, better known for military than political attainments.

Then, true to form, both party platforms were completely non-committal on the major issue dividing Congress. Vigorous antislavery men, excluded from both parties, organized a third party. The **Free Soil Party**, and nominated Van Buren under the slogan "Free soil, free speech, free labor, free men." Taylor defeated Cass by 36 electoral votes; and the South retained control of the Senate. But in the House, the Free Soilers, with only 13 representatives, held the balance of power between the Democrats with 112 votes and the Whigs with 105. The fierceness of the Congressional debates apparently was not reflected in the country's vote. Wild talk of war and secession was as yet a minority voice.

TAYLOR AND FILLMORE, AND THE LAST OF THE WHIGS

Slavery. Slavery was the dominant issue when the Congress returned to debate the Mexican Cession. New factors had arisen during the election period to make compromise still less likely. A Southern Congressional caucus had published an "Address" which accused the North of acts of aggression on matters of slavery in territories, return of fugitive slaves and slavery in the District of Columbia. The "Address" warned the North that the growing dominance of a northern majority left the South with no choice but to organize a new, sectional party—a first step in the dissolution of the Union.

California had, by virtue of the gold rush, quickly become eligible for statehood. Her population growth had been so rapid that Congress had not even organized her as a territory. Therefore the Californians organized themselves with a constitution excluding slavery and with a provisional government, thus forcing the issue upon Congress. The Mormon State of Deseret was also applying for admission. When Congress examined the Mormon appeal they were shocked to note that Deseret had defined her boundaries as including all of Utah and Nevada as well as sizeable parts of Arizona, California, Colorado, Idaho, New Mexico, Oregon and Wyoming! What was more, the Mormon constitution sanctioned polygamy! Congress eliminated the provision for polygamy and reduced the size of Deseret into smaller divisions. **Each division was organized on a non-slave basis.** The South, of course, was outraged.

The Great Debate. The action of California and Deseret had limited considerably the possibilities of compromise in the matter of the Mexican Cession. The Missouri line could not be extended to the Pacific since California had already declared herself free. With the balance in the Senate now at 14 to 14, the applications for admission of California, Deseret (Utah), Oregon and Minnesota as non-slave states would put an end to Southern control in the Senate. Only one possibility of compromise remained—the application of popular or "squatter" sovereignty, permitting the people of a territory to choose their own way of life. Even this was less than half a loaf for the South since it was clear that the Mexican Cession was not suited to the production of cotton and the use of slaves. The Southern situation grew more tense.

Clay's Proposals. As a basis for discussion, Henry Clay, on the 29th of January 1850, introduced a series of resolutions on the Mexican Cession which, since they were grouped into a single package, were called the **Omnibus Bill.** Clay proposed that California be admitted as a free state; Utah and New Mexico be organized as territories with no reference to slavery; Texas surrender her claim to New Mexico and accept an offer that the federal government assume $10,000,000 of her debts; the slave trade be abolished in the District of Columbia and, whenever Maryland would agree, slavery itself would be abolished; a more effective Fugitive Slave Law be enacted; and Congress pledge non-interference with the interstate slave traffic.

Clay defended his compromise with the argument that, since secession was impossible, slavery as a vital need of the South had to be recognized. He analyzed Northern antislavery as a product of sentiment, not necessity. (Clay ignored the fact that the issue was not slavery alone, but the North's strategy to gain political control and institute its economic program.) Calhoun, too feeble to make his own address, had it read for him. He was fully aware of the issues underlying the slavery question. He pointed to the pattern of growing Northern domination; and showed that even the slave states were tending to become free, as in the case of Delaware. He then warned that secession was not idle talk, pointing out that it had already taken place in the churches. To prevent the tragedy of secession, the North must defend slavery as a Southern necessity.

Webster joined with Clay in an appeal for North-ern restraint. He was as much in favor of the Wilmot Proviso as any in the land—*but* why apply it to the Mexican Cession if it stirred such Southern bitterness? Slavery would never take root there anyway. WILLIAM H. SEWARD of New York spoke for the Northern non-compromisers. Any legislative compromise of the slavery issue, he argued, would violate a "higher law" and be impious and morally vicious.

The Compromise. In spite of bitterness at the extremes, the Great Debate revealed that more moderate men were not yet ready for a test of secession. Compromise prevailed. The Clay proposals were adopted virtually as presented. California entered free; the territories of Utah and New Mexico were to enter after popular sovereignty had been applied; Texas surrendered her claims to New Mexico and was indemnified; the slave trade was illegalized in the District of Columbia; a new, severer **Fugitive Slave Law** was enacted making federal marshals criminally guilty if they failed to enforce the law. Under this new act, slaves could be seized without a warrant, interference with such seizure was a criminal offense, the evidence of the slave was inadmissible in court and the marshal was to have his fee doubled if he turned the slave over to the claimant. For Northerners, this law was a moral abomination.

Southern Reaction. Southern extremists called conventions in Georgia, Mississippi and South Carolina to consider anew their relationship to the federal government. South Carolina openly proclaimed the right to secede. But Georgia was more cautious. She drew up a list of those Congressional enactments which would set her on to the path of secession (for example, abolishing slavery in the District of Columbia, or the abolition of interstate slave traffic, etc.). Other Southerners, aware of the importance of the railroad in binding together the North and the West advocated southern transcontinental routes and that the South foster the growth of industry to rival the North, but this proposal met with sharp resistance. Far more Southerners gave consideration to proposals to reopen the African slave trade and thus force a reduction in the price of slaves, and to the possibility of the conquest of new cotton lands—in Latin America.

Northern Reaction. Northern extremists turned their wrath upon Daniel Webster—he was the "Benedict Arnold," the "Fallen Star," the "Judas." Some Northern states engaged in a form of nullification of their own by enacting new personal liberty laws which encouraged Northern partisans to interfere with the arrest of fugitive slaves. Antislavery newspaper circulation boomed and in one of them, *The National Era*, appeared the first installment of HARRIET BEECHER STOWE's *Uncle Tom's Cabin*. Mrs. Stowe followed closely the rules of melodrama. Her Negro prototypes were noble, pious, even majestic, and they suffered terrible fates at the hands of men like Simon Legree, an unspeakable symbol of Southern cruelty. The story of Uncle Tom, Little Eva, Cassy and Topsy shocked readers to tears and left a deposit of hatred toward the institution of slavery that had a deep and lasting effect. Not since Tom Paine's *Common Sense* had America known such a "best seller"; 300,000 copies were sold in the year 1852 alone. Perhaps as much as any single factor *Uncle Tom* disposed the North to espouse abolition.

Foreign Relations. By 1846, both Southerners and Northerners regarded the Pacific Coast as a potential trading area. The domestic market was large and there seemed every likelihood that a large Far Eastern trade would soon be centered there. Considerable discussion arose concerning the possibility of an Isthmian Canal to shorten the east-west route. Polk succeeded in securing from New Granada the rights to such a canal, and a group of American financiers undertook construction of an Isthmian railroad. England was also interested in such a project and moved to take over the Nicaraguan route. This resulted in the "Polk Doctrine," the first in a number of extensions of the Monroe Doctrine. Polk notified England that the Monroe Doctrine prevented the extension into the Western Hemisphere of foreign influence even at the invitation of a native country.

Bitterness between England and America developed and even reached the war-talk stage. Taylor, however, encouraged the negotiation of the Clayton-Bulwer Treaty (1850). By the terms of this treaty neither country was to obtain or exercise exclusive control over the canal area; both were to guarantee the neutrality and security of a canal; both agreed to keep the canal open on equal terms to either country; and both pledged not to colonize, occupy or exercise dominion over any part of Central America. The approving Senate vote, 42-10, showed that both North and South favored expansion, although their purposes differed.

Election. The disruption caused by the Compromise of 1850 was in clearest evidence at the nominating conventions in 1852: the split between Northern and Southern Whigs was complete. It took 53 ballots to nominate General WINFIELD SCOTT for the presidency. Similar confusion reigned at the Democratic Convention. Complete deadlock existed for 35 ballots and was broken only by nominating the "dark horse," FRANKLIN PIERCE, whose only qualification was his extreme opposition to abolitionism. In an election involving 3,000,000 votes, Pierce won by only 30,000, and interpreted his victory as a national repudiation of abolitionism.

PIERCE'S PRO-SOUTHERN POLITICS

Expansion. Pierce surrounded himself with Southern expansionists, men like Jefferson Davis, Caleb Cushing, James Buchanan, Pierre Soule and James Gadsden, whose aim was aggressive expansion in the interests of cotton and slavery. They encouraged expeditions into Mexico, Nicaragua and Cuba designed to overthrow existing governments there; they forced through the **Gadsden Purchase** from Mexico of 30,000 square miles to make room for a southern railroad from Santa Fe to the coast. But the limit to which they were prepared to go is best illustrated by the incidents that led to the Ostend Manifesto.

The Ostend Manifesto. Soule was minister to Spain. Without instructions to do so, he *ordered* Spain to sell Cuba to the United States. Cuba played into his hands by seizing the "Black Warrior" an American vessel suspected of carrying foreign revolutionary agents. Secretary of State Marcy, who had opposed Soule's aggressive tactics, was forced to take action. He ordered Buchanan in England, Soule in Spain and Mason in France to meet on the Cuban Question and to recommend some policy. The three ambassadors met at Ostend and issued a manifesto which is remarkable in the history of diplomacy.

In the name of the United States, it presented a most narrow sectionalist demand. After reviewing the history of the "Cuban Question," the Manifesto declared that Cuba was vital to American national security, that slave uprisings in Cuba were a menace to the United States, that Spain was powerless to control these uprisings and that, in refusing to sell Cuba, Spain was obviously "deaf to the voice of her own interest, and actuated by stubborn pride and a false sense of honor." Therefore, it continued, if Spain would not sell, the United States would seize Cuba. Under no circumstances would the United States permit Cuba to become a free, Negro Republic. One can only explain a document like this as an act of Southern desperation. Northern opposition was so immediate and strong that the policy was dropped.

Slavery. In 1854, Americans who favored compromise on the slavery issue had cause for self-congratulation. There was political peace in the land. Every square inch of American soil was covered by some measure regulating the practice of slavery. In some areas the Northwest Ordinance applied; in some, the Missouri Compromise line, and in others, popular sovereignty. But slavery was too deeply involved in other matters—railroads, for example. The Louisiana Territory contained a large area of unorganized land known as Nebraska, which was, according to the Missouri Compromise, to be a nonslave territory. Settlers in that area pressed Congress for territorial organization; and at the same time, a group of railroad promoters demanded federal asistance for a transcontinental branch to extend from Nebraska southward and westward to the coast. Southerners were in a desperate dilemma: they wanted the railroad; but a railroad meant the rapid population of Nebraska and its entry into the Union as a free state, which they did not want!

Enter Stephen A. Douglas. A way out of the dilemma was offered by STEPHEN A. DOUGLAS in 1854. He introduced a bill into Congress which would organize the Nebraska Territory into two territories, one called Nebraska, the other Kansas; the Missouri Compromise line was to be repealed and the issue of slavery settled by popular sovereignty. The South strongly supported the measure— under the Missouri Compromise they had no hope of making Nebraska slave territory; but under the doctrine of popular sovereignty they had every hope that they could fill the territory with slaveholders and win it for slavery. Whatever Douglas' motives may have been for proposing the **Kansas-Nebraska Act,** there is no doubt that the measure helped bring the slavery conflict to a climax.

Formation of Republican Party. It destroyed any middle political ground. The Whig coalition disappeared; thousands of Northern Democrats left the Democratic Party, ready for a new Northern sectional grouping that would not require compromise for political victory. In 1854 the new party was born. It sprang from a meeting in Ripon, Wisconsin, of a group of citizens from all parties who gathered to protest the pending Kansas-Nebraska Bill. They drew up resolutions protesting the opening of the Louisiana Territory to slavery and called for a new party dedicated to the Wilmot Proviso, that is, to no further extension of slavery to the territories. Five months later another meeting was held at Jackson, Michigan. Here a formal party organization was created, pledged to the repeal of the Kansas-Nebraska Act and the Fugitive Slave Law and to the abolition of slavery in the District of Columbia. They then issued a call to all states for conventions to adopt this program. The response was overwhelming. The Wisconsin and Vermont Conventions popularized the name of **Republican Party,**

and it stuck. By 1855, the Republican Party was firmly established in all of the free states.

John Brown and "Bloody Kansas." In newly organized Kansas, the slavery issue moved from ballots to bullets (hence, "Bloody Kansas"). Since squatter sovereignty was a matter of majorities, the Northerners organized an Emigrant Aid Society to send settlers into the territory, who joined with neighboring free farmers to build a large anti-slave vote. In reprisal, the Southerners organized "border ruffians" ready to pour into the territory on election days to establish a pro-slave majority. (After the election, they returned home to the slave states.) The ultimate result in Kansas was two governments and two constitutions submitted to Congress. Both Pierce and Buchanan openly favored the Lecompton or pro-slave government over the Topeka or anti-slave. Then violence broke out.

Northerners armed themselves with "Beecher's Bibles," that is, with rifles (the preacher HENRY WARD BEECHER had proclaimed the rifle as a greater moral force than the Bible). Southerners began the bloodshed with an attack on free-state leaders at the town of Lawrence. This was followed by the bloody massacre of Southerners at Pottawatomie, led by the implacable abolitionist JOHN BROWN and his sons. (Violence even entered the august Senatorial chamber when a Southern Representative, Preston S. Brooks, beat Senator Charles A. Sumner unconscious with a heavy cane for the latter's address, "The Crime Against Kansas.") Douglas had legislated—and Kansas bled.

Election. For the election of 1856, the Republicans nominated the "Pathfinder" John C. Fremont. (Abraham Lincoln was passed over for the Vice-Presidency.) The Republican platform demanded immediate admission of Kansas under the Topeka constitution, adopted the Free-Soil slogan, condemned the Ostend Manifesto and advocated federal aid to transcontinental railroads. The Democrats wisely chose JAMES BUCHANAN who had been in London, remote from the hectic national scene. Their platform denounced sectional groupings and called for economy, low tariffs and states' rights. A third party, the **"Know-Nothing,"** nominated MILLARD FILLMORE.

"The Know-Nothings." This political combination formed in about 1850 to taint the national scene. Its appearance was prompted by the arrival after 1845 of a large number of Irish Catholic immigrants who concentrated in cities and engaged actively in politics. The "Know Nothings" directed violent abuse against the "Irish Papists." Rioting against Catholic persons and property was common in America in the

1820's and '30's. Anti-Irish sentiment then broadened into strong sentiment against all immigrants and stimulated the rise of "patriotic" organizations preaching "America for the Americans."

One such group, a secret society with the password "I know nothing" entered politics as the **Know Nothing Party** and was quite successful in securing representation in the state legislatures and Congress. Its program included proposals to exclude Catholics from public office, to raise naturalization requirements to 21 years and to require its members to swear not to vote for anyone but an American-born Protestant. Since the Irish were Democrats, support for Know Nothingism came from disaffected Whigs. In 1856 the Know Nothings abandoned their secrecy and it was then revealed that they were but Whigs in another guise. They disappeared after the campaign of 1856, but left an ugly heritage for posterity.

The Democrats won the election of 1856 without much difficulty. Buchanan was elected 174-114 and both Houses went Democratic. But it was significant that they had beaten the Republicans by only 500,000 votes and that the Know Nothings had gathered 870,000 votes. Clearly, if the Know Nothings dissolved as a party, enough of the former Whig votes might go to the Republicans to give them a majority. This would become a certainty if the Democrats should split.

BUCHANAN: THE BREAK-UP OF THE DEMOCRATS

Dred Scott. Since **Prigg v. Pennsylvania**, Northern hostility to the Supreme Court had mounted; for the Court had thrown its great weight behind the enforcement of the new Fugitive Slave Law. Republicans charged that the Court had deserted the judicial chambers for the political arena. Then, in 1857, came the **Dred Scott Decision.**

Dred Scott had been a slave belonging to Dr. Emerson, an army surgeon, who had taken Scott into free territory. When Emerson died, Scott sued Mrs. Emerson for his freedom, his contention being that residence in a free state and free territory had made him a free man. A high Missouri court denied Scott's contention on the ground that return to a slave state returned Scott to slavery. To test this decision in the federal courts, Scott was sold to a New Yorker, John Sanford. Scott now sued Sanford for his freedom and the case entered the federal courts. The **Dred Scott v. Sanford**, then, was a "test case." The Supreme Court decision was five-four, four of the majority being Southerners.

Chief Justice TANEY spoke for the majority, holding that Scott was not free, in spite of his residence in a free state and free territory, since he had returned to a slave state; and that Scott could not even sue in a federal court since he was not a citizen of Missouri. The Constitution, said Taney, was made by and for "white" men. Now followed an *Obiter Dictum*, that is, a judicial opinion without effect as law. Taney held that the Northwest Ordinance was without effect under the Constitution in its abolition of slavery, that Congress could not establish a free territory since it deprived American citizens of property (slaves) without due process of law, that the Missouri Compromise was an unconstitutional act and that slaves could exist anywhere in the Union.

Consequences. The Court had not only nullified Dred Scott's freedom, but the Democratic Platform of 1856 as well. The Democrats had endorsed popular sovereignty (the right of a territory to exclude slavery by popular majority). Now under the Dred Scott decision it could not exclude slavery. No one saw this Democratic dilemma better than Abraham Lincoln whose star rose with the formation of the Republican Party. The Republicans of Illinois had nominated Lincoln to oppose Stephen A. Douglas for the senatorial seat. In his acceptance speech at the Springfield convention, Lincoln attracted national attention with this statement:

A house divided against itself cannot stand. I believe that this government cannot endure permanently half slave and half free. I do not expect the union to be dissolved—I do not expect the house to fall—but I do expect it to cease to be divided. It will become all one thing or all the other.

The Lincoln-Douglas Debates. Douglas now attacked Lincoln as an abolitionist and warmonger. As for himself, Douglas said that he stood for popular sovereignty and rule of the white man, since the Negro is inferior. Lincoln then challenged Douglas to a series of public debates; Douglas accepted. These debates were attended by thousands and were fully reported in the press of the country. The important results of the debates were that Lincoln revealed himself as a conservative on the slavery issue and therefore as an acceptable candidate for the Presidency; and that Lincoln drove a deeper wedge into the badly split Democratic Party by asking Douglas to choose between the Dred Scott decision and his doctrine of popular sovereignty.

Douglas responded with his **"Freeport Doctrine."** He said that he accepted the Dred Scott decision that neither Congress nor a territory could exclude slavery; but he added that if a territory did not want slavery, no decision of the Supreme Court could force its acceptance. A free territory could exclude slavery by local police ordinances. This satisfied Illinois and Douglas beat Lincoln; but it did not satisfy the South. Why take Douglas' compromise when they had the Supreme Court's unequivocal pronouncement.

Hinton R. Helper's "Impending Crisis." In the off-year elections of 1858, the Republicans had swept into control of the House of Representatives and were eleven short of control in the Senate. An intense battle developed over choice of the Speaker in the House. The Republican nominee, John Sherman, had endorsed a book by Hinton R. Helper called *The Impending Crisis of the South*. This book was written by a back-country Southerner and its argument was that the backwardness of the South was caused by slavery. Helper called upon poor Southerners to vote Republican. Hatred in the South was as violent toward Helper as toward Harriet Beecher Stowe; and was turned against John Sherman, so that he had to be abandoned by the Republicans until their majority was greater.

"John Brown's Body Lies. . . ." In July 1859, five miles from the arsenal at **Harpers Ferry**, Virginia, a group of about fifty men gathered, posing as farmers and cattlemen. Their aim was to seize the arsenal and launch a military maneuver to free all the slaves in the surrounding area. On October 15th, they began their attack, captured the arsenal and freed about fifty slaves. Their leaders were John Brown and his sons. A disastrous delay, however, enabled Colonel ROBERT E. LEE to rally a marine detachment and to destroy Brown's force. On December 2, 1859 Brown was hanged. A wave of admiration and pity for Brown swept over the North. Emerson hailed him as the "New Saint." His elevation to heroism and martyrdom marked the further deterioration of North-South relations.

Election. In anticipation of the decisive election of 1860, the Democrats met at Charleston, South Carolina. Douglas commanded the solid support of the conservative (majority) wing seeking for some compromise on the slavery issue. The radical Southern wing was defeated on the platform to be adopted. Thereupon Yancey of Alabama led his delegates from the convention hall in a walk-out, followed by the delegates from Mississippi, Louisiana, Georgia, Florida, Arkansas and Texas. The split in the Democratic Party was complete. Two Democratic candidates appeared—Douglas for the Northern wing and John Breckenridge for the Southern. The Republicans chose Abraham Lincoln. A fourth group appeared in the form of the **Constitutional Union Party** and selected John Bell.

Platforms. What were the choices confronting the American electorate in the momentous election?

The Southern Democrats declared that they stood for the right of all people to bring their property into the territories, for the use of the federal government to protect such property, for the admission of slave states into the Union, for the acquisition of Cuba, for enforcement of the Fugitive Slave Law and the construction of transcontinental railroads.

The Northern Democrats adopted virtually the same platform but avoided the slavery issue with a mere statement of support for the decisions of the Supreme Court.

The Constitutional Union Party stood for generalities: union and constitution.

The Republican Party platform was more comprehensive. It proclaimed adherence to the principles of the Declaration of Independence; denounced threats of disunion as treasonous; condemned the "invasion" of Kansas; attacked the Dred Scott decision; branded suggestions to reopen the African slave trade as a crime against humanity; promised, if elected, to secure passage of immediate admission of a free Kansas, of a high protective tariff, of a national exchange to secure workingmen higher wages, of a **Homestead Act** granting settlers free land, of federal appropriations for internal improvements and federal support for a transcontinental railroad system.

Results. In view of what followed upon this election, the results were most interesting. The country was Democratic. Lincoln got only 40% of the popular vote, though he received a clear majority in the electoral college. The country was for restricting slavery: this was shown in the combined Lincoln-Douglas totals. The South was for peace and union. Breckenridge got only 20% of the total vote and the combined vote for Douglas and Bell was 124,000 more than Breckenridge's vote in the fourteen slave states.

Secession. Events now began to move with a terrible momentum. In December 1860 South Carolina, by previous agreement with other Southern states, seceded. Ten others—Mississippi, Florida, Alabama, Georgia, Louisiana, Texas, Virginia, Arkansas, Tennessee and North Carolina—followed in that order. Buchanan evaded the crisis by proclaiming himself helpless. A Congressional effort at compromise, the **Crittenden Resolutions**, failed of adoption. By February 4th the **Southern Confederacy** was established. Its constitution duplicated that of the United States except for provisions guaranteeing states' rights and slavery. (To win over French and British support for the Confederate cause, a provision was written in prohibiting the importation of slaves.) JEFFERSON DAVIS and ALEXANDER H. STEPHENS were chosen provisional President and Vice-President.

The new Southern government began to seize important federal fortified posts. Buchanan made a feeble effort to supply one of them, Fort Sumter, with supplies and reinforcements, but when the United States vessel, "The Star of the West," was repulsed by Southern shore batteries, he offered no resistance. On February 11th, Abraham Lincoln began his journey from Springfield to Washington. He arrived on the 23rd. On March 4th he was inaugurated. On April 6th, he decided to send a provision ship to Fort Sumter for Major Anderson's use and notified South Carolina of his intention. On the 11th of April South Carolina demanded the immediate surrender of Fort Sumter. Major Anderson refused and on the 12th of April at 4:30 A.M. Confederate General BEAUREGARD opened fire on Fort Sumter. The Civil War had begun.

CHAPTER XI

CONSOLIDATION OF THE UNION

THE WAR ITSELF

The Line Up. The South could not hope to win the war; it could only hope not to lose. To win the war it would have had to overwhelm a region with four times the manpower, nine times the industrial power, six times the labor power, twice the transport and three times the monetary reserves. The North had most of the arsenals, the merchant marine and the navy. In spite of these material disadvantages, it was possible for the South not to lose the war if it could effect a prolonged military stalemate, or stave off a decisive defeat.

For this limited military purpose the South was well equipped. It would be able to fight defensively along interior lines of communication and on familiar terrain; it could retreat with deadly advantage. This would require brilliant tactics and Southerners were steeped in military traditions. Moreover, they could depend on an indefinite suspension of war weariness since their very lives and institutions were at stake.

The Eastern Front. How accurate Southern estimates were was shown in the early eastern campaigns. The goal of "On to Richmond" was set by the Northern press and in response an untrained army under General McDowell advanced to take that city. The Southern army under Beauregard, Joseph E. Johnston, and "Stonewall" Jackson took up defensive positions and when the Northern asault came at Bull Run (July 1861) it was smashed and turned into a rout. Fortunately for the Northerners, the Southern army was just as demoralized in victory as they were in defeat. Because of this demoralization, General ROBERT E. LEE took over command of the Virginia sector. The defeat at Bull Run at the same time showed the Northern command what would be required to effect a victorious assault on Richmond.

General George Brinton McClellan was drafted from the Ohio and Mississippi Railroad to whip an assault army into shape. He did so admirably. But when the time for the second attack came (1862) he was over-cautious, though he had a better than two-to-one advantage. High pressure tactics brought McClellan to within five miles of Richmond in what has been called the **Peninsular Campaign.**

But Stonewall Jackson conducted brilliant maneuvers in the Shenandoah Valley against the flank of the "Army of the Potomac" and threatened McClellan's force with encirclement. McClellan escaped the pincers; but political pressures forced Lincoln to remove him and replace him with General John Pope. Pope's Attempt to take Richmond resulted in a second defeat at *Bull Run;* Pope was dismissed and McClellan recalled just as General Robert E. Lee began a sensational offensive northward through Maryland.

McClellan followed the Southern armies laterally and caught up with them at Antietam; here the bloodiest battle of the war to date (September 1862) took place; Lee was stopped and driven back over the Potomac. Instead of following Lee for the kill, McClellan paused to lick his own wounds. He was removed once again from the command. (Antietam produced two important subsidiary victories —Lincoln was encouraged to issue the **Emancipation Proclamation** and England was permanently discouraged from recognizing the South as independent state.) McClellan's successors—Burnside and Hooker—turned in important but not decisive victories at **Fredericksburg** and **Chancellorsville**. So matters stood on the eastern front in 1863.

The Western Front. The Civil War began and ended in the east; but it was won in the west. The general strategy in the west was to divide the Confederacy along the Mississippi and then cut it through Georgia to the Atlantic Ocean. This would outflank Virginia. Missouri, a pivot-point on the western flank of the Northern forces was occupied. The rest was up to General ULYSSES S. GRANT.

Grant set out to release Tennessee from the Southern grip upon it. Cooperating perfectly with a naval flotilla under Flag-Officer ANDREW H. FOOTE, Grant crushed two fortified points, Fort Henry and Fort Donelson, and rolled the Confederates back to Mississippi and Alabama. In these early campaigns Grant revealed that with numerical superiority he would not hesitate to sacrifice men to win an assault and that he would be satisfied with nothing less than "unconditional surrender." He pursued his beaten foes until a decision was reached. When New Orleans fell to Admiral DAVID FARRAGUT, the Northern army was in a position to advance upon the Mississippi River from both north and south. Vicksburg was the strongest fortified point held by the Southerners on the Mississippi and became the goal of Northern maneuvering. To get there, Grant smashed a Southern stand at **Shiloh** in Tennessee and at **Jackson** in Mississippi. After a siege, Vicksburg fell on July 4, 1863.

Gettysburg. July 1-4, 1863 was the turning point in the war. Not only did Vicksburg fall, but a desperate invasion of the North by General Lee was crushed at **Gettysburg**, Pennsylvania on that very same day. Late in June Lee began an advance into Pennsylvania. Head of the Army of the Potomac, General George Gordon Meade, retreated along the path of Lee's advance until the two armies met at Gettysburg. Here a stand was made. 100,000 Union troops faced 75,000 Confederates—with this difference, the Confederates were now on the offensive! The battle at Gettysburg lasted three days. Union forces had dug in deeply on Lee's flanks leaving him but one choice—to retreat or to make a frontal assault against the Union center across an open field to Cemetery Ridge a mile away.

It was General George Pickett's unfortunate assignment to attempt the assault. After an intensive artillery barrage, Pickett began his charge. Sheer, futile slaughter resulted; three-quarters of his men killed or wounded. Lee then beat a hasty retreat. Meade, however, stayed behind to nurse his

victory. He was fired and replaced by Grant.

Completion in the West. Bitter battling characterized Union victories at **Murfreesboro, Chattanooga** and **Chickamauga**; near-rout at **Lookout Mountain** and **Missionary Ridge**—all in Tennessee. Out of these battles emerged two outstanding Union generals, GEORGE H. THOMAS (who never lost a battle!) and WILLIAM T. SHERMAN ("War is Hell!"). When Grant was removed to the eastern front, Sherman replaced him as commander in the west. In November 1864 Sherman began his "march through Georgia" virtually unopposed, the South having out-maneuvered itself by advancing northward to Nashville, Tennessee in the hope that Sherman would follow. Instead, Thomas followed the Southern force and crushed it at Nashville. Meanwhile Sherman destroyed Georgia in a war against things, not men. Roads, bridges, factories, rails, gins, livestock, houses and household furnishings were wrecked, burned, ripped up or eaten. This was "total war" and in a month Savannah fell. Now Sherman turned his forces north to the Carolinas where the tactics of war by devastation were repeated. The Carolinas fell; Virginia was outflanked.

Completion in the East. Grant was not satisfied with outmaneuvering the South. He wanted to crush their forces and concluded that only a frontal assault upon Richmond could achieve this. The strength of the Southern defenses was tested in the **Wilderness Campaign** (May, 1864) and again at **Spotsylvania Courthouse**. Union losses were large in these experimental thrusts but Grant could better afford them than Lee.

General PHILIP SHERIDAN now eliminated the Shenandoah Valley as a diversionary outlet for the South. Grant crept forward to Petersburgh, southeast of Richmond. A noose had been wound about Lee's army. It was tightened by a victory at **Five Forks** (April 1, 1865), Southern abandonment of **Petersburgh** and the retreat to **Appomattox**. With 160,000 fresh Union troups facing his 30,000 starved Confederates, Lee surrendered on the 9th of April, 1865. Two weeks later Sherman gathered in the Confederates under General Johnston; in May General E. Kirby-Smith gave up a remnant of forces in the Trans-Mississippi sector. The war was over and the armies went home—the Southerners with their side-arms and their mules. Grant felt that the latter "will be needed for spring-plowing." His generous mood, however, did not prevail in the country at large.

Reasons for the Defeat of the South. Writers are so captivated by the South's "gallant stand" during the four years of civil war, that the defeat of the

South is sometimes obscured. Rarely in the world's military history had a combatant been more thoroughly beaten. The reasons for the defeat of the South are many. **It was outfought**—in war, not maneuvering but victory counts. **It had no sea power.** Control of the ocean lanes gave the North limitless access to goods and credits abroad and a free path to sell its wheat in payment for purchases abroad. **It had no navy.** The Union navy strangled Southern overseas trade; established an effective blockade from Maryland to Texas and split the South along its Mississippi spine. Under Farragut's order ("Damn the torpedoes! Full speed ahead!") the navy took Norfolk, Roanoke Island, Wilmington and New Orleans.

Southerners tried desperate measures to avoid oceanic strangulation. They ran the perilous blockade, experimented with submarines unsuccessfully, and then successfully launched the ironclad C.S.S. "Merimac," built up—with England's aid—a fleet of sea-raiders, the most notable being the "Shenandoah" and the "Alabama." Blockade running proved ineffective; the submarines all sank; the threat of the Merrimac was eliminated by the construction by the North of the U.S.S. "Monitor" (John Ericsson's "cheesebox on a raft"). Ironclad and possessing a revolving turret, the Monitor fought it out with the Merrimac to a draw. A draw, however, was a Northern victory; after this one battle the Merrimac made no further appearance. The sea-raiders were much more effective and accounted for the destruction of 250 Union vessels. The Alabama in particular was a terror until she was destroyed by the U.S.S. "Kearsage."

The Home Front. The home front of the Southern Confederacy was unequal to the task of a four year war. War demanded national unity but throughout the South Davis' efforts at centralization were fought and stymied. Conscription of Southern manhood failed; efforts to suspend *habeas corpus* collapsed and state governors kept a strong hand upon the movements of their own militia. Taxes on tobacco, liquor, salt were unpaid; absence of specie caused bond drives to fail; printed paper money depreciated rapidly and was valueless by 1865. It cost $350 to buy a ham in 1864 and $1,200 to buy a barrel of flour. All efforts at price control failed. The South was consumed by its own philosophy of decentralization. What enabled it to hold out as well as it did was success in industrial ventures, its curtailment of cotton production for production of foodstuffs, the remarkable adaptation of aristocratic Southern women and children to the needs of war production and, ironically, the loyalty of the slaves who tilled the fields and made up the bulk of the labor of the army that was fighting to keep them in slavery.

THE FOREIGN RELATIONS OF THE CIVIL WAR

England. The American Civil War created a split in British public opinion. Those who saw the war as one for emancipation and needed cheap Northern wheat inclined to the Union; those who feared the effect of a war for emancipation on their own "lower classes," or felt kinship with the Southern aristocracy, or needed Southern cotton inclined to the Confederacy.

The English government was less riven. It protested the Northern blockade, built privateers for the South and almost declared war on the North when a Northern vessel stopped a British steamer to remove two Confederate diplomats, Mason and Slidell. (Indeed, they were released by their captors to prevent a war declaration by England.) Only Northern victories prevented the English government from taking the final step of recognizing the South as an independent nation.

France. Napoleon III of France was no less partial to the Southern cause. French industry was suffering cotton starvation as a result of the Union blockade. Napoleon sought vainly to secure a truce. When this failed, he threatened direct intervention by France on behalf of the South. Northern victories checked this move but forced him into a colonizing venture instead.

In 1861 a French force joined England and Spain in a military expedition to Mexico to collect debts due them. England and Spain left but France remained. In 1862 Napoleon III sent Archduke Maximilian of Austria to occupy the Mexican throne. Secretary of State Seward protested this occupation vigorously as a violation of the Monroe Doctrine. When the South was defeated, the United States sent a detachment of troops to the border. There was no need for them as Napoleon had begun to withdraw his troops and a Mexican underground led by JUAREZ had captured and executed the hapless Maximilian.

Russia. Only Russia gave some assistance to the Northern cause. Tsar Alexander II had freed his own serfs in 1861, had rejected French and English overtures to intervene on the Southern side and had dispatched his navy to American waters, an act which was interpreted as a counter to English or French intervention.

ABRAHAM LINCOLN

It is difficult to write temperately about ABRAHAM LINCOLN since, over the years, he has grown to epic stature. To speak of him as a skillful politician, as a sectional Republican embroiled in the large and petty issues of his day, is almost a sacrilege.

Why has this president, of all, achieved legendary dimensions? Lincoln was an example for all time of an American who by his own superb endowments could rise from complete obscurity to world renown. In the course of his meteoric rise, however, he retained the most admirable characteristics of his origin—extreme simplicity, candor, a native honesty, real humility, a plainness of approach and a deep religiosity. His mode of expression was the simple yet profound thought clearly expressed and flavored with western wit and Biblical rhythms, with the illuminating anecdote or "tall tale."

He was no philosopher, as were Hamilton and Jefferson, but he had a philosophy. It flowed from his unbounded faith in the equality of man and in **human rights** above property rights. Institutions which deform or suppress the **basic equality** of all men, he believed, are doomed to extinction and he placed himself philosophically on the side of dooming them. But to doom them did not mean violently uprooting established ways and constitutional sanction. It meant reform by **free consent of the majority** of the governed. Thus Lincoln's faith was **democratic** to the core. He believed, too, that government of, by, and for the people included the struggle of the economically lowly to rise in the social scale. Like Jackson, Lincoln was the spokesman for the average man—the farmer, mechanic, laborer (in short, the "people")—and it is the average man who has enshrined him. And when the assassin's bullet slew him, he became a martyr as well. In calling Lincoln the "greatest character since Christ," John Hay struck the dominant note in the Lincoln legend.

Lincoln and the Union. But Lincoln accommodated his ideals—for the moment at least—to political realities. He became president after the South had seceded. There was no great passion in the North for bringing the South back, especially if it took a coercive war to do so. Lincoln was convinced that disunity was wrong and that a forcible reunion would have to be made. But any aggressive move on his part would drive the border states—still in the union—into the arms of the secessionists. The dilemma could be bridged if the South were to begin an aggressive war on the North. All of these considerations were present in Lincoln's decision to notify South Carolina that he was sending an *unarmed* relief ship to Major Anderson at Fort Sumter. When South Carolina attacked Fort Sumter, the South became the aggressor in the eyes of both the Northern and border states; a coercive war by the North now became a *defensive* war.

Lincoln and Slavery. Lincoln's ideal was **union and peace**; necessity made him a man of war. In Lincoln's view war's aim was preservative not revolutionary. The South was to be brought back into the Union in the same state in which it left the Union. Lincoln was emphatic in his statement that the war was not being fought to abolish slavery but to preserve the Union. Whatever his personal feelings in the matter, Lincoln was convinced that if slavery were abolished during the course of the war the border states of Maryland, Kentucky, Missouri and Delaware as well as the Northern Negro-haters would desert the Union cause.

This, however, was no fixed position. Lincoln gauged carefully the pressures for emancipation—increased abolitionist protests, military protest against slavery as an adjunct to the Southern military arm, the voice of the workers in England refusing to mill Southern cotton, the need to recruit Negro regiments in the North following the draft riots of 1863. When military and political necessity compelled it, Lincoln acted upon emancipation.

The **Emancipation Proclamation** of January 1, 1863 did not, in fact, free any slaves. It was a war measure; it expressly omitted the loyal slave states and occupied territories from its terms; it freed the slaves in states where the people were in active rebellion, that is, where the Union government could not at the time put emancipation into effect. Northern Negro leaders protested bitterly the limited terms of the Proclamation. But this, Lincoln felt, was the most one dared undertake at the precise political moment. Later, Lincoln backed fully the **Thirteenth Amendment** which freed all the slaves. Lincoln, in sum, was an "emancipator" acting very cautiously in a complex historical situation.

Lincoln and the Draft. A war for freedom must sometimes be fought with limited freedom. To recruit armies, reliance had been placed upon volunteers and those who would fight for "bounties" or monetary rewards. This system had failed. Volunteers quit the moment their time was up—no matter what the military situation, and payment of bounties caused "bounty jumping," that is, desertion from one paying regiment to another.

Lincoln therefore in 1863 sponsored a form of Federal conscription. The draft went into effect when a state failed to meet its voluntary quota; physical and occupational exemptions were permitted. Unfortunately, a draftee could buy his way out of service if he could get a substitute by paying $300. This caused objectors to raise the cry "Rich man's war, poor man's fight." Protest against this inequitable draft was highlighted in New York City where on July 11, 1863 riots began that lasted five days. Draft offices were sacked, private homes were looted, Negroes lynched and a Colored Orphan Asylum burned.

Lincoln and the Executive Power. That a national emergency should result in an increase in executive power is a commonplace today. In Lincoln's day any departure from strict adherence to the separation of powers was a radical innovation. It is noteworthy that Lincoln, with his staunch belief in consent of the governed, was the first to increase the power of the executive.

Early in the war, Lincoln held off calling Congress into special session until the three-month enlistment of the state militias under arms was up. Congress was thus forced to act without time for deliberation in securing new forces. Meanwhile Lincoln took the constitutionally dubious, but necessary, steps of declaring a blockade and calling for 42,000 volunteers to serve three years. Normally such actions required Congressional authorization. Then, too, to deal with possible enemy agents in the North, Lincoln suspended *habeas corpus,* a move which opened the way for arbitrary arrests and wholesale suspension of due process of law. (In the case of *ex parte* Merryman, Chief Justice Taney declared that the President had no right to suspend *habeas corpus* since that right belonged to Congress alone, nor could he violate due process which is protected by the Sixth Amendment. Lincoln's answer was, in effect, that, in this emergency, he would interpret the Constitution in a manner fit to preserve it.)

Arrests and debate continued until March 1863 when Congress granted Lincoln the right he was already exercising. Then, through military orders, Lincoln drew up a list of actions to be judged as criminal and those apprehended were given military not civil trials. Neither the actions nor the trial procedures were authorized by Congress. (In the **Milligan Case** (1866), the Supreme Court held that such an extension of martial law was unconstitutional if the civil courts were to function normally.) Lincoln also proclaimed a complete censorship over communication channels; newspapers were submitted to rigid regulations and defiant editors were arrested by military authorities. Less direct, but equally forceful, was Lincoln's domination of his Cabinet.

Opposition to Lincoln. Seen from a distance, the opposition to Lincoln fades into insignificance; in his own day, however, it was most formidable and came from two sources: the "**Copperheads**" and the "**Radical Republicans.**" The **Copperheads** were recruited from disaffected Northern Democrats who were loyal to the Southern cause. It was they who provoked the draft riots in New York City; who bombarded Lincoln in the columns of the *Chicago Times* and the *New York City Daily News;* who tried, with the aid of Confederate prisoners of war, to seize Chicago in 1864; and who were behind the conspiracy that led to Lincoln's assassination.

The **Radical Republicans,** on the other hand, were those who considered Lincoln's prosecution of the war and the antislavery crusade as weak and vacillating. They demanded immediate negotiation of a cease-fire with the South.

The **Republican National Union Party,** after a struggle, nominated Lincoln. The popular vote was close, but Lincoln won overwhelmingly in the electoral college. One month after his inauguration, he was assassinated. This horrible act destroyed any middle ground between the victorious Northerners and defeated Southerners. Lincoln might have bridged the gulf of hatred.

Final Estimate. These, then, are some of the facts required to see Lincoln whole. They do not diminish his stature but make him a man of his time. He rose above his time and became a "man for the ages" by the suffering and greatness he exhibited during the course of the war. His objective was limited to re-cementing the Union and to binding up the wounds of the war. When the holocaust was over he sought to restore the secessionists with all dispatch. He proclaimed the duty of reconstruction to be his alone. The South, he argued, had never left the Union, since they could not. They were in rebellion, the government had crushed the rebellion and now must restore the rebels. If 10% of the voters of 1860 in each Southern state would pledge by oath to support the Constitution of the United States and the acts on slavery passed during the war, they might re-enter the Union. Only those who had resigned Federal military and civil posts to join the Confederacy or who had served in important positions in the Confederate government and army were to be ineligible to participate in the reconstructed governments. The South responded quickly to this program. Louisiana, Tennessee and Arkansas qualified by taking the oath, drawing up state constitutions abolishing slavery and providing for equal rights; they then elected Congressmen to the United States Congress and sought to be re-admitted to their former seats.

The bullet fired by JOHN WILKES BOOTH, an insane, fanatical secessionist, from behind a curtain in a loge at Ford's Theatre, removed Lincoln from the political scene and started him on the road to legend. The South had lost a wise and tolerant friend.

THE ECONOMIC CONSEQUENCES OF THE CIVIL WAR

Because of the violent rupture of normal relations between North and South, a severe economic depression followed immediately upon the outbreak of the war. By 1862, however, prosperity had returned.

Agriculture. The **Homestead Act of 1862** stimulated an agricultural revival. It offered to any citizen or intending citizen who was the head of a family and over 21 years old a land grant of 160 acres provided he resided on the land continuously for five years and paid a small registration fee. America's long history of cheap land thus evolved into a **policy of free land.** Railroads, immigrants and neighboring farmers rushed westward to stake their claims. Now that extensive farming was possible and many men were called off to the war, the sales of labor-saving machinery—mowers, horse-rakes, grain drills, threshers etc.—mounted rapidly. Farm prices rose as farmers undertook to supply the armed forces, the new-rising industries and an especially heavy foreign demand.

Manufacturing. The **Morrill Tariff of 1861** began a policy of high protection for infant industries. The rates in 1861 averaged only ten per cent; but by 1864, the act had been amended until the average rates rose to 47%. Extensive profiteering took place behind these protective walls—inferior goods were palmed off at high prices, wild speculation paid off because of the country's pressing need for goods, and lobbyists secured all manners of favorable legislation. With demand rising steadily, production in all manufacturing lines rose.

Labor. Workers were the hardest hit by the war. Wages did not rise equally with prices so that at the end of the war the workers were worse off than at the beginning. Jobs, of course, were plentiful; but competition for employment—a factor which tended to depress wage rates—increased with the large influx of immigrants and displaced farmhands that converged upon the cities during the Civil War.

Capital. Capital was highly favored by war de-velopments. Scores of millionaires were created. War taxes favored larger industry. The result was that business began the process of consolidation to secure the advantages of large scale organization—a process which has continued to this day. In particular, war needs forced the centralization of separate railroad lines into trunk systems. Business not only consolidated; it also expanded tremendously. The government virtually legislated expansion. In the case of the Central Pacific Railroad Company and the Union Pacific Company Congress loaned government bonds to both to complete a transcontinental line. Loans were made at the rate of $16,000 a mile in the plains, $32,000 in the hills, and $48,000 in the mountains. Each road was given ten sections of land for each mile of track; the total land grant to these two roads amounted to 33,000,000 acres.

Finance. Civil War financing had lasting effects. High tariffs were a high source of revenue. An income tax was imposed for the first time. Borrowing was the chief source of war revenue; bond loans were floated through private agents of whom JAY COOKE was the most famous. To widen the market for government bonds and to fulfil a campaign pledge to restore a national banking system, the **National Banking Act of 1863** was passed. The need for some such law was clear; in 1862 there were about 1,600 banks chartered in 29 states together issuing 7,000 species of banknotes of varying values.

The National Banking Act sought to establish a uniform and stable currency. Under this act a bank could be chartered under national authority if a minimum of five persons contributed at least $50,000. One third of the paid-in capital was to be in national bonds and these were to be deposited with the Treasury. In exchange, the bankers received up to 90% of the value of their bonds in national bank notes; these notes could be used in the payment of all debts. In 1865 the notes were protected by a 10% tax placed on the circulation of state banking notes; state banking notes were driven out of circulation. To supervise the system, a comptroller of the currency was created; and to safeguard depositors, a system of cash reserves was established. This was the American banking system until the passage of the Federal Reserve Act in 1913.

Finally, beginning in 1862 the Federal government began to issue "greenbacks," paper money without specie backing. These declined in value almost immediately upon issuance and helped produce the inflation that characterized the war period. "Greenbackism" remained a national issue until 1879.

Social Consequences. Sudden wealth accumulation produced a splurge of expenditure on luxury, gambling and conspicuous consumption. At the same time, however, philanthropic enterprise grew. Fifteen colleges were founded during the sixties; private endowments to education mounted to more than $5,000,000; the government itself in the Morrill Act of 1862 gave each state 30,000 acres of the public domain for each of its Senators and Representatives for the use of establishing **mechanical and agricultural schools.**

Sanitary and welfare work among soldiers was widened through the efforts of CLARA BARTON (who later founded the American Red Cross), the U. S. Sanitary Commission and the U. S. Christian Commission. Through the efforts of these three, $25,000,000 worth of clothing, bandages, medicine, food and tobacco was distributed; soldiers' homes were maintained; advice-agencies (on back-pay and pensions) were set up; hospitals built and the like. Funds were collected by means of newspaper campaigns, sanitary fairs, theatres, schools etc. Generosity and self-sacrifice more than matched the self-indulgence displayed during the war.

THE POLITICAL CONSEQUENCES OF THE WAR

The Problem of Reconstruction. As early as 1863 Lincoln had proposed a ten per cent plan for the readmission of the Southern states. It stirred immediate rebellion within Republican ranks in the form of the **Wade-Davis Manifesto of 1864.** This manifesto demanded that no southern state be readmitted until a *majority* had taken the oath of allegiance to the Constitution and had repudiated the Southern war debt. This latter provision would have impoverished all Southerners who held Confederate war bonds.

Johnson's Plan. ANDREW JOHNSON, who succeeded Lincoln, was not only a moderate, but a democrat loyal to the Union to be sure, but nonetheless a border Southerner. His plan for reconstruction was treated by the radical Republicans as nothing less than the continuation in high office of the Southern conspiracy. Yet Johnson's was no more than a variation of Lincoln's original proposal: a general amnesty for all Southerners but those who owned $20,000 worth of property or more; individual pardons for these latter; admission of Virginia, Tennessee, Arkansas and Louisiana immediately; the election of constitutional conventions in the other southern states by eligible voters (including qualified Negroes) who would agree to take an oath to support the Constitution of the United States; abolition of all acts of secession; repudiation of all debts incurred in the southern cause; and ratification of the Thirteenth Amendment. Southerners responded readily to this moderate and charitable program and by December 1865 all but Texas had complied with Johnson's program; they had even elected their representatives to meet with the newly assembled Congress.

Congress's Plan. Congress, in a fury, ignored Johnson's plan and turned away the elected Southern representatives. It then wrote its own program in a series of enactments, each of which had to be passed over Johnson's veto. A **Freedman's Bureau** was created to care for the socio-economic needs of the freed southern negro. Then a **Civil Rights Act** was passed; but, fearful that it might be declared unconstitutional, Congress turned this act into the **Fourteenth Amendment** and sent it to the states for ratification.

The Fourteenth Amendment made the Negro a citizen by defining a citizen as a person born or naturalized in the United States. It gave the Negro protection against discrimination by the Southern states. No state could abridge the privileges or immunities of any citizen of the United States or deprive him of life, liberty or property without due process of law; nor could it deny to him the equal protection of the laws. The "Federal ratio" was abolished and the amendment warned states that denied Negroes equal rights that they would suffer a proportionate loss in representation. The Amendment then went on to deny to prominent ex-rebels the right to hold office unless pardoned by Congress and it repudiated the Southern war debt as well as any claim to compensation for loss of slave property.

"Radical Reconstruction." The Radical Republicans won an important election in 1866 by charging the Southerners with efforts to reestablish slavery in the guise of "Black Codes." These codes were vagrancy or apprenticeship laws and followed this pattern: if a Negro was found without visible means of support, he was fined by the courts and then assigned to a planter (usually his former master) to work out the fine. Other aspects of the Black Codes (varying in the different states included: establishment of equal rights except in voting or holding office; and prohibition of landholding, intermarriage and testifying in court against whites. Southerners justified these Codes as the only way of putting millions of uprooting Negroes back to work and destroying the delusion they had of being voted by Congress "40 acres and a mule."

The Radicals rejected this argument and proceeded to place the Negro and his white allies into political office. A **Reconstruction Act of 1867** illegalized all of the reconstruction governments but Tennessee; split the South into five military districts; instructed military commanders to enforce equal rights; and made restoration depend upon adoption of a state constitution that guaranteed Negro suffrage and ratification of the Fourteenth Amendment. (The presidential election of 1868 showed that the Radical Republicans had acted none too soon for their candidate, ULYSSES S. GRANT, won by a *Negro majority* of 700,000 over the Democrat Horatio Seymour of New York.)

The Reconstruction Governments. The governments now established under military protection were composed, in the main, of Negroes and their white allies: Northern whites (derisively called "Carpetbaggers") who had drifted south to aid the Negro cause, and Southern whites (contemptuously called "Scalawags") who were up-country, anti-slavery and anti-secessionist men. What they accomplished while they ruled the South is a matter of considerable dispute. There is evidence that they undertook revolutionary social programs: establishment of equal rights, creation of free public schools with integrated populations; increased democratic rights; road and bridge-building; abolition of duelling, imprisonment for debt; increased women's rights; etc. Other evidence points to incredible extravagance and corruption; confiscatory property taxes; mounting state indebtedness; purchase of office, bribery etc. This issue still remains unresolved.

The Impeachment of Johnson. To silence President Johnson's violent opposition to their plans, the Radicals took from him the right to issue commands to the occupation troops, and in the **Tenure of Office Act (1867)** they prevented him from removing a cabinet officer, EDWIN M. STANTON, from his post without senatorial consent. Stanton was a Radical Republican directing the Congressional program from within the Cabinet. Johnson removed Stanton and now found himself subject to a House impeachment. The charges against Johnson were patently political and not at all "high crimes and misdemeanors." Some Radicals hoped to take advantage of the **Presidential Succession Act of 1792** to establish Ben Wade, president *pro tempore* of the Senate, as President of the United States; and Wade himself went so far as to create his cabinet! In the trial in the Senate, however, Johnson was acquitted by one vote. He was vindicated, but effectively silenced.

The Failure of Radical Reconstruction. In spite of these victories, Congress, in the long run, failed in its policy of reconstruction. Where they were in a majority, the large conservative planters and businessmen regained control in their states by legal and peaceful means. In states where they were in a minority, they used extra-legal and violent means. Secret societies like the **Ku Klux Klan** and the **Knights of the White Camellia** resorted to terror and murder to keep Negroes from the polls. In this way they captured the legislatures and promptly disenfranchised the Negro. Congressional attempts to suppress these terror-societies only succeeded in driving them under sheets and underground. In 1872 the Radicals themselves granted general amnesty to all ex-Confederates. Finally, in 1877 President HAYES withdrew the troops. Freed from bayonet coercion, the South settled down to Jim Crowism and a "solid South" vote for the Democrats in the presidential elections that followed.

REHABILITATION

The Wasteland. The South was an economic wasteland after the war and completely at the mercy of Northern financiers for its economic survival. Over $2,000,000,000 in slave property had been wiped out. Around and about her were denuded fields and forests, slaughtered livestock, destroyed and decayed homes, blasted cities, ripped up railroads and bridges. Banks and insurance companies were shut, currency and bonds were worthless. There was no seed with which to begin planting. Above all, there were 4,000,000 Negroes waiting for 40 acres and a mule, that is, some program of land redistribution that would enable them to begin lives anew as free farmers.

The "New South." With money borrowed at outrageous rates from Northern bankers, the South began a slow climb to rehabilitation. Significant economic changes were made. The oversized plantation was reduced. Land re-distribution doubled the number of farms. The chief beneficiaries were the former poor whites and small farmers. Sharecropping and tenant farming appeared as Negroes were allotted small shares of land in exchange for rentals in crops or cash; housing, fuel, pasture land and gardening areas were usually included. So meager were the returns to the Negroes that they were soon in "perpetual debt." Smaller scale farming, nevertheless, resulted in crop diversification and by 1880 the value of non-cotton agriculture exceeded that of cotton. But due to improved and intensive farming (that is, more per acre rather than more acres per) by 1870 the cotton crop exceeded that of 1860.

Investment capital from the North was at this

time ventured in Southern cotton manufacturing and by 1880 there were 15,000 looms and 714,000 spindles consuming 102,000,000 pounds of cotton annually. Southerners began to tap their coal and iron resources and by 1880 there were 400 coal and 200 iron concerns. With this turn to industrialism, the Northern conquest was complete. The old South receded into the imagination of the Faulkners, Warrens, Capotes and Williamses—novelists, poets and playrights of the New South.

CHAPTER XII

INDUSTRIALIZATION: CAUSES AND RESULTS

The Advance of Industry. The most significant trend in American history in the years from 1865 to 1910 was the advance of industry to first place in the employment of labor and capital. The effects of this trend upon the character of American domestic and foreign policies as well as upon American life and thought were incalculable. A great many factors combined to produce this trend.

Mechanization. Most characteristic of industrialization is the machine, the substitution of automatic, power-driven processes for hand operations. During the latter half of the nineteenth century there appeared an abundance of inventive genius which responded to increasing demands for machines by men who had the capital to finance them. This inventive genius is vividly established by the fact that from 1865 to 1900 about 640,000 patents were issued. Many of these were simply gadgets aimed at lightening labor in the kitchen and on the workbench. A good number were improvements, often revolutionary, of previously invented machines. Some, however, were basic, that is, out of these inventions grew vast industries. For example, there were ALEXANDER GRAHAM BELL's telephone, THOMAS ALVA EDISON's dynamo, incandescent lamp, phonograph and kinematascope, the WRIGHT BROTHERS' airplane, HENRY BESSEMER's open-hearth steel process, CHRISTOPHER SHOLE's typewriter, HOE's rotary press, MERGENTHALER's linotype machine, EASTMAN's camera, etc.

Financial Genius. Inventive genius must be supported. Successful exploitation of an invention often required large outlays of capital to secure a scale of production that would be profitable. This was particularly true of the "heavy industries"—steel, oil, machines and machine parts. In the steel industry ANDREW CARNEGIE was the financial genius. Carnegie amassed a huge capital supply by collecting wealthy patrons as partners rather than by selling stocks. This gave him a commanding position and liquid capital. From this vantage point he began to

unify steel production by buying out competitors, acquiring sources of raw materials and building his own transport. Between 1889 and 1900 Carnegie boosted his steel production from 322,000 to 3,000,000 tons; and at the same time invested huge sums in a drive to lower costs—chiefly by encouraging experiments in new fuels, mechanical processes, etc. Moreover, Carnegie surrounded himself with able steel men and gave them a personal stake in his success; he is said to have created forty millionaires in his lifetime.

When it was to his advantage, he applied ruthless methods of competition—forcing railroads to give him rebates, entering monopoly pools for limited periods, playing high politics to get special tariff protection, and keeping down labor costs by breaking the back of any effort to unionize the steel industry. But these tactics were not the secret of his success; rather it was the fact that he did not dissipate his profits but constantly plowed them back into more furnaces, more mills, more mines, more tracks, more ships and greater modernization.

Administrative Genius. On a par with mechanization was the "rationalization" of factory production—that is, the arrangement of processes for the achievement of maximum production at lowest cost. This required the application of the scientific method of management to industrial enterprise. Carnegie was a pioneer in such methods.

But the greatest influence was the work of FREDERICK W. TAYLOR, a young engineer, who was the first to "measure" waste motion and then retrain workers to enable them to get maximum production in minimum time. **Taylorism** became synonymous with "scientific management." The effects of Taylorism were profound: cost accounting developed; special, psychologically trained personnel managers appeared; a new approach to wages was formulated, the system of payment by "piece-rates." Opposition by unions against Taylor's "speed-up" processes was bitter. But the movement caught on.

Henry Ford, for example, applied it to produce a popularly priced car. Ford combined the **Whitney process** of standardized parts and a "conveyer-belt system" long in use in meat-packing plants. He then added his own idea of breaking the labor process down to thousands of small operations which required little or no skill. The result was an incredible speeding up of production followed by mass production. Mass production in turn reduced the cost per unit of each car and it was not to be long before the automobile would become available for a vast middle-income market.

Raw Materials. The appetite of these new industries for raw materials became insatiable. Men were encouraged to tap every inch of the continent for new sources of raw materials. In the Minnesota-Michigan belt they found an apparently inexhaustible store of iron ore—the **Mesabi Range** in Minnesota by itself was to produce one-third of the United States' supply of iron ore. Coal was found in abundance in Pennsylvania; lumber throughout the north and southwest regions; oil made an early dribbling appearance in Pennsylvania and then a gushing one in the southwest. From Colorado and Nevada came silver, from California and South Dakota, gold, from Montana and Arizona, copper. And, as the electrical industries underwent birth and growth, a call for lead, aluminum and zinc went forth, and they, too, were found in relative abundance. Each year, steadily, the amount of corn, cattle, cotton and wheat multiplied. The good earth of America responded vigorously to industrial demands.

Capital. Manufacturing processes and production of raw materials required ever greater capital investment, more capital, in fact, than was available within the United States. The decline in mercantile and commercial activity after the Civil War had released considerable domestic funds for investment and the spread of the corporation had made available relatively large pools of capital funds; so, for the most part, industrialization was domestically financed. But foreign capital played a significant part too. High interest and dividend rates were characteristic of American industry in this period and foreign investors from England, Germany and Holland were eager to share in the gains. They invested almost three and one-half billion dollars in American industrial progress.

Labor. A large supply of efficient labor was required to support industrial expansion. From 1860 to 1900 about 4,000,000 workers responded to the need and became industrial laborers. Many came from the farms for the increased use of farm machinery was already creating a rural unemployed

group. It is estimated that in the twenty years from 1870 to 1890 almost four and one-half million persons were released from farm labor; these became an important source of factory recruitment. A second major source was immigration. Between 1860 and 1900 about 14,000,000 immigrants reached American shores driven there by the too-well-advertised opportunities in the United States, by declining economic opportunities at home and by flight from persecution and the military draft.

Until 1885 patterns of the "Old Immigration" persisted, that is, most of the immigrants came from Scandinavia, Germany and Ireland. During this period, too, some 70,000 Chinese were imported for work on the transcontinental railroads. After 1885, however, the "New Immigrant" appeared. He was from Russia, Poland, Austria-Hungary, the Balkans and Italy, and he tended to concentrate within the large cities and thus provided a reserve of unskilled labor for the steel mills, mines, plants and railroads. They were not very popular with the "native" Americans for necessity compelled them to work for low wages. Employers hired them eagerly; the result was that they bore the brunt of the brutalizing work of the new industrialization. America's debt to them is inestimable.

The Market. Goods must go to market; both markets and goods must expand together. The results of the industrial expansion would have been less marked if American manufactured goods had to find their market abroad. Competition from England and Germany at this time might have been too much for America's infant industries. Fortunately, American goods could stay at home to feed the expanding home market that resulted from a tremendous increase in American population. From 1860 to 1900 the number of American people increased from 31,443,000 to 75,994,000. When one thinks of increased population in terms of new demands for food, shelter, clothing and transport alone, one can see readily why increased production had no trouble finding markets.

Transportation. Railroad transportation kept pace with the expanding industrial economy and in many ways stimulated it. Here, too, invention, administrative genius, increased raw materials and capital, steadily rising demand, plentiful labor and skilled engineers, and munificent government subsidies helped expansion. Steel rails replaced iron; locomotives advanced in size, weight and tractive power; Pullman, dining and refrigeration cars were added; block signal systems, Westinghouse airbrakes and automatic couplers increased safety factors; mechanical devices for handling bulk freight were introduced; Eads and Roebling built bridges big and strong enough to handle the heavier loads; a standard gauge of four feet eight and a half inches came into use.

Railroads began to reach into every community. By 1900 over 190,000 miles of track had been laid. The railroad magnates who accomplished this transport miracle included Commodore VANDERBILT, unifier of the New York Central; STANFORD, HUNTINGTON, CROCKER and HOPKINS, builders of the Central Pacific; JAY GOULD of the Erie; and the great JAMES J. HILL who built the Great Northern without any government subsidy.

Government subsidies were enormous; the Union Pacific got over $27,000,000 in grants and loans; the Northern Pacific secured 42,000,000 acres of land without charge. Subsidies were more often than not accompanied by corrupt practices and shameful profiteering at the expense of both customers and stockholders. But the transport was built.

Government and Industrial Growth. From 1865 to about 1890—the period of industrial expansion—the federal government pursued a policy of *laissez-faire*. Concretely this meant that there were no laws restricting business practices, no federal commissions issuing regulations or instituting investigation of violations. Paying low wages, charging what the traffic would bear, combining to establish monopolies, discriminating in rates against certain persons and places, collecting rebates or "kick-backs," or refusing to bargain collectively were not *illegal* activities.

Laissez-faire did not mean a policy of "hands-off" business; from the days of Hamilton the American government believed in state aid to business as part of its non-regulatory, laissez-faire policy. State aid took many forms: tariff and banking laws; acts distributing the public domain to farmers, lumbermen and railroaders; direct subsidies to the merchant marine and the railroads; judicial decisions protecting private property against inroads by state legislation; direct government interference with strikes by national labor unions.

Monopoly. Of great significance in the history of the country was the growth of monopolized industry toward the end of the nineteenth century. Generally speaking, a monopoly is a company or a group of companies combined which control enough of the supply of certain goods to fix the price for the goods for the whole industry. If any producer will not follow the lead of the monopolists, he will be crushed by a ruthless "price war" waged by them against him. The Standard Oil Company offers an interesting example of this form of business

organization. First drillings for oil were made in 1859 at Titusville, Pennsylvania, by Edwin Drake. To BENJAMIN SILLIMAN JR., professor of chemistry at Yale, belongs the honor of first analyzing the value of petroleum as an illuminant and lubricant. Drake was sent to dig for oil by a shrewd promoter named Bissell. The Drake-Bissell success started an oil rush and by 1872 production was in the millions of barrels. The utility of crude petroleum depends upon its being refined, and about 1862 JOHN D. ROCKEFELLER entered the refinery business by allying with SAMUEL ANDREWS who had invented an improved refining process. Centering his activities in Cleveland, Rockefeller affected his first combination by joining together five companies. This gave him needed capital and skilled managers. In 1870, this "combine" was refining about four percent of the nation's oil.

John D. By centering his operations at Cleveland, Rockefeller had located near competing railroad lines. These roads began to vie for Rockefeller's oil by lowering their rates for him. Favorable rates gave Rockefeller a competitive advantage and he now began a ruthless war against all competitors by cutting their prices until they were forced to the wall. Then he bought them out. Capital accumulated so rapidly that the depressions of the nineteenth century found the Rockefeller combine strong enough to buy out their hard-hit competitors. By 1882, the Rockefeller interests controlled 95% of all refined oil. Oil producers were forced to sell to his combine at low prices and oil consumers were forced to buy at high prices.

About forty companies were involved with Rockefeller in this monopoly. To tighten control, Rockefeller created the trust. The forty companies turned over their stock to nine trustees (selected by Rockefeller) who were endowed with an irrevocable power of attorney; the companies received trust certificates in exchange. When this trust arrangement was successfully prosecuted as illegal, Rockefeller used the **holding company** device instead. Under this form of business organization, one oil company—Standard of New Jersey—owned controlling shares of stock in each of the forty subsidiaries. This holding company was dissolved by the Supreme Court in 1911 and separate companies were re-established; but not for long. A new form of monopoly now appeared, the "**community of interest.**" Under this form, chosen individuals received controlling interests in the several companies and then got together privately on matters of production and pricing. Every effort to dissolve the oil monopoly failed.

Monopolistic Devices. In the making of combines, the means were many. Earliest was the **pool**, which appeared after the Panic of 1873. Rails led the way. Competition was eliminated by careful division of the territory, rate-fixing, pooling and sharing of profits. Pools were held together by "gentlemen's agreements" and remained together only as long as it was profitable to be a gentleman. More effective control directed to the same end was the stock exchange maneuver which produced the **trust**. Standard Oil pioneered here; but before long, there was a Whiskey Trust, Sugar Trust, Lead Trust, etc. When this device was illegalized the **holding company** appeared—a company which produced nothing but stock ownership and company control of the voting shares. The American Bell Telephone Company was one of the first to use this device; its imitators were many. Since the holding company was itself open to legal attack, many other devices were employed: **interlocking directorates**, or strategic placement of officers of the parent company on the boards of directors of subsidiaries; **mergers**, or outright purchase of one company by another; **community of interest**, or individual ownerships informally united; **dummy directorships**; monopoly through **deposits in a common bank**; and many variations of these devices.

THE MINING FRONTIER

"Strike" and "Rush." Industry needed minerals—metals, for raw material and alloy; gold and silver, for an expanding currency vital to large scale industrial operations. Uncovering the boundless (so it seemed at the time) wealth that lay buried in the lands between the Mississippi River and the Rockies was the work of the prospecting pioneer. The individual "strike" followed by a mad "rush" was characteristic of the period from 1848 to 1890. When the gold rush of 1849 petered out, prospectors fanned out eastward into Nevada, Colorado and Montana in search of new "strikes." These "strikes," however, could not provide permanently for the metal needs of an industrial economy.

Large Scale Mining. Too much of the ore was imbedded in quartz veins. This required "lode mining" (ore-extraction) not "placer-mining" (collection of pure ores on the surface). Lode mining demanded heavy machinery. The capital investments required were far beyond the resources of individual prospectors. Thus, the great wealth of the Colorado fields was not tapped until the massive GUGGENHEIM corporation took them over. It took the considerable capital of the Anaconda Copper

Mining Company to realize in full Montana's mineral wealth.

Then, too, prospectors struck for the richest metals and ignored the less spectacular ones like antimony, arsenic, manganese etc. Community patterns created by the prospectors were inadequate to conduct organized business. Wealth was wasted extravagantly; gambling was rife; thievery was organized on a large scale; murder a la Billy the Kid and Wild Bill Hickok was common; housing was inadequate and sanitation non-existent.

These "picturesque" features of the first mining communities disappeared with the appearance of the large-scale mining enterprise. The need for organized social life asserted itself and those who had a stake in a law abiding existence (the retailers, mining company officials, lawyers, news editors, etc.) formed elected groups to enforce law and order—the **vigilante committee**. Vigilante committees were a volunteer police force and applied somewhat summary justice to law violators. At the same time they pressed for more formal territorial organization and, eventually, for admission to statehood. The face of the mining community was lifted: attractive homes appeared, stage-coaching like that of the Butterfield Overland Express gave way to railroading; the "Pony Express" surrendered to both the railroad and the telegraph pole. By 1900, the mining "frontier" had faded into the romantic past.

The Heritage. This "romantic" period of the mining frontier left a rich deposit of tradition for legend to draw upon. The lone prospector facing the elements and the Indians, the deadly feuds over claims, the wars of miners and homesteaders, of miners and cattlemen, the lawlessness of temporary mining towns with their whirling rounds of gamblers, gunmen, prostitutes, and confidence men, the gun battles for law, order and morality, the dance hall, saloon, barroom and gambling joint, the outburst of street gun-fights, the attacks upon Wells, Fargo and Company stagecoaches—all of these have provided a wealth of material for retelling the story of the miner's frontier.

THE INDIAN FRONTIER

The "Vanishing American." Indians were the major victims of the march across the frontier. While America was primarily agricultural, the Indians could fight a rearguard, slow retreat against the westward movement. This became impossible when they were assaulted by advancing industrialism. For example, the large industrial demand for hides and animal bone for fertilizer led to the slaughter of an estimated 10,000,000 head of buffalo in ten years. This slaughter doomed the nomadic Indian to starvation. Therefore the Sioux, Cheyennes, Apaches and Nez Perce fought bitterly against every advance in settlement projects—railroads, highways, stagecoaches, homesteaders and miners.

At this stage of resistance the federal government turned from persuasion and treaty to war and unconditional surrender. Post Civil War Indian wars were massacres of Indians; those that did not die were herded into reservations, the first of which was in Oklahoma and into which 75,000 Indians from 22 tribes were incarcerated.

The Indian wars have been overglamorized; incidents like the sadistic **Chivington Massacre** of the Cheyenne and the massacre of Custer's men at the **Battle of Little Big Horn** have become legendary. But there were less than 1,000 men involved in these "battles." Battles with Indians have been personalized around exaggerated portraits of SITTING BULL, CRAZY HORSE, CHIEF JOSEPH and GERONIMO. What these chiefs could not understand was that the underlying clash was that of a nomadic, hunting-and-fishing civilization in possession of abundant agricultural, animal and mineral resources with an urban-agricultural civilization hungering for those riches. The Indians were compelled to yield to the more powerful civilization—as has been true throughout history. Indian resistance was heroic, but hopeless, from the start to the finish.

An Indian Policy. What was to be done with the Indians now that they were on reservations? Since they could no longer be dealt with as foreign nations, they were made "pensioners" of the Federal government and compelled, by 1885, to reside in one of 171 reservations scattered in 21 states and territories. On the reservations, vicious conditions led to a degradation of the Indians. They became a prey for every conniving trader and government agent. These degenerating conditions and foul treatment were given national publicity when HELEN HUNT JACKSON published her book *A Century of Dishonor* in 1881. As a result of Jackson's exposure humanitarian societies were organized and prominent publicists like CARL SCHURZ, editor of the *New York Evening Post*, took up the cause of Indian reform. In 1887 the Dawes General Allotment Act was passed. It directed its main effort against tribalism. Each head of a family was to get 160 acres of land with 40 acres additional for each dependent. Indians who received such land grants were granted American citizenship. They were to keep the land for 25 years. Any reservation land unsold was to be placed in the market and the proceeds were to be used for educating the Indian.

Failure of the Policy. The policy of destroying Indian tribalism and compulsory assimilation failed. White settlers in Oklahoma (the "Sooners" and "Boomers," so-called) squatted on reservation territory in spite of "efforts" of the United States army to restrain them. Indians for the most part proved unable to farm their allotments successfully and permitted their landholdings to deteriorate. Competent Indians were handicapped by the 25 year prohibition on the sale of land; they could not profit from improvements made, rise in land values, etc. Unscrupulous politicians, cattlemen, liquor salesmen and land speculators defrauded Indians without check. In 1906 "remedial" legislation was enacted—Indian citizenship was now deferred until the end of the 25 year period. This produced no noticeable improvement. Some new approach was obviously necessary.

THE CATTLE FRONTIER

Obstacles to Expansion. The treeless, semi-arid Great Plains moving eastward from the Rockies were ideal for cattlegrazing. Between 1830 and 1860 a "cattle kingdom" was founded, centered in Texas and extending into neighboring states. In these years the cattle kings were hampered in expanding their production by a great many obstacles. Because the meat spoiled, they were forced to rely upon local markets; thus they supplied emigrants, miners and transients, but were unable to tap the teeming demand of the urban areas along the seaboard. There was no profitable way to get cattle to Chicago for slaughter and trans-shipment eastward. The Ozark Trail to Missouri was overlong and the cattle were unmanageable and lost weight; besides, the farmers along the route were extremely hostile to the passage of the Texas longhorns through their land. There was ruinous competition for the open ranges; cattlemen fought each other for limited water supplies; sheepherders warred with cattlemen over grazing ground; homesteaders or "nestors" fenced their land off and thus cut off more grazing land; miners contaminated range land with slag.

Moreover, disorder ranged through the industry; herds grazed in common and the cow-brand was an ineffective means of identification; wide-ranging cattle were an easy prey for marauding rustlers like Billy the Kid and Scarface Ike; and there was no way of isolating diseased cattle.

Obstacles Overcome. The invention of the refrigerated car (ca. 1870) revolutionized the transportation of meat. Every city in the nation now became a potential market. The extension of the Kansas-Pacific Railroad to Abilene eliminated the problem of getting the cattle to shipping points. Dozens of "cow-towns" (Abilene, Dodge City, Ogallala, etc.) were founded at railroad terminals. These towns had every facility for the delivery, sale and shipment of cattle. Everywhere new trails were carved for the "long drive" to market—the Chisholm Trail, the Pecos or Goodnight Trail, etc.

Victory in the battle for the ranges went to the homesteader because he secured legal title to the land, because the ideal fence material—barbed wire —was invented in 1874, and because he was willing to "shoot it out" with the cattlemen. This and other circumstances, chiefly severe overproduction of cattle and collapse of cattle prices in the 1880's, forced the cattlemen themselves to fence in, to dig for water, and to engage in intensive instead of extensive breeding. Smaller ranges were also made possible by extension of the area of the cattle kingdom to the far north when it was found that cattle could weather the severe winters there.

Before the downfall of the cattle kingdom, cattlemen had taken the first steps to organizing their industry by forming stockgrowers corporations, employing detectives, blacklisting cowboys with bad records, supervising round-ups, inspecting brands and the like. Vigilantes waged open war on the badmen, most of whom were destroyed with the help of federal authorities. Finally, rude beginnings were made in state and federal legislation to protect animals from contagious disease.

Heritage. The present stereotype of the two-gun-toting, lean, laconic, hard-riding, fast-shooting cowhand living romantically and dangerously in the small spaces between a hail of bullets, is far from the truth. The work of the "cowboy" was hard, unrewarding, monotonous and dull and its real character is reflected in the melancholy songs and ballads which have survived from this period; their keynote is loneliness and obsession with death. More accurate is the stereotype of a cowtown with its dancehalls, saloons, gambling joints and brothels. Here all the frustration and loneliness of the cowboys, accumulated during the dull work season, could be released in acts of violence that were more sordid than romantic.

THE FARMER AND THE WORKER

Mechanization. Industrialization antiquated the horse-drawn plow, the hand-sown seed, the hand-picked cotton, the hand-sickled-and-flailed grain, the hand-milked cows and hand-churned butter.

After 1860 mechanical substitutes for every hand operation began to appear. To aid in soil preparation factories began to produce steel plows, gang plows, spring-tooth and disc harrows, and seed-drills. The result was that soil preparation was reduced from about 33 minutes per bushel of wheat to a little more than 2 minutes. For the gathering in of crops there were harvesters, reapers, wire-binders, combines, threshers, feeders, weighers, straw-stackers, corn husker-shellers and binders, and ensilage and silo-filling machines.

At the turn of the century, the chief unsolved problem was power for light and traction; the gasoline tractor and the electrified farm were products of the post World War I period. But even without these important advances, the amount of time in human labor required to produce a bushel of wheat was lowered from 183 minutes in 1830 to 10 minutes in 1900.

Consequences. Important consequences flowed from the spread of industrialization to the farm. The Department of Agriculture joined the ranks of experimenters and through the land-grant colleges and its own laboratories added to knowledge of fertilizers, dry-farming techniques and irrigation methods. Scientific farming led to crop specialization; the result was that specific regions appeared for cotton, corn, wheat and fruits. Crop specialization meant the production of a cash crop and the commercialization of farm enterprise. The farmer became primarily a business man who had to sell what he produced and to buy what he consumed.

Market factors became the arbiters of his continued existence. And, while the bulk of his market was domestic, the farmer began to depend more and more upon the sale of his surpluses abroad; the foreign market was often his margin of profits. As the size of the farm increased, the farmer became a large employer of labor in the form of share-cropper, tenant-farmer and migratory worker. Farming was on the point of becoming a large scale business itself as history moved into the 1900's.

Industrialization and the Worker. Machines displaced workers but increased work. However, the nature of the work created was far different from that which had been displaced. Formerly, the worker had been a craftsman who owned his own tools; he had a scarce skill and commanded a good bargaining position; he had pride in his craft; he was free to pursue a schedule of combined laboring and farming.

Now he became a machine-tender, mostly semi-skilled; his contribution to the end-product was unrecognizable; he became defenceless against discharge and was divorced from farming as a substitute; he became a slave to factory routine. Because he was now at the mercy of the law of supply and demand, he developed a sense of insecurity; he took whatever wages, hours and conditions of work he could get for job competition increased with each influx into the labor market of immigrants, Negroes, displaced farmhands, women and children. He was helpless when the blight of panic or depression came, or when some new technological invention momentarily displaced him. And inside the factory, he found the work monotonous, his mind wandering and the number of industrial accidents in which he was involved increasing.

CHAPTER XIII

INDUSTRIALIZATION (1860-1910): POLITICAL AND SOCIAL CONSEQUENCES

POLITICAL RESULTS

Introduction. From the administration of Ulysses S. Grant to that of William McKinley the American political system went through a period of equilibrium, one in which significant differences between the two major parties became minimal. Each party had the "solid" support of a relatively stable voting bloc. With fair regularity the Republicans rallied to their banner the businessmen who associated that party with favorable banking, tariff and monetary legislation; the grain grower reaping some of the rewards of the Homestead Act; the Negroes and war veterans. Since this group comprised a majority of the voters, the Republicans had effective control of the executive and judicial branches of government; from 1861 to 1913 the only Democratic president was Grover Cleveland.

The Democrats had their support in the "Solid South" and in the urban areas controlled by machine politicians; businessmen opposed to high tariffs also supported the Democrats. Both parties agreed on such matters as laissez-faire toward business, subsidies for private enterprise, protective tariffs, a deflationary "hard-money" policy and easing the Radical Reconstruction of the south. Opposition was largely within rather than between parties.

Machine Politics. The presidents during this period were remarkable for their mediocrity. They had no flair, refused to head any "reform" movements and seemed to agree that the President should be an honest but passive executive without responsibility in formulating national policy. In the field of government, Congress became the dominant influence. Congress, however, often had to share the rule with an "invisible government" centered in the private kingdoms of party bosses like Conkling and Platt of New York, Quay and Penrose in Pennsylvania, "Black Jack" Logan in Illinois, Morton in Indiana and an army of local city bosses of whom "Boss" Tweed of New York was the most notorious.

Corruption and Reform. Business and politics became mutually corrupting forces; politicians blackmailed businessmen, businessmen bribed politicians; the civil service was a patronage tool in the hands of the politicians. Spoilsmen in both parties brought the country into national disgrace. Without real issues, both parties turned national and local elections into campaigns of personal vilification. The private lives of candidates were exposed mercilessly; the lowest instincts of the electorate were appealed to; racial, religious and national prejudices were inflamed. Intra-party strife was as scurrilous as inter-party; in Republican ranks, for example, "Stalwart" fought "Half Breed," that is, the original spoilsmen opposed those who wanted a higher share of the spoils; and "Half Breed" fought "Mugwump," that is, those Republicans who wanted to clean up the party.

Reform movements stirred continuously within both parties and showed that, while the American social conscience was dormant, it was not dead. There were issues enough to stir up reform: political corruption, farm complaints against monopolies, worker complaints against employers, debtors complaints against creditors, and the like. But the editors, preachers, novelists and feminists who raised their voices on behalf of reform were drowned out by the great silence generated by the political equilibrium of these years.

Ulysses S. Grant (1869-1877). Grant was a brilliant general and an honest man; he was also a thoroughly incompetent President. He appointed mediocrities as aides, and when they proved criminally corrupt, he defended them out of a false sense of loyalty. He lacked knowledge of or interest in the essential business of government. During his administration railroad speculation was fostered by increased public land grants, the high protective wall was maintained, "Greenbacks" were converted into hard money and the Radical Republicans were permitted to use reconstruction politics to bolster Northern business in the South.

A low point in national corruption was reached. The American ambassador to England used his post to dispose of bogus mining stock among the English; Senator Blaine of Maine was bribed to get a railroad land grant through Congress; Butterfield of the New York sub-treasury worked with Jay Gould and Jim Fiske to corner the gold market; the Secretary of the Treasury conspired with a treasury agent to pocket $213,500 of collected back taxes; a "Whiskey Ring" made up in part of government officials milked the treasury of large sums—a deal which involved Grant's private secretary, Babcock; treasury agents accepted millions in blackmailing "hush money"; government posts were sold to highest bidders; and, in the **Credit Mobilier Affair**, centering on the building of the Union Pacific Railroad, it was revealed that Oaks Ames, Congressman from Massachusetts, had organized a firm to equip the railroad and had bribed Congressmen with shares of Credit Mobilier sold at par value (the stock was already worth twice par value) to secure fat, uninvestigated contracts for his equipment firm.

An effort to oust Grant was made in the election of 1872. Reformers organized the **Liberal Republican Party** and attracted such notables as the statesmen Charles Francis Adams, Carl Schurz and Salmon Chase and Editor Horace Greeley to its cause of the removal of Radical Reconstruction, low tariff and civil service reform. GREELEY was nominated by the Liberal Republicans and received besides the support of the Democrats; but a corrupt administration was no bar to Grant's re-election.

Rutherford B. Hayes (1877-1881). In 1876 the Republicans opposed Rutherford B. Hayes to Democrat Samuel Tilden of New York. Hayes was governor of Ohio and an advocate of civil service reform. In the election Tilden secured a majority of 242,292 popular votes and an electoral vote of 184, one short of election. There were, however, two sets of returns—one Republican, one Democratic—from three unreconstructed states—Florida, Louisiana and South Carolina. This unprecedented situation revealed an ambiguity in the Constitution. The Constitution held that "The President of the Senate

shall . . . open all the (electoral) certificates and the votes shall be counted." Counted by whom? The President of the Senate?—he was Republican and would count the Republican returns. The House of Representatives?—it was Democratic. The Senate? —it was Republican. The combined Congress?—it was Democratic. To resolve this dilemma, an Electoral Count Commission was created with eight Republicans and seven Democrats to decide which of the returns to accept. The Republican returns were accepted, 8-7, and the electoral vote went to Hayes, 185-184. Thus another weakness in the Constitution was revealed: it was possible for a candidate to be elected President **by the people** yet defeated **by the electoral college.**

Hayes had been a notable governor. As President he believed that a president "serves the party best who serves the country best." In his cabinet choices he boldly defied the "Stalwarts," particularly Conkling, and sought to give his administration a reform tinge by naming Carl Schurz as Secretary of the Interior. In the course of his administration, Hayes ended Reconstruction by recalling federal troops from the South, and following a precedent set by Andrew Jackson, he crushed the **Railroad Strike of 1877** with federal troops. His vetoes were unable to prevent a policy of the restriction of Asian immigration from being instituted as well as the policy of currency inflation through the purchase by the treasury of large amounts of silver. Supported by "Half-Breeds" and Democrats, Hayes cleaned up corruption in the New York Customs House; this act won him the bitter hatred of Conkling, Chester Arthur and other "Stalwarts." He was not renominated for a second term.

James A. Garfield (1881). For the election of 1880, the Republicans offered the voters a combination consisting of James A. Garfield, slightly tainted by the Credit Mobilier scandal, and Chester A. Arthur, deeply tainted with the New York Custom House scandal. Garfield was a "Half-Breed" and Arthur was a "Stalwart." Garfield, like Hayes, was greeted with a patronage fight involving Bosses Conkling and Platt of New York; like Hayes, too, he won the fight. But he lost his life when an insane "Stalwart," Charles Guiteau, shot him, saying "I am a Stalwart and Arthur is President now."

Chester A. Arthur (1881-1885). Guiteau's remark was not intended as irony; "Stalwarts" fully expected manna from heaven now that their man was President. But Garfield's death had produced a transformation in Arthur. His first act was to veto a "pork barrel" bill. A pork barrel bill is usually an omnibus "rivers and harbors" measure by means of which Congressmen secure "improvements" for their districts. Since such bills will not bear investigation, they are usually passed by "log-rolling" tactics, that is, "you vote for my 'pork' and I'll vote for yours." Vetoing pork-barrel legislation is a heinous party offense. Arthur also delayed by veto a **Chinese Exclusion Act**. But the highlight of his administration was civil service reform.

The idea of civil service reform was fathered by THOMAS JENCKES in a report to Congress in 1868. Grant appointed a commission to investigate the possibility of legislation on this matter, but Congress refused to appropriate funds for the commission. Hayes was powerless to revive the idea. With the assassination of Garfield, a **National Civil Service Reform League**, headed by GEORGE WILLIAM CURTIS of the *Nation*, was formed. It succeeded, in 1883, in having Congressman GEORGE PENDLETON introduce a bill for reform. After considerable debate and ridicule about "snivel service," the **Pendleton Act** was passed and created a merit system to replace the spoils system. A commission was created to draw up rules for classified lists; open competitive examinations were to be held for classified posts; appointments were to be made in order of placement; a period of probation was to precede permanent appointment; political assessments for classified jobs were prohibited; politics were banned as a cause for removal; finally, the list of classified positions could be extended by the President. Arthur's conversion to honest politics was complete; he was not renominated.

Grover Cleveland (1885-1889). The campaign choice in the election of 1884 was between a corrupt candidate and an immoral one—or so it seems if we read the campaign literature. The charge against Blaine was contained in the widely circulated "Mulligan Letters" which indicted Blaine of corrupting Congress on behalf of the Little Rock and Fort Smith Railroad. The charge against Cleveland was that he had fathered Maria Halpin's illegitimate child—a fact which Cleveland acknowledged by unconcealed financial support of the child. Cleveland supporters paraded and chanted "Burn, burn, Oh! burn this Letter"; Blaine supporters responded with "Ma! Ma! Where's my Pa? Gone to the White House, Ha, Ha, Ha!" The race was close; Blaine was in the lead when an earnest supporter, the Reverend Burchard, referred to the Democratic Party as the party of "Rum, Romanism and Rebellion." This slogan cost Blaine the Irish Catholic vote in New York. Cleveland won with a 25,000 majority in a total vote of 10,000,000. Either way, dignity lost.

Nonetheless, Cleveland made a dignified President. His guiding principle was that "A public office is a public trust." Cleveland's first administration was plagued by a treasury surplus and the eager desire of Congress to dispose of it by enacting pork-barrel and veterans' pension legislation. Cleveland thereupon established a record in the use of vetoes for such legislation. He himself preferred to dispose of the surplus by lowering the tariff, one of the chief sources of treasury income. The Congress would not hear of such heresy and the surplus remained. Congress and the President did agree on certain important measures which were signed into law: an **Electoral Count Act** to prevent duplicate sets of electoral returns, a **Dawes Act** to aid Indians on reservations, and **Presidential Succession Act** providing for succession through cabinet positions in chronological order of creation, and the all-important **Interstate Commerce Act**, the first shattering blow against the policy of federal laissez-faire.

Benjamin Harrison (1889-1893). Cleveland was defeated in 1888 by vast sums of money poured into the campaign by Republican Boss Matt Quay of Pennsylvania; by effective use of the "bloody shirt" tactic, that is, proclaiming the Republicans as the party that won the Civil War; by the circulation of a fraudulent letter supposed to have been written by an Englishman and declaring that England wanted Cleveland in office; and by a second failure in the electoral system. Cleveland got a plurality of the popular vote, but Harrison won in the electoral college. Under Harrison, Congress, not the President, dominated the national scene. "Czar" Thomas B. Reed of Maine, the Speaker of the House, assumed extraordinary powers for that office: for example, as presiding officer he recognized as present anyone seated in the Congress whether he answered the roll call or not (this prevented a minority from defeating Reed's bills by not voting and then declaring the absence of a quorum); he undertook to name the membership of the most important committees and thus ensured that only legislation he favored came before the House; all progressive legislation died in committee. The Congress, so dominated, voted the unheard of sum of a billion dollars for veterans' pensions, political postmasterships, subsidies to industry and the purchase of silver (a move designed to win the farm vote for the extraordinarily high **McKinley Tariff** in which rates were raised from an average of 38% to 50%!).

But Congress could not resist the almost universal pressure to take some action against the predatory trusts. With domestic rivals eliminated and now protected by the McKinley Tariff, the monopolies showed open contempt for legislative processes by ill-concealed bribery of officials on national and state levels, by unscrupulous price boosts and the like. In 1890 the **Sherman Anti-Trust Law** was passed declaring all combinations in restraint of trade illegal. It proved ineffective from its inception.

Grover Cleveland (1893-1897). Grover Cleveland easily defeated Benjamin Harrison in the election of 1892. His popularity was undisputed. When he left office, four years later, he was one of the most unpopular Presidents in American history. He entered his second term just as the economy collapsed in the major **Depression of 1893**, a depression brought on by farm decline, overexpansion of railroads, a gold drainage caused by the failure of the banking concern of Baring Brothers in England and the collapse of important industries in America.

In this national calamity, Cleveland's main concern was to stop the drainage of gold. With Congressional support, the Silver Purchase Act was repealed, bond sales were launched and finally the treasury borrowed $65 million in gold from the private concern of J. P. MORGAN. Cleveland was bitterly assailed for having "sold out" the government to the private bankers. Congress ignored Cleveland's appeals for a lower tariff and passed the **Wilson-Gorman Act** which averaged just a trifle below the McKinley rates. Cleveland refused to sign the bill; but, curiously, he permitted it to become law without his signature—for which he was roundly condemned.

Big Business was clearly in the ascendent. It scored heavily in two decisions of the Supreme Court. In **Pollock v. Farmer's Loan and Trust Company,** by a 5-4 decision, the Court invalidated the income tax provision of the Wilson-Gorman Tariff; and in **United States v. Knight,** the Sherman Act was held inoperative against a monopoly which combines manufacturing plants since interstate commerce was not involved *in the manufacture of goods!*

Cleveland's passivity in the face of Big Business stood in sharp contrast to his activity in the matter of unionized labor. Resisting paycuts, the workers for the Pullman Company struck under the leadership of EUGENE V. DEBS and the American Railway Union. Cleveland smashed the strike with federal troops sent in "to protect the mails." This was done over the protest of Governor JOHN B. ALTGELD of Illinois. Debs was sent to jail for violating a court injunction. Cleveland's popularity declined even more when he refused to sanction the annexation of Hawaii; it revived somewhat only when he brought the nation close to war with England over an Anglo-Venezuelan boundary dispute in 1895.

Feminism. During the course of the half century under consideration here women rejected their role of passive obedience and second class citizenship. They became increasingly active as workers, educators and philanthropists. As a result they stepped up the fight for political equality. ELIZABETH CADY STANTON and SUSAN B. ANTHONY organized the **National Woman Suffrage Association** in 1869 to secure equal political rights through a constitutional amendment. HENRY WARD BEECHER and LUCY STONE preferred working through the states and organized the **American Woman Suffrage Association** for that purpose. In 1890 both organizations merged as the **National American Woman Suffrage Association.** United, they were powerful enough to force through state laws giving women legal control over their own persons, property, earnings and children.

New Americans. The impact of the "New American" immigrant on American codes and customs was profound. In 1890 the big city became the settling ground for the immigrant; he came to represent one-third of the population of such metropolises as New York, Chicago, Detroit, etc. Gathered in ghettos, the immigrants spoke in tongues strange to American ears, ate exotic foods, practiced odd customs, constructed new temples of worship, crowded into English-for-foreigners classes, went through the twin agonies of adapting themselves to the New World and watching their children adapt more readily than they. The sudden multiplication in overcrowded slums forced city governments to cope anew with building codes, sewage disposal, water distribution, fire prevention and gang war; and, as the naturalization rolls swelled, city politicians had to cope with a new political mass. It was not long before the "new citizen" became a determining factor in urban politics and began demanding his fair share of the leadership. Longer established Americans watched the "invasion" of immigrants with increasing discontent and by the end of the century they were prepared to begin shutting the gates at Ellis Island to the "huddled masses."

Education. Demand for more schools and improved education rose steadily through the half century. From 1870 to 1910 the number of pupils in the lower grades increased from 6.8 million to 17.8 million. Per capita expenditure on pupils rose from $1.65 to $4.64. The number of high schools increased from 500 in 1870 to 10,000 in 1910. Slowly older methods and tools of instruction gave way to new: corporal punishment to child guidance, "Mc-

Guffey Reader" to objective picture-text, the 3-R's and rote-learning to "activity" methods, etc. Functional subjects like sewing, machine-and-woodshop, drawing, typewriting appeared. These changes were forecast earlier in the theoretical work of FROEBEL in kindergarten work, HERBART in the theory of interest and motivation and JOHN DEWEY in the doctrine of learning by doing and the integration of the classroom with society. These theories of education received increased attention in the teacher training colleges and the graduates of these "normal schools" went forth as pedagogic missionaries into the schools of the nation. Educational opportunity for the untrained adult grew apace with formal child education.

President Charles W. Eliot of Harvard revolutionized the college curriculum; he introduced the elective system which permitted students to pick and choose among curricular offerings. To accommodate popular demand, physics, international law, political economy, fine arts, music and modern languages were given equal status with Latin, Greek and theology. Reforms in legal and medical education followed. In both these professional schools the terms were lengthened, written examinations were introduced, apprenticeship laws were evolved and new methods—laboratory work in medicine, casework in law—were tried out. Other specialized schools followed rapidly in architecture, education, business and finance. New all-women colleges came into being—Vassar, Smith, Bryn Mawr etc.—as did all-Negro colleges—Hampton, Tuskegee etc. Finally, of especial importance for the future of American scholarship was the appearance at Johns Hopkins University under the brilliant leadership of Daniel Cort Gilman of the school for post-graduate studies granting the degrees of Master of Arts and Doctor of Philosophy.

Scholarship. Inspiration for post-graduate work came from American scholars who had been trained in Germany. The great trek of Americans to German universities began before the Civil War as a mere trickle; by 1880 it was a wave. During the 1880's more than 2,000 Americans were enrolled in German institutions of higher learning. Here they were inducted into the art and science of scholarship and they brought their knowledge and scholarly ideals back with them. The impact of this training was tremendous.

Science. American science was an early beneficiary of the new scholarship. *Chemistry.* American chemists made important advances in the study of colloidal suspensions; in improved techniques of metrical analysis; and in the formulation of chem-ical law. Josiah Willard Gibbs, for example, founded chemical energetics, extended the method of thermodynamics and introduced the "phase rule" which paved part of the way for the theory of relativity. Unfortunately American appreciation of Gibbs lagged behind European and his fame in the United States was posthumous. *Geology.* American interest in geology was by now a century old. In this period American geologists contributed important information about historical geologic strata, glacial formations and fossils. Foundations for a theory of glaciation were laid by Thomas C. Chamberlain. *Astronomy.* The tremendous, scholarly patience required by pure science was evident in the work of Harvard's Edward Pickering (1846-1919) who catalogued 40,000 stars. Other astronomers worked on methods of photographing nebulae, measuring stellar temperatures etc. *Mathematics.* Josiah Willard Gibbs contributed to mathematics with his theory of vector analysis. *Physics.* The American Michelson invented the interferometer by means of which he determined accurately the speed of light. Then with Edward Morley, he established that the speed of light was constant. This was the starting point for Einstein's Special Theory of Relativity (1905). *Psychology.* Pioneering scientific studies were made in the field of psychology by Edward Thorndike who investigated the laws of learning, by G. Stanley Hall who studied the phases of adolescence and William James who (together with Lange) made important contributions to a theory of emotions.

Social Science. Emulating the massive research of the German masters Herder, Mommsen, Ranke and others, the Americans Rhodes, McMaster, Channing and Henry Adams wrote imposing volumes on the history of the United States. They were fed by innumerable monographists who spent endless time in tracking down minutiae of historical detail. These works, however, were sparse in interpretation; they were primarily fact accumulations. When the facts were finally in, some American historians began to work boldly in the area of speculative history. They searched for some universal laws that would explain all the phenomena of American history. Henry Adams, for example, thought he found the key to all history in the law of thermodynamics; Turner, in the moving frontier; Beard, in economic determinism. In sociology William Graham Sumner studied "folkways" in the light of Darwinian laws. In economics, Thorstein Veblen, Wesley Mitchell and John R. Commons made careful analyses of the psychological forces underlying the dynamic structure of economic systems.

Philosophy. Darwinism affected all of American

thought, and American philosophy particularly. Prior to Darwin, Americans favored the philosophy of idealism. This philosophy taught that man's mind was unique and unlike anything in nature; that man was composed of a mortal body and immortal spirit; that man's immortal spirit corresponded with the real nature of the universe which also was spiritual; that God created both man and universe and was Himself the ultimate substance of all that is. Darwinism, however, suggested that man was an animal, the latest in a long line of evolutionary species; his mind was nothing more than a material adaptation to the struggle for existence; that there was no evidence of divine creation but that all that existed was the product of environment and accident. Thus Darwinism instigated a bitter warfare between both science and theology and materialism (explaining things by natural causes) and idealism (explaining things by spiritual causes). A number of philosophers were very unhappy with this ideological war and they tried to find some middle way that would make room for both science *and* theology, both materialism *and* idealism. Out of this effort at reconciliation was born the American philosophy of *Pragmatism*. Pragmatism is an answer to the question, What is Truth? According to the pragmatists there is no absolute truth, one that is good for all times, all places or all persons. What is true depends upon experimental results and *practical* outcomes. With each new discovery, the truth is modified; therefore, truth is relative. Truth is a means to a useful end; whatever works is true. These ideas were first worked out by C. S. Pierce; they were then elaborated by William James and John Dewey. Americans took readily to such a philosophy: it represented what the average man felt anyway; it was experimental and therefore it fitted in with modern science; it endorsed religious beliefs if these worked, that is, if they made the world a happier place to live in; and, finally, it was easily adaptable to any movement for social reform. Obviously, pragmatism was all things to all men; hence its popularity.

Religion. Darwinism was not all that churchmen had to contend with in these years. When scholarship was applied to the Bible in a movement called the "Higher Criticism," churchmen were faced with assertions that the Bible contained factual errors, evidences of primitive religious practices, gross contradictions, varying styles suggesting many authors and the like. Folklorists made comparative studies and argued that the stories in the Bible were like those in the mythologies of other peoples. The implications in these assertions were clear to the churchmen. The result was that many of the churches underwent a ferment of revival.

Efforts were made by theologians to reconcile evolution and religion. Some argued that science and religion were two unrelated, independent spheres; others argued that they complemented each other. Some, like Henry Ward Beecher, viewed God as the First Cause and Evolution as an elaboration of God's handiwork; others began to treat the Bible, not as a divine book invariably true but as a moral guide and literary masterpiece. Not all churchmen sought reconciliation. Sects multiplied which practiced pure religious emotionalism. Madam Blavatsky founded the Theosophists and preached occult mysteries and human brotherhood; Mary Baker Eddy started the Church of Christ Scientist and taught that evil, sickness, sin and death were products of a diseased soul and could only be healed by direct appeal to God, the Eternal Mind, through prayer; revivalists spread abroad the evangelical message. Moody, Sankey and Billy Sunday revived the techniques of the old frontier circuit riders and won thousands of public converts to repentance and faith.

All the churches made new drives to keep the poor from drifting from their parishes. This drive eventuated as the "social Gospel." For example, Josiah Strong and William Gladden found in the teachings of Jesus sanction for advocating labor's right to organize and strike, or sanction for public drives against monopoly and municipal corruption. Then, too, churches began to open their doors to the establishment of clubs, lectures, gymnasiums, libraries, sewing circles, etc. Most conspicuously successful was the Salvation Army, distinguished by uniform and brass band. In 1910 it was supporting workingmen's hotels, women's hotels, food depots, industrial homes, farm colonies, employment bureaus, second hand shops, children's homes, day nurseries, slum settlements—almost a state within a state. Less conspicuous, perhaps, but equally widespread was the work of the Roman Catholic Church whose membership had grown between 1880 and 1910 from six to sixteen million members. Caring for the needs of the poor was no innovation in this church for the great bulk of its parishioners were immigrants. The work of James Cardinal Gibbons of Baltimore was typical: he worked hard to Americanize his flock; he advocated rapid assimilation; he openly supported labor in the industrial disputes of the nineteenth century; and fought valiantly for the separation of church and state.

Literature: Popular. Journalism. Personal journalism, which distinguished the ante-bellum press, disappeared in the post-bellum world and was replaced by a highly standardized newspaper. From 1870 to 1890 the number of newspaper services by the Associated Press and United Press, jumped by 5,000. A tremendous drive to gain readers was the primary purpose of publisher and editor in the presentation of news and features. Newspapers began to exploit the society story, the scandal and the murder as the public exhibited a taste for the lurid and the intimate. Reports were encouraged to compete for "scoops" and developed irresponsible tactics in ferreting out news. Publishers used to excess sensational headlines, color, the picture and cartoon. Editorial crusades were launched—sometimes sincerely—but more often with an eye to sales; newspapers became the primary agents in "muckraking" campaigns against political bosses, trusts, bankers etc. War was good press, but the threat of war was better. News was jingoed and newspapers made sabre-rattling daily fare. In addition, the feature was exploited to the full: comic strips and feature columnists; household hints for the wives; advice for the lovelorn; sentimental verse and simple short stories. Advertisements spreading over two columns broke the monotony of the page and provided revenue for an increase in the number of pages. Big names were exploited—Stephen Crane, Richard Harding Davis and Mark Twain were attracted to newspaper work by fabulous salaries.

Magazines. The gentleman-scholarly magazine persisted—*Harper's, Atlantic, Scribner's* and the *Nation.* These were essentially literary journals supplying an outlet for American literary artists. But the future of the bulk sale of magazines lay with the application of "yellow-journal" techniques to this field. Edward W. Bok's *Ladies' Home Journal, Munsey's Weekly* and *McClure's* muckraked, crusaded, advised the lovelorn, printed recipes etc. They began to use photoengravings for the visual-minded and to exploit famous names in sentimental fiction. Circulation began to approach the million mark. In fact, by 1900, the *Saturday Evening Post* —staid, conservative, moral and very middle-class —was already at the 2,000,000 mark.

Books. Mass taste ran to the love story that ended happily; or to the historical romance spread with somewhat sticky heroes and villains; or to escape adventure with each chapter but the last ending on the note of an "approaching death"; or to "by gosh" fiction about "real clever" hayseeds from the back regions.

Literature. Serious literary artists were, however, trying to come to grips with the realities of American life. Many of them were, like the contemporary historians, fact gatherers working within a limited region. Their aim was basically descriptive; together they formed a school of "regionalists" or "local colorists." Thus Sarah Orne Jewett and Mary E. Wilkins surveyed New England and described what they found—decay, stagnating seaports, loneliness, crabbed lives. They drew no moral but wrote of what they saw. Similarly George W. Cable examined the "old Creole days" in Louisiana; Twain, Eggleston and French laid bare the Midwest; Page, Craddock and Harris worked on the South; and Bret Harte on the Far West. Mark Twain (Samuel Clemens) cannot be categorized. There was a bumptious nationalism in his *Innocents Abroad* that became biting, lampooning criticism of wealth-seeking in *The Gilded Age;* there is romantic nostalgia in Tom Sawyer, and much more realism in Huckleberry Finn; and, in his last works, Twain was deeply pessimistic.

The second important literary trend in this period was a realistic one; one concerned with recognizable people suffering through actual problems. In some of the works of Thomas Bailey Aldrich, John Hay and Jack London the unromantic laboring man became hero and villain of the story. In the works of Hamlin Garland and Ed Howe the embattled farmer held the spotlight. William Dean Howells dealt realistically with the industrialist-on-the-decline. These writers were unsparing in their portrayals, though not without a touch of pity. So, too, Ellen Glasgow stripped her beloved south of its sentiment and mint julep and showed the impact of industrialism on the decaying southern aristocracy. Completely realistic with almost no admixture of sentiment was Stephen Crane's *Maggie, a Girl of the Streets* and his *Red Badge of Courage.*

Realism led American novelists to search for some key, some law to human destiny. Some found what they sought in the "naturalism" of Emile Zola. Naturalism derived from Darwinism; it believed that environment was the sole determinant in character. Those who imitated Zola placed their characters in an environment from which they could not escape and then recorded their piecemeal disintegration. Tragedy was the essence of America's first naturalists—Frank Norris and Theodore Dreiser.

In a class by himself stood Henry James. At an early age James became acquainted with European cosmopolitan society and he felt acutely the cultural inferiority of American society. In his early works (*Daisy Miller* and *The American*) he contrasted European and American culture and it was clear that he felt himself drawn overwhelmingly by the former. In 1876 he settled abroad and remained to become a British citizen. From the remote perspective of an expatriate, he viewed the American, and not without considerable sympathy, as an innocent baffled by the sophistication of Old World culture; and, while he himself inclined to this sophistication, he was not unaware of the considerable amount of decay that underlay European culture. As his writing matured, his aim became less and less to imitate naive realism or naturalism; more and more he concerned himself with examining the consequences of the pursuit of art as a way of life and with probing into the consciousness that underlay human behavior. This required intensive experiment with a new style, with a sharper, more exact use of words. As a result, his later works (*The Ambassadors, The Wings of the Dove*) are highly complex and intricately and delicately woven. Henry James was the first American to make an art of being an artist. He could not accomplish this in a land where a barbecue of big business, big moguls and big money consumed the minds of literate men. In the mellowed civilization of Europe, he found his release.

The Arts. Painting. During the Gilded Age, American taste was tasteless. While the *nouveau riche* gave way to a collectional mania which gave to their gaudy homes the appearance of art salesrooms, the great populace insisted upon art as illustration, or as moral-bearing, or as story-telling. Both these characteristics of American taste, however, were ultimately of some value: the large collections of the rich found their way into newly built museums and served to raise the taste of the populace; and illustration became a school for artists, some of whom like Pyle, Abbey, Pennell, Remington and Kemble became brilliant craftsmen.

Generally, with no call for their work at home, American artists took to the expatriate path. Some became traditionalists and concentrated on neo-classical nudes; others, inspired by the French Barbizon school, became out-of-doors painters; still others joined the radical *impressionists*. The towering figure among these painters was George Inness who through technical ability, variety of approach and emotional power became the greatest landscapist of his day. All this was in the traditional mode, and America was ripe for insurgency. John LaFarge was the first to organize an insurgent movement through his Society of American Artists. The earliest form of insurgency was in the realistic mode. Thomas Eakins and Winslow Homer worked on American subjects and landscapes in a startlingly realistic vein. With the turn of the century appeared a "New Realism." Eschewing the trite and pedestrian, George Bellows, Robert Henri, John Sloan, George Luks and others turned their brushes to record the stark reality of urban life, the elevateds, ashcans, hall bedrooms, saloons, dancehalls, prize fights, bums and "floozies" of the city. They painted with abandoned color. Overnight, American art became "hardboiled" and slowly, the taste of Americans changed to accommodate this new mood. Meanwhile, overseas three American artists had achieved international stature: Mary Cassatt, a leader of the impressionist school; John Singer Sargent, a painter of stylized and idealistic portraits of members of English society; and James McNeill Whistler, a leader in the war on the Philistines and highly articulate advocate of art for art's sake (his "Mother" became an American byword).

Sculpture. Those who could afford it surrounded their homes with plastered sculptures of mournful females and noble males in classic Greek robes; or with iron deer. In 1876 Parisian winds blew in some new ideas emphasizing naturalism, broken surfaces and originality. A group of American sculptors responded with a series of carvings that exhibited great vitality, depth of feeling, mingled realism and symbolism and earnest nationalism. St. Gaudens, Barnard, MacMonnies and French sculptured the American great (Lincoln, Washington, Grant, etc.) in a new vein, one that inspired nationalist faith. Sculpture approached a high water mark in this period.

Architecture. So, too, did architecture. It fought its way up from vulgarity and materialism, from ostentatious scrolls, brackets, gables and turrets adjoining banks, homes, museums and college halls, and from incessant duplication of alien styles to something new. The Roeblings began this new movement when they built their Brooklyn Bridge as an art-masterpiece of steel and cable which was, at the same time, functional. The complete philosophy of functionalism in architecture was worked out by Louis Sullivan. As a result, the first American skyscrapers and steel supported buildings appeared —giant structures combining art, nature and need.

Music. America took slowly to symphonic music and it was not until the end of the century that the New York, Boston and Philadelphia symphony orchestras were well established. The Damrosches did pioneer work in this field. In 1912 Leopold Stokowski made the Philadelphia Orchestra world-renowned. Opera had better fortune and was housed in 1883 in New York's Metropolitan Opera House. Caruso sang and Toscanini conducted. Of composing, however, there was little of significance: songs and piano suites by Ethelbert Nevin and Edward MacDowell; operettas by Reginald De-

Koven and Victor Herbert; band music by John Philip Sousa; and popular songs like *After the Ball, Sidewalks of New York*, etc. America now became conscious of the deep beauty of the negro spiritual and of a new type of rhythm music called "blues" that was ascending from New Orleans. "Jazz" musicians were producing rare melancholy notes in incisive rhythms and were showing a remarkable ability to improvise on any written tune in what seemed, at the time, in the wild abandon of African Dixieland. In their day, Jelly Roll Martin and Bunk Johnson were crowned kings.

CHAPTER XIV

THE STRUGGLE AGAINST LAISSEZ FAIRE

THE FARMER-LABOR PROTEST

Causes for unrest among the farmers were numerous. Between 1870 and 1895 there was a steady and severe decline in farm prices. Farmers blamed monopolistic controls over manufactured goods, high protective tariffs and maintenance by the nation's bankers of a "hard money" policy for high industrial prices.

The monopolies that the farmers were most directly concerned with, however, were the railroads, the grain elevators and the banks. Railroad abuses were particularly onerous in areas where there was no railroad competition. In such areas, railroads were charging "what the traffic would bear" (rates in the East, for example, were far lower than those in the West); they were charging more for a short-haul where only one feeder line existed than for a long haul where there were competing roads; railroad land speculators were withholding good farmland while waiting for a rise in land values. Corrupt practices were rife among railroaders—for example, rebates to favorite shippers, free passes to government officials and other forms of bribery, fraudulent security sales, notorious market manipulations by the Goulds, the Drews and the Fiskes. "stockwatering," and the like.

Farmers felt that they were being forced to pay in high rates for these ruthless extortions and corrupt practices. Grain elevator operators were also in an advantageous position to mulct the farmer for the farmer had to dispose of his crops before they rotted. Finally, the banks benefited from deflation or declining prices. They loaned money to the farmer when money was cheap and could buy little, and were paid back when it was dearer and could buy more. The farmer, having to pay back in reality more than he borrowed, was forced into debt. Foreclosures, farm tenancy and sharecropping increased.

The Grangers. It was also clear to the farming community that political power was slipping out of their hands. To win back some of this power before it was too late, OLIVER H. KELLEY in 1867 organized the National Grange of the Patrons of Husbandry. Its program was to secure state laws regulating railroad rates and the rates of storage plants; to reduce farm costs by encouraging farm cooperatives for the purchase of manufactured goods; to pool their production and sell it as one lot in order to command a favorable bargaining position; to build their own cooperative grain elevators, insurance companies, flour mills, banks, etc. and to break down farmers' isolation by encouraging wide social activities.

The Grangers hoped to fulfill this program by influencing the state legislatures. After a brief period of organization, the Grangers did manage to win majorities in Illinois, Wisconsin, Iowa and Minnesota and there they put their programs of railroad regulation and grain elevator regulation into effect. Surprisingly enough, this legislation was upheld in the Supreme Court in two cases, Munn v. Illinois and Polk v. Chicago and Northwestern Railroad. The Court argued that regulation of private property is constitutional when that property "is affected with a public interest" and that the states were free to regulate interstate commerce where Congress has not acted. The Grangers were jubilant—but not for long.

Their ventures in cooperatives failed because of cut-throat competition from industrialists and because of poor managerial skill. Then the Supreme Court reversed itself suddenly. In Wabash, St. Louis and Pacific Railway v. Illinois (1886) the Court flatly denied the right of states to fix rates in interstate commerce; this was a power reserved to Congress alone. Granger legislation collapsed and all that was left of Kelley's dream was some success in effecting a social life for the farmer.

Inflation. Regulation of railroads and grain elevators having collapsed, the farmers advocated inflation as a cure-all. The logic of an inflationist is very simple. For example, between 1865 and 1890 currency in circulation was relatively fixed at about $2 billion; in the same period business had tripled. It stood to reason that one dollar at the end of the period was doing the work of three at the beginning. This caused the dollar to rise in value and a rising dollar meant a decreasing price. Moreover, in this period the farmers' debt remained fairly fixed in dollar value; but when prices declined his "real debt" mounted.

With wheat at $1 a bushel, one bushel pays one dollar of debt. With wheat at 50¢ a bushel, two bushels pay one dollar of debt. Therefore, the rise in the debt is one bushel. The obvious answer to this dilemma, said the farmer, is to triple the amount of currency in circulation. This would lower the value of the dollar, force prices up and enable the farmer to pay off his debt of one dollar with one bushel of wheat.

Greenbackism. Greenbacks were fiat (unbacked) money issued during the Civil War, which by 1870 had already fallen considerably in value. Following upon the Panic of 1873, the farmers organized the **Greenback Party** to get the government to increase the number of these unbacked dollars in circulation. This was contrary to the wishes of eastern bankers and industrialists who wanted to place the outstanding greenbacks on a gold standard and make them worth one hundred cents on a dollar. Since the latter were in control of Congress, they were able to push through a **Resumption Bill** in 1875 which ordered the Secretary of the Treasury to accumulate sufficient gold to redeem all greenbacks by 1879. Farmers, of course, supported the Greenback Party and in 1878 it polled almost a million votes; but when, in 1879, greenbacks were placed on a gold standard, the Greenback Party collapsed.

"Free Silver." Prior to 1873 the United States was on a bimetallic standard: paper money was backed by gold and silver. Gold and silver were in a ratio of 16 to 1. The discovery of gold, however, had cheapened that metal and made silver more expensive. Those who used silver for industry were willing to give one ounce of gold for only 15½ ounces of silver. Since the United States mint required 16 ounces of silver for one of gold, no silver was presented for coinage. Therefore, in 1873, Congress failed to provide for coinage of the silver dollar; in other words, it demonetized silver. In this very year, silver was struck at the **Comstock Lode** and began to flood the market. In the process it cheapened considerably until it took many more ounces of silver than 16 to get one ounce of gold. Farmers now

realized that if the treasury would print "silver" dollar bills at the ratio of 16 to 1, the country would soon be flooded with dollar bills and a monetary inflation would follow. They therefore raised a hue and cry about the "crime of '73"—that is, the act of Congress which had demonetized silver.

Farmers demanded a new act permitting the free, unlimited coinage of silver at 16 to 1. In 1878 the inflationists were able to pass, over President Hayes' veto, the **Bland-Allison Act** which required the Secretary of the Treasury to buy between $2 million and $4 million of silver a month for coinage; but prices failed to rise. Inflationists demanded increased purchases of silver. In 1890 the **Sherman Silver Purchase Act** was passed which required the Secretary of the Treasury to buy a minimum of 4½ million ounces of silver a month payable in Treasury notes (dollar bills). This was approximately the total production of silver in domestic mines; prices still did not respond.

Populism. During the eighties and nineties farmers continued to suffer acute distress; meanwhile, the "Billion Dollar Congress" splurged its bounties on tariffs, pensions and porkbarrels. In reaction, **Farmers' Alliances** now appeared in the North and South; their aim was to capture the national government for the farmer in a Presidential election. By 1890 the membership of the Alliances was about 5,000,000 and they were expertly led by IGNATIUS DONNELLY of Minnesota, WILLIAM PEFFER, MARY ELLEN LEASE ("raise less corn and more hell!") and "SOCKLESS" JERRY SIMPSON of Kansas, JIM WEAVER of Iowa, TOM WATSON of Georgia, "PITCHFORK" BEN TILLMAN of South Carolina and WILLIAM JENNINGS BRYAN of Nebraska. Agreement on common principles was worked out slowly as the Alliances began to attract workingmen and socialist elements as well as farmers. In 1891 the Alliances became the **Populist Party.** They met in St. Louis in 1892 where they nominated James B. Weaver for the Presidency of the United States and drew up a platform that became a great landmark in American history.

Principles of Populism. Populism was a revival of the Jacksonian protest in the context of the growth of Big Business. Its core, like that of Jacksonism, was protest against monopolization of economic opportunity which limited the possibilities of advance. Much of its phraseology was radical, but at its core it was not "radical" at all. It was primarily interested in restoring the individual freeholder to his land. Its alliance with the cause of labor was largely tactical. It did make a few thrusts in the direction of "socialist" ownership of public utilities, but its basic demand was that government intervene to curb those who tended to restrict private enterprise. In this demand for intervention it differed from the Jacksonian revolt which had sought to institute laissez faire as a defense against special privilege. By 1890 the farmers had come to the opinion that laissez faire resulted in monopolization and that the cure for monopoly was government control. The program drawn up by the Populists was regarded in its day as extremely "radical." Since then, however, it has been almost entirely enacted into law by a succession of "liberal" administrations. The program bears examination in detail.

The Populist Platform. The Populist platform called for government ownership of the roads with employees chosen by civil service. Its financial program was extensive: a safe, sound, flexible currency issued by the government and not by banks; a sub-treasury plan of distributing currency (under this scheme farmers could bring their produce to a government storehouse, secure a certificate of deposit, and then borrow up to 80% of the value of the deposit at interest not to exceed 2%); further distribution of public money through a program of public improvements; free, unlimited coinage of silver at 16 to 1; increase in the circulating medium until it reached $50 per capita; a graduated income tax; and strict state and national economies to prevent accumulation of a treasury surplus. It proposed that the government create a postal savings bank and take over the ownership and operation of the telegraph and telephone companies. It then advocated that monopolization of land for speculative purposes be abolished, alien ownership of land be outlawed and excess lands in the hands of speculators and aliens be reclaimed by the government and sold to actual settlers.

In an "expression of sentiments" which concluded this manifesto the Populists asked for adoption of the Australian or secret ballot, use of the income from the graduated income tax to reduce taxation on domestic industry, fair and liberal pensions to veterans, elimination of contract labor, restriction of immigration, shorter hours for factory workers, abolition of the Pinkerton System (private detectives who specialized in strikebreaking), support for initiative and referendum (methods of direct democracy) in introducing bills and voting upon them, one term for President and Vice-President, direct election of senators, abolition of government subsidies to private corporations, and support for the Knights of Labor and boycott of the goods of any plant that was on strike.

Labor Unrest. Workers complained that they were underpaid, had no job security and were de-

nied the right to organize into unions. In these years (1865-1890) wages rose, but very slowly. In 1890 unskilled labor averaged $10 weekly and skilled labor $20, and as a result wives and children had to work for supplementary income. Hours of work had dropped from 12 to 11 hours per day for a six-day week. The flood of the new immigration kept wages depressed and hours long. Moreover, conditions in factories, mills and mines lagged far behind recognized health and safety standards. Rapid industrial and railroad advances often resulted in overexpansion with subsequent depression and mass unemployment. At such times, meager savings were drained and workers had to fall back upon charity to survive. Increased use of mechanical equipment caused temporary but distressing layoffs. Workers had no protection against injuries, ill health or old age; nor were families protected against the death of the breadwinner.

These conditions were distressing enough; but more important for labor than even these was their legal inferiority. Since employers were not compelled to bargain collectively with a union of workers, the strike was the union's only weapon. But a striking worker had to consider the use of police, militia and troops by governmental authorities; the injunctions against picketing issued by hostile judges who regarded unions as conspiracies in restraint of trade. Employers could with impunity hire large forces of armed Pinkerton men to protect strikebreakers. Moreover, workers had no redress against the use by the employer of the blacklist, the lockout and the "yellow dog contract"—each an instrument to cripple incipient union organization.

The Knights of Labor. URIAH S. STEPHENS, a garment cutter, sought for labor a remedy based upon producers' and consumers' cooperatives, a move by which he hoped to redistribute the wealth. But "labor" to him meant *all* labor, regardless of craft or skill. As the unit of organization he chose the residential area. Within a specific land area all workers, whether they were mill-hands or independent farmers, miners or artisan shop owners, (so long as they were *not* gamblers, saloon keepers, bankers, lawyers or stockbrokers!) were to belong to one big union organized as a local assembly. Centralized control over the local assemblies was vested in a National General Assembly. By education and agitation Stephens' **Noble Order of the Knights of Labor** aimed to destroy the system of laissez-faire by securing government intervention in legislating an eight-hour day, in compelling employers to recognize unions and to arbitrate industrial disputes, in setting up minimum health and safety standards, in establishing equal wages for equal work among men and women, in abolishing child labor, contract labor and national banks; and, finally, in instituting a graduated income tax and government ownership of railroads and communications. This was to be accomplished by education and agitation—not by strikes.

Nor did TERENCE V. POWDERLY, successor to Stephens in 1878, believe in strikes. However, the membership of the Knights did. When, in 1884, a massive strike against the Missouri Pacific Railroad was successful in restoring a wage cut, the rolls of the Knights mounted. In 1886, 5,892 locals reported a membership of 702,924. But this was the pinnacle of the success of the Knights; their decline was as rapid as their rise. They were unable to solve their internal problems—the hostility of the skilled toward the unskilled worker, the visionary social idealist versus the bread-and-butter unionist, the squabbles between the local assemblies and the General Assembly. Their cooperatives went bankrupt. A major strike against the Texas and Pacific Railroad failed after draining their funds. Finally, they became identified with the radical anarchistic wing of the labor movement through participation in the **Haymarket Affair in 1886.**

The Haymarket Riots. The Knights had sponsored a nation-wide strike on **May 1, 1886 for the eight-hour day.** A small group of anarchists joined in their activities; the local police moved in to break up the meeting. There was gunfire and several workers were killed. The next evening a protest meeting was held by the anarchists in Haymarket Square in Chicago. While the meeting was breaking up the police moved in in column formation. A bomb was thrown and seven policemen were killed and sixty wounded. Whereupon eight anarchists were seized and so great was the public hysteria that they were sentenced to death even though there was no evidence that they had thrown the bomb or had been in any way connected with the bomb throwing. Four men were executed; the fifth, who was sentenced to die, committed suicide. When the hysteria had somewhat subsided and a more impartial review of the evidence was possible, the innocence of the executed anarchists was clearly established and Governor John Altgeld pardoned the other three anarchists.

These are the facts as seen in retrospect; at the time the public viewed the Knights of Labor as the breeder of violent subversion. Employers blacklisted any member of the organization. Under the pressure of being denied employment anywhere in the country, the skilled workers left the organiza-

tion in droves. The thinned ranks of the Knights then merged with the Populists and disappeared when that group vanished. They had, however, fulfilled an historic function—their ideas of government intervention in behalf of labor and the organization of labor by industry instead of craft were to bear fruit fifty years after their demise.

The American Federation of Labor. In the late '70's two workingmen, ADOLPH STRASSER and SAMUEL GOMPERS, made a careful study of the failures of the Knights of Labor. It seemed to them that its basic weakness stemmed from linking unionism with radical utopianism, preferring education and agitation to the well-calculated strike, engaging in politics rather than in labor relations, opposing the capitalist system rather than working within it and ignoring the differences among workers and their natural inclination for local autonomy. So these men planned a new type of organization which in 1886 became the **American Federation of Labor.**

The AFL rested upon the craft local and the skilled workman, even though it was organized nationally. The central body was a federation of all the separate crafts and care was taken to so divide the powers that considerable local autonomy was permitted each local group. Inter-group organization on a state-wide or city-wide basis was permitted to deal with political problems that arose in these areas. Thus a division of function was achieved.

Union objectives were narrowed and concentrated upon wages, hours and working conditions for the skilled workers in the specific shop. The ultimate weapon was the strike and for this purpose funds were accumulated and invested. Each effort was to be a major effort, there were to be no "wildcat" or unauthorized strikes. To prevent a strike, the union leader developed new collective bargaining skills which often involved cooperation with the employer—even to the extent of helping him out of financial difficulty. Successes were registered on a shop to shop, mine to mine basis. When a strike was used it was conducted with a view to winning public support for a boycott of the struck plant. Traditions were nurtured: for example, "don't buy without a union label," or "don't cross a picket line" etc. Loyalty to the union was fostered by the development of union welfare services and recreational activities. In politics, no parties but individual friends of labor from whatever party were supported.

Success came slowly to the AFL. In 1890 it had 190,000 members; in 1900, 500,000; in 1914, 2,000,000 and in 1924, 3,000,000. But what members it got, it kept; for them it was able to secure closed-shop agreements (only union workers were to be hired), improvements in hours, wages and conditions and, most important, public acceptance.

Radical Unionism. The history of the American labor movement reveals that the American worker is basically conservative. He strikes against the level of wages and not the wage system and he uses violence as a last resort. Only a very few workers have made a program of violence in the manner of the **Ancient Order of Hibernians** (the so-called "Molly Maguires.") When a wage dispute broke out in the Pennsylvania coal fields in 1876 the "Molly Maguires" committed a number of crimes, including murder, against the coal operators. Ten of their number were hanged. But they did not become martyrs in the American labor movement which did not countenance "Molly" tactics.

Socialists made a strenuous effort to "capture" the labor movement during this period. DANIEL DELEON organized the **Socialist Labor Party** in 1895 and in 1901 VICTOR L. BERGER and EUGENE V. DEBS organized the **Socialist Party.** Both of these political groups worked within the AFL in an effort to destroy "Gomperism," that is, the conservative, craft-policies practiced by Gompers. They did not succeed; so, in 1905 they met with the Western Federation of Miners (a group not averse to the use of violence) to create a new organization, the **Industrial Workers of the World,** better known as the IWW or "Wobblies." By 1908 factionalism had driven all three of these organizing groups from the IWW. The fragment which was left was led by "BIG BILL" HAYWOOD into a series of rough and tumble industrial battles. "Wobblies" violated city ordinances to get themselves arrested and to fill the jails until the taxpayers would be forced to take their side; while on strike they used mass demonstration, sabotage, and strong arm squads to resist strikebreakers and the police. The full fury of the community was turned against them when they used the same tactics in protest against the "imperialist" first World War. Eventually their organization was smashed and their leadership scattered.

Employer Weapons. The managers of America's vast new industries watched these successive waves of unionization with indignation and fear. Post-Civil War industry had encouraged the illusion among them that they were independent organizers, that any interference with business decisions was illegal, that private property was inviolable. Most business managers were determined to crush unionism with every means at their command. In this determination they found government, at first, an eager partner. Employers placed considerable reliance upon federal troops, state militia and municipal police to enforce the open shop in their industries. In the Railroad Strike of 1877 President Hayes sent in federal troops after $5 million in property damage had resulted. The strike was crushed. In the Coeur d'Alene mining strikes of the 1890's federal troops again crushed the strikers after imposing martial law upon them. State militiamen took over in the Homestead Strike of 1892 against Carnegie's Steel Company and not only was the strike suppressed but the union itself was smashed. In 1894 over the bitter protest of Governor John Altgeld, President Cleveland sent federal troops to put down the strike led by Eugene V. Debs against the Pullman Company. Cleveland's excuse for ignoring Altgeld's demand for non-interference was that he had to protect the mails. To protect the mails, the strike was broken.

In the courts the strikers were restrained by judicial application of the common law which regarded unions of workingmen as conspiracies in restraint of trade. Under such an interpretation, for example, the Coeur d'Alene strikers were sent to jail. The courts also freely granted injunctions to employers to prevent destruction of property by the union. The most famous use of such injunctive proceedings was that used to imprison Eugene V. Debs during the Pullman strike.

Employers made use of the fact that the press, the pulpit and the public were almost always on their side. Use of these forces prevented strikers from getting public financial support to sustain a long strike. In some areas, employers succeeded in organizing "citizen's committees"—in reality, vigilante committees. Over the years, then, employers made it clear that they would not easily surrender their control over wages, hours and working conditions.

The Populist-Democrat Merger. The Republican convention, in the hands of Boss "Dollar Mark" Hanna, had rolled smoothly to a nomination for William McKinley, author of the country's highest tariff and a deserter from the cause of silver. Hailing "the full dinner pail" as its goal, the Convention had adopted planks condemning free coinage of silver, hailing the protective tariff, and pledging an enlarged navy as well as the annexation of Hawaii. The labor vote was courted in a plank calling for compulsory arbitration of labor disputes in industries affecting interstate commerce. There was clearly no place here for Populism. Nor would there be any place for them in Democratic ranks if the Cleveland men controlled the Democratic Convention. Southern and Western Democrats were in full revolt against the Cleveland wing, the "goldbug" faction. Early in the Convention this faction was repudiated and the anti-Cleveland forces took control. In its platform the Democratic Convention went on record for enlarged powers for the Interstate Commerce Commission, for free, unlimited coinage of silver at 16 to 1, and for tariffs for revenue only. The Supreme Court was denounced for its income tax decision and for "government by injunction." WILLIAM JENNINGS BRYAN was nominated for the Presidency. The "Boy Orator of the Platte" was only thirty-six; but he spoke at the Convention with what seemed to the Populists to be the voice of the ages. In his still thrilling "Cross of Gold Speech" he spoke up for the wage earner, the small merchant, the miner, the farmer and the businessman who worked, not speculated, for his money. He invoked the spirits of Tom Benton and Andrew Jackson in a strong plea against the moneyed interests. "We beg no longer; we entreat no more. . . . We defy them." Then the famous lines followed:

Having behind us the producing masses of this nation and the world, supported by the commercial interests, the laboring interests and toilers everywhere, we will answer their demands for a gold standard by saying to them: You shall not press down upon the brow of labor this crown of thorns, you shall not crucify mankind upon a cross of gold.

After naming their own Vice-Presidential candidate—Tom Watson—the Populists accepted Bryan as their man and went forth into battle. Bryan made a 15,000 mile campaign. In 600 speeches he addressed about 5,000,000 people. McKinley, ably directed by Hanna, stayed on his front porch and politely welcomed delegations; meanwhile Hanna, with a war chest of millions of dollars scared out of already frightened corporation heads, rallied professors, editors, orators and authors to attack "free silver" and to castigate the Populists as vicious, subversive radicals. The "peoples' crusade" marched to defeat. McKinley won by half a million popular votes and by 271 to 176 in the electoral college. The Populists expired. But populism had come to stay.

CHAPTER XV

DAWN OF THE WELFARE STATE

THE PROGRESSIVE MOVEMENT

The Interstate Commerce Act of 1887. In the Granger Laws of the 1870's appeared the first intimations of government interventionism. State laws were framed by the legislatures captured by the Grangers which defined railroads and grain warehouses as private businesses "affected with public interest." In other words, it was the right of the public through its governmental apparatus to regulate or draw up the rules for proper practice of private business to prevent the public from being harmed.

This interventionist philosophy, that of the "welfare state," was at first upheld by the Supreme Court. But in the Wabash Case of 1886 the Supreme Court held that state intervention was incompatible with the Constitutional mandate giving the control of interstate commerce to Congress. Railroads ran interstate; therefore, it was up to *Congress* to intervene—if it would.

Demand for intervention was no novelty to Congress. All of the post-Civil War third parties had petitioned for correction of railroad abuses. In 1874 the **Windom Committee** had recommended that the government build railroads as yardsticks for the private roads and bills to that effect had been introduced; in 1886 a **Cullom Committee** exposed malpractices exhaustively and recommended that "Congress should undertake in some way the regulation of interstate commerce." Finally the **Interstate Commerce Act** was passed and signed by Grover Cleveland in 1887. It had bipartisan support for Congressmen felt that such regulation would benefit the railroad's owners as well as its customers.

Terms. This act created the pattern for the administrative board which was to become the chief means by which the American government was transformed from a laissez faire to an interventionist state. A commission of five—the **Interstate Commerce Commission**—was created to enforce the act. The act itself illegalized railroad practices of giving special rates or secret rebates; rate-discrimination among persons, places or goods; charging more for non-competitive short hauls than for competitive long hauls; and forming pools to divide territories and thereby eliminate inter-road competition. Railroads were required to publish schedules and rates. To enforce these regulations, the commission was empowered to supervise the accounting system of the railroads, their rate schedules, and their business methods. The commission could sit as a court of complaints, make rulings on the complaints, and call upon the Attorney General to enforce their rulings in the courts.

Weaknesses. Attempted enforcement revealed basic weaknesses. The Commissioners were not given power to compel the testimony of relevant witnesses; the railroads could continue their malpractices until the courts ruled otherwise; railroad attorneys were able to tie up cases in the courts for years; and the courts themselves were hostile to abandonment of the philosophy of laissez faire and gave the Commission adverse decisions in rate-making violations (as in the **Maximum Freight Rate Case of 1897**) and violations of the long-haul-short-haul regulation (as in the **Alabama Midlands Case of 1897**). Congressional clarification of the Act and a reversal of attitude of the bench were required before this first venture in intervention could succeed. With its built-in weaknesses, however, the ICC became deadwood by 1900. But a shattering precedent had been established.

The Sherman Anti-Trust Law. Monopolies increased in strength and number in the two generations following the Civil War. Well protected by tariffs against foreign competition, American industries like oil, tobacco, steel, sugar etc. engaged in financial and business practices that crushed marginal producers and forced those more powerful to combine or fight it out to the death. Legal devices like pools, trusts, holding companies, interlocking directories and mergers were invented to form combinations. And while some states tried regulation of monopolies, others deliberately avoided regulatory practices to encourage incorporation within their jurisdictions for tax benefits. The Supreme Court, too, came to the aid of the monopolist when, in **Santa Clara County v. Southern Pacific Railroad**, it held that a corporation was a person and therefore protected by the 14th Amendment. Since, by this interpretation, no state might deprive a person or corporation of "life, liberty or property without due process of law," many state laws regulating monopolies were invalidated.

But protests against monopolies, mostly from small businessmen and consumers, would not be stilled. In 1884, the more vocal of these elements formed the **Anti-Monopoly Party** which won considerable attention though few votes. About 1890 a group of indignant publicists joined the crusade. Edward Bellamy in *Looking Backward*, Henry Demarest Lloyd in the sensational *Story of a Great Monopoly*, Henry George in *Progress and Poverty* each used monopoly both to expose capitalistic evils and to advance their own philosophy of reform. Farmer and labor organizations joined the protest. Some states enacted legislation making corrupt practices restraining free competition illegal. By 1890, neither President Harrison nor Congress could ignore the many-sided protest.

The Law. The result was the **Sherman Anti-Trust Law of 1890.** This law declared that "every contract, combination in the form of trust or otherwise, or conspiracy, in restraint of trade or commerce among the several states, or with foreign nations" was illegal. Violators were subject to a fine of $5,000 and one year imprisonment. Federal district attorneys could take action and those injured by trade restraints could sue for damages.

The Intellectual Background. "Social Darwinism" was the general target of American intellectuals. The doctrine of survival of the fittest in an unavoidable struggle for existence applied to man and society seemed inhumane and immoral. Equally erroneous, they felt, was the related thesis that the state must remain neutral while men struggled—a powerful few to victory and the great mass to certain defeat.

In 1879 HENRY GEORGE preached in *Progress and Poverty* that men could reconstruct society by intelligent political action; and in 1888, EDWARD BELLAMY (*Looking Backward*) showed—to the satisfaction of millions—what such a reconstructed society would be like.

In 1883 LESTER WARD in his *Dynamic Sociology* challenged Herbert Spencer's contention that mankind was the helpless victim of senseless evolution and argued that the human species survived because it *combined* to control its environment.

In 1885, a number of American economists challenged the doctrines of the "classical" economists who held that there were automatic laws regulating economic life; and they formed the American Economic Association to propagate the doctrine that the state must intervene to ensure human progress.

In 1889 THORSTEIN VEBLEN turned his great critical intelligence upon the concept that American capitalists had contributed to American progress. He credited American economic greatness to the engineers and managers of industry, and not to those who supplied the capital. In *The Theory of the Leisure Class* he portrayed capitalists as wasteful consumers, not producers, of wealth, interested only in acquisition and prestige, in having more than the next one, only to show it off.

WILLIAM JAMES and JOHN DEWEY developed the philosophy of **Pragmatism** and convinced many Americans that there are no fixed truths, that whatever works is right—particularly if it works for the majority of people, and that ideas are instruments and useful only when they help to transform society.

In his *An Economic Interpretation of the Constitution*, CHARLES A. BEARD led a major assault upon one of the holiest and most cherished American ideas: that the American Constitution was a sacred document, the almost divine product of our sainted forefathers. Beard produced evidence to show that the constitutional founders were self-interested groups working selfishly to secure their position as merchants, landowners, money lenders and land speculators. Beard did not draw the inferences; in fact, he later repudiated all inferences which were drawn from his thesis. But others did conclude that, far from being a sacred document, the Constitution was a "class" document to protect the interests of the propertied groups in the country. This led to the further conclusion that it could be amended to serve the interests of the many as well as the few.

Finally, in three very widely read books—Herbert Croly's *The Promise of American Life*, Walter Weyl's *The New Democracy* and Walter Lippmann's *Preface to Politics*—these points were hammered home: that laissez-faire had served its purpose and was now the source of all national evil; that, if permitted to continue, it would lead to violent overthrow of American democracy by the dispossessed; and that, therefore, the only alternative was a "planned society" using the best brains of the country to produce objective, scientific legislation which would preserve democracy while eliminating the abuses of laissez faire.

The "Muckrakers." Between 1900 and 1914, publicists translated these doctrines into popular terms. The inexpensive magazines developed by S. S. McClure (*McClure's, Cosmopolitan, Munsey's*) proved an ideal medium for public exposure of monopolies. "Muckrakers" were reporters who made a profession of exposing political evil and corruption and of espousing the cause of the unfortunate and oppressed. Henry Demarest Lloyd had fathered the movement in his two exposures of the Standard Oil Company. Building upon this early study, Ida Tarbell composed her *History of the Standard Oil Company*, a cold, objective study, carefully documented, which revealed the vast array of unscrupulous business tactics used by Rockefeller to crush his competitors. She made "John D." into "the symbol of financial Caesarism." Municipal corruption and corrupt alliances between politicos and businessmen were fully uncovered by Lincoln Steffens in his *Shame of the Cities*. The business tactics of Amalgamated Copper were bared by Thomas Lawson (a former president of the company) in his *Frenzied Finance*.

Ray Stannard Baker wrote *The Railroads on Trial* and *Following the Color Line*, a pioneer study of racial attitudes; Norman Hapgood went after patent medicines and William Randolph Hearst; Burton J. Hendrick tracked down the activities of the New York Insurance Companies; George Kibbe Turner turned a lurid spotlight on the connection of the Chicago police with organized prostitution; Edward Russell opened the public eye to the beef trust, a trust which was even more dramatically exposed by Upton Sinclair in his influential study *The Jungle*; and, finally, Gustavus Myers threw a merciless beam on all of the capitalists in his *History of Great American Fortunes* and then made similar special studies of Tammany Hall and the Supreme Court. (Today historians, in evaluating these exposures, are in fair agreement that, though there was much that was true in these books and pamphlets, the muckrakers overstated their case by fitting the facts to their biases and by omitting other, more favorable information.)

Until 1910, the muckrakers indulged in careful studies intended to clean house; and they were read eagerly by the literate. Thereafter exposure turned into sensation-mongering. But muckraking had served a purpose: the squalid relations of business and politics had been revealed and this led to demand for reform. Most of all, it forced businessmen to realize that they could not avoid forever the demand of social responsibility.

Literature in Revolt. The Progressive period coincided with the rise in America of the realistic and naturalistic novel. Novelists like FRANK NORRIS, THEODORE DREISER, JACK LONDON, UPTON SINCLAIR and STEPHEN CRANE went to the environment about them for material. Their aim was to record the environment objectively, accurately and in the greatest detail. Thus, Dreiser in a trilogy—*The Financier, The Titan* and *The Genius*—fictionalized the career of Charles T. Yerkes, a Chicago traction magnate; Norris lay bare the operations of the Southern Pacific Railroad magnates in *The Octopus*; Alfred Henry Lewis, Brand Whitlock, Henry Adams and Booth Tarkington used themes centering upon political corruption; various aspects of capitalism was the framework of the novels of Robert Hunter, Ben Lindsay, John Spargo, Jack London and Upton Sinclair; and all of them drew upon farmers, trappers, workers, seamen, the frustrated white-collar class and the fallen woman for their heroes and heroines.

THE CRUSADE FOR SOCIAL JUSTICE

Pioneers. In 1890 Jacob Riis had to write *How the Other Half Lives* to convince the American people that there were evils that had to be wiped out; in the 1890's the social conscience of America was still dormant.

The work of transforming the social conscience of America, begun during the Jacksonian Era, was resumed by a number of American ministers, priests, rabbis and social workers whose flocks and charges lived in the slums about 1900. These men and women were able to convince philanthropists to support surveys of existing conditions in order to accumulate data with which to urge remedial legislation. When collected, these data revealed that more than 8,000,000 women were at work mostly in abysmal sweatshops, that 1,700,000 children under sixteen were at work in cotton mills and on farms, that the death rate in slum areas was four times that in non-slum, and so on. They also collected facts about juvenile gangs, organized crime, prostitution and police corruption. When publicized, these facts shocked Americans to action.

Charity. Private philanthropies and agencies acted before the government intervened. Private clinics, orphanages, and childrens' aid societies were formed. Jane Addams organized Hull House in Chicago and Lillian Wald, the *Henry Street Settlement* in New York—educational and recreational settlements built in a slum area and devoted to providing children with remedial health measures and organized play. Visiting Nurses' Associations, YMCA's and the Boy Scout organizations were founded. Reforms, too, were begun in the treatment of criminals. Inspired by experiments at the State Reformatory at Elmira and by the penal philosophy of Thomas Mott Osborn first offenders were separated from habitual offenders; experiments were made with indeterminate sentences; early release under parole; special institutions for female offenders; fair intramural treatment; industrial training programs, special juvenile courts, etc.

Remedial Legislation. Under continuous pressure from the National Child Labor Committee, by 1914 every state had established a minimum labor-age limit, usually fourteen; many other states had prohibited children between the ages of fourteen and sixteen from working at night or at dangerous occupations. In 1914 the Committee sponsored the **Keating-Owen bill** which would have prohibited the shipment in interstate commerce of goods manufactured in whole or in part by children under sixteen. In 1916 this bill became national law, but was declared unconstitutional. Other legislation followed: Illinois pioneered with an eight hour a day law for women (1893); between 1909 and 1917 thirty-nine states had enacted hours-legislation. Inspired by British and Australian practices, agitation was begun for minimum wage legislation. Massachusetts framed such law and eight western states followed. By 1916 thirty states and territories had established systems of accident insurance or Workman's Compensation Laws which made an award for accident automatic instead of requiring, as in the past, a suit against the employer to establish his negligence.

The Supreme Court as a Barrier. The courts proved to be the formidable barrier to social reform. To lawyers and jurists who revered property rights as synonymous with liberty, legislation for social rights seemed anarchistic, an unwarranted extension of governmental power. Their attitude was clearly revealed in the case of **Lochner v. New York** decided in the Supreme Court in 1905. The question before the Court was the legality of a New York statute which limited the hours of bakers to ten a day and sixty a week. By a 5 to 4 decision the Court held that the statute limiting hours was a meddlesome interference with the rights of the individual worker to make a labor contract. In this case, Justice OLIVER WENDELL HOLMES JR. dissented. Holmes pointed out that the Fourteenth Amendment did not enact any particular economic theory and defended the right of the government to intervene and limit liberty if it was necessary to correct some current evil.

In the case of **Muller v. Oregon**, however, the Court did respond to the pleading of Attorney LOUIS D. BRANDEIS, who rested his case chiefly upon a sociological study of the economic and social consequences of overlong hours of work for women (the case involved an Oregon ten-hour law for women), or the "logic of facts" as he labeled it rather than legal precedent. When the Court accepted Brandeis' plea, it took its first stand in support of social legislation and **sociological jurisprudence.**

Municipal Reform. City government was the disgrace of democratic politics. Representative government had been replaced by machine government. An army of precinct captains and "ward-heelers" was ruled over by an all-powerful political boss. It was the political boss who decided upon the election of aldermen to office, distribution of patronage, contract awards and the like. Loyalty to the machine was fostered among the people by careful distribution of small favors and by giving slum-dwelling immigrants a sense of belonging to the community. Behind this benevolent "front" bribery and graft were rife in such matters as the protection of criminals, prostitutes or saloon-keepers, or in awarding franchises and contracts for railways, sewage systems, gas and electric lines, garbage disposal, etc. Corruption caused the rise of "civic leagues" or "reform movements" or "non-partisan groups" or "municipal voters' leagues." In this form, an aroused citizenry cleaned Chicago of its political machine subservient to the utilities magnate Yerkes; defeated Tammany Hall in New York City (1913) by electing a "reform" mayor, John Purroy Mitchell; imprisoned Mayor Ames of Minneapolis. A new municipal leadership arose in the persons of such men as "Golden Rule" Jones of Toledo and Tom Johnson of Cleveland who introduced such vital reforms as readjustment of tax burdens, reduction of tramcar rates, fostering of city-owned public utilities to correct franchise evils, expansion of city social services, and the like.

Stepped-up war on the machine was waged by introduction of the direct primary for nominating candidates, by securing increased powers of "home-rule" to break the hold of state politicians over the city, by experimenting with initiative, referendum, recall and new forms of city government. Under the system of **initiative** the citizens could, by petition, introduce bills into the municipal legislature; with the **referendum** they could compel the legislature to submit issues to the people for decision; and by **recall** they could force an incompetent official to run again for office before his allotted term was completed.

Frontal assaults were launched on the mayor-council type of check-and-balance city government. Galveston, Texas, in 1903 began to experiment with a **commission type** of municipal rule. The people elected five commissioners, experts in city management, to reconstruct the government when the old type proved helpless to cope with the problems that resulted from a hurricane and tidal wave. When it was discovered that the commission government failed to centralize responsibility sufficiently, cities tried a new plan, the **city-manager plan**, first adopted in Dayton, Ohio. This plan retained the commissioners but had them choose a city-manager who exercised over-all responsibility. By 1916 reform had succeeded in large measure. Though corruption persisted, it was driven underground. City administration had been professionalized and made efficient.

State Reform. Conditions in the state governments between 1900 and 1914 were no better. Political power was concentrated in two interlocked agencies, the state lobby and the state party committee. The lobby was maintained by the big business interests. The state committee operated through the party caucus in the legislature. By bribing a majority of the caucus through the state party committee, the lobby could in effect, write or kill legislation at will or have its own agents appointed to cabinet posts, state boards and judgeships. The wave of reform produced many state crusaders: Robert LaFollette in Wisconsin, Albert Cummins in Iowa, Albert J. Beveridge in Indiana, Charles Evans Hughes in New York, Woodrow Wilson in New Jersey, Hiram W. Johnson in California and William S. U'Ren of Oregon—to cite a few of the outstanding. These men had no easy task; they had to battle vested railroad and public utility interests; they had to push through reforms like direct primaries on a compulsory, state-wide basis; the short ballot; corrupt practices laws to limit and control campaign expenditures; direct election of senators; initiative and referendum (first in South Dakota, 1898) and recall (first in Oregon, 1908). Once the structure was overhauled, the more "progressive" states began to regulate public utilities and railroad to secure reasonable rates and prompt service for the public. By 1914, then, laissez-faire was an expiring attitude on municipal and state levels; and the federal government was not far behind.

THE SQUARE DEAL OF THEODORE ROOSEVELT

The "Square Deal." In his inaugural address THEODORE ROOSEVELT made a passionate plea for federal intervention to eliminate evils and abuses in the nation. Congress was dominated after 1902 by the Old Guard Republican dictator Uncle Joe Cannon who, as Speaker of the House and as chairman of the all-powerful Rules Committee, determined absolutely the composition of committees, the measures which would be permitted to come before the House, and those Representatives who might speak on the floor! The Senate was similarly dominated by Old Guardsmen with Hanna as their leader. These legislators viewed Roosevelt's program for government intervention with hostility. Roosevelt, therefore, took his case to the people in an extensive speaking tour. He called for a "square deal" for the harassed small businessman and the oppressed worker and farmer.

Congress might still have ignored him, but the

Anthracite Coal Strike of 1902 played into his hands. The United Mine Workers, led by John Mitchell, had struck for union recognition, higher wages and shorter hours. The mine operators refused to negotiate or arbitrate and the country was faced with a coal-less winter. Roosevelt offered to mediate. The miners accepted his offer, but the operators refused. Furious, Roosevelt threatened to call out the troops, take over the mines and arbitrate for the operators! The bewildered operators had to capitulate to this threat of intervention *on behalf of the miners*. The people of the country acclaimed this champion against the Old Guard; in 1904 despite bitter Old Guard opposition Roosevelt was overwhelmingly re-elected. Like the coal operators, the Congressional Old Guard had to capitulate. Therefore, when his two terms were completed, Roosevelt had fixed firmly and apparently unalterably the pattern of federal intervention upon the constitutional processes of the United States.

Regulation of Trusts. Roosevelt was not a "trust-buster." He felt that there were good trusts and bad trusts and that the Sherman Act was a useful weapon with which to *threaten* the bad trusts. Accordingly, he had a **Department of Labor and Commerce** created with a Bureau of Corporations in it that could investigate business practices and warn those engaged in harmful operations.

His fame as a "trust-buster" rested upon his prosecution in the **Northern Securities case.** James J. Hill and Edward Harriman were both battling for control of the Burlington Railroad. Hill, backed by Morgan, controlled the Great Northern and the Northern Pacific Railroads; Harriman dominated the Union Pacific; both wanted the Burlington as a Chicago link. By aggressive stock purchases (which pushed the price from $110 a share to $1,000!) Hill and Morgan won a majority of the stock and organized the Northern Securities Corporation as a stock holding company. Roosevelt began prosecution of the Hill-Morgan combine to restore competition between the two great northern transcontinental lines. In a 5 to 4 decision the Supreme Court in 1904 upheld the government and ordered Northern Securities dissolved. Having thus asserted the power of the federal government Roosevelt wielded the anti-trust club during the remainder of his administration; the Beef Trust was forbidden to engage in certain practices restraining competition and suits were begun against Standard Oil and American Tobacco. The "malefactors of great wealth" learned that Roosevelt's bark was worse than his bite; but they were forced to tread more cautiously.

Regulation of Railroads. Roosevelt led Congress to strengthen the Interstate Commerce Commission in its dealing with the railroads. The **Elkins Act** (1903) increased the Commission's power over illegal rebates by providing that both the grantor and recipient of rebates could be punished. In 1907, for example, Standard Oil was fined $29,000,000 for violation of this law. (A higher court set aside this fine.) This was followed by the **Hepburn Act** (1906) which enlarged the Commission from 5 to 7 members; extended its jurisdiction over express companies, pipe lines, ferries and terminals; gave it power to fix rates; forced the burden of a judicial contest on the carriers (that is, the Commission's rates went into effect immediately until a court reversed them); made it illegal for a railroad to carry goods which it had produced—business combinations of production and transportation were common, for example, steel production and Great Lakes shipping, oil production and pipe lines; set up a uniform system of accounting as an aid to determining uniform rates; and forbade the issuance of free passes to any but railroad employees.

Regulation of Resources. The first warnings that America's resources were being depleted by reckless railroad, lumber and cattle magnates were sounded during Cleveland's first administration by Secretary of the Interior Lamar. Not only were private owners in illegal possession of more than 80,000,000 acres of public domain, but no effort was being made to protect existing resources against natural destruction or to replant what was being cut down. Public conscience was unaffected by Lamar's revelations.

In 1891 came a first faint beginning in conservation when a **Forest Reserve Act** was passed; this was followed in 1894 by the **Carey Act** under which the government aided private contractors who constructed irrigation projects to reclaim bad land. However, not until Roosevelt had dramatized the destruction of natural resources and had blasted the "predatory" private interests was Congress moved to enact meaningful conservation legislation.

By the end of his administration Roosevelt had effected a revolution in public protection of natural resources. In the **Newlands Act** of 1902 the government used funds from the sale of public lands to reclaim large amounts of "bad" lands by dam construction and irrigation. Farmers who received water from these projects paid for it, and thus a revolving fund was created for new projects. By 1907, 28 projects were under way in 14 states. To protect the forests, the Forest Reserve Act of 1891 was revived and 148,000,000 acres of timber land was set aside; this land was turned into national parks and placed under the supervision of Gifford Pinchot who, in turn, founded the **Federal Forest Service**. Roosevelt devoted the annual message of 1907 to the problem of conservation and thus brought it to national attention. He then called a Conservation Conference in 1908 that was attended by state governors, legislators, scientific experts and prominent citizens. This conference laid down some basic principles of conservation: extension of forest fighting forces; protection of navigable waterways; control over timber-cutting; retention of government rights to coal, oil and natural gas. Pinchot became the head of the **National Conservation Commission**. While this commission soon expired for lack of Congressional financial support, its work was carried on when, by 1909, forty-one state conservation commissions were created. Finally, an **Inland Waterways Commission** was to determine best use of the nation's waterways for transportation, irrigation and water power. Historians are virtually unanimous that these were Roosevelt's greatest achievements.

Regulation of Foods and Drugs. "Muckrakers" Mark Sullivan and Samuel Hopkins Adams made a careful analysis of the manufacture of patent medicines and showed that in hundreds of instances the public was being either defrauded or harmed. They were being defrauded in that they were being sold "panaceas" which contained useless ingredients; harmed, in that medicines contained unadvertised alcohol, opium, corrosives, etc. When Dr. Wiley, chief chemist of the Department of Agriculture, confirmed these revelations, Roosevelt pressured Congress to pass a **Pure Food and Drug law** (1906) which forbade the use of certain narcotics in patent medicines; restricted the use of preservatives and adulterants in foods; and forced manufacturers to list all ingredients on labels. (Since there were no regulations covering false advertising, the size of print on the label, the intelligibility of the language used, the act was easily evaded.)

Meat manufacturers had already been denounced for "embalmed beef" sold to the armed forces during the Spanish-American War. When, in 1906, Upton Sinclair's *The Jungle* appeared, Roosevelt had an official survey made of the meat-packing industry, a survey which revealed that Mr. Sinclair had been conservative in his revelations. Congress responded with passage of the **Meat Inspection Act** of 1906 which provided that all meat in interstate commerce had to meet government specifications and had to be examined and approved by federal inspectors. The meat packers had no choice but to clean up their establishments.

The Administration of William Howard Taft. His progressive work done, Theodore Roosevelt named WILLIAM HOWARD TAFT as his successor and went off to Africa to hunt lions. Taft won the election of 1904 handily against William Jennings Bryan, a third-time contender. There was very little of the militant progressive about Taft, but the achievements of his one term added considerably to the accretion of progressive legislation and governmental action.

Trusts. A number of Roosevelt's policies were continued. The **Mann-Elkins Act** of 1910 corrected some of the faults of the Hepburn Act; ICC jurisdiction was extended to telephone and telegraph lines, no automatic rate increases were permitted without ICC consent and a special court was created to expedite appeals from ICC decisions. Taft's anti-trust division instituted twice as many suits as had Roosevelt's. Important victories were won over Standard Oil and American Tobacco for in these cases the Court ruled that the Sherman Law made it illegal for a monopoly to exist in manufacture of goods as well as in interstate transport of goods. The Court also limited prosecution of "restraint of trade" to unreasonable restraint, the so-called "rule of reason." (This ruling, often condemned, in reality made the Sherman Law workable. Many legal business contracts have the effect of restraining trade without primarily intending to; therefore, the Court held only such contracts illegal where the primary intent was to restrain trade and effect a monopoly.) In the field of conservation Taft had important oil lands removed from sale and, to guard over other mineral resources, the **Bureau of Mines** was created.

Reforms. Taft not only continued Roosevelt policies, but added his own. He divided the Department of Commerce and Labor into two for more efficient administration; signed into law an act limiting campaign expenditures and forcing them to be publicized; encouraged the addition of the **16th Amendment** to the Constitution legalizing the income tax; created a postal savings bank and parcel post system; extended the eight-hour day to workers on government contracts. Here was evidence indeed of the extent to which federal intervention had become accepted. Clearly, Taft was in the progressive tradition.

Criticism. Many historians, however, deem otherwise and argue persuasively that Taft continued support of the high protective Payne-Aldrich Tariff (1909) which most progressives—now calling themselves "insurgents"—had opposed. When Pinchot accused Richard A. Ballinger of the Department of the Interior of leasing public waterpower sites and coal lands to private syndicates like the Guggenheim-Morgan combine, Taft removed Pinchot. The evidence never sustained Pinchot's charge, but Taft, nonetheless, was regarded with hostility by the conservationists.

A full-fledged revolution, led by George W. Norris begun in 1910, to oust Uncle Joe Cannon from his privileges as Speaker, met with Taft's silence and this was considered by the progressives as siding with Cannon. The revolution succeeded for the Speaker was stripped of his power to appoint the standing committees and to serve on the rules committee. Now the opprobrious title of "Standpatter" was applied by the insurgents to Taft. Then the farmers deserted him when he worked out a reciprocity treaty with Canada under which Canada lowered her tariff on American manufactured goods and the United States lowered hers on Canadian wheat. (Taft lost additional stature when the Canadian Parliament rejected this treaty after the United States Senate approved it.)

Campaign of 1912. The upshot of Taft's inconsistencies was a serious split in Republican ranks during the election of 1912. The "Standpatters" took over the Republican Convention and nominated Taft. The Insurgents, led by ROBERT M. LAFOLLETTE, left their ranks and regrouped as the **Progressive Party** with the Bull Moose as their symbol and Theodore Roosevelt as their standard bearer. Incorporating his doctrine of government intervention under the slogan **"The New Nationalism,"** Roosevelt marched to battle on two fronts, against the Old Guard Republicans and the professional governor of New Jersey, Woodrow Wilson, the Democratic choice.

The "Great Commoner" William Jennings Bryan himself had had Wilson nominated at the Democratic Convention. To meet Roosevelt's "New Nationalism" Wilson put forward his own "New Freedom." Although he received only 40% of the popular vote, Wilson won overwhelmingly in the electoral college. The combined Republican vote was in a clear majority; but so was the combined progressive vote. Wilson for the progressive Democrats, Roosevelt for the insurgent Republicans and Debs for the Socialists polled 75% of the vote. The election of 1912 was a requiem for laissez faire.

WOODROW WILSON AND THE NEW FREEDOM

Politics and Morality. The progressive movement reached its first climax during the first administration of WOODROW WILSON. Wilson saw politics as a war of moral forces in which righteousness was on the side of reform. Unrighteousness, he felt, stemmed from extremes of plutocracy and mobocracy. The government must steer a middle course between big business and popular excess, either of which could destroy free, competitive enterprise. The "New Freedom" was to be for the "man who is on the make rather than the man who is already made" and since those who are on the make are in the majority, the machinery of government had to be put in their hands. With government in the hands of the people (that is, in Wilson's hands) each institution in America, whether derived from capital or labor, was to be called to the bar of judgment to state "by what principle of national advantage, as contrasted with selfish privilege" it drew upon the resources of the government. In this spirit, the "money trust" was called to the bar of judgment, and found guilty.

Regulation of the "Money Trust." In 1907 the country was economically sound, yet a "Banker's Panic" occurred which brought about the usual collapse of business followed by severe unemployment. One of the causes was overspeculation by private banks in stocks and bonds; but another flowed from a basic flaw in the National Banking Act of 1863. This law provided that an expansion of currency could take place only by purchase of government bonds. In good times, the government paid off its debts, hence it sold no bonds. But it was precisely in good times that more currency was needed. Therefore, as America entered into a prosperous period, it had insufficient currency to sustain that prosperity. (The situation reversed itself in bad times; the currency was "inversely elastic," that is, too little in good times and too much in bad times.)

Passage in 1908 of the **Aldrich-Vreeland Act** permitted national banks to make emergency issues of currency in good times. This was patchwork; somehow or other the currency had to be made directly elastic so that it would expand with prosperity and contract with recession. This evil of inverse elasticity was only one of seventeen defects in the banking structure uncovered by a Congressional investigation in 1912. More sensational, however, was the revelation by the **Pujo Committee** of 1911 of the control of banking by a few financiers and the control, through interlocking directorates, of almost all big business by the same few financiers. These investigations produced major and permanent legislation to correct these tendencies toward plutocracy.

The Federal Reserve System. Banking was placed under federal regulation and forced to assume national responsibility in the **Federal Reserve Act** of 1913 drafted by Senator CARTER GLASS. This act made currency elastic, centralized bank deposits so that stronger banks could help the weaker, and compelled private bankers to share their control over money with the government. To effect these purposes, the country was divided into twelve districts in each of which was a central bank. National banks in each district had to deposit with the Federal Reserve Bank a percentage of their cash reserves; thus an immense pool of money was created for emergencies. Banks in trouble could apply to the Federal Reserve Bank for help. To secure an elastic currency, the Federal Reserve Bank was permitted to issue Federal Reserve Notes backed up by gold and commercial paper (promissory notes, drafts, etc.) When a business needed cash, the private banks could take commercial paper to the Federal Reserve Bank, pay a rediscount rate, and get Federal Reserve Notes (cash). If private banks had too much cash, the process was reversed. To prevent overspeculation with depositors' money by banks the Act created required ratios between loans and cash. Finally, to manage and supervise this system, a Federal Reserve Board of Governors was established.

Regulation of Tariffs. Wilson called a special session on April 8, 1913 to consider important legislation. The importance was underscored by the personal appearance of the President before Congress (the last President to have appeared before Congress was Thomas Jefferson). Wilson asked Congress to reduce American tariffs so that American industry might be placed on a truly competitive position with Europe. Congress responded with the **Underwood Tariff.** Products manufactured abroad which competed with those produced by the "trusts" (iron, steel, etc.) were permitted free entry into the United States or charged nominal sums. The over-all average of duties was lowered from the Payne-Aldrich rates of 40% to about 25%. And, to make up for the loss of revenue, new income tax schedules were introduced with progressively higher rates on higher incomes. In this legislation, Democratic bias against big business was clear.

Regulation of the Trusts. Wilson felt that the failure of the Sherman Act was its failure to define "combination" and "restraint of trade." He sought a law which would contain precise definitions of these concepts and thus make it easier to prosecute unlawful combines. The **Clayton Anti-Trust Act (1914)** undertook this task: it forbade stock holding where the intent was to lessen competition; it for-

bade interlocking directorates in competing concerns with assets exceeding $1,000,000 or banks with assets exceeding $5,000,000; it outlawed numerous practices which made for unfair competition including price discrimination, tie-in agreements and the like; it made officers of corporations liable for illegal acts committed by corporations; it spelled out methods for securing relief from malpractices; and it exempted labor unions and farm associations from anti-trust prosecutions.

The Federal Trade Commission Act of 1914. In the **Federal Trade Commission** a watchdog for anti-trust violations was created. The FTC was given the responsibility of investigating complaints about unfair practices or to institute its own investigation wherever monopoly was suspected. If it found monopolistic practices, it could issue "cease and desist" orders to the offender and then, if necessary, secure judicial injunction to enforce its orders.

Regulating Labor Practices. Labor was assisted at Wilson's "bar of justice." Wilson felt that unions were being victimized by the courts that had been too willing to jail prominent labor leaders for violating arbitrary injunctions against striking. Debs had gone to jail in 1894; now in 1911 Gompers received a jail sentence (later set aside) for advocating in print the boycott of a company for unfair labor practices, an advocacy that encouraged violation of a judicial injunction.

But far more menacing for organized labor than these occasional jailings was the decision of the Court in the **Danbury Hatters' Case.** The Union, United Hatters of America, was hauled into court during a strike for being a combination in restraint of trade, hence a violator of the Sherman Anti-Trust Law. The union was found guilty and was wrecked by the imposition by the court of a $235,000 fine. Thus an act patently intended to curb employer monopolistic practices, and ineffective against the employers, was made deadly effective against labor. The New Freedom moved to correct this injustice.

In the Clayton Act—hailed as Labor's Magna Carta—unions were exempted from the provisions of the Sherman Anti-Trust Law; the use of injunctions in labor disputes was restricted, and—most important—strikes, boycotts and peaceful picketing were legalized. Other legislation followed: the **LaFollette Seaman's Act** of 1915 established a minimum wage and improved working conditions for seamen sailing under American registry; the **Keating-Owen Act** of 1915 forbade the shipment in interstate commerce of goods made by child-labor. (This was declared unconstitutional in **Hammer v.**

Dagenhart 1918.) **The Adamson Act** of 1916 established an eight-hour day for workers in interstate transport.

Regulating the Farm. What farmers, in this period, needed most was long-term loans at low rates of interest. This was difficult to secure from private banks. In 1916, therefore, a **Federal Farm Loan Act** was passed which created **Federal Loan Banks** empowered to make long-term loans on mortgages at reasonable rates to farm cooperatives. Farmers rapidly organized such cooperatives to take advantage of the law.

CHAPTER XVI

AMERICAN EXPANSION OVERSEAS

Challenge to Isolation. By 1898 America had turned from isolation to overseas expansionism. What brought about this transformation?

Civil War Legacies. As a result of the Civil War a number of issues arose that forced America to concern itself with the activities of foreign powers. Secretary of State Seward had employed vigorous means to force Napoleon III to abandon his Mexico conquest and Maximilian: Napoleon acceded in 1867. That done, the United States had to deal with the damages done by the British-built Confederate cruiser, the "Alabama." Convinced that England had violated its own neutrality laws, the United States sought $2,200,000,000 in payment of direct and indirect damages or, as Senator Sumner preferred, the cession of Canada to the United States. In 1871 both countries signed the **Treaty of Washington** which provided for arbitration of the Alabama claims and then settled additional matters of the Newfoundland fisheries and a Vancouver Sound boundary. In the case of the "Alabama," an arbitration tribunal met in Geneva, heard both sides, and awarded the United States $15,000,000 in direct damages. In 1867 Alaska was purchased from Russia.

Hawaii. Following the Civil War, American foreign trade and investments expanded overseas. Some of America's surplus capital went into Hawaiian sugar and pineapple plantations. (New England missionaries had paved the way for American interests in Hawaii as early as 1819.) Since the 1840's Americans had considered Hawaii as within the Western Hemisphere and therefore subject to the restrictions of the Monroe Doctrine, that is, there was to be no further colonization there by European powers. To ensure this doubly, a **Reciprocity Treaty** was signed with Hawaii which permitted Hawaiian sugar to enter the United States duty-free; it also forbade Hawaii to make a similar arrangement with any other power or to grant or lease to another power a port, harbor, territory or special privilege.

The American Hawaiian sugarmen were quite content with their economic domination until the McKinley Tariff of 1890 removed sugar from the free list; now they felt the solution lay in annexation of Hawaii by the United States.

When they could not convince the ruling monarch, Queen Liliuokalani, of the desirability of annexation; when, moreover, she acted to strip them of the political power they now possessed—then they organized a native "revolution" with the unofficial aid of the United States Navy. In turn, President Cleveland learned of the Navy's role in the revolt and withdrew a treaty of annexation he had drawn up. When McKinley became President the sugarmen found that he did not have Cleveland's scruples. The treaty was resubmitted by McKinley and the Senate approved it. These were the reasons given for annexation: Hawaii was a strategic necessity for the American Navy; America would have a tremendous outlet for their surplus capital; the American people had a moral obligation to the Hawaiians to protect and nurture them; America must fulfill its "manifest destiny" overseas; and, anyway, if America did not annex the islands, some other country would. On July 7, 1898 Hawaii was joined to the United States by a joint resolution of Congress—the two-thirds vote being unattainable.

Samoa. Actually, arguments for American imperialism had made their appearance somewhat earlier. The American Navy, such as it was in the 1870's, regarded the harbor of Pago Pago on the Samoan Island of Tutuila as an ideal South Pacific naval base. In 1878 "Pango Pango" was acquired as such by formal treaty. Securing a remote naval base proved incompatible with isolationism when the United States was challenged for possession of Samoa by both England and Germany. In 1889 a three-cornered war was shaping up among the naval squadrons of the three powers when a hurricane wrecked all the ships. This had a sobering effect and the three would-be belligerents made a tripartite division of the islands. What now of "no permanent, entangling alliances?"

Latin America. With the Pan-American Conference of 1889, Secretary of State Blaine sought to correct an unfavorable balance of trade. The bulk of Latin American exports were to the United States and 87% of these entered duty free; the bulk of Latin American imports were from European countries. This was desirable while the United States had no exportable surplus. Now that she did have such a surplus, she insisted that this imbalance be adjusted by a policy of reciprocity; but the Latin Americans were unsympathetic to this demand and the conference failed.

Latin Americans had taken note, at this conference, of a new attitude emanating from the United States State Department, an attitude bordering on the aggressive. They were confirmed in their feelings as a result of an unpleasant incident with Chile which occurred in 1891. Two American sailors were killed in a barroom brawl in Valparaiso—an event that normally would have been ignored. President Harrison, however, chose to blow it up into an international incident and the two countries came close to war. War was averted when a new government was elected in Chile. But Latin Americans noted with great alarm what seemed a "new look" in American foreign policy.

Conflict with England. If the Chilean episode disturbed Latin America, that concerning the Anglo-Venezuelan boundary dispute (1895) doubled its anxiety. Gold had been discovered in a disputed border region between Venezuela and British Guiana. Each party to the dispute intensified its land claim. Venezuela then appealed to the United States to arbitrate the matter; but England refused to arbitrate. President Cleveland and Secretary of State Olney then composed a tough note to England which charged that England was violating the Monroe Doctrine and insisted that England arbitrate the disputed area. In the note, furthermore, the United States stated that her position in this matter was not that of an invited *neutral* third party; American interest stemmed from the "fact," said Cleveland-Olney, that the United States "is practically sovereign on this continent and its fiat is law upon the subjects to which it confines its interposition."

Prime Minister Salisbury of England was startled but unmoved; Latin America was outraged. Here was an extension of the Monroe Doctrine that it had not foreseen. When Salisbury dismissed Olney's note, Cleveland, in undiplomatically blunt language asked Congress to ignore the British rejection and to set up a *compulsory* arbitration commission; the United States, he said, was prepared to take the consequences—the Navy was in readiness. War loomed. But England backed down because trouble was brewing with the Boers in South Africa and with Germany. American businessmen and churchmen helped to mollify Cleveland. The commission went to work in 1899 and in its findings awarded most of the disputed area to England!

THE FORCES UNDERLYING AMERICAN EXPANSIONISM

America obviously, was by 1898 involved in a split-policy: officially isolationist, unofficially involved in economic expansion, political assertion and "entangling" alliance. What had brought about this condition?

Rise of Imperial-Mindedness. Imperialism is the conscious creation of an empire, a deliberate expansion of a country's domain and dominion. Factors which produce such territorial aggrandizement are many. A rapidly growing domestic industry may require cheap sources of raw materials from foreign lands, especially when they are unavailable at home. That this factor was already operating in the American economy is attested to by the growth of American imports from $363,000,000 in 1860 to $850,000,000 in 1900. A nation may produce an exportable surplus which, though not large when compared with its domestic market, may often be the margin between profit and "break-even." Thus, United States exports rose from $333,000,000 in 1860 to $1,400,000,000 in 1900.

Accumulated investment capital may be searching for more profitable areas. American surplus investment capital mounted from almost nothing in 1860 to $500,000,000 in 1900. Finally, a sudden growth in naval strength may create the need for supply bases in the major seas and oceans; from 1883 to 1900 the United States navy rose to third position among those of the world's great powers.

THE SPANISH-AMERICAN WAR

Cuba. In 1898 Spain owned Cuba. To many Americans and most Cubans this seemed outlandish. Spain's ownership was of profit neither to herself nor to the Cubans. Furthermore all of the 16th and 17th century conquerors had been driven from the western hemisphere but Spain. (England's Canada had become virtually independent. There were, of course, British Honduras and British, French and Dutch Guianas; but Americans felt that such small ownership did not materially alter the argument.) Cuba looked more to the United States than Spain anyway: American investments were over $50,000,000 there by 1898 and Cuban trade with the United States was at least $100,000,000 annually. Yet Spain owned Cuba and was in a position to choke off this economic investment at will.

Cubans, for their part, were in an almost constant state of revolt against the Spanish authority, an authority guilty of corruption and economic exploitation. It was inevitable that a sympathetic bond should have been forged between the Americans and the Cubans, as evidenced by the establishment of a revolutionary Cuban "junta" on American shores, by popular American support for filibustering expeditions to overthrow Spanish rule, and by Congressional efforts to recognize the rebels as belligerents. When a filibustering vessel, the "Virginius," was seized in 1878 and eight Americans were executed as participants, the United States and Spain almost went to war. Spain apologized and paid indemnities.

In 1894 the United States decided that Spain did not deserve a privileged position in Cuba's economy since all Cuba's exports went to the United States, but all her imports were forced to come from Spain. In the Wilson-Gorman Tariff, Cuban sugar was removed from the free list and made to pay a 40% impost. Since Cuba's economy was based on this one crop, economic ruin followed. Open warfare ensued. The Spanish general, Valeriano Weyler, was sent over to crush the rebellion. As part of his campaign he built concentration camps into which the rebels were driven. In one province 50,000 of the incarcerated died.

The American "jingo" press reported one atrocity story after another, *invented* one atrocity after another, drew lurid cartoons, smuggled victims out of Cuba and took them on exhibition tour around the country. President McKinley, however, preferred to mediate through normal diplomatic channels.

The DeLome Letter. On the ninth of February, 1898 Hearst printed the "DeLome" letter which was stolen from a Havana post office. DeLome, Spanish minister to Washington, wrote in this letter to his Government an appraisal of McKinley as "weak and a bidder for the admiration of the crowd, besides being a common politician who tries to leave a door open behind himself while keeping on good terms with the jingoes of his party." This was, of course, built up into a gross, contemptuous insult to the national honor of the United States and the war fever rose.

"Remember the Maine." On the fifteenth of February, 1898, the battleship "Maine" was sunk by an internal explosion. 260 Americans died. Theodore Roosevelt expressed the popular view that the "Maine was sunk by an act of dirty treachery on the part of the Spaniards." It did not matter that investigation (to this day) could not place the guilt for the explosion. The case was tried in the press headlines. The *Journal's* circulation rose during this period from 416,885 to 1,025,624. War fever rose even higher.

The Small Voice of Peace. American business leaders were opposed to war. The financial press waged an anti-war crusade in its editorials; the stock market slumped with every war scare. It seemed to the business community that, having finally emerged from the depression of 1893, prosperity should not be jeopardized over the pittance represented in Cuban investments. President McKinley did not want war. As a matter of fact, to avoid war he had sent the Queen of Spain an ultimatum demanding a settlement with the Cuban rebels *and she had acceded.*

Yet, with the Queen's acceptance of American demands in his desk drawer, McKinley sent to the Congress a message asking for the right to use military and naval forces to end the Cuban hostilities and to establish a stable government there. Why? The answer seems to be that some powerful elements wanted war and the Republican Party could not, if it sought to be re-elected, afford to ignore the demand. On April 20, 1898 Congress declared war. Simultaneously, it adopted the **Teller Resolution** which renounced any American claim to the territory of Cuba and promised to turn the island over to the Cubans as soon as Spain was defeated.

The War Itself. Active operations did not begin until May; by August 12th, the war was over. The American all-steel navy was organized into an Atlantic Fleet under Admiral Sampson, a Flying Squadron under Commodore Schley, an Asiatic Squadron under Commodore Dewey and more than 100 auxiliary craft were ready for battle. But the 200,000 army volunteers were not; nor was the War Department which, under unaccustomed pressure, broke down. The result was that more casualties resulted from poor food, improper clothing, inadequate medical equipment and deficient armament than from battle casualties.

Commodore DEWEY secured victory in the Pacific by destroying the Spanish fleet in Manila Bay and then conquering the Philippines when Army reinforcements arrived. In this conquest, Americans made an effective alliance with Filipino guerrillas led by Emilio Aguinaldo.

In the Atlantic, Spanish Admiral Cervera took

shelter in Cuban waters under protection of powerful shore batteries. Sampson and Schley therefore could do no more than hold the Spanish fleet captive by instituting a blockade. With the Spanish navy pinned, the American army under Generals Shafter, Kent and Wheeler (and Colonel Roosevelt's Rough Riders) assaulted and captured Cuba; General Miles occupied the flank at Puerto Rico. His protective covering of the shore batteries lost, Admiral Cervera had no choice but to capitulate or make an effort to escape from the blockade. He tried the latter and was destroyed utterly.

War Against Disease. The greatest battle in the war was waged after the war was over. The enemy was malaria or yellow fever. The hero of that battle was Dr. WALTER REED. Following up a brilliant deduction of the Cuban Dr. CARLOS FINLEY, Reed proved that yellow fever was transmitted by the mosquito. The attack on malaria was therefore turned to eliminating mosquito-breeding swamps. Reed's discovery opened vast areas of tropical lands to human exploitation and habitation.

The Treaty of Paris 1898. In the peace treaty signed at Paris, Spain was forced to relinquish all claim to Cuba; to cede to the United States the islands of Puerto Rico and Guam; and to turn over to the United States the Philippine Islands for which the United States agreed to pay $20,000,000. Pending the establishment of a Cuban government and independent state, the United States was to occupy Cuba. The appearance in the treaty of the cession of the Far Eastern Philippines was a considerable shock to many Americans and to the Filipinos. In fact, Emilio Aguinaldo turned his guerrillas on the American occupation forces and began a bitter three-year war for independence that required the use of 70,000 American troops before the island was "pacified." A war of liberation then, had turned into a war of conquest.

Many anti-imperialist voices cried out; among them were the voices of Cleveland, Bryan, Schurz, Mark Twain, William Dean Howells and William James. They insisted that conquest of the Philippines would make a mockery of democracy and establish America as a nation of immoral hypocrites. McKinley denied this and the campaign of 1900 was waged on the issue of imperialism, the "paramount issue" as Bryan, the Democratic candidate would have had it. McKinley won. The American people had clearly endorsed imperialism.

The Panama Canal. The Spanish-American war was clear evidence of the need for an Isthmian canal. The U.S.S. Oregon was in Puget Sound when the war broke and it was ordered to Cuban waters. The trip was 14,000 miles around Cape Horn to the battle area. This was unthinkable from the point of view of an adequate defense. Either an Isthmian Canal or a two ocean navy would have to be built; the Canal was the cheaper of the two. But there were three major obstacles to building a canal at the Isthmus: England, Colombia and Nature.

England. In 1850 the United States had placed a barrier in the way of England's construction of a canal by getting her to sign the Clayton-Bulwer Treaty which provided that any canal across Central America should be jointly built and left unfortified. In 1898 this treaty became a millstone around America's neck. To win a friend in her time of trouble (the Boer War, etc.), England informed the United States that the Clayton-Bulwer Treaty might be re-negotiated. Thereupon Secretary of State Hay and Ambassador Sir Julian Pauncefote negotiated a new treaty. The **Hay-Pauncefote Treaty** of 1901 provided that the United States could build, own and fortify a canal; and that the use of the canal was to be accorded to all nations on equal terms.

Colombia. FERDINAND DE LESSEPS, renowned builder of the Suez Canal, had decided in the 1880's to undertake building a canal at Panama. He had organized a French company, secured a franchise from Colombia, who owned the Isthmus, and had begun building. His effort proved an utter fiasco; millions of francs and thousands of lives were lost. A new company, formed in 1890, had but one hope —that the United States would buy up the franchise. After the Spanish-American War the French asking price was $109 million; it was indignantly rejected by the Congressional Walker Commission which had been set up to investigate possible routes; the Commission recommended a Nicaraguan route instead. A most unusual public relations man, Philippe Buneau-Varilla of Panama, now entered the negotiations; his assignment was to sell the Panama project to Congress. He won Roosevelt support and then had the asking price lowered to $40 million. Effective lobbying did the rest. The **Spooner Bill,** passed by Congress, authorized the Panama route if the franchise could be bought and if authority to build were secured from Columbia.

It was now 1903 and the French contract was due to expire in 1904; Buneau-Varilla realized—as did Theodore Roosevelt—that Colombia had to act immediately. Thereupon Hay negotiated a treaty with a Colombian diplomat, Tomas Herran, which provided for a six-mile wide zone through the Isthmus for $10 million and an annual rental of $250,000. This was submitted to the Colombian Senate for ratification; it was rejected by that body. The Colombian Senate preferred to wait until 1904 when the French contract had expired and thus to get for Colombia the extra $40 million. Roosevelt was furious and Buneau-Varilla panic-stricken. Therefore Roosevelt did not balk when Buneau-Varilla suggested that the Panamanians were ripe for revolution from the tyrannical rule of Colombia.

Buneau-Varilla then sat down and composed a declaration of independence, a constitution and a flag for the as yet unborn Panama Republic. Meanwhile Roosevelt dispatched the U.S.S. Nashville to Panama to guard freedom of transit across the Isthmus, should any barrier happen to be interposed; the United States' right to do this was based on a treaty with Colombia signed in 1846. The revolution took place as scheduled on November 3, 1903. Colombian troops were prevented by the American navy from making a landing on the Isthmus to suppress the rebellion. On November 4th the new republic was proclaimed. On November 6th the United States recognized the independence of Panama and a week later Buneau-Varilla was accepted as the Panamanian envoy to the United States. On November 18th the **Hay-Buneau-Varilla Treaty** was signed which allotted the United States a ten-mile zone for $10 million and an annual rental of $250,000. The French Company got its $40 million.

Roosevelt denied any part in preparing, inciting, or encouraging the Panama Revolution. Some years later, however, when he had left office, he said, "I took the Canal Zone and let Congress debate." (In 1921 the United States paid Colombia $21 million for damage to her rights and interests in the canal; some historians see in this move the pangs of a bad conscience.)

Nature. The formidable obstacle represented by Nature is evidenced in some construction figures. The Canal took seven years to build (1907-1914); the total cost was $336.6 million; 240 million cubic yards of earth was removed; a set of three locks on the Atlantic side (the Gatun locks) had to be constructed to achieve an elevation of 85 feet above-sea-level; another set of three were required on the Pacific side. This colossal undertaking was planned and executed by Colonel GEORGE WASHINGTON GOETHALS and his Army engineers and remains their enduring monument. It would not have been possible to build the Canal, as French experience had shown, without the elimination of malaria. Dr. WILLIAM GORGAS accomplished this feat and virtually eradicated yellow fever in that area.

Canal Problems. Construction of a canal and defense of it were related problems. The first requirement was to remove all foreign economic and political influence, direct and indirect from the Caribbean area. This led to an aggressive Caribbean policy. The second requirement was to fortify the approaches to the Canal. For this reason the United States purchased the **Virgin Islands** from Denmark in 1917 for $25 million. A third requirement was to ensure that alternative routes like the proposed sea-level canal through Nicaragua would be built by no one but the United States. For this purpose, the **Bryan-Chamorro Treaty** of 1916 was forced from Nicaragua. It provided that Nicaragua was to cede to the United States the right of way for a canal, a lease on the Corn Island in the Atlantic Ocean and a naval base in the Gulf of Fonesca. In exchange for these privileges the United States paid Nicaragua $8 million. Finally, to establish complete sovereignty over the Canal, Congress in 1914 drew up the **Panama Canal Tolls Act** which exempted American coastwise traffic from the payment of tolls—a clear violation of the equality provision of the Hay-Pauncefote Treaty. Only the most strenuous efforts of President Wilson prevented its passage.

Cuba and the Platt Amendment. It has been seen that American investments in and trade with Cuba grew enormously during the period that Cuba was under Spain's rule, and that in the Teller Resolution the United States promised Cuba freedom when she was "ready" for it. Under General Leonard Wood, American occupation forces did a thorough job in rehabilitating that war-torn area and in restoring normal conditions. He overhauled its administrative machinery and its financial system; constructed roads, bridges, schools and hospitals; provided the means to clear out yellow fever. In spite of these clear benefits of the occupation, Cubans were eager for their freedom.

In 1901 the Cubans were asked to draw up a constitution as a pre-condition of freedom; they did. No mention was made in their constitution of future relations with the United States; if Cuba was a free country, there was no need to do so. Congress, however, took offense and as an amending rider to an Army appropriations bill it included a resolution submitted by Senator Platt of New York defining United States-Cuban relationships. (Later, the Cubans were forced to add the "Platt Amendment" to their constitution.) The **Platt Amendment** stipulated that

Cuba was to make no treaty with a foreign power which might impair her independence; nor was she to permit any foreign power to alienate any of her territory. Cuba was not to borrow beyond its income.

The United States was to be permitted to intervene with armed forces to preserve Cuba's independence, to protect life, liberty and property, and to enforce the provisions of the Treaty of Paris.

The United States could lease or buy naval and coaling stations.

Secretary of State Elihu Root assured Cuba in 1901 that this was but a normal extension of the Monroe Doctrine. But it should be obvious that the Platt Amendment represented a severe restriction upon Cuba's freedom, particularly the third item. Under this provision, the American marines were sent into Cuba in 1906 to supervise orderly elections; they remained until 1909. In 1912 the marines landed again to put down race riots; again in 1917 to suppress election disorders. Cuba was virtually under permanent American occupation.

This occupation was exceptionally profitable for American business interests in Cuba. Capital investments rose from $50 million in 1898 to $1 billion in 1924. While the bulk of American investment was in sugar plantations, it had also penetrated into railroads, tobacco, public utilities, government bonds, mines, mills, etc. In 1924, 83% of all Cuba's exports went to the United States and 75% of all her imports came from there. But the source of Cuban hostility to the United States did not lie in these capital and commercial investments but in the limitation to her freedom. (Since the abrogation of the Platt Amendment in 1934, there has been little change in America's dominant position in the Cuban economy; but Cuba is now a free nation, free to withdraw, tax, limit and share in this wealth according to laws of her own making.)

Stretching the Monroe Doctrine. Economic expansion was not the only force in this period disrupting America's isolationist policy. Ownership of the Panama Canal forced America to become concerned with the stability of the Caribbean area, with keeping war, revolution and foreign intervention out of the western hemisphere. Latin American countries did not share this concern and engaged in practices which openly invited European intervention. Most Latin American economies were based on a single crop which had to be sold abroad. All other economic ventures in industrialization had to be financed through the sale of government bonds abroad. Thus, Latin American countries were continuously in debt to foreign financiers; and when they did not pay their debts—as often enough they did not—foreign countries were privileged to collect them by force, a fact well-recognized in international law until the adoption at the Hague Conference of 1907 of the **Drago Doctrine** which provided that default of debt was not a sufficient reason for intervention.

Why were Latin American governments so frequently unable to pay off their obligations? Property in Latin America was badly maldistributed; ownership was concentrated in the hands of a very tiny minority of native aristocrats and of foreign investors. Government was brutal and wasteful. From among the aristocracy came the *caudillo,* the Latin American dictator whose support rested upon army bayonets. These caudillos treated their countries as private possessions, disposed of its wealth irresponsibly, and punished native protest with incredible brutality. The connection between them and foreign investors was close; the latter could easily organize a "revolution" and place into power some caudillo who would then shut his eyes to the most ruthless exploitation if handsomely bribed to do so. Exploited wealth did not remain in the Latin American country from which it was extracted but was removed to the foreign banks of the foreign investors. The result was pervasive and continuous bankruptcy.

Out of this miserable state of affairs came war, revolution and foreign intervention. Thus, in 1902 the Venezuelan caudillo, Gastro, refused to meet his obligations to Great Britain, Germany and Italy. These three powers, ignoring the Monroe Doctrine, sent warships into the Caribbean, blockaded the Venezuelan coast and fired on some fishing villages. Theodore Roosevelt had at first consented to the collection; but so strong was the American reaction against the bombardment of the fishing villages that he was forced to intervene and secure arbitration of the dispute.

American Intervention. Obviously there was neither liberty, nor peace, nor security in this part of the world where American economic and political stakes were so great. When he abandoned the policy of non-intervention, so vital a feature of America's isolationist policy, Theodore Roosevelt was seeking a democratic way out of the dilemma. Intervention flowed from an extension of the Monroe Doctrine.

The Roosevelt Corollary. During the Venezuelan Debt Dispute of 1902 England had suggested that she would accept the enforcement of the Monroe Doctrine in the Caribbean area if the United States would guarantee that the need for intervention would not arise. After the German bombardment of the fishing village, Roosevelt, "speaking softly but carrying the big stick," assigned Dewey to command of the Atlantic Fleet and then demanded that the foreign powers arbitrate the debt dispute in the Hague Tribunal. When they accepted this demand, the European powers at the same time accepted American supremacy in the Caribbean area. With the United States to protect them now, unscrupulous caudillos realized that they could default on all their obligations with impunity. Thus in 1904 Santo Domingo defaulted on a debt of $32 million owed to Europeans, a default which was preceded by a prolonged civil war. On the island's own request, the American State Department negotiated an agreement with Santo Domingo which provided that customs receipts be placed in receivership, with the United States as receiver and responsible for the prompt liquidation of the debt. The American Receiver General was able to get the debt reduced from $32 million to $17 million and then refunded into a 50-year loan held by an American bank at a much lower rate of interest than the original. The great gainers in this intervention were the people of Santo Domingo. While negotiations were pending, Roosevelt took the occasion of his annual message (December 2, 1904) to announce his corollary to the Monroe Doctrine:

If a nation shows that it knows how to act with reasonable efficiency and decency in social and political matters, if it keeps order and pays its obligations, it need fear no interference from the United States. Chronic wrong doing, or an impotence which results in a general loosening of the ties of civilized society may in America, as elsewhere, ultimately require intervention by some civilized nation, and in the Western Hemisphere, the adherence of the United States to the Monroe Doctrine may force the United States, however reluctantly, in flagrant cases of such wrongdoing or impotence, to the exercise of an international police power.

Secretary of State Elihu Root invoked this "police power" sparingly; interventions in Cuba, Panama and Santo Domingo were limited to specific purposes; and where possible, other Latin American powers were invited to collaborate in intervention.

Protest. Latin American reaction to the Corollary was intensely bitter. Poets, publicists and historians led the protest. America was painted as a crude, materialistic power forcing its will upon the refined and spiritual Latins; America was dominated by "Yanqui" imperialists; it had become the "Colossus of the North." Propagandists revived the Spanish past of Latin-America and fostered Pan-Hispanic and Pan-Latinist movements. Latin Americans were whipped up into a frenzy against American culture, that is, against a business and machine culture. Americans were painted (from that day to this) as barbaric, Wall-Street dominated brutes—drunken, immoral conquerors spreading the rule of white supremacy over the Latin World. The fact is, nonetheless, that neither Theodore Roosevelt nor Elihu Root sought intervention; it was the United States

that sponsored Drago's Doctrine of non-intervention for the collection of defaulted debts when it came up at the second Hague Conference of 1907.

Dollar Diplomacy. Latin American bitterness was more justly leveled against President William Howard Taft and his Secretary of State Philander C. Knox than against Theodore Roosevelt and Elihu Root. These men realized that Roosevelt's Corollary was a perfectly designed instrument for gaining absolute political and economic control of the Caribbean World. Knox undertook, on behalf of American business interests, to oust all European concessionaires and creditors from that region. To effectuate this, the State Department organized American banking groups to take over Latin American obligations; it then placed political and military pressure on Latin American governments to refund existing obligations into American bonds which were then turned over to the American bankers. In a similar fashion, the State Department secured mines, banana plantations, railroad construction privileges etc. for American investors. The marines were used to place puppet caudillos into office and to war against all "rebels" who objected to United States selection of Latin American heads of state. Haiti, the "banana republic," and Nicaragua felt the full brunt of this policy of "dollar diplomacy" or the use of the government of the United States abroad to foster the very private interests of Americans at home. Latin American fears concerning the Roosevelt Corollary were thus justified.

Woodrow Wilson and Latin America. In an encouraging address at Mobile, Alabama, in 1913, Wilson proclaimed a "new freedom" for the oppressed Latin American protectorates (for such had they become). Human rights were to be set above material interests and American conquest was repudiated forever. And, to hammer home the point of these two principles, William Jennings Bryan, the country's outstanding anti-imperialist was chosen as Secretary of State. What resulted? When Haiti was involved in revolution in 1915, Wilson and Bryan sent in the Marines to establish order and, of course, to take over the finances. American occupation lasted ten years as Haitian "rebels" waged relentless guerrilla war against the United States. Then, in 1916, Santo Domingo (the Dominican Republic) was subjected to a Marine occupation.

In both these countries American occupation did produce an efficient constabulary, law and order, better roads, honest customs collections; but the price was American supervised elections and the suspension of all the basic freedoms. Occupation of Nicaragua in 1916 resulted in the forced Bryan-Chamorro

Treaty. Latin Americans, with some justice, denounced Wilson; but Wilson was caught in the same dilemma as his predecessors. Mexico is a case in point.

Mexico. Wilson's Mexican difficulties began when the Mexicans sought to choose a ruler after having overthrown the caudillo, Porfirio Diaz. Diaz had been particularly brutal. He had deliberately fostered serfdom and industrial slavery while prodigally giving away the nation's resources to himself and foreign investors. Americans shared in his "generosity,"—about one billion dollars worth, largely in oil resources. When Diaz, pursuing a divide-and-rule policy, began to favor English over American investments, the American investors openly supported the revolution (1911) which resulted in the downfall of Diaz.

The revolution was at first in the hands of the idealist, Madero, but he was murdered by the supporters of a new "Diaz," Victoriano Huerta. Condemning Huerta as "unspeakable," Wilson refused to recognize the new regime. This reversed a policy begun by Thomas Jefferson of recognizing any *de facto* government, that is, one which is *actually* though not legally in control.

In effect, Wilson was perpetuating the Mexican Revolution and thus resorting to indirect intervention. He blockaded the Mexican coast and gave open support to Huerta's opponent's Carranza and Pancho Villa. Wilson called this policy of indirect intervention "watchful waiting." Waiting was temporarily suspended when, to avenge the arrest of some American sailors and to secure a public apology from Huerta for an insult to the American flag (and to stop a shipment of German arms to Huerta!), the Marines were sent in to occupy Vera Cruz. A shooting war was prevented by intercession of the "ABC powers" (Argentina, Brazil and Chile) who suggested mediation. Wilson accepted their intervention, but before any solution was reached, Huerta resigned and Carranza took over.

Pancho Villa. Now it was Pancho Villa who incited intervention. With the support of the United States Pancho Villa and the great revolutionary leader EMILIANO ZAPATA had set up a provisional government in the northern provinces to oppose Huerta. Villa turned against Carranza. To bring the Americans into Mexico, Villa killed 18 of them within Mexico and then crossed over the Rio Grande to kill more on American soil. Wilson ordered General John Pershing to get Villa and the American army crossed the Mexican border to do so. War between the United States and Mexico was narrowly averted during this invasion, as American pursuing forces committed one aggression after another on Carranza's troops. The American army of invasion was still looking for Villa in 1917 when America's entry into the first World War forced Wilson to recall the troops. With America at war, Wilson reversed his policy and extended to Carranza *de jure* (legal) recognition.

Mexico was now free to pursue an independent existence in the community of nations. As an independent nation, Mexico proclaimed a new constitution. It revolutionized the social structure of Mexico: church and state were separated; education was secularized; labor was granted constitutional protection by guaranteed conditions of work, workman's compensation, compulsory unionization and legalization of the strike; the large estates of the church, the aristocrats and the foreign corporations were confiscated and distributed in small parcels to the serfs and tenant farmers. Then, of utmost significance to the United States, a provision was written in which gave to the Mexican nation the title of all subsoil properties (oil etc.). All foreign holdings in Mexico were jeopardized by this provision.

The American Empire. Americans were confronted with the problem of reconciling democracy and imperialism in the overseas areas ceded to them by force, treaty or purchase. She could free or subjugate these territories as she pleased. Of course, old and tested precedents could be followed in the territories of Alaska, the Philippines, Puerto Rico, Guam, Hawaii, Samoa or Midway. They could be placed under the terms of the Northwest Ordinance under which population would determine the degree of local autonomy; the goal would be statehood.

But objections arose almost immediately to applying the Northwest Ordinance to these areas. It was argued that these territories were non-contiguous; they were not likely to be settled by an overflow of Americans; they were composed of peoples of the most diverse races, religions, languages, social customs and stages of civilization. Contrary arguments pointed out that these territories were important and should be kept as part of America; if kept, then their populations became Americans; as Americans, they were entitled to the rights and privileges of citizenship under the Constitution of the United States and the right to be admitted as states. It was not long before these opposing ideas were contending in the Supreme Court.

"Does the Constitution Follow the Flag?" A number of insular cases arose and the Court had an opportunity to take decisive stand on these matters. It resorted, instead, to ambiguities. In the matter of the relationship of the United States to its possessions, the Court established two kinds of territorial status: an **incorporated territory**, one entitled to full citizenship and eligible for membership in the Union—Alaska and Hawaii became such; and an **unincorporated territory**, one that had limited citizenship and, while privileged with certain rights like life, liberty and property, did not enjoy common-law privileges like trial by jury, freedom of the press etc. unless the Congress voted these privileges. As "appurtenances of the United States" unincorporated territories could look forward to independence, not statehood—if Congress so willed. Congress and not the Courts was made the arbiter of the fate of these dependencies.

Still another irritating problem arose. Did exports from Puerto Rico and the Philippines enter the United States free of duty? The Constitution provides that duties must be uniform throughout the United States. In the case of **DeLima v. Bidwell** (1901) by a 5 to 4 decision the Court held that Puerto Rico did not have to pay a duty; then, in the same year, the Court reversed itself and held that tariff equality was not a "fundamental" right and that Congress could discriminate against the products of Puerto Rico and the Philippines (**Downs v. Bidwell**). From these cases onward, the extent to which the Constitution followed the flag was left entirely to Congress.

Congress Disposes. As residents in incorporated territories, the people of Alaska and Hawaii enjoy limited freedom under Congressional grants: they are American citizens, are protected by the Constitution, elect both houses of their Congress and send a voteless, territorial delegate to the American Congress; but their governors are appointed and the President of the United States may veto the legislation they adopt. They can look forward to becoming states of the United States. As unincorporated territories, Puerto Rico and the Philippines could look forward to emancipation. As temporory dependencies both the Filipinos and the Puerto Ricans were given considerable local autonomy; in fact in 1917 the latter were made citizens of the United States. While the Philippines went on, in 1946, to become an independent state, Puerto Rico remains a dependency. Her position today is that of "Commonwealth" for she enjoys *virtual* independence and is free to leave the orbit of the United States if she wills; her "dependency" is voluntary. By such forward looking political measures Congress reduced and eliminated imperialism from the "American Empire."

CHAPTER XVII

THE ORIGINS OF AMERICAN COLLECTIVE SECURITY

FAR EASTERN POLICY

Imperialism. The Sino-Japanese War of 1895 had revealed that China, under the Manchu Dowager Empress, Tzu Hsi, was a corrupt and backward nation. Japan had defeated her armies with ease and had secured the independence and cession of the Lioatung Peninsula, Korea, and Taiwan (Formosa). Their own imperialist hopes threatened by this aggression, the great European powers had set aside Japan's conquests and had then proceeded to partition China for themselves into **spheres of influence**. Within each sphere, the great powers collected customs duties and harbor fees and distributed to its own nationals desirable mining, railroad etc. concessions.

Enter the United States. The United States was on the periphery of these events. During the 19th century, there was no formed American Far Eastern policy. With the acquisition of the Philippines and Guam, however, the United States entered the Far Eastern arena. It found that spheres of influence had closed all the doors to opportunities in trade there; the powers were rattling sabres at each other; and a new warlike Japan was being driven by expansionist urges to satisfy her enormous need for raw materials and population outlets. What policy or policies were required in this situation?—logically, any policy that would reduce foreign threats to the safety of the Philippines and which would, at the same time, make for increased commercial opportunities. Secretary of State JOHN HAY drew up an **"Open Door Note."** This note was sent to all the powers with interests in China and it asked that within a sphere of interest

there be no interference with the twenty-two ports already opened by treaty;

Chinese tariffs were to be applied equally and collected by China; and

no nation was to discriminate in behalf of its own citizens in harbor dues and railroad charges.

The answers to Hay's note were cold, evasive, indifferent and qualified; Russia did not answer at all. But Hay announced (20 March 1900) that the **Open Door Policy** was accepted by all the powers and was "final and definitive." This was a high point in diplomatic bravado.

The "Boxer" Rebellion. In its original formulation, the Open Door Policy seemed to accept the division of China into spheres of influence, provided equal commercial opportunity was preserved. This interpretation was tested in the spring of 1900. The reactionary Chinese anti-imperialists led by a society called the "Boxers"—really the "Patriotic Order of Harmonious Fists"—began a revolt against the "foreign devils." The result was wide destruction of all properties designed to "westernize" China (railroads etc.). The Boxers occupied Peking, and placed foreign legations under siege. Hay insisted that an international relief force be organized to save the besieged legations. About 20,000 such troops representing all the western powers were gathered and suppressed the revolt brutally.

Hay now began to fear that a Frankenstein's monster had been created in this international expeditionary force and that the powers, now finally united, would go on to make a political partition of China. He therefore quickly circulated another note (3 July 1900) which stated that the United States had joined the expedition "to seek a solution which may bring about permanent safety and peace to China, preserve Chinese territorial and administrative integrity, protect all rights guaranteed to friendly powers by treaty and international law, and safeguard for the world the principle of equal and impartial trade with all parts of the Chinese empire." The Open Door, Hay asserted, could rest only on China's "integrity"—that is, independence.

By taking a firm stand against the dismemberment of China, the United States once again faced a dilemma; for the United States was still determined to make no foreign alliances—yet, what if some power or combination of powers were to threaten China's integrity? Was the United States prepared to fight alone? Or would the United States agree now to some form of "collective security" against an aggressor in China? (The United States had first to demonstrate that its own hands were clean. An outrageous indemnity of $330 million had been levied by the united interventionists against China for damages done by the Boxers. $24.5 million went to America. This was scaled down to $12 million and then in 1924 the unpaid balance was remitted. China used the returned American share for scholarships for Chinese to American universities.)

The Threat to China's Integrity. In 1895 Russia had loomed as the chief threat to China's integrity. They had penetrated Manchuria, seized the Liaotung Peninsula with its valuable port of Port Arthur. This was exactly the territory seized by the Japanese following the Sino-Japanese War of 1895. Relations between Russia and Japan deteriorated rapidly. One day, in 1904, a Japanese torpedo squadron moved without warning against the Russian fleet at Port Arthur and sank it. This was followed by a declaration of war (10 February 1904). Rapid Japanese maneuvers on land and sea gave her a victorious lead but brought her to the point of economic exhaustion.

Theodore Roosevelt was aware that both Russia and Japan menaced the Open Door; while both were powerful, he felt they served to balance one another and to prevent any territorial grabs by either. Therefore, the military destruction of either was not to the interest of the United States. Accordingly Roosevelt offered to mediate. Russia accepted because she was unaware of Japan's state of exhaustion and because the Tsar was being threatened at home with revolution; Japan had taken the initiative in inviting Roosevelt to mediate.

In the **Treaty of Portsmouth** (N. H. 1905) Roosevelt consented to a modification of the Open Door Policy. Japan received dominant rights in Korea, a leasehold on the Liaotung Peninsula and the southern half of Sakhalin. Roosevelt turned down Japan's demand for an indemnity as well. For his work as mediator, Theodore Roosevelt was awarded the Nobel Peace Prize (1906), but, unfortunately for China, he had made the Open Door a less absolute policy, one that could apparently be modified with a little pressure.

The Threat to the Open Door. Roosevelt was anxious to keep Japan friendly, but not too strong. The **Taft-Katsura Memorandum** signed in 1905 showed why. In that agreement America acquiesced in Japan's proposed seizure of Korea in exchange for her recognition of American control of the Philippines.

Japan, too, felt friendly to America—for a while. But her hostility bristled when America's jingo press found a new issue on which to increase circulation—the "yellow menace." On the west coast the press was in a frenzy over the "yellow menace," that is, Japanese immigration into the United States. Spurred by prejudice, the San Francisco school board segregated 93 Japanese children; west coast labor unions organized a Japanese and Korean Exclusion League; and hoodlums sacked all Japanese owned stores. Roosevelt had to promise some form of international restrictive action on Japanese immigration in order to get the school board to rescind its policy of segregation.

Such action was finally secured in the **Gentleman's Agreement of 1907**. Japan promised to withhold passports from laborers intending to enter the United States; the United States agreed not to bar the Japanese completely. With this face-saving maneuver, Japan's ruffled temper subsided somewhat and Japan agreed to the **Root-Takahira Agreement in 1908**. By this agreement both powers proclaimed the Open Door Policy in effect while they simultaneously pledged to recognize Japan's priority in Manchuria and to keep *status quo* in the Pacific (!) Japan could see nothing wrong in an Open Door which sanctioned the piecemeal partition of China —first Korea and now Manchuria.

The Twenty-One Demands. Taft's efforts to extend "dollar diplomacy" to the Far East failed miserably when American bankers refused to enter into competition with European and Japanese bankers for Chinese railroad securities. Wilson openly repudiated "dollar diplomacy" in both Latin America and China and kept his word in China. With the outbreak of World War I, American attention was distracted to Europe; thereupon, Japan declared war on Germany and seized all German holdings in China as well as the German islands in the Pacific north of the equator. With all the great powers away, Japan in 1915 made her brutal **twenty-one demands** upon China which, in effect, converted all of China into a Japanese protectorate. The United States protested strongly against this wholesale violation of the Open Door Policy and forced Japan to hesitate before implementing the twenty-one demands. But by 1917 the United States had entered the European War. Japan took new courage and forced the United States into the **Lansing-Ishii Agreement** of 1917 in which both powers solemnly reaffirmed China's territorial integrity and the Open Door, and then with equal solemnity, recognized that Japan had "special interests" in all of China because of her "territorial propinquity." Here was a strange doctrine indeed—conquest justified by geographical closeness! In the Lansing-Ishii Agreement Americans agreed to closing the Open Door. World War I permitted her no choice.

THE UNITED STATES AND THE FIRST WORLD WAR

"He Kept Us Out of War." World War I began on July 28, 1914. On the 4th of August, President Wilson issued a **Proclamation of Neutrality;** on the 19th,

he demanded that Americans be "impartial in thought as well as in action." Thereafter, every violation of the "rights of neutrals" was formally protested. Protest notes were sent to England when she made arbitrary extensions in the contraband list, or invoked the doctrine of "continuous voyage" which permitted her to seize neutral ships going to Germany or Germany's neighbors, or blockaded German ports, or rifled American mails. Somewhat stronger protests were sent to Germany when that country proclaimed the waters around England a war zone within which enemy ships would be sunk at sight without regard for the safety of the passengers or the crew, and when the **Lusitania** with 123 Americans aboard was sunk (indeed, one of Wilson's protests was so strong that Bryan, fearing war, resigned rather than sign it).

Wilson attempted to bring the warring powers to their senses. He sent Colonel EDWARD M. HOUSE on a mission to Europe to seek a negotiated peace; he called, in 1916, upon all the powers to state their war aims as a basis for possible mediation; he called again upon them for a "peace without victory" to be maintained by some international organization which the United States was prepared to join. That America wanted to stay at peace in the warring world was evident in the re-election of Wilson over Charles Evans Hughes in 1916; for Wilson made "He kept us out of war!" his platform. Six months after the election, despite neutrality laws and peace resolutions, the United States was at war. Why?

Un-neutral in Thought. The cause for America's entry into the first World War remains one of the most complex problems in American history. Many hypotheses have been advanced. One is that Americans, even in the early years of the war, were un-neutral in thought. They felt much closer to the Anglo-French cause than the German, so the argument goes, because English was a common tongue; England was the "mother country"; American and Anglo-French institutions were democratic; and Germany and Austria-Hungary appeared to be the aggressors when they refused to negotiate the Serbian crisis.

Though un-neutral in thought, Americans were not ready to desert their non-belligerent status because all the powers were on a war footing and none sought actively to avoid war—the Tsar was hardly a democrat; the British and French were imperialistic; and the Germans were such a highly cultured people that to war against them seemed incredible. Whatever doubts America may have had, however, dwindled once the British cut the Atlantic cable and war news began to pour into America from censored British sources only. Slowly the complexities of the war were re-structured into simple black-white patterns. Now the Germans became mad, ruthless "Huns" murdering Belgian babies, trampling on neutral countries, slaughtering nurses like Edith Cavell; and the British became the defenders of democracy, the French became a nation of Lafayettes and the Russian aristocrats became the people who had befriended America during the civil war. When, out of desperation caused by the British blockade, Germany began unrestricted submarine warfare against Allied shipping, many Americans were convinced of the truth of Allied propaganda and were ready to enter the war.

Un-neutral in Action. Another line of argument stems from the charge that Americans were not only un-neutral in thought but very un-neutral in action as well. Wilson tried to get England to accept the **Declaration of London** of 1909 which guaranteed neutral trading rights with respect to contraband goods. This would have permitted shipment of food and raw materials intended for civilian use to the Central Powers. England refused and seized all goods enroute to Germany and her allies. Wilson then accepted British restrictions; this meant, in fact, that the United States was imposing an embargo on German trade.

In 1914 American trade with the Central Powers amounted to $169,290,000; by 1916 this fell to $1,-150,000. At the same time American trade with the Allied Powers rose from $824,800,000 to $3,214,-500,000. There was no doubt where American economic sympathy lay. Similarly, when the war broke out, loans to the belligerents were discouraged by the administration in order to preserve neutrality and to restrict the flow of gold out of the country. As Allied purchases mounted, pressure for extension of credit to them increased. In 1915 the bar on loans was lowered and within a year and a half American bankers had extended more than $2 billion in credit to the Allies. These factors, so goes the argument, tied the American economy to an Allied victory. With production, employment and profits at record heights, any German move to cripple production and the flow of war goods could have serious consequences.

The German Reaction. Still another argument has it that Germany herself was responsible for America's entry into the war against her. Germany's answer to America's un-neutral trade was the submarine, now being used against all ships supplying her enemies. Early in 1915, Wilson had warned the Germans that they would be held to strict accountability for illegal destruction of American ships and lives. The sinking of the Lusitania put this doctrine to the test. In a series of notes Wilson demanded that German submarine commanders warn their victims and provide safety for passengers and crew; any other type of sinking would be regarded by the United States as "deliberately unfriendly." When the passenger liner "Arabic," was then sunk (Aug. 1915) Germany, seeking to avoid an American declaration of war, submitted to the "Arabic pledge" not to sink unresisting liners without warning. The "Arabic pledge" was itself put to the test when a torpedo sank the French liner, Sussex, in February 1916. Wilson sent an ultimatum to Berlin threatening the severance of diplomatic relations. Once again Germany pledged to cancel unrestricted submarine warfare—if the United States would force England to abide by international law.

In spite of commitment to the Allied cause and provocation by the Germans, Americans did not seem to want to go to war. For two years Wilson had resisted the pressure by the National Security League of industrialists and munitions manufacturers, the Navy League, the Army League, Theodore Roosevelt's blustering, and General Leonard Wood's demands to begin a preparedness program. The submarine menace and the approaching election of 1916 forced Wilson to abandon his resistance.

In 1916 he advocated an increase in the army and navy. After a furious legislative struggle Congress passed a **National Defense Act** which increased the size of the army, placed the state militia under national control and inaugurated a program of military training in the schools and colleges; and a Naval Appropriations Bill for construction of dreadnaughts and auxiliary vessels to accommodate the flood of goods being sent overseas.

But these apparently warlike moves were accompanied by Wilson's most intensive peace efforts. Elected on a platform of peace, Wilson started a round of negotiations to secure the consent of both belligerents to a negotiated peace. Colonel House was sent on a mission to England and Germany to discover some common basis for a peace conference. When neither country would accept the other's terms, Wilson drew up his own in a memorable address to Congress (January 1917). He called for peace without victory, for the abandonment of secret treaties and balance of power politics, for recognition of the rights of self-determination and equality of all nations, for arms limitation and the guarantee of freedom of the seas and, finally, for a league of nations to enforce the peace. But these idealistic proposals were drowned in a new clash of arms and explosion of torpedoes newly launched by the German submarines. Was not Germany to blame, so the argument ends, for not accepting American good will?

America Enters the War. On April 6, 1917 Congress declared war on Germany and thus became associated with the Allied cause. What, then, happened between January and April to cause this radical shift from peace to war? Was it the resumption of unrestricted submarine warfare begun by the Germans on February 1st? The Germans sank the U.S.S. **Housatonic** on February 3rd after warning the vessel. Wilson then broke off diplomatic relations with Germany and armed all merchantmen by executive order, when Senator LaFollette's filibuster prevented Congress from taking such action. Other sinkings followed immediately.

Was it the **Zimmerman Note?** This was a code message sent by the German Foreign Secretary Zimmerman to the German Minister to Mexico (March 1917) proposing a Mexican-German Alliance and promising to Mexico the restoration of New Mexico, Arizona and Texas if the United States were defeated. British intelligence intercepted and decoded it and then released it to the American press.

Was it mounting German sabotage and espionage? Documents planning such sabotage had been discovered in the possession of Austrian and German diplomatic personnel; a munitions dump was exploded on Black Tom Island, N. J. and another at Kingsland, N. J. and both were attributed to German agents. Damages ran to $75 million.

Was it the Russian Revolution of March, 1917? This revolution had put into power a liberal-democratic government and made the Allied cause truly democratic. Whatever the cause, it can be stated with a fair degree of certainty that in 1917 the majority of Americans had come to the conclusion, however, false, that booted and helmeted Kaiserism menaced the world. This explains the highly idealistic note, the crusader's cry, with which Americans went into battle; for the American people who fought the war, this was truly a battle for a freer, safer world for all mankind.

THE HOME FRONT

Manpower was mobilized by a **Selective Service Act.** It provided, eventually, for universal registration and conscription of all men between 18 years of age and 45. 2,810,296 men were inducted; combined with the regular army and units of the national guard, the total number of men under arms amounted to 4,800,000. Two million were sent overseas. 32 training camps were set up fairly well equipped with small arms, but woefully deficient in artillery and such new weapons as tanks and airplane bombers. Fortunately, the British and French were able to make up the deficiency. By the time American factories had converted to the production of heavy artillery, the war was over.

Industry was mobilized by the **War Industries Board** under Bernard M. Baruch. Production was organized, industries converted by fiat, and production boosted about 20% before the war was over.

Water Transport was mobilized by a **War Shipping Board** under Edward N. Hurley who increased American tonnage from one to ten million.

Land transport was mobilized by a **United States Railroad Administration** under William J. McAdoo. Treating the lines as a single system, McAdoo eliminated excess lines, constructed interlocking links, improved rolling stock, etc.

Farmers were mobilized under a **Food Administration** headed by Herbert Hoover. Production was increased by price inducements and consumption was reduced by voluntary wheatless and meatless days. Food exports doubled in volume.

Resources were mobilized by a **Fuel Administration** under Harry A. Garfield. In this area, too, production was increased while consumption was decreased. Fuelless Mondays, gasless Sundays, and daylight saving time were some of the devices used to control consumption.

Labor was mobilized by a **National War Labor Board** under Frank P. Walsh and William H. Taft. This agency sought to keep men on the job while wage disputes were negotiated. A **War Labor Policies Board** under Felix Frankfurter attempted to standardize wages and hours and helped to create a **United States Employment Service** which placed over 3,700,000 workers in vital industries.

Finances were mobilized by enormous increases in the percentages and varieties of tax rates and taxes; by vast numbers of Liberty bonds sold. Government appropriations amounted to $35.4 billion. $11.2 billion was raised by taxation—higher rates, surtaxes, excess profits taxes, luxury taxes and sales taxes; five bond drives netted $21.4 billion. Each drive was oversubscribed.

Morale was mobilized by the **Creel Committee on Public Information** which effectuated a voluntary press censorship and engaged 150,000 lecturers, actors, artists and scholars to participate in a propaganda campaign to expose the Germans as the enemies of democracy and civilization. They were too successful. Anti-German feeling reached hysterical proportions; the teaching of the German language was suspended in the schools; the playing of

German music was prohibited; statues of German heroes were removed from public view; sauerkraut became "liberty cabbage" and German measles was dubbed "liberty measles."

Voluntary organizations put the country on a vigilante footing. An Espionage Act (1917) imposed heavy fines and long imprisonment terms for any person who aided the enemy, incited rebellion in the armed forces, or obstructed recruitment. Eugene V. Debs was sent to prison for ten years for violating this law with an anti-war speech in 1918. The Postmaster General could deny the use of the mails to anyone suspected of violating the Espionage Act; socialist and anti-British publications were effectively banned. A Sabotage Act (1918) made willful sabotage of war materials, utilities or transport a federal crime. (The Act was used to break the I.W.W.) In 1918, too, a Sedition Act was passed. Under the Espionage Act the state had to prove that injurious effects resulted from seditious utterances; now, under the Sedition Act the mere utterance or printing of any disloyal, profane, scurrilous or abusive statement about the American form of government, flag or uniform or any words intended to obstruct the war effort were punishable—whatever the effects. Finally, an Alien Act in 1918 provided for deportation without jury trial of any alien advocating the overthrow of government.

America's Military Contributions. Before the American fighting forces moved into action, Allied prospects were bleak indeed. Great Britain and France were scraping the bottom of their manpower barrels; French soldiers were mutinying; the Russians were in the throes of revolution; German submarines were sinking Allied vessels ten times faster than they were being built. By the time the first American military operations had begun, the Italians had been routed at Caporetto, Russia was in the hands of the Bolsheviks and out of the war as a result of the Treaty of Brest-Litovsk (3 March 1918); and the Germans had shattered the quiet on the western front with a tremendous offensive which brought them within "Big Bertha" artillery range of Paris.

At this point the American Navy came to the rescue. It made possible protective convoying (the 2,000,000 American soldiers sent overseas, for example, suffered the loss of only one transport with 210 men aboard!) as anti-submarine mines, the renowned "ash-cans," took heavy toll of the German submarines. The German Navy no longer dared to engage in direct combat; when ordered to do so, a suicidal order, the men mutinied.

The American Army made significant contributions. General John J. Pershing and his men first saw action at Chateau Thierry on the Marne where they bolstered the French against a heavy German thrust. They then participated more fully in the counteroffensive that followed the weakening of the last German drive. The first independent American action was in the St. Mihiel sector and then in an extremely costly operation through the Argonne Forest along the Meuse River. This operation broke the southern flank of the German salient and paved the way for successful French and British offensives in the north. While it may be debatable whether the American Army won the first World War, no one can quarrel with the statement that it shortened the war considerably.

The American Peace. In 1917, the Communists (Bolsheviks) were in power in Russia and had withdrawn from the war. Hoping to spread discontent among allied soldiers, the Bolsheviks began to publish a number of inter-Allied secret treaties to which Tsarist Russia had been a party. These treaties had arranged for a redivision of colonial holdings at the expense of Germany, Austria-Hungary and Turkey, if the Allies were victorious. Wilson felt impelled, therefore, to make America's war aims and peace goals clear and unmistakable.

The Fourteen Points. On January 22, 1918 he set fourth his **Fourteen Points** which framed the American peace. No settlement was possible, said Wilson, until the troops of the Central Powers had been evacuated from Belgium, France, Rumania, Serbia, Montenegro and Russia. Once the troops had been removed, a peace would be made by eliminating the causes of future wars. Open covenants openly arrived at would replace balances of power secretly arrived at; the seas would be made free both in peace and war; the removal of trade barriers would end economic warfare; the arms race would be ended and all nations would disarm; imperialism would be eliminated by some "absolutely impartial adjustment of all colonial claims;" restoration of Alsace-Lorraine and the creation of an independent Poland with access to the sea would remove two threats to the peace of Europe; the principles of nationality would be applied to Austria-Hungary and Turkey to put an end to the nationalistic contention within those empires; no decision would be made without the self-determination of the peoples concerned.

As a crowning glory, a **League of Nations** would be created to preserve for all time both the political independence and territorial integrity of all nations, large and small. Thus Wilson shaped a vision of a wonderful new world and his message swept like a beacon over the world's exhausted armies, even those of the Central Powers. Wilson's Fourteen Points, in fact, became the basis upon which the Germans finally, on November 11, 1918, accepted Allied terms for an armistice.

The Great Blunder. The Peace Treaty and the League of Nations negotiated at Versailles between January and June 1919 went down to defeat in the American Senate in November 1919 in a renewed wave of isolation. Here was a drastic shift indeed. There is virtual unanimity of opinion that the responsibility for this defeat lay primarily with Wilson. The President, who broke all precedents and left the country to attend the Peace Conference in person, ignored some obvious facts. The Congressional elections of 1918 had given the Republicans control of both Houses of Congress. Why, then, did Wilson, in selecting a delegation for the Versailles Conference, fail to include a single Republican Congressman? Did he feel that he, and only he, could write an effective treaty? Or was it that Wilson was determined to convert America's military victory into a victory for the Democratic Party? There are no ready answers to these questions even at this late date. Once in Paris, Wilson confronted a triumvirate of bitter men—GEORGE CLEMENCEAU, LLOYD GEORGE and VITTORIO ORLANDO—each determined to exact a terrible vengeance upon Germany and to secure for France, England and Italy the territories promised in the secret treaties. (This would, of course, have made a mockery of the Fourteen Points.) How did America's peace fare at Versailles in the face of such determined opposition?

The provisions in the Treaty which restored Alsace-Lorraine to France, disarmed and demilitarized Germany, created a mandate system for the eventual elimination of imperialist control of backward areas, constructed Poland with a corridor to the sea and set up a League of Nations based on the sovereign equality of all states large and small—all accorded well with the Fourteen Points.

But Wilson's failures were serious ones: the unnecessary punishment of Germany by assigning to her the total guilt of the war and making her pay an astronomical bill for reparations (about $62 billion); the post-war occupation of Germany by French troops; the stripping of German territory, railroads, livestock, ships and coal—all this seemed not a peace treaty, but a revenge treaty. Then, too, there were Germany's overseas possessions handed over to Japan, England and France; a mere exchange of im-

perial rule, it appeared. Wilson's surrenders on these points seemed to the Americans completely abject; he did not once leave the Conference in a dramatic protest; he preferred behind-closed-doors diplomacy and did not, at any time, take the American press into his confidence.

The League of Nations. Wilson could and did say that what he had surrendered were sacrifices to secure a League of Nations, which became Article 1 of the Treaty of Versailles. The purposes of this covenant of nations were to protect its members in their political independence and territorial integrity (that is, to preserve the results arrived at Versailles); to force the submission of all disputes to the League for settlement thus preventing war; to reduce armaments, eliminate imperialism by gradual means through mandates and to improve social and economic conditions, thus eliminating the causes of war; and to provide for political, economic and as a last resort, military sanctions against any aggressor that disturbed the peace. The agencies by which these purposes would be realized were an **Assembly** of all the member nations, a **Council** of five powerful permanent members and four elected non-permanent members, a **Permanent Court for International Justice**, a **Secretariat** and an **International Labor Organization**.

Back to Isolation. On March 19, 1920, the Treaty of Versailles and the League of Nations went down to defeat in the Senate; it had failed of two-thirds ratification by a vote of 49 for and 35 against. The battle for ratification had been dramatic and bitter but the isolationist forces of Hiram Johnson, William Borah, Henry Cabot Lodge and other "irreconcilables" and "reservationists"—that is, those who would under no conditions agree to support the League of Nations, and those who would support with decisive qualifications—proved stronger than Wilson and the many pro-League forces. Ratification failed for many reasons: Wilson's refusal to compromise with Lodge; isolationist fears for the Monroe Doctrine and the power of Congress to declare war; hatred of the German-Americans and Irish-Americans for any association with England; revulsion toward the punitive Treaty of Versailles; postwar disillusionment, and the like. Wilson made the election of 1920 a popular referendum on the issue of joining the League. Republican isolationists under Harding seeking a return to normalcy were overwhelmingly elected. The League of Nations was permanently shelved and Congress, by joint resolution, concluded a separate peace treaty with Germany and Austria-Hungary on 2 July 1921.

CHAPTER XVIII

THE TWENTIES

THE AFTERMATH OF PROGRESSIVISM

The Progressive Period and the war left the American people with contradictory moods. On the one hand, the move to extend democracy and government welfare intervention was brought to completion. In 1919 and 1920 the manufacture, sale and transportation of intoxicating liquor was forbidden in the **18th Amendment** to the Constitution. Prohibition was almost universally considered as a crowning achievement of social welfare, a measure that would improve the health, safety and morals of the American people. The right to vote was given to women in the ("Susan B. Anthony") **19th Amendment**, an act which doubled the electorate and rewarded women for their extraordinary activities during the war.

While rejecting the Plumb Plan for government ownership of the badly battered railroads, the government returned the roads to private ownership and in the **Esch-Cummins Transportation Act of 1920** made the ICC virtual ruler over the industry, just short of nationalization. The ICC now had complete control over rates, supervised the sale of railroad securities, could recapture all profits over six per cent, approved or rejected proposed expenditures and consolidated systems at will to achieve economy and efficiency. Finally, in the **General Leasing and Water Power Act of 1920** the government extended its controlling hand over oil and mineral reserves, removing them in the public interest from private exploitation; control extended, too, to water areas which might be used for conversion to electric power. Measures like these could easily have fitted into the "Square Deal" of the "New Freedom."

POLITICAL PARTIES

The Republicans. There was no serious opposition to Republican domination of the Presidency during the Twenties. In 1920 WARREN G. HARDING won easily over the Democrat James M. Cox. He died in 1923 and was succeeded by his Vice-President CALVIN COOLIDGE. In 1924 Coolidge defeated Democrat John W. Davis without difficulty; in 1928 HERBERT HOOVER for the Republicans swamped Alfred E. Smith.

Harding and Coolidge were exceptionally mediocre men committed to a do-nothing policy. Harding's do-nothingism, his almost helpless reliance upon subordinates gave rise to a wave of corruption in high office equalled only by Grant's administration. Thus, Charles R. Forbes, Director of the Veterans' Bureau, was found guilty of reckless waste, misconduct and dishonesty in administering construction contracts and in purchasing supplies. Attorney General Daugherty was accused of illegal withdrawals of alcohol to enrich his friends and himself, and of criminal neglect of duty. One of Daugherty's friends, Thomas W. Miller, the Alien Property Custodian, went to jail for fraud in the sale of an alien metal concern. Secretary of the Interior Albert B. Fall managed to get Harding to transfer naval oil reserves at Elks Hill, California, and Teapot Dome, Wyoming, from the Navy Department to the Interior. He thereupon leased these reserves to his oil friends E. M. Doheny and Harry F. Sinclair. It was Fall's sudden wealth (since he was well known to be in financial straits) that caused a Senatorial investigation and exposure of the "Teapot Dome Scandal." As a result of this exposure, Secretary of the Navy Denby and Fall both resigned; Fall was prosecuted, convicted, fined and sent to jail for one year. Sinclair and Doheny were acquitted of the charge of conspiracy. Little public indignation followed these events for the public itself had just begun a speculative spree of its own and had little moral energy to spare.

Populist-Progressivism. The only real challenge to Republican standpattism came from within the Republican Party. A solid phalanx of the Populist-Progressive past remained in the persons of La-Follette, Wheeler, Norris, Walsh, Cutting, Cousens and Shipstead. In 1924 these men organized the **Conference for Progressive Political Action** and received the solid backing of the farmers, the powerful Railway Brotherhoods, the AFL and the Socialist Party. What resulted, then, was a "farmer-labor" party within staunch Republican ranks! In the election of 1924, however, LaFollette was chosen to oppose Coolidge and Davis. The platform on which he ran was far too radical for him to win the support of the American people—government ownership of waterpower, railroads and financial credit; legalization of labor's right to organize and bargain collectively; popular election of the federal judiciary and abolition of its right to declare laws unconstitutional; declarations of war by popular referendum; and absolute disarmament. It was Coolidge all the way —and then Hoover.

Democrats. Democrats provided little opposition to Republican ascendancy in the Twenties; but they did supply spectacular political drama. Prohibition offers an excellent example. The "Solid South" was the element in the Democratic Party that fought through the 18th Amendment. (In the **Volstead Act** of 1920, an intoxicating beverage was defined as any with more than 2.5% alcohol.) But another important wing of the Democrats, centered in the larger cities of the North, were largely hostile to prohibition. Thus the Democrats split into Northern "wet" and Southern "dry." They fought each other bitterly.

A further schism occurred in party ranks over the revival of the **KKK** with its violently anti-Negro, anti-Catholic and anti-Semitic program, a program, that is, directed against almost the entire Northern wing of the Democratic Party.

An additional split took place over party emphasis: Southerners were pro-farmer and anti-labor; Northerners, the opposite. When these two groups met in nominating convention, the fur flew. In 1924, for example, Southerners supported William G. McAdoo, Doheny's lawyer during the Teapot Dome Scandal; Northerners supported Governor Alfred E. Smith of New York, a prominent Tammany Hall man an Irish Catholic. When the Smith forces sponsored an anti-KKK resolution for the platform, it was defeated 543 to 542; nor could any agreement be reached on the issues of prohibition, the League of Nations, etc. Since a nominee had to get ⅔ of the convention vote, neither group could get its man nominated even though 95 ballots were cast. Finally on the 103rd ballot a "dark horse" John W. Davis was chosen.

In 1928, however, Smith had gained so greatly in popularity that he was named on the first ballot. The campaign of 1928 was conducted on the lowest, most personal level (there was little in the platforms of both Parties to distinguish them). Forces of religious bigotry and social snobbism (Smith was from New York's lower East Side) were unleashed against Smith to a shocking extent. Protestant clergy made Smith's defeat the object of virtually a religious crusade. Republicans hammered at Smith's "wetness," his tie-in with Tammany and his Catholicism. When the votes were in, it was found that the "Solid South" for the first time in fifty years had split from the Democratic fold. Prejudice carried the day in Texas, Virginia, North Carolina, Tennessee, Florida and the border states. Needless to say, Smith was defeated.

POLITICAL ISSUES

The Veterans' Problem. In 1919 the American Legion was formed and became almost immediately a powerful pressure group to secure special benefits for veterans. In 1917 provision had been made for permanent care of totally disabled veterans and for the sale, on easy terms, of life insurance to all service men. In 1918 and 1919 compensation terms were liberalized; in 1921 a Veterans' Bureau was organized. But the American Legion sought additional benefits, particularly for non-disabled ex-soldiers. Agitation for a "bonus bill" was successful in 1924 when Congress passed, over Coolidge's veto, the Adjusted Compensation Act which provided for adjusted service certificates in the form of 20-year endowment policies. Veterans could borrow against these policies at 6% interest.

An important further gain was registered in 1930 when a civil disability pension law was passed which provided that certain non-service connected physical and mental disabilities were to be considered service-connected and to be compensated for by monthly payments. In 1931, again over the President's veto, a Bonus Law was passed which permitted immediate redemption of the 20-year policies for cash. The power of the American Legion, thus matured during the Twenties, became a powerful force in the American legislative process.

Power. During the Twenties there were demands for federal **regulation** of all power production and federal **ownership** of some. Leadership for government ownership was provided chiefly by GEORGE W. NORRIS of Nebraska. Norris selected as his target the **Muscle Shoals** plant in Alabama, on the Tennessee River which had been constructed by the United States government in 1917 to provide nitrates for the manufacture of explosives. In 1925 the project was turned over to the United States Corps of Engineers. Power generated at Muscle Shoals was sold to private utility for distribution. Considerable pressure now developed for the sale of all the government owned properties to private interests; Norris, however, was an impassable barrier. In 1928 and again in 1930 and 1931 Norris bills for public ownership of Tennessee River power projects were vetoed, the last with President Hoover's stinging rebuke: "This is not liberalism; it is degeneration." So the matter stood when the Democrats took over in 1932.

Railroads. While electric power came under government ownership, the railroads returned to the status of government regulated private industry. Long struggles for control over the railroads had culminated in the power of the ICC to fix railroad rates based upon physical valuation and to recapture profits over 6%. But, beginning in 1923, the Supreme Court ruled that the Commission, in determining physical valuation, must consider not only the orginal value of the property, but also what it would cost to reproduce existing properties anew. (Since reproduction costs were far higher than original investment costs, the rates would necessarily be higher.)

Of particular importance in this matter was the **O'Fallon decision** of 1929. Throughout the Twenties, the railroads fought the commission with all the means at its disposal. But, as the decade ended, a new note was heard. Competition from pipelines, buses, trucks, autos, steamships and planes reduced railroad revenues to a point where the railroads themselves began to clamor for more government regulation and aid.

Merchant Marine. The merchant marine moved in the Twenties from outright government ownership to private ownership. By authorization of the **Merchant Marine Act** of 1920, the Shipping Board sold $258 million worth of vessels to private lines for $23 million. By such generous disposal, an American merchant marine was kept afloat, which freed American exporters somewhat from dependence upon British and other ships. Not for long, however; for competition from foreign ships prevented any capital accumulation by the private owners; lack of capital prevented new construction. Therefore, in 1928, Congress passed the **Jones-White Bill** which provided for federal construction loans up to three-quarters of the cost of each vessel, for long-term mail carrying contracts and for continued cheap sales of government owned vessels.

Prohibition. The noisiest political issue of the Twenties was that of the enforcement of the 18th Amendment. The amendment was designed to eliminate barrooms; instead there arose "speakeasies," "beerflats" and "blind pigs" where bad liquor was sold under the benevolent eyes of a corrupted police force. More important than the actual consumption of bad liquor, however, was the growth in contempt of law as evidenced in the spread of "bootlegging," racketeering, murderous gangs (symbolized by Al Capone), and almost universal police corruption. The "wet-dry" issue was clamorous in local and national political elections. In 1931 President Hoover's **Wickersham Commission** reported that the "noble experiment" had broken down; and with the election of the Democrats in 1932 the era of prohibition came to an end. By December 1933 the **21st Amendment** repealed the 18th; the problem of liquor control was turned over to the states; and the problem of alcoholism moved from the moral to the medical area.

ECONOMIC DEVELOPMENT

The Technological Revolution. The Twenties were characterized by increasing mechanization in the basic industries; by improvements in existing machines; by wider application of electric power; by radical innovations in standardization of parts and assembly belts, particularly in the production of consumers' durable goods, e.g., automobiles. Increased mechanization and standardization resulted in increased productivity per man hour; in mounting mass production; in reduction of fixed costs per unit and therefore in larger profits—which were constantly reinvested in expansion. These were the good results.

On the debit side of the ledger, problems arose over the elimination of the skilled job and the resulting monotony of factory labor; over technological unemployment which caused great distress; and over the increasing size of industrial combines and the gradual disappearance of the small, independent producer.

The Rise of New Industries. Auto. Automobile production was easily the most prominent industry of the Twenties. By 1929 a total of 5,000,000 vehicles had been produced. The three major producers—Ford, General Motors and Chrysler—were giant corporations organized both vertically (from raw material to finished product) and horizontally (producing different brands within one corporation). Auto's effect on steel, glass, oil, rubber, asphalt and cement production was immense. Highway construction and traffic management became major problems; new patterns of indebtedness (chiefly installment buying) developed; and the social effects of putting most Americans on wheels were incalculable.

Radio. Out of Marconi's invention of wireless telegraphy and Lee DeForest's audion tube came the radio; and out of radio came General Electric's giant subsidiary, Radio Corporation of America. The possibility of widespread ownership of radio receivers stimulated the business of radio transmission. In 1920 the first commercial long-wave station was set up in Pittsburgh (KDKA). It was soon obvious, with a rapid multiplication of broadcasters, that the air waves would require policing. Therefore, in 1917 Congress created the Federal Radio Commission to assign both power and frequencies to broadcasters. The impact of radio upon advertising, recreation habits, political campaigns, national defense need not be detailed.

Chemicals. Production of chemicals mounted rapidly when German goods were cut off by World War I. The Alien Property Custodian permitted American producers to buy up German patents and once the industry was launched, total protection was granted to the industry by the **Fordney-McCumber Tariff** of 1922. By heavy subsidies to colleges, the chemical industry turned thousands of "chem labs" to its own use and profit.

Movies and Aviation. Finally, note must be made of the rise in this era of the motion picture industry which went from silent to sound in 1926; and of the aviation industry growing up slowly and painfully on government mail subsidies.

Increased Concentration of Wealth. By 1929, 594 corporations owned 52.2% of all corporate assets. This amazing concentration of ownership had been achieved in various ways. Automobile production was featured by the horizontal and vertical combination; cross-licensing enabled the Radio Corporation of America to control over 2,000 patents; holding companies featured in the public utilities (for example, with the ownership of 23,000 shares of the voting common stock in a parent holding company, the Standard Gas and Electric Company was able to control $1.2 billion in corporate assets!); mergers were dominant in the chemical and banking industries; the "chain" (the so-called "circular merger") appeared in movies, groceries, drugs, shoes, etc.; in all industries the "trade association" flourished, an organization which advised its members on anti-unionism, industrial practices, market controls, research, standardization, credit information, fair trade practices, and the like.

This pyramiding of business created a great chasm between the owners of industry (that is, the millions of small stockholders) and the managers (owners of blocs of voting shares). Virtually unchecked, the managers were able to vote themselves excessive bonuses, inequitable division of the dividends, fat contracts for services to their own subsidiaries, etc.

Patterns of Finance. The philosophy of Andrew Mellon dominated government finance. In brief, Mellon believed that it was the duty of the government to create funds for investment by reducing the tax load on big business. If, at the same time, government economized by pursuing a strict laissez-faire policy, the budget could be balanced. In the **Budgeting and Accounting Act** of 1921, a **Bureau of the Budget** headed by a Comptroller had been set up. It was to make annual reports to Congress of budgetary needs and advise Congress on a policy of expenditures balanced against expected receipts.

Mellon's withdrawal from regulating business, then, was deliberate; the Federal Reserve Board's withdrawal was inadvertent and due to a fault in the Federal Reserve Act. The fault lay in the fact that the FRB did not control the banks. The new giants of industry no longer required financing through the banks; their own reserves were large enough. The banks, therefore, turned their own surpluses into stock purchases through stock security affiliates which they created in the Twenties. The health of the banks thus came to depend to an unhealthy degree upon the stability of the stockmarket. There was little the FRB could do to stop the banks from gambling with "other people's (depositors') money."

Agriculture. Deepening depression characterized agriculture all through the Twenties. During the war farm production skyrocketed as the all-purpose tractor was put into use; as new plows, harvesters, threshers multiplied; and as scientific methods of farming increased the yields of wheat, corn and animals. With the war's end, the farmer's guaranteed market, both at home and overseas, disappeared, surpluses piled high, prices plummeted and market shifts created havoc (that is, autos reduced the need for animal feed, the population rate slowed, high caloried foods were rejected as slender figures came into vogue, as women's clothes shrank at both ends etc.). Once again came the round of debt, foreclosure and tenancy.

Outside Congress non-partisan leagues and farmer-labor parties took root; inside Congress a powerful "farm bloc" appeared—that is, representatives from farm regions who ignored party lines in matters of aid to the farmers. Suggestions for aid took many forms; increased tariffs, government aid to farm cooperatives, government purchase of the surpluses, government storage, sale and export of the surpluses, easier access to credit etc. In 1929 came the **Agricultural Marketing Act**—a timid effort to cope with surpluses: a **Federal Farm Board** was created to make loans to cooperatives so that the cooperatives might buy up the surpluses. That, of course, was all the encouragement the farmers needed to produce super-surpluses and the meager allotment to the Farm Board was used up in a short time.

LABOR

Immigration. Labor attained one of its primary goals during the Twenties—the elimination of labor competition from immigrants. Economic argument against immigration was only one objection. Another stemmed from prejudiced hostility to the "new immigrant." After 1880 the number of immigrants from the north of Europe dwindled to a trickle while those from the south and east of Europe rose to a flood. Between 1906 and 1914 immigrants from Austria-Hungary, the Balkans and Russia reached 1,000,000 in each of six separate years. In 1914 73.4% of the total immigration came from southern and eastern Europe as against 13.4% from northern and western Europe. Moreover, most of these immigrants were Roman and Greek Orthodox Catholics and Jews.

Some of the irrational racist stereotypes that prevailed in the early Twenties were: the new immigrant was "racially inferior" to the "superior Nordic" type; he was unassimilable; he "caused" slums; he was a "radical" etc. The result was that in 1921 quota restrictions were imposed; each group was allowed 3% of their nationals resident in the United States in 1910. Since this allotment still permitted too many of the "undesirables" to enter, the law was changed in 1924 to 2% of those registered in the census of 1890. Asians were now barred completely. (Natives of the western hemisphere, on the other hand, were free from quota restriction.) In 1929 the *National Origins Act* was passed and established a permanent formula for admission:

$$\frac{Quota}{150,000} \text{ equal } \frac{\text{Nationalities in the U. S. in 1920}}{\text{Total population in the U. S. in 1920}}$$

Cheaper Labor. Employers were somewhat hard pressed by this legislation for it tended to make labor more expensive. Other factors were increasing the cost of labor. The eight-hour day became standard in most industries; mechanization tended to eliminate the cheap unskilled worker (semi-skilled workers at the machine got more pay); welfare legislation forced employers to make provision for health and sanitation; and unions had grown powerful enough in some areas to compel steady wage increases. In an effort to counteract labor costs employers began widespread hiring of Canadians, southern whites, Mexicans, women and southern Negroes.

The Labor Movement. Failure of great strikes in coal, steel, meatpacking and railroads from 1919 to 1922 broke the back of organized labor. To prevent a revival of the trade union movement, employers experimented with welfare plans like group insurance, pension schemes, stock ownership etc. (so-called "welfare capitalism") while, at the same time, they used the traditional methods of company unions, blacklists, lockouts and the like. Established unions became conservative during the Twenties and concentrated their attention on developing union welfare schemes. Union inactivity gave the opportunity to communists to penetrate successfully into the leadership of the textile, coal, food, fur and furniture unions.

FOREIGN POLICY

Disarmament in the Far East. A foreign policy cannot safely ignore the realities of the international scene. America wanted to scrap its armament and to avoid new construction so that the national debt might be paid off and taxes reduced. How could this be done unilaterally without leaving oneself open to attack? The aggressor the United States feared most was Japan. How could Japan be curbed and isolation maintained? It was to resolve this dilemma that the United States in the summer of 1921 invited Great Britain, France, Italy, Japan, Belgium, the Netherlands, Portugal and China to consider stabilizing the Far East and limiting armaments. After prolonged negotiation, three treaties were drawn up.

The Five Power Treaty. The United States made extraordinary concessions in this treaty. A ratio of tonnage was drawn up. The United States and Great Britain were permitted 500,000 tons apiece; Japan, 315,000 tons; and France and Italy, 172,000 tons each. For the United States this meant junking 30 existing warships and 9 in construction; England had to scrap but 4 in construction; and Japan destroyed one 20-year old battleship! Since the 500,000 American tons had to be divided into a two-ocean navy, Japan secured a clear edge in the Pacific.

The Four Power Treaty. Japan, China, England and the United States agreed to maintain the status quo in fortifying insular possession; to respect each others' possessions; and to consult if a conflict broke out among the signers. Practically, this meant that the American defense string from Samoa to the Aleutians remained unfortified—since the United States kept its pledge, while Japan fortified its mandate islands. Furthermore, since the United States was not a member of the League of Nations, it had no right to check on the fulfillment of Japanese mandatory obligations. (The abrogation, in this treaty, of the Anglo-Japanese Pact of 1902 was a gain, however.)

The Nine Power Treaty. All the powers agreed to respect the sovereignty, territory, integrity and independence of China; to help China set up an efficient and stable government; to guarantee equal opportunity for all commerce in China and to refrain from seeking special privileges and rights which would abridge the rights of others. These excellent sentiments of the Open Door, however, would be only as strong as they were enforced. By withdrawing into isolation, the United States was withdrawing from enforcement and no country knew this better than Japan.

Further Conferences. Further conferences had to be called, however, to correct the deficiencies of the Washington Arms Conference. One at Rome in 1924 and another at Geneva in 1927 were fruitless. A third was held in London in 1930. Once again the United States favored disarmament. She granted Japan new ratio—10 to 6 for big gun cruisers, 10 to 7 for small gun cruisers and parity (10 to 10) in submarines; she agreed to six more years of a naval holiday (no further construction beyond treaty limits); she renewed her pledge of non-fortification of her island possessions, limited heavy cruiser construction and permitted an "escalator clause" to be included in the treaty which would permit England to have a navy equal in size to that of any two great powers.

Post War Debts. The United States was committed to collecting its war debts from the Allied powers. But the Allies made debt payment contingent on the receipt of German reparations payments. Therefore, to collect its debts, the United States undertook to finance Germany's reparations payments! Germany used the loans given to her in the **Dawes Plan** (1924) and in the **Young Plan** (1929) partly to pay her reparations bill and partly to rebuild her army in defiance of the Treaty of Versailles. When the depression overwhelmed Germany in 1931, the United States was forced to declare a moratorium on the payment of both Allied debts and German reparations. Actually this was the end to all payments.

At Lausanne, in 1933, Adolph Hitler repudiated all reparations payments; and, since the Allies had hitched debt payments to reparations, they repudiated their debts (already considerably scaled down). This, then, was the ironic situation in which the United States found itself: victor in World War I, the United States footed both the reparations bill as well as the Allied debts—that is, for all the Allied powers but Finland which paid its debt in full.

The League of Nations. Isolationism prevented American participation in the League of Nations. But how could America ignore so vast a body of combined nations? In fact, it did not. In 1923 unofficial American observers began to sit in on League committees which were considering non-political matters. In 1924, official American delegates were sent to League conferences. The government of the United States signed nine international draft conventions on such matters as narcotics control, control of slavery and forced labor etc.

But while it sought the benefits from League activities, the United States was unwilling to assume the responsibilities. Harding, Coolidge and Hoover were very much aware of this failing and urged that the United States enter, at the very least, the World Court and party platforms echoed this sentiment. The American Elihu Root had helped to frame the charter of the World Court; four Americans—John Bassett Moore, Charles Evans Hughes, Frank B. Kellogg and Manley O. Hudson—had sat as jurists there. But every proposal in the Congress to join was rejected by the Senate. Each of these proposals was accompanied by remarkable reservations which the League of Nations was ready to accept. For example, under the "Root Formula" if the United States joined the World Court, she would be informed of any opinion given by the Court which affected the United States; it would then be permitted to state its case against the Court's opinion to the League Assembly or to the Council; and if the opinion was nonetheless to be given against the United States, the United States could leave the World Court so that the opinion would have no effect. Even with these amazing concessions, the Senate rejected the Root Formula.

The Kellogg-Briand Pact. America did enter into a commitment for peace. Together with France, the United States made an anti-war pact (The Kellogg-Briand Pact) which condemned any recourse to war, renounced war as an instrument of national policy and pledged itself to peaceful settlement of all disputes. There was no provision enforcing these noble sentiments, so that it was easy to get 62 nations to join and to get the Senate to approve (81 to 1).

Latin America. Isolation did not mean a withdrawal from Latin America. Intervention and control continued through the Twenties in Haiti, the Dominican Republic, and Cuba. Restrictions were placed on the economic activities of these areas and American customs receivers were stationed there. In Nicaragua, active guerilla warfare was waged against American occupation. Relations with Mexico, however, improved considerably. In 1923 Mexico year leases only to properties acquired before 1917, should be respected and expropriated land paid for. This resulted in the recognition of Obregon as President of Mexico.

Two years later the Mexicans passed a Petroleum Law which vested ownership rights of subsoil resources in Mexico, demanded that foreigners abide by the law or forfeit their properties, granted fifty year leases only to properties acquired before 1917, limited the amount of grazing and agricultural land foreigners might own and forbade foreigners to apply to their home governments for protection. There was violent protest in America from the Secretary of State, Frank Kellogg, and from the Hearst press. Instead of intervening the United States sent Dwight Morrow on a mission to President Calles. By skillful diplomacy Morrow secured from Calles the following concessions: oil titles acquired before 1917 were legalized; Mexico's anti-clerical program was modified to permit religious services to be held in public. Hard feeling subsided.

In 1929 came a harbinger of the future in Latin-American relations—the **Clark Memorandum.** This memorandum repudiated the Roosevelt Corollary. It reaffirmed America's right to be the sole interpreter of the Monroe Doctrine but it denied that the doctrine sanctioned intervention in Latin American affairs. The Monroe Doctrine, it said, was intended for Europe, not Latin America.

SOCIETY AND CULTURE IN THE TWENTIES

No generalization about social and cultural trends in the Twenties can safely be made. It was an era of contradictions, of continuous ferment, of re-evaluation of values, of trial and error. But it left a profound mark upon American institutions and American thought.

Intolerance. One is struck, as one studies the record, by the many instances during the Twenties of undemocratic intolerance. The "Red scare" that began in the Twenties clearly got out of hand. Under the leadership of state legislatures and "Palmer raids," thousands of "radicals" were rounded up; they were often denied the most elementary civil liberties; they were "third-degreed" and, if aliens, deported. Out of the thousands apprehended, 500 were convicted and sentenced under the wartime Espionage and Sedition Acts. Five socialists were removed from the New York State legislature. Congress refused to seat the elected and re-elected Socialist, Victor L. Berger. Two innocent men, Sacco and Vanzetti, were tried and executed for a payroll robbery-killing they did not commit; what was really on trial in this case were their anarchist and pacifist sentiments.

Religious intolerance matched this political intolerance. Henry Ford sponsored the publication and distribution of a vicious, obviously forged and fraudulent, anti-semitic tract called "Protocols of the Elders of Zion" purporting to prove that the Jews were planning to conquer the world. To his eternal credit, Ford later withdrew his support and apologized for his mistaken judgment. This had little effect on the unpublished "quotas" that Jews encountered when seeking admission to colleges, professional schools and jobs. Anti-Catholicism was also rife and was revealed in all its ugliness in the election of 1928 involving Alfred E. Smith.

Worst of all, as we have seen, was the treatment of the Negro who had begun a mass movement northward. He was greeted in St. Louis, Omaha, Detroit and Chicago with fearful riots, and when these had settled down, with restrictive covenants forcing him into "ghettos" and with Jim Crow restrictions (both North and South) on the use of public places, educational facilities and employment opportunities. In the South, the KKK was revived and began an orgy of lynchings, floggings and terrorizations unparalleled in American history. No completely convincing answer has yet been given to the question: Why was there this post-war upsurge in intolerance?

Religion. The Twenties recorded no sensational growth in the religious spirit. Church membership grew; evangelists like "Billy" Sunday and Aimee Semple McPherson drew thousands of worshipers and auditors to their revivalist meetings; and the trial of John Scopes (1924) showed how deep-grained was the fundamentalist doctrine in American religious life in the South. Tennessee had outlawed the teaching of the theory of evolution.

Scopes, a science teacher, challenged the law. To the defense of Scopes came Clarence Darrow; to the defense of the law came William Jennings Bryan. The match between these two giants, one representing the skeptical spirit of Science and the other the dogmatic spirit of Religion, attracted international attention. Scopes was convicted; the conflict of science and theology remained unresolved.

Sex. The Twenties were marked by a self-concious revolt against Puritan restraints. Young women adopted the new "flapper" mode of dress; used gaudy cosmetics; participated in "wild parties"; danced the "Charleston" and "Big Apple"; devoured "confession" magazines and books; imitated the movie "vamp" and "it-girl." Young men were not far behind: raccoon coats; bell-bottom trousers; flask-on-hip; outlandishly decorated "tin-lizzies." Moral standards relating to courtship and marriage changed radically within a generation.

Ballyhoo. The advertiser and the public relations men were the kings of the Twenties. It was they who built the businessman into a myth; who created the American "standard of living"—as consisting of everything from a second car in a double garage to the mink coat; who built up the "million-dollar" gate for a prize fight, baseball game, football game or six-day bike race; who made Babe Ruth, Jack Dempsey, Red Grange and Shirley Temple national idols; who set the sheik and "flapper" styles; who promoted every kind of zany—the flagpole sitter, the Brooklyn Bridge jumper, the marathon dancer and the like.

Lawlessness. No sooner was the 18th Amendment passed and enforced by the Volstead Act when systematic violation of it began. Enforcement was non-existent; home brews multiplied; bootlegging became a major industry; gangsterdom flourished. King of gangsterdom, Al Capone, had a private army of thugs who conducted his businesses which embraced not only bootleg whiskey, but "collections" for "protection," sale of narcotics, extortion and prostitution. Enemies were "rubbed out" or "taken for a ride." Yet the American public remained either apathetic toward gangsterdom, fearful of it, or secretly sympathetic. Many of the gangsters fostered this attitude by appearing to be latter-day Robin Hoods. In fact, in a veiled form, the gangster became a kind of popular hero.

Social Advances. The seamy side of the Twenties is the "interesting" side; but some rather dull, solid gains were also registered. Considerable money was poured into the building of churches and synagogues; businessmen's associations like the Kiwanis, Elks and Rotary began a number of extensive service programs; living standards did rise and with them came a new freedom in the home; hundreds of new vocations were opened to enterprising women; the Model "T" and Model "A" Fords opened up all of America to travel and recreation; colleges expanded their physical facilities to accommodate a tremendous upsurge in enrollment.

Popular Reading. The most sensational development in popular literature was the appearance of the tabloid, an illustrated and heavily featured press that specialized in the lurid and sensational news story, and the racing tip. Daily circulation of these small-size newspapers was in the millions. Standard magazines kept pace. But they were being hard pressed by the "confession" magazines, the western pulps and the magazine tabloids called "digests."

Popular Music. Music entered the jazz age and composers began to exploit its possibilities. George Gershwin, Irving Berlin, Cole Porter, Hoagy Carmichal and William C. Handy produced songs that have endured as "jazz classics." With his "Rhapsody in Blue" Gershwin began to extend the American jazz idiom into quasi-symphonic form; but fulfillment of this form did not come until a later day.

SCIENTIFIC AND CULTURAL ADVANCE

Medicine. By the end of the twenties, diphtheria, and typhoid had succumbed to vaccines. Life expectancy continued to rise. Harvey Cushing advanced the frontiers of neurological surgery. Vitamin E was isolated. Drinker and Shaw invented the iron lung. American medicine had clearly come of age.

Physics. So, too, had the pure science of Physics. Nobel Prize winners Robert A. Millikan and Arthur Compton made basic discoveries. Millikan measured the charge of an electron and found it constant. Elaborating his findings, he was able to prove an Einstein equation and to evaluate Planck's constant. Compton showed that X-rays had a corpuscular structure (the "Compton effect").

Biology. Thomas Hunt Morgan, an American experimenter in heredity, made basic contributions to the science of heredity. Most of his studies on the gene, chromosomes and sex-characteristics were completed before 1920. However, during the Twenties, his students continued to expand his findings in these fields. Of particular importance was the discovery by H. Muller that X-rays increase the rate of mutation among fruit flies.

Psychology. John B. Watson provided an exciting moment in the field of psychology as he elaborated Pavlov's "condition reflex" into the science of "Behaviorism." In Watson's psychology man was reduced to mechanical-neural activity, a reduction which eliminated "consciousness," "free will," etc. While Watson's publicity was immense and had the good effect of encouraging laboratory experiments in psychology, most American psychiatrists were turning to the epoch-making studies of Sigmund Freud and beginning to apply his theories in psychotherapy.

Fine Arts. The turning point in American painting and sculpture was the controversial Armory Show in New York City in 1913, America's first view of the European revolution in the fine arts. Exhibited were Renoir, Roualt, Picabia, Picasso, Brancusi, etc.—names which no longer shock, but once shook the world. Following this showing, many Americans joined the cause of free expression as impressionists, expressionists, cubists, futurists, abstractionists—in short, as "modern" artists. These works resolved forms into abstracted planes and curves; distorted perspective to achieve esthetic tension; made color and line independent of theme. Among the many who became famous in the Twenties were Kroll, Kuniyoshi, Sheeler, O'Keefe, Davidson, Manship and Borglum. Their works are now featured in museums all over the world.

LITERARY ADVANCES

Fiction. With the war's end, the American novelist began a period of self-conscious revolt as a "lost generation" of sad, young men. Disgust with the war was universal when these writers discovered that the war was not a crusade, as Wilson had painted it; that war was mass slaughter, pain and agony, was destructive of artistic values and humane ideals, and death to the free mind. In the war tales of JOHN DOS PASSOS, E. E. CUMMINGS, and ERNEST HEMINGWAY, American protagonists (in the novels) are detached, disillusioned, sensitive observers of life.

Generalizing from this bitter experience, American novelists came back from the wars with the message that *all* ideals are shams, and that only he is "free" who lives permanently detached from them. They received considerable support for these beliefs from the sudden spread in America of Freudianism (in its most imprecise and popularized forms). A misreading of Freud led American novelists to the conclusions that absolute freedom of the individual and unlicensed self-expression were the only roads to stability and mental health, the only way out of the quagmire of pessimism and nihilism (that is, expect the worse and believe in nothing). So these writers in their texts preached the right to sexual license, and damned as "puritanical inhibition" any protest against such activities.

SHERWOOD ANDERSON (*Winesburg, Ohio; Triumph of the Egg*) at forty left his job, wife and family to become a novelist and short story writer. Out of his observation, his deep introspection, and cursory knowledge of Freudianism, he produced a gallery of fumbling adolescents, eccentrics, old and bitter failures—most of them homeless, rejected, impotent, frustrated, pursuing mangled dreams and private obsessions. They all grasp for something beyond their reach and their failures end in confusion. Anderson had no "message" but he did elaborate the method of the interior monologue for others to improve upon in a more hopeful vein. Because his types were so extreme ("grotesques") Anderson did not unduly disturb Americans.

SINCLAIR LEWIS did; (*Main Street; Babbitt; Arrowsmith; Elmer Gantry; Dodsworth*). In 1920 he began to hurl his bombs at American complacency and before he had done, he had ripped the closets open on small town life; he had exposed its unbearable drabness and narrowness; he had assaulted the "boobus americanis" of H. L. MENCKEN (perhaps the most influential social critic of the decade) in the form of George Babbitt, an American stereotype—the backslapper, go-getter, booster, joiner type, completely devoid of any insight into his own essential hypocrisies; he had exposed the idiocies and corruptions in fields as diverse as science and religion. In 1930 he won the Nobel Prize for literature, the first American to do so. Lewis, however, satiric and sarcastic though he was, did not hate the types he trampled on; on his own word, he loved them. His aim was to improve the community, the people and the faiths with which he identified himself. His was a reformer's goal, a fact revealed by the almost invariable "happy ending" to his books. But so vitriolic and loud was the contempt in his books, that his affection is barely noticeable.

Ernest Hemingway (*The Sun Also Rises; In Our Time; Men Without Women; Farewell to Arms*) created characters who were casualties—physical and spiritual—of the first World War. They follow a rigid code; drink to excess; are laconic; engage in violent sport; distrust intelligence and resist sentiment; believe in nothing. Hemingway's style matched his credo—it was bare; devoid of literary embellishment; reportorial; and transcriptive. Early Hemingway, therefore, became the prototype of the "lost generation," pessimistic, nihilistic, expecting nothing but sudden death.

Hemingway's heroes were young men grown old too soon. F. SCOTT FITZGERALD's would simply not grow old. (*Flappers and Philosophers; Tales of the Jazz Age; This Side of Paradise; The Beautiful and the Damned.*) Fitzgerald molded his characters in the image of himself—young, handsome, clever—and then projected his own conflicts and desires into them—his sensibilities; inordinate longings to be eternally young and rich beyond all care and responsibility. His style was elegantly shaped and mannered.

Finally, John Dos Passos (*Three Soldiers; Manhattan Transfer*) and WILLIAM FAULKNER (*The Sound and the Fury*) and THOMAS WOLFE (*Look Homeward, Angel*) began their work in the Twenties but came to their fulfillment in the Thirties. At this time, Dos Passos wrote of the artist struggling to free himself from a machine society; Faulkner began his intricate studies of Southern violence and decadence; and Wolfe made his first plunge into the past in an effort to recapture his experience.

Poetry and Criticism. During the Twenties American poets continued to experiment in verse forms begun in the previous decade. Most impressive was the work of E. E. Cummings who showed his contempt for an aspect of the received past by a singular assault upon the English language. In his poems he assailed mediocrity and celebrated the individual's right to love; he employed sometimes eccentric typographical devices to represent and extend meaning.

Hart Crane (The Bridge) selected the Brooklyn Bridge as the symbol of his attitude toward American values in a machine age, an attitude that oscillated sharply between exultation and despair (he eventually committed suicide).

Extending into the Twenties was the influence of Ezra Pound and T. S. Eliot. Pound combined in his poetry an extreme modernism with a profound sense of the past. Strikingly, he used obscure allusions to and quotations from ancient and medieval writers (often in their original language) and coupled this with direct English colloquialism.

Eliot was profoundly affected by Pound; he too sought for a simultaneity of the past and present. Eliot, however, more than Pound, was determined (e.g., in *The Sacred Wood*) to re-establish the values and traditions of the past, particularly those of the Christian heritage. It was in pursuit of this traditionalism that Eliot began, in the Thirties, his attempt to revive poetic verse-drama.

The "traditionalism" of the Twenties was part of an effort by some American intellectuals to find values in the American heritage by which to live in the present. The advance of science and mechanics had been deeply disruptive of a sense of values. In his *The Modern Temper*, Joseph Wood Krutch made a list of the "illusions" that would have to be dismissed now that science and mechanics ruled the universe of the mind: God, love, tragedy, esthetics, etc.

There arose a group of writers who indignantly rejected this gloomy appraisal of the present. Stuart Sherman, Irving Babbitt and Paul Elmer More, who called themselves the "New Humanists" urged Americans to return to Emerson and Thoreau and Melville, to established religion and philosophy, to a more abiding faith in democracy and the values of Puritanism. This return to the past, they argued, would produce in all Americans an "inner check" on their undisciplined emotions.

By similar reasoning Allan Tate, John Crowe Ransom and Robert Penn Warren evoked in their writings the Southern agrarian past when people had, they argued, a sense of propriety, rules of conduct, codes of manners. Willa Cather returned to the pioneer past where she could study nobility of character as it struggled against primitive natural forces; Stephen Vincent Benet wrote *John Brown's Body*, an evocation of the Civil War past; Ellen Glasgow and Edith Wharton wrote sadly, ironically but lovingly of the vanishing aristocracies, the former of the South and the latter of the North.

But these seekers of the American past were overshadowed in the Twenties by those who rejected America, past and present. Such were the thirty intellectuals whose essays appeared in 1921 in a volume called *Civilization in the United States* edited by Harold Stearns. They wrote in the spirit of disillusionment with their country. America, they charged, was a failure, culturally immature, preaching a false and hypocritical morality, crass, materialistic; a land that was death to its creative artists. What was a "free spirit" to do? He could drink himself to death, or write books full of self-pity, or expatriate himself to Europe where the artist had status, or create a small part of Europe called "Bohemia" in some Greenwich Village in America where he could practice his art.

Theatre. The "commercial" theatre of Broadway was dead—empty and exhausted. Off-Broadway the "little theatre" movement could experiment freely. From these experiments came Eugene O'Neill, who absorbed European influences and combined realism and expressionism. He sought to write American tragedies out of such themes as the struggle for dominance between a father and son, both competing for the father's wife and farm; a genius defeated by a mediocrity; a steamboat stoker who finds that no one will accept his humanity; a beautifully, emotionally sterile woman who dominates three men—her husband, her lover and her bachelor uncle; a modernized version of the tale of Electra, Orestes and Clytemnestra.

In his treatment of these themes and characters, O'Neill tried to portray the events as they were seen by the participating characters and not by the neutral spectators. In the inner life of his characters, O'Neill thought he had found the essential sickness of his time: "the death of the old God and the failure of science and materialism to give any satisfactory new one for the surviving primitive, religious instinct to find a meaning for life in and to comfort its fears of death." O'Neill, too, joined the disillusioned, the lost and the disinherited of the first World War.

CHAPTER XIX

THE NEW DEAL

The Great Collapse. President Herbert Hoover, inaugurated on March 4, 1929, inherited a deluge. On October 24, 1929, the stock market collapsed; within two weeks the value of securities shrank by $25,000,000,000; within three years, 110,000 businesses had closed their doors; 5,000 banks had failed; national income had toppled from $88 billion to $42 billion. Prices hit bottom: cotton dropped from 16¢ a pound in 1929 to 5¢; wheat from $1 a bushel to 32¢. More than 10,000,000 workers were unemployed. Wages for those fortunate enough to have jobs fell 55%. New investments in business fell from $10 billion in 1929 to $1 billion in 1932, not even enough to maintain existing plants. On the farm crops were rotting and farmers were dumping their milk; in the cities breadlines and souplines grew longer.

The dispossessed and adrift, the penniless and hungry were congregating in "Hoovervilles" and "hobo jungles"; in patchwork shambles that served as shelter. Desperate veterans formed a "bonus army" to demand full payment on their service certificates and then marched on Washington where they established headquarters on Anaconda Flats along the Potomac. At first the nation was stunned by this tragedy of poverty in the midst of plenty, of hunger in the midst of surplus. Then protesting voices were raised—from churchmen, from industrialists like Gerard Swope, from labor unions, from radicals, from men-and-women-in-the-street—agonized voices demanding that someone "do something."

"Prosperity is Just Around the Corner." Herbert Hoover, too, was baffled. He had no experience, as we have today, with the many indicators of a coming collapse: the chronic agricultural depression; the limited "depression" in coal, textiles and railroads; the unequal distribution of income leading to wild speculation; the widespread underconsumption since one-half the income receivers were getting less than subsistence earnings; the large withdrawals of foreign funds; the unusual "bull" or inflated market; the rigid, overmonopolized economy; the large numbers of unemployed even during "prosperity." Signs like these today would stimulate immediate government action; but Hoover firmly believed that "natural laws" should operate without government interference. But when the full impact of the collapse could not possibly be ignored any more, Hoover did move, and inaugurated the "Little New Deal."

The Little New Deal 1929-1932. Hoover's program for recovery was founded on the belief that government must first rescue the capitalist from distress. In 1932 the huge **Reconstruction Finance Corporation** was launched with a capitalization of $500 million and a borrowing capacity of $1.5 billion. Its purpose was to save from bankruptcy the banks, railroads, building and loan, and other businesses of the country by government sustaining loans. The **Glass-Steagall Act** of 1932 expanded the currency by permitting the issue of Federal Reserve notes with only government bonds and commercial paper only as backing; it also acted to stop the drain of gold by foreigners.

A **Federal Home Loan Bank** was established to halt the flood of foreclosures on mortgages. To bolster relief to the unemployed, the RFC might lend up to $300 million to the states whose treasuries were exhausted. Farmers were getting additional aid by the **Agricultural Marketing Act** of 1929 under which the government bought up surpluses in an effort to prop farm prices. Hard pressed foreign governments were given one year's moratorium on the payment of their debts to the United States. Outside of direct legislation, Hoover appealed to the heads of corporations to have faith, to keep producing and to refrain from wage cutting and layoffs. Nothing availed.

The Election of 1932. It was in his speech accepting the nomination that FRANKLIN DELANO ROOSEVELT created the slogan for his administration. "I pledge you," he said, "I pledge myself, to a new deal for the American people." Not much of a "New Deal" was apparent in the Democratic platform: a promise to balance the budget, to reduce federal expenditures, to remove government from fields of private enterprise except for public works and conservation, to maintain a sound currency, to reform the banking system, to lend relief money to the states and to control crop surpluses. All these were echoed in the Republican platform. Outright repeal of the 18th Amendment was purely a political issue; only an endorsement for unemployment and old age insurance sounded new. Republicans, nominating Hoover again, fought the campaign with the onus of the depression on their backs. Roosevelt waged a confident campaign and in his speeches became much more specific in discussing his reform program: a **crop control** program for the farmer; hydroelectric **projects**; full production, full employment, control of the stock exchanges and so forth. But more forceful than his program was his personality which inspired confidence wherever it was heard or seen. The electoral vote was overwhelmingly in his favor—672 to 59; only six northeastern states were in the Hoover column. Roosevelt had a clear mandate to construct his New Deal.

The General Staff. In his first inaugural address, Roosevelt proclaimed that "the only thing we have to fear is fear itself." What the nation needed was leadership. Roosevelt flayed the "rulers of the exchange of mankind's goods," the "unscrupulous money changers" and "self-seekers." He called for a spiritual rebirth—and for jobs. Action was to be placed on an emergency war-footing; the people would move as a trained disciplined force under his leadership and that of the "General Staff."

Strong administrators filled the cabinet posts: Secretary of State Cordell Hull, Treasury Henry Morgenthau, Jr., Arigulture Henry A. Wallace, Interior Harold L. Ickes, Labor Frances Perkins—the first woman cabinet member in American history—and Postmaster General James Farley. Then, from the nation's universities and other intellectual centers, Roosevelt gathered a "brain trust" consisting of Raymond Moley, Thomas Corcoran, Benjamin Cohen, Jerome Frank, Rexford Tugwell, Robert Sherwood, Hugh Johnson, Louis McHenry Howe, Samuel Rosenman and others. While far from unanimous in opinion, this group brought to the administration a high level of idealism and intellectual gifts.

New Deal Measures. Congressional legislation passed during the period of the New Deal fell into four categories: **emergency legislation** which became inoperative when the emergency passed; **trial and error legislation** which was abandoned when it produced failure; **reform legislation** which redesigned existing law to eliminate weaknesses exposed during the onset of the Depression of 1929; and **new legislation** which protected the physical resources of the country, redistributed the wealth of its citizens, and extended the protection of the government to new groups.

EMERGENCY LEGISLATION

Opening the Banks. By March 4, 1933 virtually every bank in the country was closed as a result of state-ordered "bank holidays." Roosevelt, invoking the "Trading with the Enemy Act of 1917," thereupon proclaimed a four-day **national bank holiday.** This was coupled with an embargo on the export of gold, silver and currency. Congress then passed an **Emergency Banking Act** under which the Treasury officials and the RFC could begin to reopen sound banks and to liquidate those that were insolvent. On the 12th of March, the President had his first "fireside chat" with the people and informed them in simple language of what the government had done and what *they* must do, namely, return to normal banking habits. The people did so and by April 1st one billion dollars in currency and gold was dehoarded and returned to the banks. The banking emergency was resolved.

The Unemployed. By 1933 unemployment stood at about 16,000,000 and with each passing month thousands of young people were entering the labor market, swelling the total. Private, municipal and state relief funds were exhausted and emergency measures were required to stave off hunger. On the 31st of March, therefore, Congress enacted the **Civilian Conservation Corps Reforestation Relief Act** which authorized the creation of work camps for 250,000 jobless male citizens between 18 and 25 years of age. These young people were housed and fed, given $30 a month (part of which went to their dependents), and set to work under Army supervision planting trees, draining swamps, and combating soil erosion, poison ivy and hay fever weeds.

The following May, the **Federal Emergency Relief Act** provided a half-billion dollar allotment to states and municipalities for the creation of work relief projects. When a temporary business revival in mid-1933 collapsed, the **Civil Works Administration** under Harry Hopkins was created to provide federal employment for four million jobless persons. Almost a billion dollars was spent on CWA for 180,000 work projects before this phase of relief was abandoned (March 1934).

The "WPA." In 1935 Congress produced the **Works Progress Administration**—the highly controversial WPA. WPA lasted until 1943 and, in the course of its existence, it cared for 8,500,000 people. Part of WPA funds went to the states to place unemployables on relief. Another part was devoted to the **National Youth Administration** which removed students and unemployed girls from the labor market by subsidizing them in such tasks as clerkships, library assistants, etc. The bulk of the money, however, went for employing adults on projects which would not compete with private industry and would not require large expenditures on capital equipment. Such projects included construction of schools, playgrounds and airports; maintenance of roads, water mains and sewers; flood relief, snow removal and the like.

Special attention was given to unemployed artists, actors, writers and scholars who produced hundreds of murals and statuary for public buildings, a **Federal Theatre Project** that educated millions in great drama and did special research that produced guidebooks, dictionaries and the like. The WPA never became more than an employment dole and for this reason was severly criticized as "boon doggling" and demoralizing to the individual (even though it fed him) and as non-contributary to economic recovery, if the cost were considered.

Foreclosures on Farm Mortgages. With surpluses on their hands, with prices at rock bottom, farmers were unable to meet their debts. Foreclosures multiplied; 25% of the farm families of the nation were on relief and a large number had been reduced to tenancy or to grubbing a bare subsistence from submarginal lands. Congress, therefore, acted to halt further foreclosures. Measures were adopted which extended funds to Federal Farm Loan agencies enabling them to refinance mortgage payment which had come due but could not be met. Then Congress enacted a foreclosure act which permitted farmers to renegotiate mortgages which had already been foreclosed. But the most radical approach to foreclosure was the **Frazier-Lemke Act** of June 1934 which placed a five-year moratorium on foreclosures and provided a method for repurchase of lost properties. Enraged creditors went to the courts and won their case on the unconstitutionality of the law (**Louisville Joint Stock Land Bank v. Radford 1935**).

Congress struck back at the Supreme Court with the **Farm Mortgage Moratorium Act** of 1935. Under this law (which was upheld by the Court) the courts could grant to a farmer three years' grace against foreclosure if he paid rent or repossessed his property. Creditors could force a sale at auction, but the farmer might then redeem his farm at auction price. Finally, for those who had been permanently displaced and were now tenants or farm laborers, Congress experimented with creating subsistence homesteads and resettlement projects. A number of such efforts were consolidated in the **Bankhead-Jones Farm Tenancy Act** of 1937.

A **Federal Security Administration** was set up and empowered to make loans to help tenants buy land, to build camps for migratory workers, and to build subsistence homestead projects. FSA measures met the same hostile criticism of "paternalism" and "socialism" and "demoralization" as did the WPA. Few men in public life were more abused than Rexford G. Tugwell, head of the **Resettlement Administration**, as he sought to establish "Greenbelt Towns" (subsistence homestead communities in suburban areas) and to promote cooperative farming and soil conservation projects.

"Priming the Pump." Business revival hinged on the ability of solvent enterprises to make short-term and long-term loans. The banks were unable to make them, and the savings banks, insurance companies, trust companies, title and mortgage companies were unwilling to do so. Therefore the New Deal began to "prime the pump." It shot funds into sick industries. The RFC was expanded and given the right to make direct loans to private businesses, municipalities and public corporations for housing projects, electric power projects and the like. In Title II of the National Industrial Recovery Act a **Public Works Administration** was created (the PWA). Secretary of the Interior Ickes was placed at its head and given $3 million to spend on projects which would put private contractors back into business. They, in turn (it was hoped), would begin to employ labor and thus the pump would be primed through an increase in consumption power. Unfortunately, more money was consumed in purchase of capital goods than in employment of labor.

"TRIAL AND ERROR" LEGISLATION

Inflation. With low prices plaguing the land, the time seemed ideal to many New Dealers to make a national experiment in **monetary inflation.** The first step was to abandon the gold standard. This required an embargo on gold shipped abroad, an order to all holders of gold coin, bullion or certificates to turn in their holdings for currency, and a further order permitting anyone bound by contract to pay a debt in gold to substitute currency for gold. (The Supreme Court upheld the legality of the **Gold Clause Repeal Act** by a 5 to 4 decision, 1935).

With the government in control of all gold stocks, the President proceeded to reduce the gold content of the gold dollar to 59.06 of its former weight. Since each paper dollar was now backed by a little more than half the former gold content, the number of paper dollars could be almost doubled. The paper profit in this manipulation was $3 billion. $2 billion of this became a "stabilization fund" to deal in gold, government securities and international currencies. (The cheap dollar had little effect on domestic prices, but it did stimulate foreign trade since a foreign buyer could get almost $2 where he formerly got only $1.)

The "silver bloc" in Congress forced through a silver purchase act which required the President to buy silver at a high artificial price until silver constituted one-quarter of the monetary stock, and to pay for it in silver certificates. It was hoped, of course, that a flood of silver certificates would make for a sudden inflation; it did not. Finally, the **Thomas Amendment to the Agricultural Adjustment Act of 1933** permitted the President to issue $3 billion of fiat (unbacked) currency. But the President was at most a "relationist," that is, a mild inflationist and never implemented the Thomas Amendment. Controlled inflation proved a disappointing failure.

The NIRA. The greatest failure of the New Deal, however, was the **National Industrial Recovery Act of 16 June 1933** which created a **National Recovery Administration (the NRA)** under HUGH S. JOHNSON. Its stated aims were all-embracing: to free commerce; to secure cooperative action among trade groups; to achieve united action of labor and management; to eliminate unfair competition; to promote full production; to increase purchasing power; to reduce unemployment; to improve labor standards; to rehabilitate industry; and to conserve resources—in a word, to end the depression.

How was this omnibus goal to be achieved? Antitrust laws were suspended for the duration of NRA; men of good will in all industries were to submit voluntarily to "codes of fair competition" drawn up by themselves. Voluntarism and cooperation were the keynotes; but, if any group proved stubborn and would not agree to a code then the government might impose a code upon it. The codes provided for self-regulation through production controls, minimum prices, assigned quotas, quality controls, minimum wages and maximum hours and, in the highly significant Section 7A, the specific recognition of labor's right to organize and to bargain collectively. Those who submitted to a code were permitted to display a "Blue Eagle" and those who did not were publicly condemned by Mr. Johnson and were prosecuted in the federal courts.

From their inception, the codes were attacked furiously. Large producers sought to dominate or destroy them; small businessmen charged that the codes were simply legalized monopolistic practices; labor complained that employers had only been driven to more ingenious methods of destroying unions and that minimum wages were fast becoming maximum and that maximum hours were becoming minimum; consumers complained that restricted production resulted in price increase without compensating employment wage increases.

Non-compliance became the rule by March 1934 and Congress was seething with discontent; relief was general when the Supreme Court declared NRA unconstitutional in the **Schechter Poultry Case** (1933) because it was an improper extension of Congress' power over interstate commerce. NIRA was the widest deviation of the federal government from traditional American free enterprise; in declaring it unconstitutional, the Supreme Court prevented the first major effort of the central government to dominate industry completely.

REFORM THROUGH REGULATION

Transport and Coal. The Interstate Commerce Commission had its powers increased as New Deal economists strove to eliminate the weakness in government regulation of basic industries. The plight of the railroads, for example, was pitiful. They were harassed by accumulated fixed debts that could not be reduced, by duplication and waste of services, and by competition from autos, buses, water transport, pipelines and planes. An epidemic of bankruptcy threatened the entire industry in 1931.

In 1933, therefore, Congress passed the **Emergency Railroad Transportation Act** which created a Federal Coordinator of Transportation whose task was to aid the roads by consolidating them into three major systems. At the same time, the ICC was given control over railroad holding companies to prevent their corrupt "milking" operations. The Federal Coordinator had little success for he was powerless to overcome the railroad's inability to compete with cheaper means of transport.

To counteract this defect, in 1935 Congress extended the power of the ICC over the rates and finances of airlines and motor carriers and then in 1940, over water transport. The commission was now in a position to distribute government aid impartially to the weakest sectors of transport. Rate-making was separated from the value of the investment and designed to make all traffic profitable. As in railroads, so in coal; coal, too, suffered from reduced demand, overcompetition, heavy fixed costs etc. The **Guffey-Vinson Act of 1937** created a code of fair competition for the entire industry and sought to improve its position by restricting output.

Monopoly Price Fixing and Quality Control. Few subjects so preoccupied the New Deal theoreticians as monopoly. In 1938 Congress decided to make a massive inquiry into American monopoly and set up a **Temporary National Economic Committee (TNEC)** to investigate. This committee conducted a three-year inquiry, heard more than 550 witnesses from every walk of life, and collected 17,000 pages of testimony plus 43 volumes of special monographs by outstanding economists, sociologists and political scientists. This mountain of research produced a mouse of remedial legislation. In convening the investigation President Roosevelt had declared that there "is a concentration of private power without equal in history" in America; the TNEC proved there was. The Department of Justice proceeded with enforcement of anti-trust prosecutions. But many Americans considered the anti-trust laws antiquated.

The New Deal itself established rigid prices in an effort to prevent cutthroat competition which would drive out the small businessman. In the **Miller-Tydings Act** (1937) it sanctioned state laws which enforced the monopolistic practice of price-fixing to protect small retailers against chain stores; in the **Robinson-Patman Act** it amended the Clayton Anti-Trust Act to protect wholesalers against the buying power of chain stores and mail order houses by once again maintaining retail prices and eliminating discounts for large scale purchases. The FTC was empowered to enforce uniform discounts. In other words, price-fixing was not the evil here; the destruction of competition was, and if fixed prices will protect a competitor—then fix them. Was uncontrolled competition the answer? Certainly not where the health of the public was concerned.

The New Deal was particularly active on the consumer front and this required severe control over quality. Under the **Commodity Exchange Act** of 1936 the Secretary of Agriculture could set standards for agricultural produce traded on the Exchange. In 1938 a **Food, Drugs and Cosmetics Act**, under a Food and Drug Administrator, enforced standards for all three products; subjected them to inspection; no new drugs could be offered for sale until tested and found harmless; all drugs and cosmetics had now to carry informative labels. In the same year the power of the FTC was extended to advertisements of drugs, cosmetics and therapeutic devices by the **Wheeler-Lea Act**. In 1939 quality standards and labeling was extended to wool products; manufacturers had to indicate whether the wool was new, reprocessed, reused, adulterated.

In practice, then, the New Deal found no over-all approach to the problem of monopoly. In some cases, monopoly proved desirable (coal, railroads); in others, monopolies could be limited by government monopolistic practices (price fixing, quality controls). Monopolies were enmeshed in the total economy; they had to be balanced with the needs of consumers, workers and small businessmen. Perhaps the best answer lay in regulated co-existence.

Public Utilities. Unregulated monopoly had produced extraordinary evils in the area of public utilities. Holding companies milked their operating subsidiaries; magnates like Samuel Insull were concerned only with stock manipulation and not with services; subsidiaries refused to expand electric facilities to low income groups; outrageous rates could be enforced upon helpless consumers. In 1935 Congress passed the **Wheeler-Rayburn Public Utility Holding Company Act**. To the Securities and Exchange Commission was given the power to regulate the service, sales, construction contracts, loans, dividends, etc., of the public utilities. The SEC was further ordered to simplify the sprawling pyramids of holding company control by lopping off subsidiaries which were neither economically nor geographically justified. (Utilities called this provision of the Act the "death sentence" clause.)

At the same time the power of the PFC was broadened to control interstate commerce in power. Utilities had now to file their rate schedules and the FPC could suspend unwarranted rate charges. New power projects on public lands and navigable rivers required the consent of the FPC. In 1938 similar FPC controls were extended to the natural gas industry. Federal control over these varied utilities worked well: more realistic values of the utilities' properties were established; consumers secured lower rates. Is this then the answer to the monopoly problem: coexistence plus adequate regulation?

Securities and Exchanges. The most obvious areas for extension of government control were the stock and commodity exchanges. The rise and fall of economic values has been most sensational in these areas. One of the earliest acts of the New Deal Congress was the **Truth-in-Securities Act** of 1933. The FTC could require every corporation offering new securities for sale through the mails or in interstate commerce to register them with the Commission. This function was transferred in 1934 to the Securities and Exchange Commission. Besides requiring registration of securities, the SEC was empowered to license exchanges; to define the function of members, dealers and brokers; to require annual reports; and to investigate unfair market practices. To the Federal Reserve Board, however, was given the function of regulating margin requirements (that is, buying stocks on the installment plan with a down payment), though the SEC could investigate excessive trading on margin. The SEC soon acquired other powers: control over unlisted securities; regulation of corporate bankruptcies involving more than $3 million; enforcing the "death sentence"; investigation of investment trusts.

NEW LEGISLATION

Protecting the Physical Resources. Besides being great avenues of transport, rivers are sources of hydroelectric power. At favorable water sites huge dams can be constructed to supply the water to power plants; power plants can then generate and distribute electricity. In the **Federal Water Power Act of 1920** the United States government had announced its ownership of all water power sites on public lands and navigable rivers. A **Federal Power Commission** was created to license private power companies, state government or municipalities for the use of such sites. There was no legal bar to federal use. In fact, in 1917 a project had been started at Muscle Shoals to generate the power to produce military nitrates. There was no legal bar—but a considerable traditional barrier existed: it was generally held that federally generated power was a venture into "socialism," that is, government ownership and operation of industry. So felt Presidents Coolidge and Hoover and they vetoed the bills sponsored by George W. Norris for the complete development of the Tennessee River Valley. Norris argued that the demands of the nation for cheap electricity and the conservation of natural resources could best be met only by a legitimate extension of the federal authority.

Conservation needs bulked large in New Deal thought. Electricity and flood control were vital needs in the Tennessee Valley; as were electricity and irrigation along the Columbia and Colorado Rivers. Therefore in 1933 Congress passed the act creating the **Tennessee Valley Authority** which was empowered to construct dams, reservoirs, powerhouses and transmission lines; to produce, distribute, and sell electric power; to produce nitrates for military and agricultural purposes; to control floods; to make rivers more navigable; to engage in soil conservation by extensive reforestation.

As implied extensions of its stated powers TVA has in fact sold electrical appliances and established industries in order to foster the sale of electricity; it has pushed electrification in rural areas; it has removed marginal lands from cultivation and encouraged crop diversification; it has constructed towns and all the dwellings in them. TVA's rates were to serve as a "yardstick" for private utility rates, but events were to show that no private utility could hope to compete with TVA. Thus in the Tennessee Valley the huge corporation, Commonwealth and Southern Public Utility, was forced to sell out all its properties to TVA.

Private companies had hopes that the government could be stopped in the courts. But in **Ashwander v. TVA** (1936) the Supreme Court found that federal sale of power to municipalities was constitutional; in **Alabama Power Co. v. Ickes** it upheld the construction of city plants to receive TVA power; in 1939 in **Tennessee Electric Power Co. v. TVA** the court supported government competition with private power provided the primary purpose was navigation, flood control, national defense or conservation. Having launched public ownership along the Tennessee with construction of the Norris and Wilson Dams and seven others, the New Deal extended its program to the Columbia River (Grand Coulee, Bonneville) and to the Colorado River (Hoover). Opposition to these extensions was fierce and as a result regional planning remained limited during the New Deal period.

Soil Conservation. TVA was not alone in the war on waste. New Deal agricultural programs also contained conservation features. One of the most pressing problems was the appearance in the Thirties of huge "dust bowls"—eroded areas with their top soils washed or blown away. The **Soil Conservation and Domestic Allotment Act of 1936** offered farmers benefits for planting soil restoring crops; the CCC and TVA engaged in large reforestation programs; the Resettlement Administration concerned itself with reclamation as a measure of conservation; the Department of Agriculture organized technical assistance teams which toured the farm country to teach new methods of contour and terrace farming to the farmers. War on waste was many-sided, and remains so.

Redistributing the Wealth. In the Revenue Acts of 1935, 1936 and 1937 the New Deal undertook to tap more heavily the large incomes in the country. Revenue laws, said Roosevelt, "have operated in many ways to the unfair advantage of the few." As a result surtaxes on high incomes were increased; normal taxes were more steeply graduated; gift and estate taxes were raised; undistributed profits were taxed; and loopholes in the tax laws were plugged up. One purpose in the "soak-the-rich" program was to redistribute wealth to raise consuming power—thus priming the pump; another was humanitarian—to ameliorate conditions for "one-third of the nation" who were "ill-fed, ill-clothed and ill-housed."

Relief measures costing millions were adopted to provide food and work for the unemployed; but there were many others whose plight was not specifically depression-born, many who suffered loss of income even in the best of times and who, in the best of times, were forced to live in unhealthful environments. These were the widowed, the orphaned, the discarded old-age, the underfed, the illiterate and the slum-dwellers. This humanitarian impulse in the New Deal resulted in legislation which became a permanent feature of American life.

Social Security. Federal aid was made available to needy dependent children (the crippled, the blind, etc.) and the needy widowed. Federal funds were offered to states. With these funds, states launched large scale public health, child, crippled, and blind service programs. Needy persons, sixty-five years old or older (in 1935) were able to secure old age pensions if they could prove that they had no dependents. This, too, was a matching program with Federal aid limited to $15 per person per month.

The heart of the New Deal social security scheme, however, was an **insurance** program covering the aged, and survivors without support. The insured were those who worked in their life time and paid insurance taxes out of their earnings; the amount of the insurance tax was matched by the employer. In this manner a fund was created and when a worker reached 65, he was entitled to retirement benefits (not pensions). If he died before he retired, his widow or dependents received benefits. There were other features to the law that have remained to this day: there were to be minimum and maximum benefits; minimum periods of work were required before benefits could be secured. The same law provided for an unemployment insurance plan to be worked through the states. The federal government collected from each state a special payroll tax. 90% of this tax was returned to the state if it enacted an unemployment insurance law. The fund for unemployment insurance benefits was to be contributed by the employers of labor alone. Any worker who became unemployed could draw, depending on the length of time he worked, certain minimum and maximum amounts (states differ in the amount of their payments). To secure payment, a worker had to make himself available for another job, if the job met certain prescribed standards. Government planners were somewhat uncertain of the constitutionality of this law but the Supreme Court upheld it on the ground that the federal government may tax for the purposes of social welfare.

Housing. In the depression hundreds of thousands of Americans were either in danger of losing their homes or being forced by loss of jobs to dwell in the slums. President Hoover had already acted to save the homeowner with a Home Loan Bank System. But its capitalization at $125 million was as nothing compared to the $3 billion expended by the **Home Owners Loan Corporation** (HOLC) which had been set up by the **Home Owners' Refinancing Act** in the early days of the New Deal.

The full extent of this humanitarian effort was revealed in the terminal report of HOLC in 1951. 800,000 foreclosures had been staved off and 1,017,-321 mortgages had been refinanced. The psychological gains cannot be estimated. For the "ill-housed"

a **National Housing Act** was passed in 1934 which created a **Federal Housing Authority** with power to stimulate residential housing construction. This was to be done by an elaborate insurance system for mortgages incurred in new building as well as for modernization and repair measures. In 1937, the New Deal began a direct assault on the slums. For every substandard building torn down, a newly created United States Housing Authority would build a new tenement project with occupancy limited to low-income groups. "Housing projects" began to appear everywhere on the urban landscape.

Minimum Wages-Maximum Hours. In 1938 the concept of an established minimum wage and maximum hour load—first forecast in the NIRA—was written into law as the **Fair Labor Standards Act.** Forty hours became the maximum beyond which employers were compelled to pay time-and-a-half. 40¢ an hour was made the minimum wage. The FLSA also limited child labor. In **United States v. Darby** the Supreme Court upheld these social measures too.

The Farm Problem. By 1933 violence had flared up in the mid-west as commercial farmers struck out against shrinking farm income land values; against mounting surpluses and foreclosed homesteads. Vigilante committees were formed to see that food was withheld from market, that milk was dumped, that purchasers were frightened away from forced auction sales, and that judges about to foreclose on homesteads were intimidated. They marched on state capitals and assaulted agents of the insurance and mortgage companies. To halt this violence, the New Deal resorted to stop-gap measures.

Private banks were clearly unable to finance farmers for any extended period. Congress, therefore, created a public bank, the **Farm Credit Administration,** which paid off the farmers' creditors and then took over his mortgages. It then made loans to farmers unable to offer any kind of security. But so great was the number of mortgages threatened with foreclosure that the Congress enacted moratoriums on mortgage payments (the Frazier-Lemke Act of 1934, declared unconstitutional was upheld in 1935. Further aid was given to farmers stricken by natural disaster. Farmers not threatened with collapse were protected by liberal extensions of credit from this government bank.

Control of the Surplus and Parity Price. All of the basic crops were in excess for commercial purposes (although there was widespread hunger in the land). What does one do with more crops than one can sell? One can destroy them; and in 1933 and 1934 the New Deal paid farmers to plow under cotton and to slaughter 6,000,000 pigs. This caused moral revulsion. Or, the government might store the surplus or give it away and, at the same time, grant the farmers loans on their storage. A Commodity Credit Corporation was set up in 1933 for precisely this purpose. But wasn't there a danger that farmers would begin to overproduce deliberately for storage?

It became clear to New Deal planners that the only solution to the problem of surplus was nonproduction. Such was the purpose of the Agricultural Adjustment Act of 1933 (declared unconstitutional in the Hoosac Mills Case), the Bankhead Cotton Control Act, the Kerr-Smith Tobacco Act and the Soil Conservation and Domestic Allotment Act of 1936. All of the specific features of these laws were included in the comprehensive Agricultural Adjustment Act of 1938.

The logic of this law rested upon three goals: to attain for the farmer a "parity price," that is, a price at such a level that agricultural products would have the same purchasing power with respect to the goods farmers buy as they had in the years from 1909 to 1914. In those years, when a farmer sold his crops, he received prices that enabled him to buy all he needed and to discharge his debts. This relationship of goods sold to goods bought was to be reestablished. But how?—by curtailed production paid for by the government; by deliberately not planting a surplus and getting paid for not planting.

The AAA paid a benefit to a farmer who took a basic crop out of production and substituted soil-conserving crops like hay or alfalfa. Others were paid benefits if they accepted acreage quotas, that is, planting a *limited* amount of acres. Intensive farming of limited acreage might still produce a surplus; therefore two things were done to cope with this possibility: surpluses could be stored in a government granary to be sold in the market whenever shortages appeared (under this arrangement, a farmer could not lose: if prices were depressed, he would store his crop and receive a loan rate higher than market price; if prices were higher than the loan rate, he would redeem his stored crop and sell it at market price); or surpluses could be prevented from reaching the market by marketing quotas. The AAA provided that such marketing quotas could be set up if two-thirds of the farmers voted for them. Anyone violating his marketing quota would be punished by a tax on all excess sales. If after all this prices still were below parity, the government would dip into the national treasury and pay the difference. Finally, if nature struck the wheat farmer down, there was a Federal Crop Insurance Corporation that would make up his losses.

Government warehousemen had the problem now of what to do with the surpluses. They experimented in give-away programs. Foreign markets were sought out in Reciprocal Trade Agreements; food was handed out in direct relief; and a large amount went into school-lunch programs.

Criticism. These restrictive measures (the basis for the current farm program) registered some important gains. There was a sizeable rise in farm income and a somewhat more moderate decrease in farm mortgages. But criticism of the program was severe and manifold. It was charged that crop curtailment at a time of hunger was immoral; the farmers were being made into a privileged class supported by all other sectors of the economy; and that by no means all farmers were benefited. The program centered upon the *commercial* farmer. But what of the tenant farmer, the migratory dust-bowl "Oakies" and "Arkies," and the marginal back-country farmers? What of the sharecroppers and farm laborers? There were at least 5,000,000 of these underprivileged rural groups in the country in 1935. In 1934, 3,500,000 rural families were on relief.

The War on Rural Poverty. The rural underprivileged had either no land or land too poor to farm profitably. Government donated seeds and tools were of no use to them. The obvious solution seemed to be to resettle them on better lands. The Resettlement Administration (1935) and the Farm Security Administration (1937) wrestled with this problem, for in their resettlement projects they were creating a new set of producers at a time when curtailment was the order of the day. Submarginal lands were bought up; cooperative farms were set up on fertile lands and farmers were given money, seeds, tools and instruction in farming techniques; subsistence (non-commercial) farms were created in "Greenbelts" located in the suburbs of the large cities; camps for the migratory workers were built; and farm tenants were encouraged to borrow for land purchases. Thus, under the guidance of Rexford G. Tugwell, valiant but uncoordinated efforts, running counter to the chief farm programs, were made to save the rural poor.

Indians. Special beneficiaries of the policy of resettlement were the Indian tribes living on reservations. In 1924, whether members of tribes or not, they had been made American citizens. Attempts to individualize land holdings had failed utterly. Therefore, in 1934, the Wheeler-Howard Act permitted whole tribes to buy land and engage in business as a corporate body. Severe restrictions were placed on the resale of land by the tribes. The total value of the land so assigned was estimated in 1934 as worth about $2 billion. Some of it was rich in oil, minerals, and timber; but most of it was poor. The result was that considerable supplemental aid had to be given the Indians by the state and federal governments.

Labor and the New Deal. Organized labor felt that it had been lost in this new shuffle. Roosevelt was more humanitarian, they felt, than Hoover, a great many New Deal acts (the CCC, the Emergency Relief Act, the Public Works Program of Title II of the NIRA, and the Civil Works Administration) took care of the workingman's immediate needs; the housing measures, too, benefited him in the longer run. But labor chafed, nonetheless, NIRA, they felt, favored the employer over the worker; few changes in wages and hours resulted despite grandiose "code" provisions; and Section 7A guaranteed nothing since employers began to outmaneuver it with every known anti-union tactic. To give point to its grievances, labor began a series of bloody strikes immediately following the adoption of the codes. In coping with the problems created by these strikes, Robert F. Wagner, Sr., Senator from New York, came to the conclusion that government must ally itself directly with the cause of labor. The result was the **Wagner-Connery National Labor Relations Act of 1935.**

The NLRA. This act began with an accusation. Denial by employers, it said, of the right of their employees to organize and refusal by employers to bargain collectively with unions is the cause of strikes, of obstructions to the free flow of commerce, and of a fall in wage rates and employment. The act then proposed to correct these abuses. It created a **National Labor Relations Board** to enforce the act; legalized the right of employees to organize and bargain collectively through representatives of their own choosing; outlawed as unfair labor practices interferences by the employers with efforts to unionize, establishment of company unions, discrimination in the hiring and firing of union labor and refusal to bargain collectively. To determine who the bargaining representatives were to be, the NLRB was empowered to hold elections in the plants concerned. And to insure that the law was obeyed, the NLRB could make investigations of complaints and hold hearings on them. Decisions of the NLRB were enforceable in the courts.

AFL and CIO. Employers did not accommodate to this new emphasis in government easily as is evidenced by the fact that from 1935 to 1940 the NLRB handled more than 30,000 cases and reinstated 21,000 fired workers. Some leaders in the AFL felt that the time was ripe to organize the unorganized and pressured the AFL President, WILLIAM GREEN, to do so. But Green moved warily. Into what crafts would the unorganized fit? While Green

hesitated, JOHN L. LEWIS took the leadership. His own United Mine Workers were organized fully on an industrial union basis, not according to what each man did, but according to the industry in which he worked. In his fight against Green, Lewis advocated industrial unionism, more militant strikes, mass picketing and intensified political activity; and to achieve this, a **Committee for Industrial Organizations** was formed within the AFL, in 1936. In 1938 a **Congress of Industrial Organization (the CIO)** was formed when its predecessor within the AFL was expelled from that organization in 1936. Lewis became the CIO's first president and remained that until 1940 when he quarreled with FDR and resigned his post in the CIO which supported FDR; PHILIP MURRAY (of the Steelworker's Union) took his place.

From 1936 to 1938 the CIO conducted a series of sensational "sit-down" strikes. Strikers ousted the plant management and locked themselves in the plant. Neither the police nor the militia could oust the workers without doing considerable damage to the plants and employers themselves opposed military action against the workers' seizure. Sit-down strikes brought the new CIO unions tremendous victories: Goodyear Tire & Rubber, General Motors, "Big Steel" were the first to capitulate. ("Little Steel" was far more resistant; efforts to organize this part of the steel industry resulted in the "Memorial Day Massacre" in which Chicago police fired upon and killed a number of picnicking pickets and their wives who were on strike against Republic Steel. Loss of Little Steel was a serious blow to the CIO; even FDR's sympathy began to wane.) In the **Fansteel Case,** the Supreme Court outlawed the sit-down strike.

But the sit-down had served labor's purpose; in two years the numbers of unionized workers jumped from three to nine million, the AFL having a slight edge, for it, too, had begun to organize workers on an industrial basis. And the organized workers, were no longer politically inactive. In many of the large cities the CIO organized "Non-Partisan Leagues" which generally supported the Democratic Party. In New York City they put a labor party in the field, the **American Labor Party,** and ran their own candidates when dissatisfied with the choices offered by the Republicans or Democrats. Thus the New Deal worked a profound revolution in labor's relation to capital and to American society. But it left America with two huge national labor organizations bitterly antagonistic, a situation which was to act against labor itself and lead in 1955 to a re-merger of the two groups.

Opposition to the New Deal. Of those who felt

that the New Deal had gone too far, the Supreme Court was the leader. In the early years of the New Deal, the Court had struck down the NIRA, the AAA, the Railroad Pensions Act, the Bituminous Coal Act, the Municipal Bankruptcy Act and the Frazier-Lemke Farm Bankruptcy Act. FDR decided on what proved to be a rash plan—in view of the American tradition of separation of powers—to "democratize" the Court. To his opponents, it was "packing" the Court.

His plan (1937) was to force judges to retire at age 70 by permitting the President to appoint one judge (up to a maximum of 15 justices) for each member of the Court over 70 who did not retire; to speed up decisions involving constitutionality; to prevent the Court from issuing injunctions against the government, in cases involving constitutionality, before the governments case was argued. The fight for this bill became deadlocked because of a serious split in Democratic ranks. The Supreme Court, too, confused the issue by suddenly upholding a minimum wage law for women, the second Frazier-Lemke Act, the Social Security Act and the Wagner Labor Relations Act. As a result, Roosevelt's Supreme Court Reform Bill died in committee. In the long run, it didn't much matter, for, during the course of the New Deal, FDR filled seven vacancies. No important New Deal law was thereafter overruled.

The Politics of the New Deal. As in the case of Andrew Jackson, FDR was able to weld a tremendous coalition of potentially hostile elements around the Democratic Party. At its height, the New Deal contained the "Solid South" as well as the Northern Negro Bloc (the latter had been staunchly Republican since the Civil War); the conservative farmer and normally liberal urban worker; the "white collar" middle class; the intellectuals in the universities and the arts; the city and state political bosses. This coalition held solidly during the election of 1936. To oppose FDR the Republicans chose Alfred M. Landon of Kansas. The Democrats stood on their record. The Republicans, powerfully supported by elements of big business, Al Smith and a majority of the press hammered at the theme that the New Deal was destroying the American way of life and depriving Americans of their freedom as individuals. FDR carried every state but two—Maine and Vermont.

SOCIETY AND CULTURE OF THE THIRTIES

Population. Population, during the Thirties, continued to rise, but by a mere 7% as compared with 16% during the Twenties. There was no large scale immigration to offset this decline. In fact, during the years from 1931 to 1935, 103,654 more people left the United States than came into it! Hitler's persecutions, however, brought to America Thomas Mann, Franz Werfel, George Grosz, Walter Gropius, Paul Hindemuth, Bruno Walter, Albert Einstein and other distinguished men and women. The decline in the death rate helped swell the population. The depression, apparently, put a heavy premium on raising a family and prevented millions from being born; and since it was too expensive to get married or divorced, both figures declined in the Thirties. Within the home, tensions mounted as wives were discharged from jobs to favor unemployed men. Unemployed husbands became strained with anxiety and injured pride. Overcrowding was frequent as hungry, unemployed relations "moved in" to reduce the cost of living. Increased tension was registered in the mounting load of mental patients and in the increased sale, when money was so scarce, of cigarettes.

Education. Schools bore a heavy load during the depression. They lived in continual financial straits; their plant and equipment deteriorated; pupil-loads increased as boards of education reduced hiring; but total school population increased as the labor market rejected child labor. Secondary schools were now faced with the problem of educating all the children. Uniform methods and standards had to be dropped for differentiated programs, homogeneous groupings based on intelligence testing, and the like.

Vocational education grew apace both on the high school and college levels as students sought specific skills that would get them jobs. As the colleges adjusted to this demand, a profound controversy broke out over the nature of a college education. Robert Hutchins and Mortimer Adler led their colleagues in the University of Chicago in a battle for the traditional disciplines; St. John's introduced a "Great Books" approach to the Humanities; most colleges, however, watered down their curricula to meet the need of the day for employment skills.

Religion. Depression did not result in a sharp increase in church membership and attendance, as might have been anticipated. Clergymen, however, redoubled their social activities in the areas of relief and welfare work. Two new sects made their appearance. Father Divine's following, largely Negroes ("Peace, it's wonderful!") and Jehovah's Witnesses, a group of Christian literalists who, among other beliefs, would not bow down to any graven images, including the flag of the United States, and they were upheld in their refusal by the Supreme Court.

Reading. Magazines held up well during the depression for they were one of the cheapest means of escape from depression drabness. The appearance of *Life* and its immediate popularity was indicative of the role to be played by the picture story as a substitute for reading. But reading standards were somewhat modified by Henry Luce's *Time* and *Fortune;* and by *The New Yorker*, which provided an outlet for some of America's best short story writers and cartoonists.

Newspapers, on the other hand, were hard-hit as advertising declined. The public opinion polls of George Gallup and Elmo Roper became popular. At the end of the decade, there was an interesting but short-lived experiment in "high brow" tabloidism. Marshall Field III's *PM* tried to operate, under Ralph Ingersoll's editorship, without advertising or sensation. It didn't. American literary preferences ran to detective stories, westerns, Dale Carnegie's *How to Win Friends and Influence People* and to historical novels of awesome length.

Literature. "Proletarian" novels made their inevitable appearance in the Thirties. They were written by Grace Lumpkin, Albert Halper, Meyer Levin and Albert Maltz, and others. Most of them were simple tracts about "good guys" (labor leaders and radicals) and "bad guys" (capitalists and their agents) and had small literary value.

Far superior novels were written by independent social critics like John Dos Passos (*USA*), Erskine Caldwell (*Tobacco Road*), William Faulkner, James Farrell (*Studs Lonigan*), Ernest Hemingway and John Steinbeck (*Grapes of Wrath*). For, while unsparing in their criticism of the society which could produce the human wreckage caused by the depression, these men continued the search begun in the Twenties for American values, for the meaning of the American past. Thomas Wolfe fulfilled himself in the Thirties. His novels were formless; but no one could miss his deep, abiding love for America. Willa Cather and Ellen Glasgow continued in their vein of the Twenties; and Sinclair Lewis, Eugene O'Neill and Pearl Buck won Nobel Prizes.

Among the poets, Edna St. Vincent Millay, Archibald MacLeish and Carl Sandburg affirmed their faith in the American people. Robert Frost wrote with wonderful irony and pathos of the New England "common man."

Theatre. The American theatre experienced something of a Renaissance as a result of the gifted productions by Maxwell Anderson, Clifford Odets, Elmer Rice, Robert Sherwood, Paul Green, Sidney Kingsley and Thorton Wilder; and the continued productivity of Eugene O'Neill. These playwrights wrote mostly in the traditional vein but did not neglect the theatrical innovations of the Twenties. Folklore, contemporary problems, historical events were subordinated to the creation of living characters. Meanwhile, the Federal Theatre Project proved a valuable medium for producing the classics and experimenting with new forms. Out of its experimenting came the "living newspaper"—dramatic and experimental presentations of the topical themes (*Triple A Plowed Under, One Third of a Nation*).

The movies made great efforts to produce an equally vital theatre which grappled with "real" problems. Films were made that dealt with problems of hunger, the dispossessed, of racial intolerance, of slums, of the old-aged and the like, Poetic documentaries like "The River" and "The Plow that Broke the Plains" were made. But the escapist element predominated in the usual run of penthouse frolics, song and dance, and slapstick comedy. Walt Disney's rise to fame on the animated cartoon was spectacular; more Americans knew the names of his Seven Dwarfs than those of the President's cabinet.

Radio, too, had its more intellectual and artistic moments in the Thirties, though it was still dominated by the soap-opera, the murder tale, the sports event and the "comedy" show. It experimented with serious forums, high-brow quiz programs, broadcast symphonic concerts and operas, etc.

Music. Jazz gave way to swing and to the swingmasters like Benny Goodman, Tommy Dorsey and Artie Shaw. In Aaron Copland, America produced a very competent modernist; Roy Harris, Virgil Thomson and others made important contributions to the modern musical idiom. Native artistic talent became more numerous and internationally renowned.

FINE ARTS

Painting. Three painting trends characterized the Thirties: some painters began the rediscovery of American regionalism and history—the most publicized being Thomas Hart Benton and Grant Wood; others became involved with the social scene —outstanding were William Gropper, Raphael Soyer, Peter Blume, Jack Levine, Ben Shahn, etc., and a third group continued in the modernist manner—among the better known were Marsden Hartley, Walt Kuhn and Stuart Davis. Not all of these works were uniformly excellent, but all were competent and their work is widely exhibited today.

Sculpture. Sculptors in the Thirties definitely

grew more abstract, more concerned with their medium than with representation. Alexander Calder produced metal shapes called "mobiles" delicately balanced in space; Noguchi and Robus practiced a severe and classic abstractionism in the manner of Brancusi.

Architecture. Raymond Hood constructed the clean lines of the *Daily News* and McGraw-Hill buildings and collaborated in the construction of Rockefeller Center. **Function** was more nearly related to form in these structures. Prodded by Lewis Mumford and Frank Lloyd Wright, however, architects were still struggling for some synthesis that would merge the repeated area with the unique, that would flow from its surrounding, that would relate the interior and exterior of a building.

Science. Americans scored heavily in Nobel Prizes for science during the Thirties. Major contributions were made in the field of atomic research. Langmuir investigated the chemical activity of an element. Lawrence constructed the first cyclotron. Urey discovered heavy hydrogen; Hess and Anderson, the positron; Anderson and Neddermeyer, the Meson; Davisson and Thomson, the diffraction of electrons by crystals, etc. These discoveries brought Americans six Nobel prizes.

CHAPTER XX

NEW DEAL AND WORLD AFFAIRS

FOREIGN POLICY

Reciprocal Tariff Program. Consistent with determination to shape America's foreign policy to the nation's depression needs, FDR kept Hoover's pledge to attend a 1933 World Economic Conference; Secretary of State CORDELL HULL was instructed to discuss nothing but bilateral tariff treaties which would increase foreign trade. In June of 1934 a **Trade Agreements Act** was passed which provided that the President could cut American tariffs by 50% if other nations would do likewise. Hull began to negotiate bilateral treaties almost immediately, thus revolutionizing America's tariff policy.

Recognition of the Soviet Union. For seventeen years America had refused to recognize the Soviet Union; the reasons were many, e.g., the U.S.S.R. had refused to pay Tsarist debts, pressing instead their own claims for damages incurred during American intervention of 1917-1920. Russia's willingness to negotiate these matters and America's hopes that a new understanding might result in an American-Russian trade boom led to the **Roosevelt-Litvinov Agreement** in 1933, in which the U. S. formally recognized the U.S.S.R.

The Good Neighbor Policy. In his inaugural address President Roosevelt had said: "In the field of world policy, I would dedicate this nation to the policy of the good neighbor." At the Inter-American Conference at Montevideo in 1933 Hull spelled out the meaning of "good neighbor." "No state has the right to intervene in the internal or external affairs of another."

Cuba. Cuba was torn by a revolt that had overthrown Machado, a particularly brutal dictator. The American ambassador, Sumner Welles, proposed "limited intervention" but Secretary Hull refused to intervene. When a temporary government under Mendieta took over, Hull granted it immediate *de facto* recognition. Hull then negotiated a treaty with Cuba to abrogate the Platt Amendment; thus he destroyed America's legal right to intervene. A tariff treaty favorable to Cuba was then agreed to bilaterally. Hull had shown Latin America concretely that America had every intention of living up to her "good neighbor" pledge.

Haiti. In 1934 all American troops were withdrawn from Haiti—never to return.

Panama. After a prolonged battle in the Senate, the Hay-Buneau-Varilla Treaty was modified to give Panama the commercial rights of a sovereign state in the Canal Zone.

Mexico. Mexico put the good neighbor policy to a severe test. Under Lazaro Cardenas, in 1936, Mexico adopted a six-year plan which called for nationalizing American oil companies, redistributing the land, secularizing the state completely and the like. In spite of heavy pressures to intervene, Secretary Hull openly acknowledged Mexico's right to expropriate properties worth half a billion dollars; but he did insist upon a fair compensation. To secure the latter, Mexico was cut off from America's silver-support policy. Negotiations as equals followed and eventually Mexico paid for the expropriated properties and the United States, in turn, supported Mexican silver prices and made large loans to her through the Export-Import Bank.

Montevideo, 1933. When the Inter-American powers met at Montevideo in 1933 to consider matters of Hemisphere peace and trade, Secretary Hull made a firm declaration not to intervene in the affairs of the Latin American nations. He then went on to lead that conference to approve tariff reductions, conciliation treaties and other matters of significance to the Latin Americans. This change in policy came none too soon for Inter-Americanism was taking on new meaning as Hitler and Mussolini began their physical assault on Europe and Africa and their economic-propaganda assault in Latin America.

Buenos Aires, 1936. The direct link between South America and Europe was the French, Dutch and British Guianas. Should these European powers fall into German or Italian hands, their South American holdings would become overseas bases for the German and Italian armies. Aware of these possibilities, F.D.R. suggested in 1936 that a conference be held to consider the maintenance of peace in the Western Hemisphere. At Argentina's request the conference met at Buenos Aires. There the Inter-American powers agreed that they would consult in the event of an international war which might menace the peace of the Americas. It was also agreed that territorial acquisition made by force would not be recognized; nor would intervention, or the forcible collection of debts, or violent settlement of Inter-American disputes.

Effects of the Second World War. This agreement was implemented at Lima, Peru in 1938 when the Inter-American powers agreed that if European hostilities broke out, the foreign ministers of the twenty-one republics would devise methods of countering any attempt to "invade" the Western Hemisphere. War broke in 1939 and the foreign ministers met in Panama and drew sea-safety zones around the Western Hemisphere and warned belligerent vessels to stay out of the proscribed waters; announced that American republics would administer any European possession in the New World which was endangered by aggression (Havana 1940); recommended, after the United States became a belligerent in 1941, that all the Americas break diplomatic relations with the Axis (all but Chile and Argentina did so immediately; Chile followed in 1943; Argentina, in 1944), and that materials, bases and manpower be supplied in behalf of the common cause.

Isolation: Neutrality. American isolationism took the form of neutrality. Though fully aware of the threat of Hitlerism, the United States chose a policy designed to keep America out of all wars. In deciding what neutral course to take, Congress followed the lead of Senator Nye's investigation into the causes for American entry into World War I. Nye's Committee had concluded that trading in munitions, loans to belligerents, travel by American citizens in war zones and machinations by American and international munitions makers were the primary causes. Therefore, in 1935 Congress drew up the "fool-proof" Neutrality Act which provided that upon outbreak of war, the President was to prohibit export of implements of war to any belligerent; American ships could not carry such goods to or for a belligerent; and the President might warn American citizens that they would travel on belligerent ships at their own risk.

The Test of Neutrality. The Italo-Ethiopian War and the Spanish Civil War put these provisions to the test. In the former, F.D.R. invoked the Neutrality Act. But what Italy needed was oil not guns, and oil was not classified as an "article of war." Roosevelt called upon American producers for a "moral embargo" on oil; this failed miserably. In the Spanish Civil War, the Neutrality Act was not even invoked. Both wars confirmed the American Congress in its desire to "stay out of war" and in 1936 the Neutrality Act of 1935 was "strengthened" by a new provision: loans to belligerents were forbidden through purchase of their securities or otherwise.

"Permanent" Neutrality, 1937. In 1937, Congress undertook "permanent" neutrality. Provisions of the acts of 1935 and 1936 were extended to apply to civil as well as international wars; American citizens were now forbidden by law to sail on belligerent ships; and a temporary "cash and carry" feature was added, that is, before goods could be exported to or for a belligerent the ownership of the goods had to be transferred to the foreign purchaser. This latter provision ended America's traditional doctrine of the "freedom of the seas"; and the entire act served notice to the aggressors that America would do nothing to oppose their plans of conquest. However, one year after their adoption, the permanent neutrality laws began to disintegrate.

"Quarantine the Aggressor!" In 1936 Japan and Germany signed the Anti-Comintern Pact; in 1937 Italy joined this pact and it became the Rome-Berlin-Tokyo Axis. In 1937 Japan conquered China's coastal regions and the main railways. In the course of this assault, Japan bombed open cities, closed the Open Door, set up a puppet Chinese government, sank an American gunboat (the "Panay"—apologies were made and damages paid), and bombed and strafed American and foreign schools, hospitals and churches. Roosevelt did not proclaim a state of war so that China might be able to buy war-goods; but he did label Japan a treaty violator and on October 5, 1937 deplored the "epidemic of lawlessness" in the world and asked the peace-loving powers for a "quarantine of aggressors." Japan was told flatly that the United States would not recognize her "New Order in Asia" in areas over which the Japanese had no sovereign right and would insist on enforcement of the Open Door Policy. These executive proclamations shook the policy of neutrality.

From "Appeasement" to War. Prime Minister Chamberlain of England and Premier Daladier of France were determined to purchase peace at any price. Therefore, they did not oppose Hitler's policy of rearmament, his occupation of the Rhineland and annexation of Austria; they consented to his absorption of the Sudetenland and were silent when the German armies occupied all of Czechoslovakia and the Italian armies took over Albania. Such was the policy of "appeasement"—a policy whose primary aim was to instigate a mutually destructive German-Russian war. But in August 1939 Russia and Germany signed a "non-aggression" pact and a secret protocol to partition Poland. England now warned Germany that an attack on Poland would mean war. The attack came on September 1, 1939. France and England declared war.

In response to these events, F.D.R. asked Congress, in January 1939, to revise the Neutrality Laws so that America might more effectively meet the challenge. This request touched off a great debate between the "isolationists" and the "interventionists" in America. The interventionists, led by the President, had their way, and America moved from a policy of neutrality to one of non-belligerency.

From Neutrality to Non-Belligerency. In 1939, the Neutrality Law was amended to repeal the embargo on war goods; sales to belligerents were put on a cash and carry basis. Following the blitzkrieg attack on the Low Countries and Scandanavia, the Italian "stab in the back" attack on France and the fall of France, the President promised all-out aid to France and England. At home, the first peace-time draft was enacted (1940) and American rearmament began in earnest. A "destroyer-base" deal was then concluded with England in which the President exchanged fifty over-aged destroyers for eight Atlantic military bases. Then, on March 11, 1941, Congress adopted the **Lend-Lease Act** which made America into an "arsenal of democracy" and permitted the President to make available to any country vital to the defense of the United States all war materials on a loan or lease basis. (Eventually $50 billion in supplies was shipped by America to its beleaguered allies; the United States received about $10 billion in "return" lend-lease.) In August 1941 came the Atlantic Charter.

The Atlantic Charter. Though not yet a belligerent, the United States joined with England to proclaim the peace-aims of the warring powers and their non-belligerent allies:

they will seek no aggrandizement, territorial or otherwise;
territorial changes will be made in accord with the freely expressed wishes of the people concerned;
people will choose the form of government under which they will live;
they will see to it that people who have forcibly lost their self-government will get it back;
with due respect for existing obligations, they will see to it that all States have access, on equal terms, to the trade and raw materials of the world;
they will get nations to collaborate to improve labor standards, economic advancement, and social security;
they will establish a peace in which men may live out their lives free from fear and want;
they will assure freedom of the high seas; and
they will disarm aggressors and will remain armed themselves until permanent security is established.

This proclamation was followed by American occupation (with permission) of Greenland and Iceland; the arming of merchant ships; repeal of "cash-and-carry" and permission of American ships to sail in all waters.

Pearl Harbor. In 1939 the Japanese seized Pacific islands close to the Philippines; created a "Greater East Asia Co-Prosperity Sphere" which excluded the United States from all of Asia; seized French Indo-China from its Vichy French rulers; and concluded a tripartite military pact with Germany and Italy aimed directly at the United States. American policy toward Japan toughened. Petroleum, scrap metal and aviation gasoline were embargoed; Americans in the Far East were recalled; loans were made to China; Japanese funds in America were seized; and Japan was warned to end her aggressions. The Japanese were ordered to withdraw from French Indo-China, from China itself and from the Tripartite Pact. Following this ultimatum the Japanese war-lords decided to attack the United States. Saburu Kurusu was sent to Washington as a decoy envoy to negotiate the ultimatum. While the negotiations were in progress on December 7, 1941, the bombs fell on Pearl Harbor, Hawaii, with devastating effect. Two hours before the attack Japan had declared war on the United States; on December 8th Congress declared war.

The Second World War. When the United States entered the war, the Axis triumph was near its peak.

German submarines dominated the Atlantic; England was reeling under murderous air bombardment; all of Europe was a Nazi fortress; Nazi armies were slicing into Russia and heading eastward to India; Japanese armies, now dominating all of southeast Asia, were advancing westward on India to make a decisive link with the Nazis.

First Phase. The worst came in the summer of 1942. Japan took Guam, Wake, Hong Kong, the Philippines, the Dutch East Indies and (after annihilating an Allied naval force in the Battle of the Java Sea) New Britain and the Solomon Islands; now they threatened southern New Guinea and Australia.

Nazi subs sank 8,000,000 tons of Allied shipping in the North Atlantic; Nazi General Rommel drove the British to El Alemain in Egypt, 75 miles from Alexandria; Nazi armies swung south into the Caucusus and entered Stalingrad.

In a **Declaration of the United Nations,** signed on January 1, 1942, twenty-six nations formed a Grand Alliance to fight under joint command until Germany was crushed.

A Japanese convoy was sunk in the Battle of Macassar Strait; Admiral Halsey bombed the Marshall and Gilbert Islands; General Doolittle bombed Tokyo itself in a daring raid; and thousand-bomber raids were begun over Germany.

On May 7-8, 1942, a Japanese task force bound for Australia was sunk. This was followed by the Battle of Midway, a battle fought with dive-bombers only, which resulted in a catastrophic defeat for the Japanese navy. The way was now paved for an offensive; this began when Tulagi and Guadalcanal were taken and held by the American marines.

Second Phase. General Montgomery (October 1942) broke through Rommel's siege at El Alemain forcing him to retreat; American forces landed in North Africa and won important victories.

At the Casablanca Conference, January 1943, it was decided to invade Sicily and demand unconditional surrender.

American armed forces took the Solomon and Admiralty Islands; moved into the Marshall Islands in the Central Pacific; cleaned the Japanese forces from the Aleutians; and began the attack on the Mariannas.

Third Phase. In September, 1942 the Russians captured the Nazi army besieging Stalingrad and launched a counter-offensive that ended in Berlin. The Allies crushed the submarine menace in the Atlantic, attacked (July 1943) Sicily; and then (September 1943) mainland of Italy.

An armistice was concluded with Italy. At an important conference in **Moscow** (18 October 1943) the Western Allies and Russia agreed to the unconditional surrender of Germany; the destruction of Nazism; the establishment of a democratic government in Germany; the destruction of the German General Staff and war production capacity; the separation of East Prussia from Germany; reparations in kind from Germany; and punishment of all German war criminals. Austria was to be "liberated." On November 23, 1943 Roosevelt, Churchill and Chiang Kai Shek met at **Cairo** and planned the defeat of Japan and the disposal of Japanese held territory after the war. Finally, at **Teheran,** on November 27, 1943, Roosevelt, Churchill and Stalin met to discuss all the major issues, including strategy to end the war.

Victory. June 6, 1944 was D-Day, the landing on Normandy. On August 25th Paris was liberated and by March 7, 1945 the Allies were poised for a breakthrough to Berlin. General Eisenhower arranged to meet the Russian forces at the Elbe to the south of Berlin. This permitted the Russians to take all of East Germany. On April 12, 1945, Roosevelt died. President Truman agreed with Eisenhower's plan of attack; the Allied forces moved south into Bavaria while the Russians moved east through Czechoslovakia. On April 27th the Russian and Allied forces made contact; on the 28th Mussolini was killed by Italian partisans; on the 29th Hitler "committed suicide"; surrender came on May 8, 1945. This was V-E Day, Victory in Europe.

Pacific Theatre. In the summer of 1944 the Mariannas fell to the Americans. A Japanese fleet was destroyed in the Battle of the Philippine Sea. On the 20th of October, 1944 the counter-attack on the Philippines began and by the 5th of July, 1945 they were taken. Iwo Jima and Okinawa fell. On July 26th the **Potsdam Conference** demanded unconditional surrender; it was rejected. Nine days later the first atomic bomb fell on Hiroshima; three days after that another fell on Nagasaki; two bombs killed 100,000 people. On Nagasaki Day, Russia entered the Japanese war. V-J Day came on the 14th of August and the surrender of Japan was completed aboard the U.S.S. Missouri on September 2, 1945.

Postscript. The total agony suffered in the second World War cannot be calculated; statistics are but cold indicators. It was a global war. It was the most lethal war in history—at least 20,000,000 soldiers and civilians were killed. It manifested incredible brutalities—6,000,000 Jews burned in the furnaces, Japanese "death marches" in the Philippines, and 100,000 Japanese killed by two bombs. Damages were astronomical, whole cities became rubble and desert. Americans paid heavily for their participation—1,120,000 casualities, 300,000 dead. War costs in the United States alone were $341 billion. But an immense evil—world enslavement—had been prevented.

The Home Front 1940-1945. 15,000,000 men were recruited under the Selective Service Act. A Woman's Army Corps of 250,000 was established for clerical and non-combatant work. In 1944 Congress passed the "GI Bill of Rights" which provided veterans with educational and other benefits.

Production. Production miracles were effected. The government poured billions into the construction of new factories. Anti-trust laws were suspended for the duration. Farmers vastly increased production.

Labor. The War Manpower Board moved millions of workers from civilian to defense jobs. A National War Labor Board kept strikes down to one per cent of all the workers employed. Devices like the "Little Steel Formula"—that is, linking wage rises to cost-of-living indexes—failed; some strikes took place; and Congress passed the Smith-Connally Act which required a thirty-day notice before striking, permitted the government to seize strike-bound factories and made fomenting strikes in war plants a criminal offense.

Inflation. Shortages of goods and increased income and credit sent prices sky-high. The government therefore increased tax-rates on a "pay-as-you-go" plan of prior tax deductions; launched eight bond drives; enforced wage ceilings; created the Office of Price Administration which placed ceilings on rents and retail prices, rationed goods by a stamp system and eliminated installment buying. Widespread "blackmarketing" successfully and shamefully evaded these regulations.

American Japanese. Civil liberties were fully protected during the war for all but Japanese-Americans on the West Coast, which was declared a "theater of war." Without charges of disloyalty, the Japanese-Americans were forced into "relocation centers" in the swamplands of Arkansas. The action of the army was upheld by the Supreme Court in the case of Korematsu v. U. S. (1944).

Politics. In 1940 President Roosevelt broke the two term tradition by defeating Wendell Wilkie for the presidency. Roosevelt's personality; the split in Republican ranks—isolationism versus interventionism; the absence of any real difference between Roosevelt and Wilkie on both domestic and foreign issues; the fear of "changing horses in mid-stream" with the war raging in Europe—all these account for Roosevelt's victory. In 1944 FDR easily defeated

Governor Thomas E. Dewey of New York. When Roosevelt died suddenly of a cerebral hemorrhage on the 12th of April, 1945, he was succeeded by Harry S. Truman, his Vice-President.

The Grand Design. President Truman inherited the herculean task of completing the unfinished work begun by Roosevelt. There was a Grand Alliance of major powers working within a broader alliance now called the United Nations. Unity was achieved by "summit meetings" of the heads of states. At these meetings, Roosevelt had committed the United States to a number of post-war pledges. For example, at Moscow (1943) the United States accepted the Moscow Declaration which proclaimed the "necessity of establishing a general international organization . . . for the maintenance of peace and security"; at Cairo (1943) the United States agreed to stripping Japan of all Pacific Islands, to restoring to China all the territories taken from her and to granting Korea independence; at Yalta (1945) the United States consented to granting Russia the Kuriles Islands, southern Sakhalin, an occupation zone in Korea, privileges in Manchuria, recognition of Outer Mongolia, occupation of eastern Poland. In exchange for these concessions, Russia agreed to enter the Pacific War, to support postwar popular governments, to accept America's veto proposals for the new United Nations Organization.

Truman strove faithfully to fulfill these many commitments. At the Potsdam (Berlin) Conference (July-August 1945), he agreed to dividing Germany into four occupation zones; to eradicating Nazism and bringing to justice Nazi war criminals; to the complete demilitarization of Germany and destruction of her war industries; to a plan of reparations heavily favoring the Russians; to the future unification of Germany on an undefined "democratic basis"; to a Council of Ministers to draft peace treaties with Italy, Rumania, Bulgaria, Austria, Hungary and Finland; and to a mandatory transfer of 6,500,000 Germans out of Hungary, Czechoslovakia and Poland into Germany.

By 1947 peace treaties with Italy, Hungary, Bulgaria and Rumania were completed, submitted to the Senate and ratified. A short draft treaty providing for the independence of Austria was rejected. The result was that Austria remained divided into four zones until February 1955 when, in a sudden reversal of tactic, Russia proposed a treaty that set Austria free.

War Crimes. An International Military Tribunal was established in Nuremburg, Germany, with Supreme Court Justice Robert H. Jackson as chief American prosecutor. As a result of the Nuremburg trials, twelve Nazis were sentenced to be hanged. In twelve additional trials in the United States zone, 503,360 were convicted, 430,890 were given light fines, 27,413 were sentenced to "community work," and 7,768 were sent to "labor camps." In a series of Tokyo trials, on the other hand, of 4,200 convicted (1949), 720 were executed.

THE UNITED NATIONS

A United Nations Organization had been projected as early as 1941 in the Atlantic Charter. At the Moscow Conference in 1943, the need for such an organization was officially proclaimed and the basic principle of the equality of states was announced. At Teheran (1943) a planning committee was projected; it met at **Dumbarton Oaks** (1944) and consisted of the Big Four—the U. S., the United Kingdom, the U.S.S.R. and (later) China.

Ninety per cent of the Charter of the United Nations Organization was hammered out at Dumbarton Oaks. The remainder was completed at **Bretton Woods** (N. H.) where an International Bank for Reconstruction and Development and an International Monetary Fund to stabilize world currencies were set up; at **Yalta** where the formula on voting procedures in the Security Council was worked out and each of the great powers was given an absolute veto on all matters except procedure; and at **San Francisco** (April-June 1945) where the important addition of Article 51 was made, an article that provided for regional pacts for individual or collective self-defense pending action by the Security Council. To avoid the error committed at Versailles in 1919, all the American delegations to these meetings were bipartisan. The Senate approved the United Nations Charter on July 2, 1945 by a vote of 89 to 2.

Purposes. Article I of the Charter of the UN sets forth the major goals: "To maintain international peace and security, and to that end: to take effective collective measures for the prevention and removal of threats to the peace . . ."; and "To achieve international cooperation in solving international problems of an economic, social, cultural or humanitarian character. . . ."

Membership. All independent, peace-loving nations are eligible if they accept the obligations of the UN and are able and willing to carry them out. By January 1, 1956 there were 76 member nations.

Structure. There are six main organs of the UN: **The General Assembly.** This is composed of all member states. Each state may send five representatives but is entitled to only one vote. On most matters a two-thirds vote prevails. The Assembly must meet at least once a year but may meet in special session. After the creation in 1947 of an interim committee called the "Little Assembly" one may now say that the General Assembly is in continuous session.

The Security Council. This was to have been the leading organ of the UN. It consists of eleven members, five (U. S., U. K., France, China, U.S.S.R.) with permanent seats and six elected by the General Assembly for two-year terms. It is in continuous session and has the primary responsibility for maintaining peace and security; all other members of the UN are bound to carry out its decisions. But its decisions have been few, for each of the permanent members has an absolute veto on all substantive matters. In procedural matters, any seven votes prevail. (Since the Soviet Union has employed the veto almost eighty times in ten years, the Council has been rendered impotent, thus far. Should it spring to life in the future, its powers to investigate, recommend and enforce are virtually limitless.)

The Economic and Social Council (ECOSOC). Its eighteen member council is chosen for staggered three-year terms by the General Assembly. It is charged with carrying out programs for the international economic and social improvement. ECOSOC coordinates the work of specialized agencies which implement its purposes: the International Labor Organization (ILO), the Food and Agricultural Organization (FAO), the United Nations Educational, Scientific and Cultural Organization (UNESCO), the International Civil Aviation Organization (ICAO), the International Bank for Reconstruction and Development (IBRD), the International Monetary Fund (IMF), the International Telecommunications Union (ITU), the World Health Organization (WHO), and the International Trade Organization (ITO). The United States is an active member of each.

The Trusteeship Council. This organ supervises territories previously administered by the League of Nations as mandates or territories voluntarily placed under trusteeship with the UN. Six UN members are at present charged with advancing the political and economic development of 20,500,000 people in eleven African and Pacific areas. It sends out questionnaires, hears reports, listens to complaints from natives and sends out on-the-spot investigating committees—unless the trust-holding country designates the territory as "strategic."

The International Court of Justice, (World Court). This court of 15 judges is charged with settling legal disputes between nations. A legal international dispute may involve territorial waters, treaty violations, boundary disputes and the like. If the contesting parties agree to submit the dispute to the Court, the Court will render a decision; but the Court may also render an advisory opinion if called upon by the UN to do so. Theoretically, all decisions of the Court are enforceable by the Security Council.

The Secretariat. This composes the civil service at the UN. The Secretary-General who heads it is not only the chief administrative officer but is empowered to bring any situation threatening the peace to the attention of the General Assembly and to make his own efforts at peace-making.

The United Nations at Work. American foreign policy is intimately related to the collective policy of the UN. While the work of the UN in the last ten years has been eclipsed by "cold-war" politics, it has made an impressive showing.

A number of new states have been born as a result of the efforts of the United Nations: Israel, Indonesia, Libya and the Republic of Korea.

It has checked warfare between Israel and the Arab powers, between Pakistan and India over Kashmir, and between the Netherlands and Indonesia.

It has forced alien armies to leave the soil of free countries. The French were removed from Syria and Lebanon; the Russians from Iran.

It has restrained Communist aggression in Greece and Korea and was the primary instrument in securing the release of American prisoners of war from Chinese Communist prison pens.

These were among the more sensational successes. But the unpublicized work of the UN is probably more effective—the technical assistance teams working in the backward areas bringing improvements in health, food supply, housing and education; the release of thousands from the bondage of illiteracy and ignorance; the care and feeding of war-uprooted families; the 8,000,000 children vaccinated (by 1953) against tuberculosis and the 20,000,000 protected against malaria. The General Assembly has served as a world forum for the conscience of humanity.

ARMAMENT AND DISARMAMENT

With the launching of three Sputniks in 1957-8, Russia assumed the leadership in the field of rocket-propelled missiles. The ability to thrust an object weighing 3000 pounds into orbit was evidence that the Russians possessed a universal intercontinental ballistic missile (ICBM). The United States had several intermediate range missiles but it was still at work on its ICBMs. Both countries, however, were in possession of enough thermonuclear warheads to destroy civilized life as we know it today. This gave a sense of gravity to disarmament talks which had been in progress since the end of World War II. Additional urgency was provided by the revelation that thermonuclear tests were poisoning the world's atmosphere with radioactive fallout.

Some unity among Russian and American scientists was achieved by common participation in the International Geophysical Year (1957-8) and in an atoms-for-peace program. Out of these proposals came an International Atomic Energy Agency, an exchange of information on the peaceful uses of atomic energy and the creation of a nuclear fuel pool. Attempts to terminate the testing and production of thermonuclear bombs were unsuccessful.

Russia insisted upon immediate outlawing of the bomb, limited inspection and retention of any agreement within the framework of the Security Council where the veto would operate. In general, these reservations were also maintained with respect to control over bomb-testing. The United States, on the other hand, made full-scale and unimpeded inspection the core of any program of disarmament. The United States felt that an agreement to outlaw the bomb should be the last stage of an effective disarmament program.

THE WESTERN HEMISPHERE

The framework of a united Western Hemisphere was designed between 1945 and 1948. In the **Act of Chapultepec** (1945) the American nations agreed that any act or threat of aggression against one American nation would be considered as such against all of them. The **Treaty of Rio de Janeiro** (1947) provided that an attack on one nation would be considered an attack on all and that appropriate steps would be taken if the representatives of two-thirds of the American nations voted it. Use of armed forces, however, required the approval of the United States Congress under the Constitution of the United States. At Bogota (1948), this collective security pact was transformed into the **Organization of American States** and was defined by a written constitution which created four organs: an Inter-American Conference to meet at least once every five years; a Consultation of Foreign Ministers to meet as the occasion required; a Council consisting of one representative from each of the 21 states to be in permanent session; and a Secretariat (the old Pan-American Union) also in permanent session.

In general terms, the major problems confronting the OAS were as follows:

Internal instability: Inexperience with democracy, the absence of a stabilizing middle class, the influence of the Army and the Church in politics, the persistence of the dictators and the military cliques, and the existence of highly organized and militant student bodies combined to produce a succession of civil wars in many of the member nations. Some of these civil wars resulted in the defeat of such dictators as Perón in Argentina and Batista in Cuba and the beginning of more democratic regimes. Cuba under Fidel Castro became a center of revolutionary activity for the entire Caribbean, but the threat of counterrevolution remained ever-present. **Economic instability:** One-crop economies, complete dependence on the shift of world prices, low standards of living, poor distribution of property holdings and inadequate foreign aid persisted in most of the Latin American countries. This resulted in nationalization of basic industries in Cuba, Mexico and Bolivia. The industries which were nationalized were usually those controlled by American corporations and the efforts of the United States government to secure fair compensation for confiscated properties caused anti-American reactions. **Threat of Communism:** Communist parties existed in many of the Latin American countries and unsuccessful bids for power were made in Cuba and Guatemala. **United States Aid:** Latin Americans insist that United States foreign aid has been too exclusively concerned with Asia, Africa and Europe; that a greater share of American foreign aid must be poured into many developmental programs that have been started in Latin America to achieve diversification of the economy. The United States has made money available through the Export-Import Bank. Private capital, however, is reluctant to enter markets where there is a constant threat of confiscation.

CHAPTER XXI

POST-WAR FOREIGN POLICIES (1945-1960)

THE "COLD WAR"

Within two years of the end of the Second World War the ideal of a Grand Alliance of great powers shaping the dream of "One World" was shattered; in its place arose the "Cold War" between the two most powerful nations—the United States and the Soviet Union. The Cold War originated in post-war conflict of interests between the U.S. and Russia.

Soviet Imperialism. Soviet imperialism had begun in 1940 with the annexation of Lithuania, Latvia and Estonia. In 1945 the Red Army was in full occupation of Poland, Rumania and Yugoslavia; these were precisely the nations that became "satellites." At Yalta, Stalin had promised self-determination and free elections in these countries and for a brief period did permit coalition governments of "governments-in-exile" and Communist Parties to exist. But within the coalition Communists were invariably given the police apparatus. This enabled them to destroy non-Communist opposition. With electoral victory thus assured, "people's republics" or satellites were created. Eastern Europe was thus sovietized. Elsewhere in the world Communist influence increased substantially.

The Truman Doctrine. Determined that Communism should make no further advances, President Truman declared to Congress that "it must be the policy of the United States to support free peoples who are resisting attempted subjugation by armed minorities." He asked Congress for $300 million to help Greece put down a Communist-led rebellion and $100 million to help Turkey resist Russia's territorial demands. A bipartisan majority of Congress approved, the money was voted, and men and materials began to move into these threatened areas. America thus inherited the British mantle in the Balkans and made it clear to the Soviet Union that she would act to "contain" Communist expansion.

The Marshall Plan. Military aid was followed by the **Marshall Plan** for economic aid, the assumption of which was that Communism fed upon "hunger, poverty, devastation and chaos." Moreover America felt that Europe should be discouraged from returning to the ruinous pre-war policy of economic nationalism. Humanitarianism dictated that the starved be fed and the uprooted sheltered. Europe was America's best customer; her post-war economic collapse had already brought a mild recession in America; her revival might have the opposite effect.

General George Marshall therefore proposed in June 1947 that the Europeans meet and decide in a body what their chief economic needs were. The United States, he declared, was prepared to supply the funds and goods to meet these needs. Sixteen nations met and decided that their needs amountd to $21,780,000,000. In April Congress voted the **Foreign Assistance Act** which launched the **European Recovery Program.** The act created

an Economic Cooperation Administration to carry out the law;

an Organization for European Economic Cooperation (OEEC) made up of the 18 members receiving aid. They were to distribute the funds according to a plan approved by the ECA;

"counter fund"—the aided government would buy goods with American money and resell them for local currency. The local currency would then be placed in a fund to prevent monetary inflation in the aided country.

Results: The Marshall Plan hastened European recovery and helped maintain American prosperity. Industrial production in Europe rose significantly; inter-European trade increased; European agriculture was revived and expanded; the dollar-gap was considerably narrowed.

The Marshall Plan fostered European integration. Belgium, Netherlands, Luxemburg (the Benelux nations), France, Italy and West Germany united in a **European Payments Union** designed to alleviate currency and exchange difficulties; in the **Schuman Plan Community,** to pool coal and iron resources; in **Euromarket,** for the gradual abolition of all tariffs within the community; in **Euratom,** for common sharing of nuclear energy construction; and in the **Council of Europe,** an advisory political group to resolve differences among the partners. The United States supported this community of continental nations. England opposed it and began to organize a **European Free Trade Area,** aimed at abolishing tariffs within the area, which would include Britain, Norway, Sweden, Denmark, Portugal, Switzerland and Austria. This community was also supported by the United States, but reconciling the hostilities between the two groups became a vital element in United States foreign policy.

The Marshall Plan initiated the policy of American foreign aid and over the years this policy became quite complex. President Truman's "Point Four" Program started technical assistance to backward areas; a Mutual Security Agency concentrated upon military assistance to all nations opposing the Soviet bloc; an Agricultural Trade and Development Act authorized the sale of surplus farm products for foreign currencies; and friendly nations were permitted to suspend payments on loans. Meanwhile, new loans were extended through a Development Fund created in 1957; through the International Bank for Reconstruction and Development; and through the Export-Import Bank. Outright grants were bestowed upon many countries whose economies could not support large military establishments. The United States also participated actively in financing projects originating outside her boundaries: For example, support for the British sponsored Colombo Plan for aid to southeastern and southern Asia; support of regional development agencies in Latin America and the Middle East; support for U.N. agencies such as the U.N. Technical Assistance Program or the U.N. Special Fund for a survey of resources. In the earlier stages of this foreign aid program, European nations received the bulk of the aid. But as the Sino-Soviet bloc launched its own programs of foreign aid to compete with the United States, more and more aid was given to the Far East, Middle East and Pacific Regions. The future may see a significant increase in aid to Latin America.

MILITARY PACTS

NATO. The North Atlantic Treaty Organization was formed on the 4th of April, 1949 when twelve nations (Belgium, Canada, Denmark, France, Iceland, Italy, Luxemburg, Netherlands, Norway, Portugal, the United States and the United Kingdom) signed a treaty which provided that for twenty years the signatories keep peace among themselves; would give each other military and economic aid; and, in Article 5, would consider "an armed attack against one or more of them . . . an attack against all of them." If an attack occurred each would avail itself, under Article 51 of the United Nations Charter, of the right of individual and collective self-defense and would take such action as it deemed necessary. When Greece, Turkey and West Germany later joined NATO, the "North Atlantic" area embraced more than 400 million people, with a *potential* army of 7,000,000.

Greece and Turkey were added to the alliance only after strenuous objection from the most northerly members. An effort to create a unified European armed force (the European Defense Community) failed when it was vetoed by the French Parliament.

Most successful, however, was the creation in the United States of the **Mutual Security Agency** (1951) to replace the Marshall Plan. This Agency was headed by the Foreign Operations Administration and provided funds for military assistance to NATO and other powers.

Problems of NATO. NATO was brought into existence to meet the threat of Communist aggression. Since 1954, however, there has been a sharp reduction in international tension. The end of the Korean and Indo-Chinese Wars and Russia's moves for peaceful coexistence have resulted in a lessened fear of new Soviet aggressions. What role, then, does a military alliance play in a peaceful world?

THE UNITED STATES IN EUROPE

NATO Successes. NATO developed into a highly organized and effective European defense system with permanent Civilian and Military Councils meeting regularly to develop new and expand old facilities. It had Supreme Headquarters established in Paris and a Supreme Commander-in-Chief to execute policies. Under NATO's jurisdiction was a vast network of airfields and communication facilities as well as a potential fighting force of 30 motorized infantry divisions, 5000 aircraft and several fleets centered in the Atlantic and Mediterranean regions. NATO was the concentration point for the collection of nuclear warheads and short-range ballistic missiles. It had, moreover, expanded its activities to include pooling of scientific information and collective support for the economies of its member nations.

Germany. Admission of Germany into NATO was indicative of the switch in policy which the United States made on the German question. American goals affecting Germany were originally proclaimed at Yalta and Potsdam (1945): disarmament, dissolution of the German General Staff, demilitarization, denazification, democratization and the reunification of Germany. Pending these achievements, Germany was divided into four zones under American, British, French and Russian military rule. This program was drastically revised to meet the challenge which came from the Soviet sector. The Russians confiscated private property, nationalized all means of production, did away with Germans who favored liberal democracy, took control of existing factories, introduced mounting obstacles to reunification and attempted to force the Allied powers out of Berlin which was divided into four zones even though well inside the Soviet sector. Airlift aid to West Berlin almost resulted in a military showdown between Russia and the Western powers. To counteract the Russian moves, the Western powers united their three zones into the independent state of West Germany with a new democratic constitution, an elected parliament and a responsible ministry under Konrad Adenauer. West Germany was given substantial financial aid to rehabilitate her economy; she was permitted to reform the General Staff and to rearm; she was admitted into both NATO and the Schuman Plan Community; in effect, West Germany became a full-fledged partner in the Western alliance.

Russia. The Soviet Union countered the Western moves by establishing East Germany as a satellite state; rearming and launching her on a series of Five Year Plans for the industrialization and collectivization of her economy. At the same time, all of the eastern European satellites were united into the WARSAW PACT, a military alliance that unified the armed commands and distributed thermonuclear warheads and ballistic missiles to each of the member countries. A huge military balance of power was effectuated: NATO versus THE WARSAW POWERS.

France. France became the weak link in the NATO pact. Both before and after the rise of General De Gaulle, France's NATO contributions were weakened by incessant warfare, first in Indo-China, Morocco, Tunisia and Algeria and then in Algeria alone. She was unable to supply NATO with armed forces or to make her financial contributions to the common pool. With the rise of De Gaulle came new complications because the General insisted on complete parity in NATO with the other powers, particularly in the distribution of commands and in the possession of complete atomic information and installation. This insistence, coupled with France's continued inability to make her full contribution to NATO, created a serious rift in NATO's unity.

England. American economic aid enabled England to stave off some of the worst consequences of the post-war disintegration of her overseas empire. England then permitted the United States to assume leadership in the events centering about Germany, Austria, Greece, Palestine and the Middle East generally. She cooperated fully in the establishment and elaboration of NATO, METO, and SEATO. Nevertheless, England, too, has weakened the effective unity of the Western powers. She refused to cooperate with plans for European integration; waged a fisheries dispute with Iceland; alienated Turkey by her attack on Egypt and her efforts to retain control of Cyprus. In the course of time, Anglo-American differences have appeared on such matters as the recognition and the admission of Communist China into the U.N.; the acceptance of Russia's proposals for a demilitarized Germany in exchange for German unity. None of these disputes, however, altered England's fundamental support of European military unity.

The Berlin Crisis. Premier Khrushchev's threat to transfer all Soviet functions in Berlin to the East German government and to sign a peace treaty, unilaterally, with East Germany, put Berlin back on the critical list and provoked a four-power conference in the summer of 1959.

THE UNITED STATES IN THE FAR EAST

President Truman had made Europe his prior objective in the struggle against Communism; he rejected Chiang Kai Shek as a fit instrument with which to oppose Communism in China; and decided that a restored Japan would serve as a stabilizing force in the Far East.

Japan. General Douglas MacArthur secured the assignment to democratize, demilitarize and decartelize Japan. In pursuing these objectives MacArthur had to override opposition from a four-power Allied Council in Japan, from Russia, from Filipinos and Koreans demanding huge reparations, and from Australians and New Zealanders seeking to cripple Japan forever. To rehabilitate Japan, MacArthur stopped reparation payments, granted Japan economic aid, helped her recapture some of her former overseas markets and prohibited strikes. To democratize Japan, a new constitution was drawn up which provided for a bicameral parliament based on universal suffrage; lowered the voting age from 25 to 20 and granted women the right to vote; removed the emperor's divine sanction and made him a figurehead; granted the Japanese a Bill of Rights, and separated church and state.

To demilitarize Japan, conscription, the General Staff and war were abolished; war criminals were tried and executed; former war officers were excluded from holding political office. Finally, to decartelize Japan, the Zaibatsu (a vast holding company dominated by five families) was dissolved and its shares of stock were sold to the public; redistribution of large landed estates was effected; and free enterprise was encouraged through a program of loans to small businessmen.

China. At Cairo, Yalta and Potsdam, the United States envisioned the formation of a strong Chinese state under Chiang Kai Shek within which the Chinese Communists would have the status of a minority party. The Stalin-Chiang treaty of "friendship and alliance" signed in 1945 gave substance to this vision. In October 1945 American Ambassador Patrick Hurley induced Chiang and Chinese Communist Mao to settle some of their differences.

The conflict between them, however, was fundamental and clashes became more frequent. Efforts by special ambassador George Marshall to secure a truce failed; and, in a Civil War, the Chinese Communists completed the mainland conquest of China. Chiang Kai Shek was forced to flee to Formosa. Inside China, a Communist "people's republic" was created. The Soviet Union and its satellites promptly recognized the new state and on February 14, 1950 a Sino-Russian Alliance was completed, an alliance against "aggression" by Japan "or states allied with it."

U. S. Response. President Truman's response to these provocations was non-recognition of the Chinese Communist state and active opposition to its admission into the United Nations. But he also informed Congress that the United States would not establish bases on Formosa or provide Chiang Kai Shek with military aid. And, in defining the American "defensive perimeter" in the Far East, Secretary of State Dean Acheson deliberately omitted Formosa and Korea.

The Korean War. As a military measure, Korea had been divided at the 38th parallel by Russian and American troops. This military separation became a political division when Russia instituted a "people's republic" in North Korea and when the United Nations, in free elections, created the Republic of (South) Korea. After a number of border incidents, the North Koreans attacked across the 38th parallel on June 25, 1950 in a gamble for conquest. President Truman made an instantaneous reversal of policy. He announced that Korea and Formosa would be defended by the United States. He convoked the Security Council and, Russia being absent, had a resolution adopted (9-0) declaring North Korea guilty of aggression and demanding that it withdraw behind the 38th parallel and calling upon all members of the United Nations to render every assistance in carrying out this resolution. The American navy and air force were promptly moved into a "police action" and gave cover and support to ROK forces south of the 38th parallel. On the 27th of June, the Security Council endorsed President Truman's military actions and appointed General Douglas MacArthur commander-in-chief of the UN forces in Korea. Military action in Korea was characterized by initial North Korean successes, United Nations counteroffensives that carried the war to the northern border of Korea (the Yalu River), invasion by Chinese Communist "volunters" and then a stalemate at the 38th parallel. When

General MacArthur publicly protested the official American policy of a limited war in Korea, he was relieved of his command. Peace came to embattled Korea on July 27, 1953 when the issues of a demarcation line, demilitarized zones, and prisoner exchange were finally negotiated.

Cold War in the Far East. The Korean War caused the United States to extend its European policy into the Far East and eventually into the Near East; the pattern of foreign policy gradually became global. And, as Germany became the pivot of the American policy in Europe, so did Japan become pivotal in the Far East.

Japan. On September 8, 1951 the United States together with 48 other states concluded a peace treaty with Japan which reduced Japan to four main islands, ended the occupation, returned her prisoners of war, relieved her of the burden of reparations, permitted her to join regional security pacts and contract for occupation troops to assist in her defense.

Defense Pacts. This "peace of reconciliation" with Japan left the Filipinos, Australians and New Zealanders unconvinced; Japan was now free to rearm. The United States, therefore, signed two reassurance treaties of defense with them; a **bilateral pact** with the Philippines (August 1951) and the **ANZUS treaty** with Australia and New Zealand. These treaties were not quite so clear cut as that of NATO: an armed attack on one would be "considered dangerous to the peace and safety" of the others; each would act, in the face of common danger, "in accordance with its constitutional processes." This formula for a defense pact was eventually signed with Korea, Iran, Thailand, Pakistan, Saudi Arabia, India, Israel, Japan and Iraq. The pact with Japan was signed on the same day as the peace treaty and provided that the United States could deploy its armed forces inside Japan. American forces were similarly stationed by treaty inside the Philippines and Korea.

Military Assistance. Japan was converted into an American military bastion. She was granted large sums in economic and military aid; to strengthen her naval defenses the Amani Islands were returned to her in 1953. Formosa also became a great American base. Chiang Kai Shek's half-million man army was brought into full strength and was serviced by the American navy. America also undertook to bear 70% of France's costs in waging her Indo-Chinese war against the Communist forces. American ground crews were sent into the battle area to help maintain and repair damaged aircraft. The U. S. warned the Communist leaders that America was ready to apply "massive retaliatory power"; despite these threats the French forces were disastrously defeated. It was at Russia's suggestion that a truce was effected in Indo-China and at Geneva in 1954 Indo-China was divided at the 17th parallel; 12,-000,000 more people were added to the Communist fold.

SEATO. For some time Secretary Dulles had been urging a **South East Asia Treaty Organization** based on the model of NATO. With the fall of Indo-China, eight governments were stirred into action (the United States, the United Kingdom, France, Australia, New Zealand, Pakistan, the Philippines and Thailand) and in the **Manila Pact** adopted the formula of the bilateral agreements made by the United States in the Far East. The absence in SEATO of India, Burma and Indonesia ("neutralist" nations) made the pact considerably weaker than NATO.

Far Eastern Policies. The policy of the United States in the Far East was influenced by the growing strength of Communist China, persisting border raids between communist and free countries, and widespread neutralism. Communist China's power was reflected in the bombardment of Quemoy and Matsu, threatening tactics used against Taiwan (Formosa) and the United States Seventh Fleet, and economic dumping activities in Hong Kong, Burma, Malaya and elsewhere. Border raids continued in Viet Nam and Korea; and a tense situation was narrowly averted when the Dalai Lama escaped from Tibet into India. India, Burma and Indonesia assumed the leadership in building up a neutralist "third force" in the world which refused to take sides in the cold war, and which, nonetheless, united with African, Near Eastern and Soviet-bloc powers at Bandung (1955) to aggressively oppose "colonialism." United States foreign policy had to steer carefully through these turbulent waters. Economic aid and military preparedness were kept in balance as the pivot of American policy. Economic assistance was given to India and other countries of southern Asia through the Colombo Plan. Meanwhile, SEATO was formed; a military defense alliance concluded with Taiwan; and South Viet Nam, Japan and the Philippines were fully armed.

THE UNITED STATES IN THE MIDDLE EAST

Even more complex were the problems that riddled the Middle East. Arab nationalists first concentrated upon eliminating England as a Middle

Eastern colonial power. Iran nationalized British oil (1951); Egypt seized the Suez Canal and forced British military withdrawal (1954); the Sudan won its independence (1955); British military advisers were driven from Jordan (1956); Cyprus loosened English control (1959). To fill the vacuum created by the loss of English prestige, the United States encouraged the creation of the Middle East Treaty Organization (the Baghdad Pact 1955). Of the Arab states proper, only Iraq joined (only to withdraw in 1959 following the Kassim Revolution); the United States itself did not join. This left only England, Turkey, Pakistan and Iran to defend the Middle East against further infiltration.

The Soviet-bloc nations also rushed in to fill the vacuum of British withdrawal. In 1955, Gamal Nasser of Egypt concluded an arms deal with Czechoslovakia and began to negotiate with the Soviet Union for a loan to build the Aswan Dam, the United States having offered such a loan and then withdrawn the offer. Syria was similarly armed. Russian technical assistants flooded into the Middle East; underground communist parties emerged and prepared to make a bid for power in some Arab countries.

At the same time, the creation of Israel by the United Nations in 1948 intensified the anarchy in the Middle East. The Arabs attacked Israel and were defeated (1948-9); Israel invaded Egypt and defeated her (1956); Egypt barred passage of Israeli ships and goods through the Suez Canal; border warfare raged in the Gaza Strip (between Egypt and Israel) and along the Syrian-Lebanon frontier. Israeli military activities had the support of the British and French. The United States, however, worked for peace between Israel and the Arabs through the United Nations and supported the efforts of Dr. Ralph Bunche to effectuate a truce between the conflicting parties in 1949. The United States was instrumental in halting the tripartite invasion of Egypt (England, France and Israel) in 1956; in establishing a cease fire and withdrawal, and creating the United Nations Emergency Force (UNEF) to supervise the withdrawal and maintain vigilance against other invasions.

Russia's threat to send "volunteers" to help Egypt; Nasser's tactics in merging Egypt and Syria to form the United Arab Republic; his verbal assaults on King Hussein of Jordan and King Faisal of Iraq; and threatening civil war in Lebanon resulted in the **Eisenhower Doctrine.** Approved by Congress, this doctrine authorized United States armed assistance, if requested by a Middle Eastern nation, to repel aggression by a Soviet-bloc nation (1957). As a result of the Iraqui **coup** of July 14, 1958, at Lebanon's request, United States marines were landed in Lebanon to prevent the spread of revolt. When it became apparent that Karim Kassim, leader of the Iraquis, would not permit a communist-backed government to be established, the marines were withdrawn. Moreover, as Nasser himself became disillusioned with Soviet-bloc aid and apprehensive of Russian moves throughout the Middle East, the United States returned to its former policy of wide-scale economic aid to Egypt and other Arab nations.

How to curb the more violent aspects of Arab nationalism, to diminish Soviet infiltration, to dispose of the Arab refugees, and to raise the standard of living in the Middle East were the continuing problems that faced Middle Eastern foreign policy makers.

CHAPTER XXII

DOMESTIC AFFAIRS (1945-1960)

HARRY S. TRUMAN (1945-1952)

Demobilization and Reconversion. Deflationary tendencies marked the immediate post-war scene. The armed forces were so rapidly reduced that on the eve of the Korean War the armed forces contained only 600,000 men; military expenditures had been reduced to $13 billion. Taxes were reduced $6 billion and the government sold $15 billion in government-owned plants to make up the loss. To head off an anticipated post-war recession, Congress passed the Employment Act which created a **Council of Economic Advisers** to study the economy, analyze weaknesses and propose measures for stabilization.

The President and the Congress. Truman's annual message in 1945 set the stage for a bitter struggle with Congress. He asked for legislation which would revive the New Deal program—extension of Social Security, increase in the minimum wage, national health insurance, slum clearance, more "TVA's" and an extension of government controls through the period of reconversion. Republicans and Democrats in Congress combined against him and forced the abandonment of price controls, passed the **Taft-Hartley Act** (curbing labor unions) over the President's veto, crippled the President's anti-inflation program, reduced his housing program and rewrote the agricultural law substituting "flexible parities" ranging from 60% to 90% for Truman's "fixed parity" of 90%.

The Election of 1948. Optimism prevailed in the Republican convention which nominated Thomas E. Dewey. Truman's New Deal program had been stopped; the Roosevelt coalition was broken when Ickes and Wallace resigned from the cabinet; Wallace organized the Progressive Party which would draw from the Democratic votes; extreme Southern Democrats under J. Strom Thurmond seceded from Democratic ranks and organized the "Dixiecrats." Defying the "experts" who had predicted his defeat, Truman triumphed.

The Fair Deal. Truman regarded his "miracle election" as a popular mandate to enact a **"Fair Deal"** program which consisted of: repeal of the Taft-Hartley Law; sweeping civil rights legislation (anti-lynching laws, anti-poll tax laws, fair employment practices, etc.); expanded and more generous social security, minimum wage and housing legislation; compulsory federal health insurance; federal aid to education; increased protection of natural resources; authority for the government to build industrial plants to overcome national commodity shortages; effective enforcement of the antitrust laws to protect small business; high farm subsidies; and a sweeping anti-inflation program. Little success attended Truman's program: minimum wages were raised from 40¢ to 75¢ per hour and coverage under the Social Security Act was extended to domestic workers and employees in non-profit organizations. But his "Brannan" farm plan was rejected, his civil rights program filibustered to death by the Southerners, his health insurance program lobbied to death by the American Medical Association, his education program destroyed by religious groups and his demands for Taft-Hartley revisions, anti-inflation measures and a Universal Military Training law ignored. Instead, the Congress passed *over his veto* the McCarran-Walter Immigration Act and the McCarran Internal Security Act requiring the registration of the Communist party. Only in foreign affairs did the country follow President Truman's lead.

DWIGHT D. EISENHOWER (1953-1960)

The Election of 1952. It was "time for a change." As nomination year rolled around, the Democrats were revealed by congressional investigation to have engaged in corrupt practices. Links were discovered between Democrats and "five-percenters" who "sold influence." Corruption was exposed in the Internal Revenue Service and the RFC. Senator McCarthy of Wisconsin investigated the State Department, Senator Millard Tydings, General Marshall, and the Army and accused them all of being "soft on Communism." While the charges were exaggerated and often irresponsible, they made good campaign material. The ticket of Dwight D. Eisenhower and Richard M. Nixon defeated the Democratic slate of Adlai E. Stevenson and John J. Sparkman by an electoral vote of 442-89.

The "New Republicanism." "New Republicanism" was characterized chiefly by the fact that it accepted the main features of the New Deal as part of the American way of life. Eisenhower continued many of the policies of his Democratic predecessors: billion-dollar foreign aid; liberalized immigration laws; reciprocal trade agreements; increased Social Security benefits; minimum wage laws; increased unemployment insurance payments; federal aid to housing, etc.

The Election of 1956. In 1952 Eisenhower had picked up the votes of millions of discontented Democrats; in 1956 he secured the votes of millions of Negroes pleased by the epochal Supreme Court school desegregation decision in *Brown v. Board of Education of Topeka* which was given in 1954 and associated with his administration. His heart attack made it uncertain whether he would be available for a second term, but by January 1956 he had eased himself back to work. His State of the Union address that year showed how far the "New Republicanism" had gone in four years. Eisenhower proposed a very ambitious program: farm aid; development of highways and waterways; aid to education; expansion of Social Security to include medical care through voluntary health insurance; increased public housing; reform of the labor laws; and anti-discrimination measures. His budget request soared to $66,000,000,000. He and Nixon were nominated by acclamation and again administered a smashing defeat to Stevenson, this time running with the popular Senator Estes Kefauver. Much of this victory was due to Eisenhower's personal popularity, for in the same election the Democrats were able to win control of both houses of Congress.

Republicanism. Eisenhower modified but did not abandon his conservatism. His general policy was that of retrenchment in domestic expenditures and of a *laissez-faire* attitude of "less government in business and more business in government." For example, price controls were ended, parity payments reduced, tidelands oil returned to the states, private enterprise admitted into atomic-energy production, government-owned plants sold to private industry, and high political offices filled by executives of large business enterprises. Stronger measures were taken against Communists: their party was outlawed (although membership in it was not made a crime), the death penalty was prescribed for peacetime espionage, persons convicted of conspiracy to overthrow the government had their citizenship revoked, and the FBI was protected against unrestricted use of its files.

Achievements of the Eisenhower Administration. In the area of human welfare: refugees were admitted above the quota limits; public housing was provided for federal slum-clearance projects; Social Security benefits were increased and extended to 10,000,000 more persons; the minimum wage was boosted to $1 an hour; another housing bill provided $1,800,000,000 to stimulate construction; aid to the jobless was extended by 50% for those who had exhausted their benefits; veterans' pensions were boosted, as was the pay of federal employees; a modified program of health care for the aged was passed, covering about 1,400,000 needy persons over 65.

In the agricultural area: farmers lost rigid price supports, and a gradual reduction in cotton, corn, and rice supports from 75% to 65% of parity was permitted; however, in the Soil Bank Act of 1956 $1,200,000,000 was set aside to encourage farmers to cut their production and plant trees and soil-conserving crops.

In the labor area, the Landrum-Griffin Act democratized unions and protected them against racketeers but placed further curbs on secondary boycotts and picketing. The President scored heavily in the field of civil rights: the 1957 act protected the Negro's right to vote; the use of federal troops in Little Rock, Arkansas, upheld the Supreme Court's decision that schools must be integrated; the act of 1960 brought further federal intervention in state voting practices where these were designed to prevent Negroes from voting. A modest beginning was made in federal aid to education: Korean veterans received G.I. Bill of Rights benefits and loans and fellowships were created for education in science and languages.

In other significant acts, Alaska and Hawaii were admitted as the forty-ninth and fiftieth states; construction of the St. Lawrence Seaway was begun; an International Atomic Energy Agency was set up to explore peaceful uses of atomic energy. The XXIII Amendment gave residents of the District of Columbia the right to vote in national elections. The newly created federal space agency launched a number of satellites. Finally, Senator McCarthy was crushed by Senate condemnation and "McCarthyism" slowly left the American scene.

JOHN F. KENNEDY (1961-1963)

The Election of 1960. During the presidential primaries of 1960 candidate John F. Kennedy seemed to be handicapped by both his youth and his religion—he was forty-three years old and was a Roman Catholic. Yet he won the Democratic nomination on the first ballot. Lyndon B. Johnson, the Senate majority leader from Texas, was nominated for the Vice-Presidency. The Republicans chose Vice-President Richard M. Nixon for the presidential post and Henry Cabot Lodge, Jr., as his running mate. The election resulted in an extraordinarily close popular vote: out of 68,836,000 ballots cast, Kennedy received 49.7% and Nixon received 49.5%. The spread in the electoral college was wider, however: 303 to 219. The Congress remained dominated by Democrats, although the effective voting bloc remained that of the Southern Democrats and the Republicans. President Kennedy was confronted from the start with a bumptious, conservative coalition.

Inauguration. The new President took little cognizance of these political realities in his now immortal inaugural address. In this address he probed into the underlying purposes uniting the groupings and jugglings of political subgroups. All the issues of the day, he said, flow into one—that of survival. In the hands of man "is the power to abolish all forms of human poverty and all forms of human life." To keep the peace and to abolish hunger were the parameters of the "New Frontier." Because it was the depository of all the ideals of freedom, America must become the strongest free nation; priority must go to solving the problems of defense.

Because it had the greatest productive machine on the globe, its economic wealth must be shared with the needy at home and abroad. Out of a position of military and economic strength, America could and wanted to negotiate with the hostile Communist world. This guideline set the tone of the Kennedy administration and created a fever in much of the country to get on with building the New Frontier.

Cabinet and Consensus. A superb politician, Kennedy understood the politics of consensus. He realized that it had to be built on the presence in America of hardening pressure blocs—liberals and conservatives, labor and management, ethnic groupings, religious groupings, etc. Consensus dictated that some of each of these groups be permitted to share in the government, regardless of party label, and his Cabinet choices reflected this political philosophy. The liberals were represented by Chester Bowles, Dean Acheson, and Adlai Stevenson, although many observers felt that these men were given relatively minor government posts. The conservative group was pleased with the appointment of Douglas Dillon, a Republican banker, as Secretary of the Treasury and Robert McNamara, president of the Ford Motor Company, as Secretary of Defense. The neutral, non-controversial Dean Rusk was made Secretary of State. The appointment of Arthur Goldberg, the AFL-CIO general counsel, must certainly have pleased the Jewish and organized labor blocs. An offer of the Postmaster Generalship to a Negro undoubtedly excited the Negro community, although the offer was eventually rejected. The Catholic bloc got an additional boost when the President appointed his brother, Robert, as Attorney General. Although this was the most controversial of the appointments, Robert Kennedy overcame the objections because of his brilliant exposure of James Hoffa of the Teamsters Union. A "kitchen cabinet" of prominent intellectuals—Arthur Schlesinger, Jr., Theodore Sorensen, McGeorge Bundy, and others—was invited to the White House to help shape the New Frontier.

Setting the Stage. In his message to Congress, Kennedy spelled out the details of the New Frontier. It was a cautious message and did not exceed the demands of Truman's Fair Deal. It emphasized, however, the need for governmental planning to achieve a steady and high rate of economic growth. As a major force in the American economy, government can divert large sums into human welfare and national defense. Therefore, the President called for medical care for the aged, federal aid to all types of education, better use of natural resources,

provision of housing and community development, highway construction, increased national defense expenditures, and increased foreign military and economic aid. It was not the best of times for these proposals. Congress felt no sense of urgency; there was a wave of prosperity on; employment was high and the gross national product was mounting. A few pockets of permanently depressed areas in the country hardly constituted a crisis. The President had to use all his skill as a politician dispensing patronage to muster slim majorities for his legislative program when he did break through Congressional inertia.

Achievements of the Kennedy Administration. The legislative achievement of the Kennedy administration was spotty. Two major bills, one for Medicare and another for federal aid to education, went down to defeat and created the impression of failure for the entire program. Actually, some important new legislation was passed and old measures extended. To accomplish this, however, Kennedy had to overcome the opposition of the very conservative Congressman Howard Smith, chairman of the House Rules Committee, where so much of the progressive legislation had been delayed. Kennedy allied with Speaker Sam Rayburn to break Smith's power by adding three members to the committee, putting control into the hands of the moderates. This done, Congress went on to pass a minimum wage law that raised the hourly rate from $1 to $1.25 over a period of four years and added more than 3,500,000 workers to the list of those covered by this law. It also increased Social Security benefits, provided for children of needy unemployed, permitted men as well as women to retire at age sixty-two, and created a retirement fund for the self-employed. Slightly less than $5,000,000,000 was allocated over a four-year period for slum clearance, FHA housing projects for middle income families, urban renewal projects, student housing, housing for the elderly, and loans for repairs.

Other major accomplishments were the establishment of area redevelopment and manpower training programs to retrain workers whose skills had become obsolete and who had joined the strange new army of the permanently unemployed despite the fact that over-all employment increased; the allocation of money for the relief of businessmen and unemployed persons in depressed areas; aid for the mentally retarded; tightening of controls over the manufacture and distribution of drugs; expansion of trade by giving the President power to reduce tariffs 50% over five years, to eliminate some tariffs altogether, and to protect industries and workers injured by such tariff reductions. Congress also approved measures to aid medical education, programs for college construction, relief of areas impacted by federal projects, and defense education. Using his executive powers, the President created a task force which was the first to explore combining housing with health, education, and welfare, and he forbade racial discrimination in the sale or rental of federal housing projects built since 1961.

Planning. Behind Kennedy's legislative requests was his deeper desire to move the U.S. closer to a managed economy. The economist Paul Samuelson's idea was that this could be accomplished by direct intervention of the federal government to stimulate economic growth with heavy aid to distressed areas and for residential construction, by raising unemployment compensation allotments, by securing lower interest rates to encourage mortgage investments, and, these failing, by cutting taxes to increase effective demand. These expenditures, Kennedy realized, would create inflationary pressures. To counteract them he persuaded the United Steel Workers, for example, to keep their wage demands low. When the steel industry raised its prices, the angry President brought every pressure to bear to compel a retraction; he succeeded, but became more unpopular with big business. As a last resort, he suggested a $13,000,000,000 income tax reduction.

The Surge to Freedom. Kennedy's administration saw a proliferation of the tactics adopted by Negroes and their white supporters to break the power structure that upheld racial discrimination and segregation. New Negro organizations appeared to reinforce the contingents from Roy Wilkins' NAACP, Martin Luther King's Southern Christian Leadership Conference, and the Urban League. The Congress of Racial Equality, the Black Muslims, and the Student Nonviolent Coordinating Committee launched a number of integrationist moves: "sit-ins" to integrate restaurants and parks; "pray-ins" to integrate churches; "freedom rides" to integrate transportation facilities and to supply the South with workers whose job it would be to get out the Negro vote; and picketing and boycotting of *de facto* segregated neighborhood schools. The movement reached its high point in the celebrated March on Washington (August 1963) in support of pending civil rights legislation. It was a typical American irony that all this motion resulted in Congress' failure to pass a comprehensive Civil Rights

Act proposed by President Kennedy; furthermore, Congress refused to grant to the city of Washington, D.C., the home rule demanded because a majority of the residents were Negro.

Southern white supremacists fought back. They formed White Citizens' Councils, rejoined the Ku Klux Klan, attacked demonstrators, murdered Northern civil rights workers, intimidated liberal Southern newspaper editors and owners of radio stations. The segregationist element in the South was so strong that federal troops were required to implement a court order integrating the University of Mississippi.

A Political Revolution. In *Baker v. Carr* (1962), the Supreme Court ordered the Federal District Court of Tennessee to reapportion the Tennessee state legislature if it found that the Constitutional requirement of representation according to population was being violated. In most states of the union fewer than 40% of the voters chose the majority of representatives of the Legislature as a result of the unequal size of legislative districts. Another reapportionment case then extended this principle of "one man-one vote" to congressional districts. Most states revised their apportionment formulas to eliminate the imbalance between the voting strength exercised by rural and urban dwellers.

Defense. Secretary of Defense McNamara modernized the Department of Defense with computers and cost-analysis techniques, which had as their objectives elimination of any missile gap between the U.S. and the U.S.S.R. and providing a firmer foundation to the new politics of "the balance of terror." Nuclear weapons were widely deployed and readied for instant retaliation. The administration realized that if the balance of terror held, new wars could assume guerrilla as well as conventional forms, so much of the military was trained in "counterinsurgent" tactics. So, too, were large numbers of American allies who were also supplied with the latest military equipment. All of these measures pushed the annual military expenditure close to the $50,000,000,000 mark so that to an increasing extent the prosperous economy of the U.S. became linked with expenditures on armaments.

Vast sums of money were also poured into the space race. The Russians, having taken the lead with the launching of Sputnik, held it through 1963. Their rocket booster was more powerful; they orbited the first cosmonaut; they established a long-distance record in orbiting the earth; and they launched two cosmonauts on succeeding days who were able to bring their vehicles close together. The

American effort seemed unspectacular in comparison, but astronauts were launched, devices were developed to register the essentials of space probes (solar radiation, magnetic fields, etc.), and communication satellites such as Telstar were successfully orbited. To overcome the space gap with Russia, Kennedy recommended the $20,000,000,000 Apollo project, designed to land an American on the moon. With no reluctance whatever, Congress voted $3,000,000,000 to $5,000,000,000 a year for this program.

The Dallas Bullets. On the afternoon of Friday, November 22, 1963, while riding in a motorcade through Dallas, Texas, President Kennedy was assassinated. Governor John Connally of Texas, riding alongside the President, was wounded. The murder was attributed to Lee Harvey Oswald, but two days later, while he was being transferred from one jail to another, Oswald was shot and killed by Jack Ruby, a Dallas restaurant owner, in full view of the police and millions of television watchers. Thoughts of a broad conspiracy filled the air, not only in America but throughout the world, where they persist to this day. President Kennedy was buried in Arlington National Cemetery on November 25, 1963 in a funeral attended by officials of almost every country in the world.

LYNDON B. JOHNSON (1963-   )

The Interim President. With John F. Kennedy dead but two hours, the Vice-President, Lyndon B. Johnson, was sworn in as thirty-sixth President of the U.S. Johnson proceeded to make the transition as smooth as possible: he called upon Congress to fulfill the Kennedy program by passing the legislation he wanted with respect to civil rights, federal aid to education, foreign aid, and a tax cut. Then he added something of his own, a program spelling out the "war on poverty." He announced that he would retain the Kennedy Cabinet and such of Kennedy's advisers as cared to stay on. National tension relaxed as the country witnessed Johnson's assurance, born out of long political experience. With the help of the Eighty-eighth Congress, Johnson was able to accomplish in his first hundred days what Kennedy could not in three years: a tax cut, the Kennedy 1963 foreign aid bill, several education laws, and a broad-based Civil Rights Act.

The Civil Rights Act of 1964. Southerners filibustered the proposed civil rights bill in the Senate for three months—the longest filibuster in American history; the rarely-used parliamentary technique of cloture eventually ended the filibuster. The act that finally passed both houses had these five principal sections: (1) prohibited racial discrimination in restaurants, theaters, hotels, and other places of "public accommodation"; (2) authorized the Attorney General to initiate suits or otherwise intervene on behalf of victims of discrimination, including school children; (3) prohibited discrimination by employers or labor unions; (4) withheld funds from federally supported projects practicing racial discrimination; and (5) compelled uniform standards for voting for whites and Negroes.

Reactions to these anti-racist legislative proposals were varied. Many parts of the South integrated public accommodations without fuss or protest; fewer, however, undertook to integrate schools. Two Negroes defeated their white opponents in a city council race. The white supremacists embarked on a reign of terror: Negro homes and churches were bombed; civil rights volunteers were murdered; Southern juries acquitted even self-confessed killers. In the North, Negroes responded with racial riots in the ghetto areas of New York City, Rochester, N.Y., Philadelphia, and Jersey City. Millions of dollars' worth of property was damaged and where local police were unable to curb the riots the National Guard was called in to do so. Now it was the turn of the Northern whites to experience this "backlash." They fiercely protested proposals to integrate *de facto* segregated neighborhood schools by bussing children to and from other districts.

Tax Planning. Early in 1964 Congress provided for more than $9,000,000,000 in tax reductions on individual incomes and $2,400,000,000 on corporate profits. This reduction came at the same time that federal revenues fell $8,400,000,000 short of expenditures, thus adding even more to the $300,000,000,000 public debt. The tax cut, however, was deliberately designed to brace the lagging economic growth with a large shot of spending power. And it worked, for the next year the gross national product boomed again.

War on Poverty. The Economic Opportunity Act of 1964 was Johnson's follow-up to his "undeclared war on poverty." Rural conservation camps and urban training centers were established to help school dropouts obtain job training. Part-time employment was provided for students so that they would be less inclined to quit school. Local communities with their own anti-poverty programs were given federal aid. Farmers received grants to improve their productivity, and small businesses were given incentives to employ the so-called "chronically disemployed." Heads of families receiving public assistance were offered job training. All this, Johnson said, was for the "forgotten fifth" of the American people.

Completing the Outline of the "Great Society." Before the election of 1964, Congress followed Johnson's leadership by setting up a 9,000,000-acre wilderness preserve for conservation and recreation; by passing a Housing Act for construction of 35,000 units of low-rent dwellings to aid the poor and clear the slums; by providing cities with federal aid to solve their transit problems; by helping school districts whose population had increased because of federal facilities in the area; by extending the National Defense Education Act to improve instruction. However, the Eighty-eighth Congress refused to act on the President's proposal for Medicare under Social Security and on his request for $1,000,000,000 to abolish poverty in Appalachia.

Labor. The labor movement appreciated Johnson's tax cut. It favored his intervention in a railroad dispute since the result was increased pay, more paid holidays, and expenses for time spent away from home; in return, the railroad obtained control over the size of crews and work assignments. There was no need for presidential intervention in the massive automobile labor-management negotiations of 1964. Labor did very well in all areas —pensions, wage increases, insurance, and paid holidays. The President was, however, criticized for invoking the Taft-Hartley Act in a longshoremen's strike.

The Warren Report. The uproar over President Kennedy's assassination continued; there was no conclusiveness about the charges against Lee Harvey Oswald. A commission headed by Chief Justice Earl Warren was established to review the evidence against Oswald. After ten months, the commission confirmed his guilt and denied any evidence of a conspiracy. The Secret Service and the FBI were mildly reprimanded for inefficiency. The full report was then published, but a surprising number of people were skeptical of its conclusions, which, it was felt, were contradicted by the evidence.

The Election of 1964. The Republicans, in a convention dominated by the conservative wing, nominated Senator Barry M. Goldwater and Congressman William Miller to run against President Johnson and Senator Hubert Humphrey, the vice-presidential choice. Goldwater was defeated by the largest margin in the history of presidential elections. The popular vote was 42,700,000 to 26,900,000. The Republicans received 52 electoral votes from the South, now voting Republican to register its protest against the civil rights movement. But thousands of Republicans crossed party lines to vote for Johnson in protest over the tactics of the right-wingers who captured the Republican party and the convention. Many of Goldwater's adherents were extremists who wanted to end the Social Security program, withdraw the U.S. from the United Nations, allow field commanders in Vietnam to use nuclear weapons, make civil rights legislation exclusively state matters, sell TVA to private interests, and end farm price supports. Johnson won handily by striking out for peace and for the "Great Society" without urban slums, with clean air and water, without poverty or crime or delinquency, and carried into office an overwhelmingly Democratic Congress. The Democratic landslide extended also to most of the state legislatures and gubernatorial races.

The Elected President. President Johnson felt, justifiably, that his massive victory was a mandate to get on with the Great Society. He therefore brought to the Eighty-ninth Congress a legislative program which made it the most revolutionary Congress since Franklin D. Roosevelt's time. The laws passed by this Congress aimed at a guaranteed income for every American. Logically, this is what the call for the abolition of poverty entails.

The Third Immigration. The immigration law of 1965 returned America to its origin of indiscriminate immigration. While a limit on total immigration was retained, and even extended to Latin America, it was separated from the racist system of "national origins" to which it had been pegged since 1921. In the new law, the classification of immigrants by national origins was abolished beginning in 1968. Until then, the unused quotas could be assigned to low-quota countries. No nation was permitted more than 20,000 emigrants to America. Total immigration per year was fixed at 170,000 for all countries outside the Western Hemisphere and 120,000 for those within. Admission was on a first come-first served basis, with exceptions being made for close relatives of American citizens and for scientists, artists, professional people, and workers who could fill U.S. shortages. Up to 60,000 close relatives could come in, even if a country's quota had been reached.

Education. An important federal law to help education was enacted. It is weighted in favor of states with large numbers of students from low-income families, but all states benefit to some degree from its provisions affecting higher teachers' salaries, additional school buildings, better equipment, and more textbooks. Aid was to be extended to parochial schools if they set up centers for special instruction on a shared-time basis. Over a period of three years $2,300,000,000 was to be spent on higher education, including opportunity grants for needy college students, continuing federally guaranteed tuition loans, and generous grants to colleges for equipment and construction. A National Foundataion on the Arts and Humanities was established to help scholars and artists.

Health. An allocation of $1,000,000,000 was earmarked for research on major diseases. For those aged sixty-five or more, a medical care program was created as part of the Social Security system. Known as Medicare, it includes payment for hospitalization, nursing homes, post-hospital care, etc. A voluntary medical insurance plan for doctors' fees and surgical costs was made available for $3 a month. Related to health was a bill to control air and water pollution by scientific disposal of waste.

Appalachia. In an effort to revive a poverty area extending over eleven states in the southeast, $1,000,000,000 was voted for roads, construction of health centers and land improvement.

Cities. Urban problems received much attention in the President's program. For their solution a Department of Housing and Urban Development was created and the Cabinet post of Secretary was given to Robert Weaver, a Negro housing expert. The Congress passed a housing act which included the radical feature of having the federal government pay the rent of low-income families who could not afford to live in low-income housing projects. The real objective of Johnson's program was to get at the high human costs of intensive urbanization. This, however, had to wait for the second session of the Eighty-ninth Congress.

Minimum Wages. This is a perennial feature of any progressive program. The base pay was to be increased to $1.40 by February 1967 and from $1.40 to $1.60 by February 1968. But a major breakthrough occurred when farm laborers, workers in small retail shops, and hospital workers were placed under the minimum wage law. They had been systematically excluded from all previous wage legislation.

Food for Freedom. The war on poverty resulted in an important reversal in farm policy. Farmers were now encouraged to increase their planted acreage. Price supports were sharply reduced and production was planned with an eye to all domestic and foreign demands.

Civil Rights. After the comprehensive bill of 1964, the Act of 1965 implemented an important area of voting rights. In those areas where 50% or more of the adults were not registered or did not vote in the 1964 elections, all literacy tests and other voting qualifications were suspended. The Attorney General could send federal examiners into these areas to register qualified voters. A sixth-grade education was considered a presumption of literacy. And, while Congress was thus engaged, the Supreme Court held that the imposition of poll taxes was unconstitutional.

Transportation. In a Mass Transport Act, $375,000,000 was allocated over three years for railroad service. The objective was to attract new passengers with high-speed, jet-propelled railroads, surface and underground, permitting speeds of up to 300 miles per hour. Somewhat less functional was a beautification bill eliminating billboards and junkyards from interstate highways.

The Lesser Eighty-ninth. A sharp change in the congressional attitude toward the Great Society occurred between 1965 and 1966. There were to be elections in November 1966 and Congressmen were concerned with the effects of their radical welfare programs; President Johnson seemed to share their mood. Besides, he had become so bound up with the war in Vietnam that he could not work up enthusiasm for a domestic program, especially one that had, along with the war, unleashed an inflation that destroyed the guidelines he himself had set for advances in prices and wages.

Some important legislation was turned out by this session, but the most exciting in terms of the Great Society went down the drain. President Johnson got only $1,000,000,000 for his Demonstration Cities plan of total urban renewal; two laws were passed to enhance traffic safety; and a twelfth Cabinet position was created, the Department of Transportation. A G.I. Bill of Rights was voted for post-Korean War veterans; deceptive packaging and false labeling were outlawed; bills were passed for regulation of election expenditures and the elimination of water pollution. The Job Corps and Project Head-Start, key programs in the war on poverty, were continued. Finally, $58,000,000,000 was voted for defense, the largest appropriation since World War II; and $2,900,000,000 was voted for foreign aid, the smallest appropriation since 1957.

Defeated Legislation. What certainly was the most important civil rights act yet conceived was defeated after considerable debate. It attacked the heart of the ghetto problem by making illegal racial discrimination in the sale or rental of dwellings in large housing and apartment developments. It also outlawed discriminatory juries. But Congress could not cross the boundary that would destroy the housing pattern that perpetuates segregation. Condemned to slums, Negroes began to talk of "black power" in segregated areas. Their aim was elimination of the white power structure within the ghetto.

Labor's plea for abolition of section 14b from the Taft-Hartley Act (guaranteeing states the right to pass "right-to-work" laws) was again defeated. No action was taken on the President's requests for streamlining Congress, lengthening terms of office to four years for representatives, eliminating the electoral college, creating new machinery to deal with labor-management disputes, and controlling the sale of firearms.

Election of 1966. The reasons for Congress' reluctance to enact much of Johnson's program in the second session of the Eighty-ninth Congress were made apparent by the November election that year. The Republicans scored a major resurgence of power, gaining a number of congressional seats, winning twenty-three of the thirty-four governorships that were contested, and regaining control of several state legislatures that they had lost in 1964. Furthermore, the feeling of despair caused by Goldwater's defeat two years earlier was overcome and there was optimistic talk of winning the presidency in the future. There were a number of reasons for the Democrats' defeat: "white backlash," the feeling by a large segment of the white population that too much was being done for Negroes; the impression held by many middle-class citizens that Johnson's program was moving the country too close to a welfare state where it is easier to sit back and let the government provide than to work for one's own living; and by increasing concern over the Vietnam war and the feeling that the U.S. was becoming more and more involved in what would turn out to be a long-term military commitment with no prospects for an easy and quick victory.

Space. Nearing its tenth year, the Space Age had witnessed placing more than a thousand man-made satellites in orbit. These fell into the categories of communication satellites, weather satellites, planet probers, military satellites, and moon probers. Some of these have been highly successful: Early Bird, located 22,300 miles above the Atlantic, sends television programs from Europe to America. Essa 3 relays weather information by flashing pictures of cloud formations all over the world. Mariner IV probed Mars and sent twenty clear pictures back. Undoubtedly, both the U.S. and the U.S.S.R. have "spies-in-the-skies" satellites reporting on missile placements and troop movements. The U.S. is well on its way to putting a manned orbital laboratory into space. In the race to put men on the moon, the U.S. is ahead of the Russians. More astronauts have been in flight, and for longer periods, and the U.S. has made more progress in space maneuverings—rendezvous, docking, and spacewalking. Both countries have taken moon pictures, have made soft landings on the moon, and have placed a satellite in orbit around the moon.

CHAPTER XXIII

FOREIGN POLICY SINCE 1960

LATIN AMERICA

In 1959, the Cuban dictator Batista was overthrown by opponents of his totalitarian regime, led by Fidel Castro. As Castro's extremely left-wing program became apparent, the U.S. severed diplomatic and economic relations with Cuba because of the disquieting prospect of a Communist state located only ninety miles from our own shore. The attempt to prevent a similar recurrence elsewhere has characterized U.S. Latin American policy. The U.S. supported an invasion by Cuban refugees at the Bay of Pigs in April 1961. Although the operation was a disaster and was a serious blow to American prestige throughout the world, President Kennedy accepted full responsibility for it. Thereupon, however, he ordered increased vigilance, especially by air reconnaissance, and thus discovered in October 1962 that the Russians were building missile bases in Cuba. Kennedy placed a blockade around

Cuba to prevent Soviet ships from entering Cuba's waters and demanded that the missiles be removed. After some tense maneuvering, during which it appeared that the world stood at the brink of war, Soviet Premier Khrushchev retreated, announced that he would dismantle the bases, and did so.

Prior to this crisis, Kennedy had realized that all of Latin America could become prey to Castroism unless the roots of revolution were removed. In 1961 he had proposed an "Alliance for Progress" which would cost the U.S. $20,000,000,000 over a ten-year period in aid to expand Latin American trade, stabilize prices, and help with social and economic reforms such as abolishing illiteracy, eradicating native diseases, building adequate housing, redistributing the land, and revising the tax structure. This program continues and has even been expanded despite bitter criticism of Latin American dictators who have been receiving aid and have been frustrating every attempt at social or economic reform.

Military dictatorship has been the response of much of Latin America to Castroism. In fact, it was the response of the United States as well. When the Dominican dictator Trujillo was assassinated in 1961, political unrest surged through the Dominican Republic. In 1965 this unrest turned into a civil war between a military junta and the followers of Juan Bosch, the elected but exiled President. Frightened by the thought of another Castro-type takeover, President Johnson rushed a contingent of U.S. marines there, ostensibly to protect American civilians. What resulted was a crude occupation by American forces who were unable to find the Communist revolutionaries who were supposedly preparing for the coup. At this point the matter was turned over to the Organization of American States (OAS) and in 1966 American troops were withdrawn. But the sudden reversal of a policy of multilateralism, established in 1933, was carefully noted by all the Latin Americans.

ASIA

The major influence on U.S. policy in Asia has been Communist China. Korean War memories have been kept alive by the uneasy truce that hung over the border, the 38th Parallel, that separates North and South Korea. In the Korean War, Communist China had inflicted wounds on the Americans that still rankle and it has become the determined policy of the U.S. to keep China isolated. Several methods have been used: diplomatic non-recognition, economic boycott, economic and military aid to China's enemies, preventing her admission to the UN, and building naval and military bases around her. When, in 1962, China lashed out at India and broke through her frontier defenses, America rushed military aid to India.

Vietnam. A second major encounter between the U.S. and Communist China, however, seemed to be developing in Vietnam. With the defeat of the French at Dienbienphu in 1954, the Geneva Accord had divided Vietnam (formerly French Indo-China) into northern (Communist) and southern (non-communist) territories and called for national elections under neutral supervision. The U.S. had already intervened in this "war of liberation" by lending France millions of dollars and giving her special military advisers. After the French left, American assistance was given to the U.S.-chosen President, Ngo Dinh Diem, who repudiated the elections and established himself as dictator. In response, the Communist Vietcong army in the south began an assault on Diem's government. They were aided by the Buddhists, who had also been alienated by Diem. Diem was assassinated and political chaos ensued. Thereupon President Kennedy increased the military aid and dispatched the first U.S. combat troops to serve as advisers. After eight successive governments were formed and overthrown, Nguyen Cao Ky was selected for the President's post. He disposed of all internal opposition by force, including the powerful Buddhists. President Johnson began to send in combat troops, assumed command of what was essentially a civil war, and permitted bombing of both South and North Vietnam, widespread napalm assaults, defoliation procedures, and tear gas attacks. Never was so much firepower hurled at so few, but the war persisted as the U.S. found it difficult to counter the guerrilla tactics of the Communists.

Throughout the escalation, the U.S. proclaimed its peaceful intentions and its willingness to meet the North Vietnamese government at any time and at any place. A major offer, made at a seven-nation conference in Manila in October 1966, called for withdrawal from South Vietnam of all troops within six months after the Communists stop fighting, end their aggression, preserve the territorial integrity of South Vietnam, reunify Vietnam, resolve internal problems, and give effective guarantees that the peace will be kept. North Vietnam rejected the offer and insisted that the war would not end until the American "aggressors" left the country. Throughout the struggle, the U.S. has declared that Communist China is the real culprit behind the North Vietnamese, who in turn are supporting the Vietcong of the south.

EUROPE

Although American-Soviet confrontations have reached the crisis stage on a number of occasions, relations between the two countries have since moved into a detente position. There has been considerable coexistence since the missile affair in Cuba. The new Soviet government has encouraged interchanges of scholars, doctors, scientists, athletes, and artists. Both countries signed a limited nuclear test-ban treaty in 1963, to the amazement of the world; both are seriously engaged in halting the proliferation of nuclear powers. Space cooperation includes the exchange of moon photographs and weather information. This improvement in relations may be due to a number of problems that are keeping the Russians too busy to bother with continuation of the Cold War: polycentricity among her former satellites; the serious schism with Communist China; crop failures and a sudden decline in economic growth rate; or just plain fear of those who so blithely bombed Hiroshima and Nagasaki. It is too soon to speak with certainty.

Yet Charles de Gaulle of France does speak with certainty. He is convinced that the Cold War is over and that Europe no longer needs the U.S. What Europe needs is France as a third force between the two giants, and it must be France since it must never be Germany, who cannot be trusted, and cannot be England, who is nothing more than an American satellite. De Gaulle's counter-American foreign policy has been: (1) to keep America's "satellite," England, out of the Common Market; (2) to remove NATO from Europe by withdrawing France from NATO; (3) to secure from West Germany, Russia, and Communist China approval of de Gaulle's European leadership (hence his opposition to arming Germany with nuclear weapons, to American intervention in Vietnam, etc.); (4) to woo Latin America away from both Castroism and Americanism and turn it to Gaullism.

The United States has been helpless in the face of de Gaulle's assaults. Its only response to date has been to move NATO's headquarters from France to Belgium. There is talk of withdrawing American troops from Germany, mostly to save the drain on dollars. Nor have the West Germans been helpful in this crisis. They have virtually refused to pay for military equipment bought in the U.S. under agreements to do so; they are clamoring for the right to possess nuclear weapons; they have used the Common Market to discriminate against the sale of American products in German supermarkets; they are worrying the world with the election to high offices of neo-Nazi National Democrats and former members of the Nazi party.

ELSEWHERE

Middle East. In the Middle East the U.S. has urged stability in the relations between Israel and the Arabs; it has supported the United Nations peace force that has struggled to maintain the truce; it has condemned belligerence on both sides. This policy of non-alignment was abandoned when Lebanon asked for help against a threat from the Communists. Russia, on the other hand, has sided with the Arabs and condemned Israel. The Middle East gets a substantial share of American military and economic aid.

Africa. Since 1960 the U.S. has cooperated with the UN in its missions to bring peace to the Congo and to Cyprus. However, it has not followed the lead of the African bloc in their assaults on the racially discriminatory (apartheid) policies of the Union of South Africa and Rhodesia. On the other hand, it did alienate its NATO ally, Portugal, by calling for the freedom of Angola and Mozambique. It has refused to permit the UN to negotiate a peace in Vietnam and received a bitter attack from Secretary-General U Thant for its aggression there. In Africa, the United States has given every encouragement to the new states, provided they were not aligned with Communism. Such aid has come in the form of grants, technical assistance, and the Peace Corps volunteers.

AN OVER-ALL ESTIMATE

Although American foreign policy has undergone an important change of *emphasis* since 1960, it would be a mistake to say that a change of *policy* has occurred. What has happened was implicit in the policy of containment of Communism begun in 1947. Containment means the maintenance of the situation that prevailed in 1945. At the end of World War II there were two huge spheres of influence—Communist and non-communist. America was prepared to help countries in the non-communist sphere retain their status as non-communists. This did not mean that the countries could not alter their forms—for example, from colonial to independent status, as in Africa, or from military dictatorships to democracy (or vice versa), as in Latin America, or, indeed, from aligned to non-aligned powers. They would still receive American foreign aid and be treated as friendly powers. The only change not permitted was from a non-communist to a Communist regime, as occurred in China, the Eastern European countries, and in Cuba. Such countries could expect to encounter American hostility in the forms of non-recognition, economic sanctions, indirect military intervention, and, when invited by some legitimate government, no matter how unrepresentative, direct military encounter.

The "sleeper" in this policy is the unasserted corollary of unilateralism. Until recently, the U.S. seemed wedded to the multilateral good-neighbor approach—hence the UN, NATO, SEATO, CENTO, the OAS, etc. What has changed is the still-unasserted policy of abandoning the multilateral approach to containment of Communism and the adoption of a unilateral stance instead. The U.S. is determined to police the earth with its armed might to combat the spread of Communism, as once she policed the Western Hemisphere to keep it isolated. We could call this policy the Johnson Corollary as, long ago, we spoke of the Roosevelt Corollary. Our speech is soft but the stick we carry is bigger than ever.

INDEX